DOCTOR WHO CLASSICS

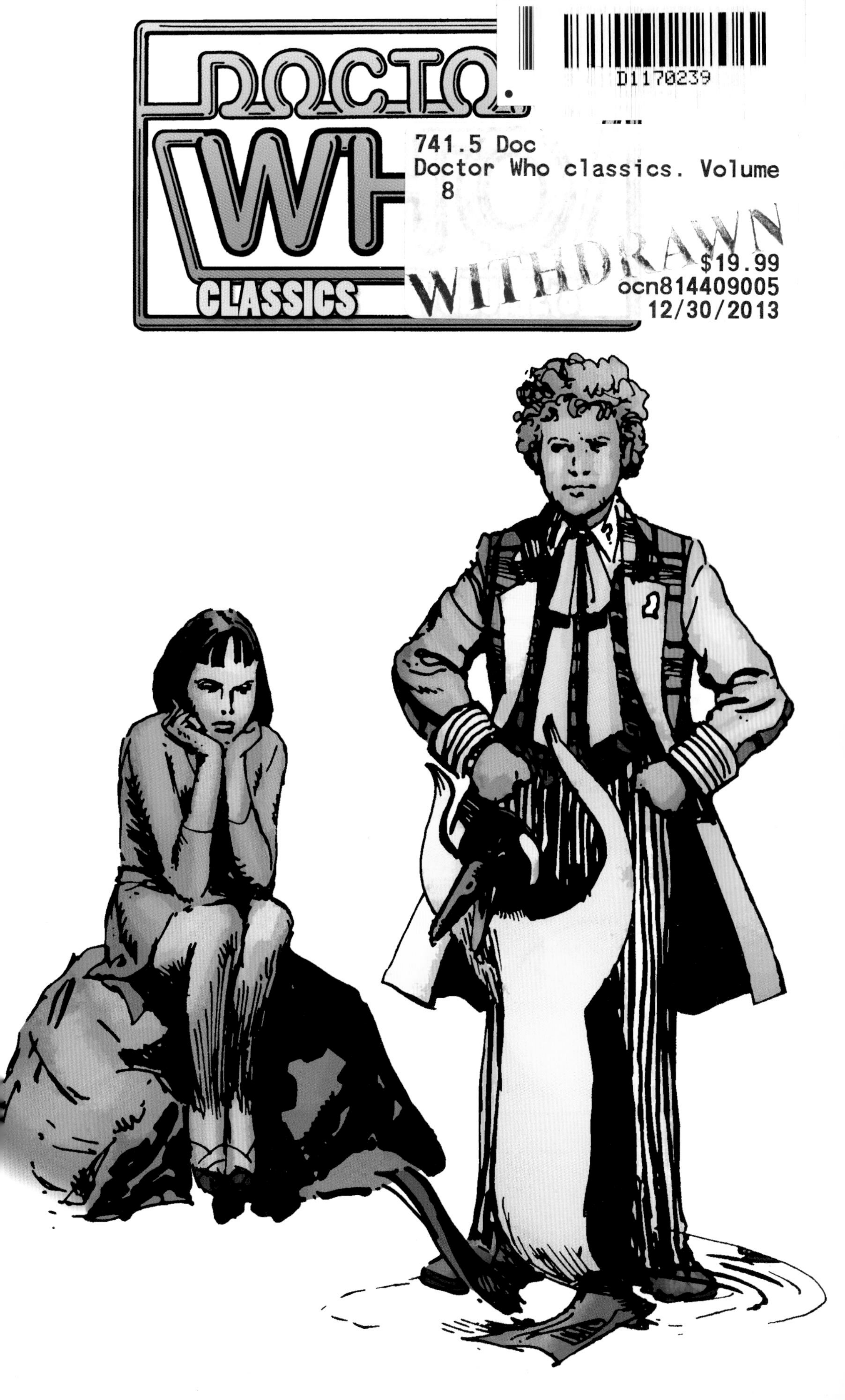

DOCTOR WHO CLASSICS VOLUME 8

"Exodus"
Originally printed in *Doctor Who Magazine #108*
Written by Alan McKenzie
Art by John Ridgway

"Revelation"
Originally printed in *Doctor Who Magazine #109*
Written by Alan McKenzie
Art by John Ridgway

"Genesis"
Originally printed in *Doctor Who Magazine #110*
Written by Alan McKenzie
Art by John Ridgway

"Nature of the Beast"
Originally printed in *Doctor Who Magazine #111-113*
Written by Simon Furman
Art by John Ridgway

"Time Bomb"
Originally printed in *Doctor Who Magazine #114-116*
Written by Jamie Delano
Art by John Ridgway

"Salad Daze"
Originally printed in *Doctor Who Magazine #117*
Written by Simon Furman
Art by John Ridgway

"Changes"
Originally printed in *Doctor Who Magazine #118-119*
Written by Grant Morrison
Art by John Ridgway

"Profits of Doom"
Originally printed in *Doctor Who Magazine #120-122*
Written by Mike Collins
Art by John Ridgway

"The Gift"
Originally printed in *Doctor Who Magazine* #123–126
Written by Jamie Delano
Art by John Ridgway
Letters by Richard Starkings

Letters by Annie Halfacree
Original Edits by Sheila Cranna
Colors by Charlie Kirchoff
Series by Edits by Denton J. Tipton
Collection Cover by John Ridgway
Cover Colors by Charlie Kirchoff

Collection Edits by Justin Eisinger & Alonzo Simon
Collection Design by Amauri Osorio

Special thanks to Kate Bush, Georgie Britton, Caroline Skinner, Denise Paul, and Ed Casey at BBC Worldwide for their invaluable assistance.

IDW founded by Ted Adams, Alex Garner, Kris Oprisko, and Robbie Robbins

ISBN: 978-1-61377-484-7

16 15 14 13 2 3 4 5

IDW®

Ted Adams, CEO & Publisher
Greg Goldstein, President & COO
Robbie Robbins, EVP/Sr. Graphic Artist
Chris Ryall, Chief Creative Officer/Editor-in-Chief
Matthew Ruzicka, CPA, Chief Financial Officer
Alan Payne, VP of Sales
Dirk Wood, VP of Marketing
Lorelei Bunjes, VP of Digital Services

Become our fan on Facebook **facebook.com/idwpublishing**
Follow us on Twitter **@idwpublishing**
Check us out on YouTube **youtube.com/idwpublishing**
www.IDWPUBLISHING.com

Originally published by Marvel Comics UK as DOCTOR WHO MAGAZINE Issues #108–126.

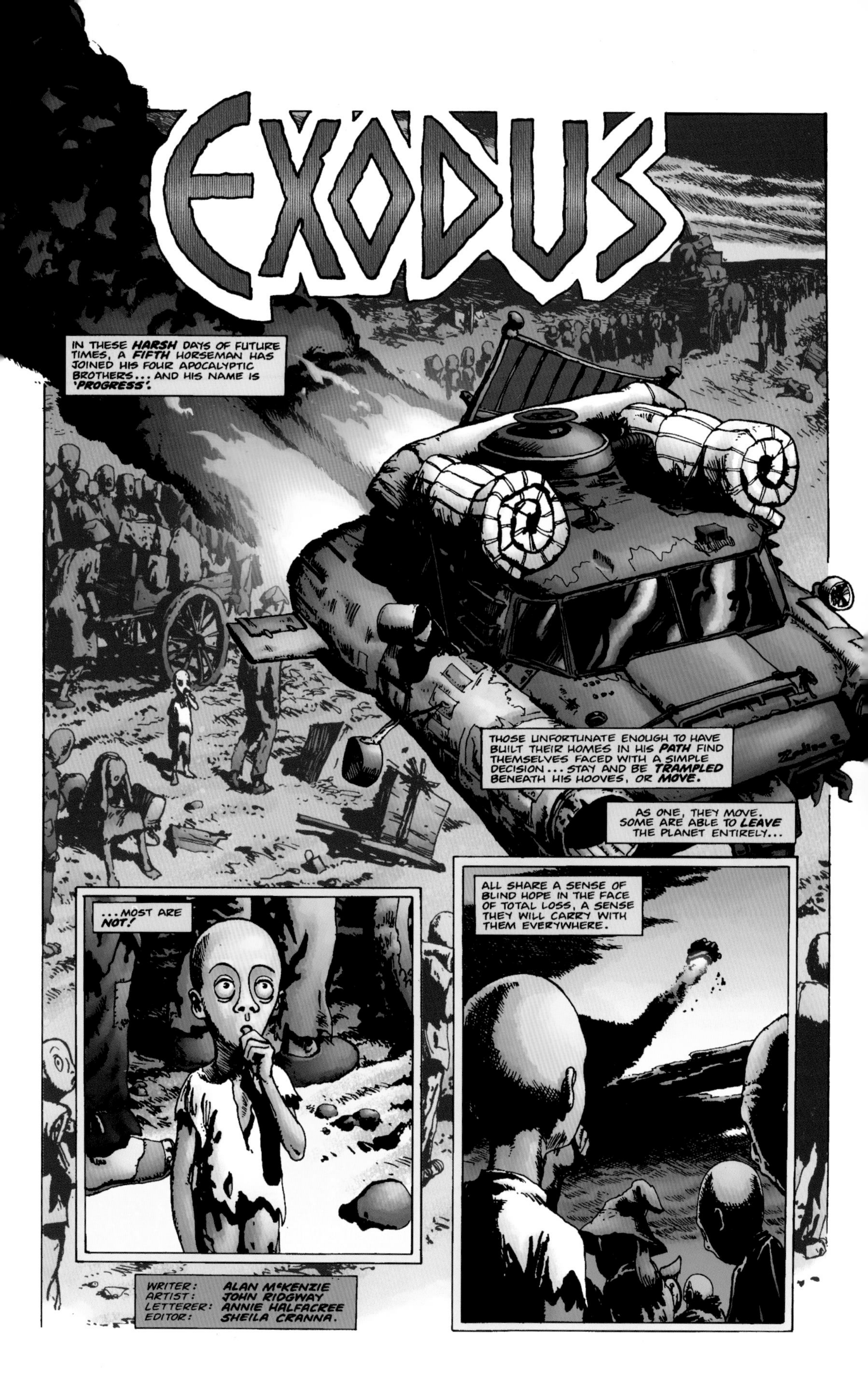
EXODUS
IN THESE HARSH DAYS OF FUTURE TIMES, A FIFTH HORSEMAN HAS JOINED HIS FOUR APOCALYPTIC BROTHERS... AND HIS NAME IS 'PROGRESS'.
THOSE UNFORTUNATE ENOUGH TO HAVE BUILT THEIR HOMES IN HIS PATH FIND THEMSELVES FACED WITH A SIMPLE DECISION... STAY AND BE TRAMPLED BENEATH HIS HOOVES, OR MOVE.
AS ONE, THEY MOVE. SOME ARE ABLE TO LEAVE THE PLANET ENTIRELY...
...MOST ARE NOT!
ALL SHARE A SENSE OF BLIND HOPE IN THE FACE OF TOTAL LOSS, A SENSE THEY WILL CARRY WITH THEM EVERYWHERE.
WRITER: ALAN McKENZIE
ARTIST: JOHN RIDGWAY
LETTERER: ANNIE HALFACREE
EDITOR: SHEILA CRANNA.

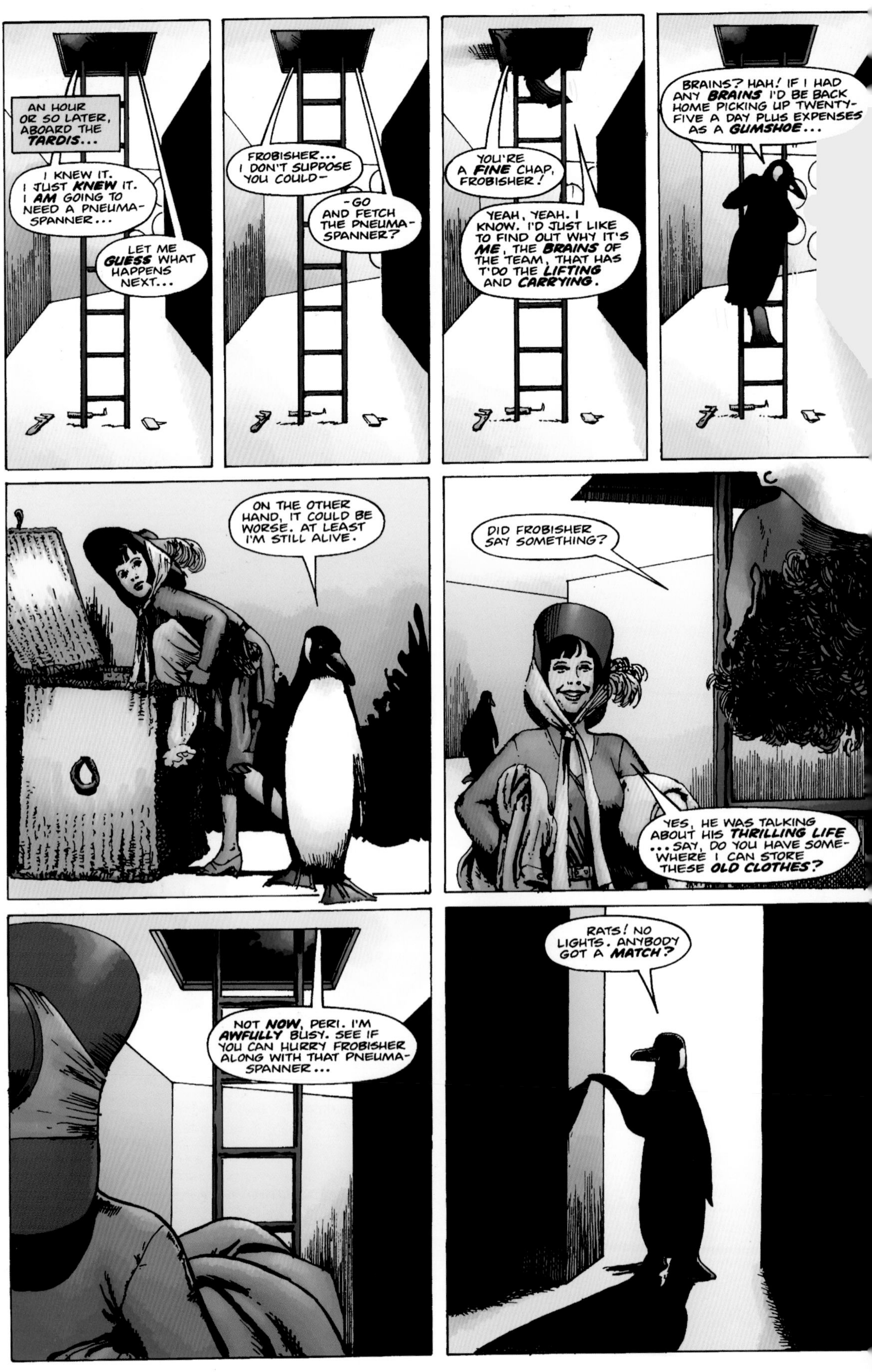

AN HOUR OR SO LATER, ABOARD THE TARDIS...
I KNEW IT. I JUST KNEW IT. I AM GOING TO NEED A PNEUMA-SPANNER...
LET ME GUESS WHAT HAPPENS NEXT...
FROBISHER... I DON'T SUPPOSE YOU COULD-
-GO AND FETCH THE PNEUMA-SPANNER?
YOU'RE A FINE CHAP, FROBISHER!
YEAH, YEAH. I KNOW. I'D JUST LIKE TO FIND OUT WHY IT'S ME, THE BRAINS OF THE TEAM, THAT HAS T'DO THE LIFTING AND CARRYING.
BRAINS? HAH! IF I HAD ANY BRAINS I'D BE BACK HOME PICKING UP TWENTY-FIVE A DAY PLUS EXPENSES AS A GUMSHOE...
ON THE OTHER HAND, IT COULD BE WORSE. AT LEAST I'M STILL ALIVE.
DID FROBISHER SAY SOMETHING?
YES, HE WAS TALKING ABOUT HIS THRILLING LIFE ... SAY, DO YOU HAVE SOME-WHERE I CAN STORE THESE OLD CLOTHES?
NOT NOW, PERI. I'M AWFULLY BUSY. SEE IF YOU CAN HURRY FROBISHER ALONG WITH THAT PNEUMA-SPANNER...
RATS! NO LIGHTS. ANYBODY GOT A MATCH?

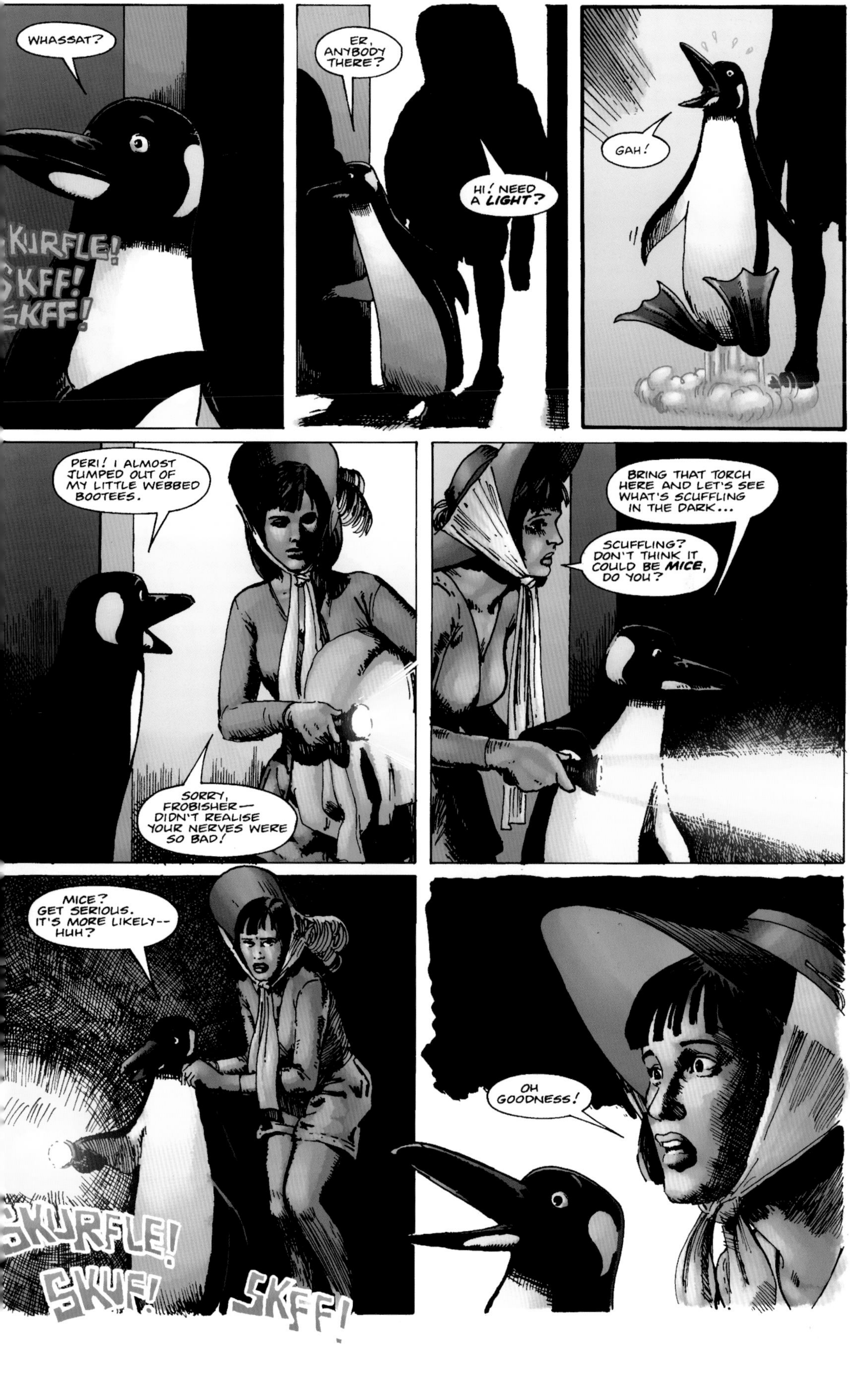
WHASSAT?
SKURFLE! SKFF! SKFF!
ER, ANYBODY THERE?
HI! NEED A LIGHT?
GAH!
PERI! I ALMOST JUMPED OUT OF MY LITTLE WEBBED BOOTEES.
SORRY, FROBISHER— DIDN'T REALISE YOUR NERVES WERE SO BAD!
BRING THAT TORCH HERE AND LET'S SEE WHAT'S SCUFFLING IN THE DARK...
SCUFFLING? DON'T THINK IT COULD BE MICE, DO YOU?
MICE? GET SERIOUS. IT'S MORE LIKELY-- HUH?
SKURFLE! SKUF!
SKFF!
OH GOODNESS!

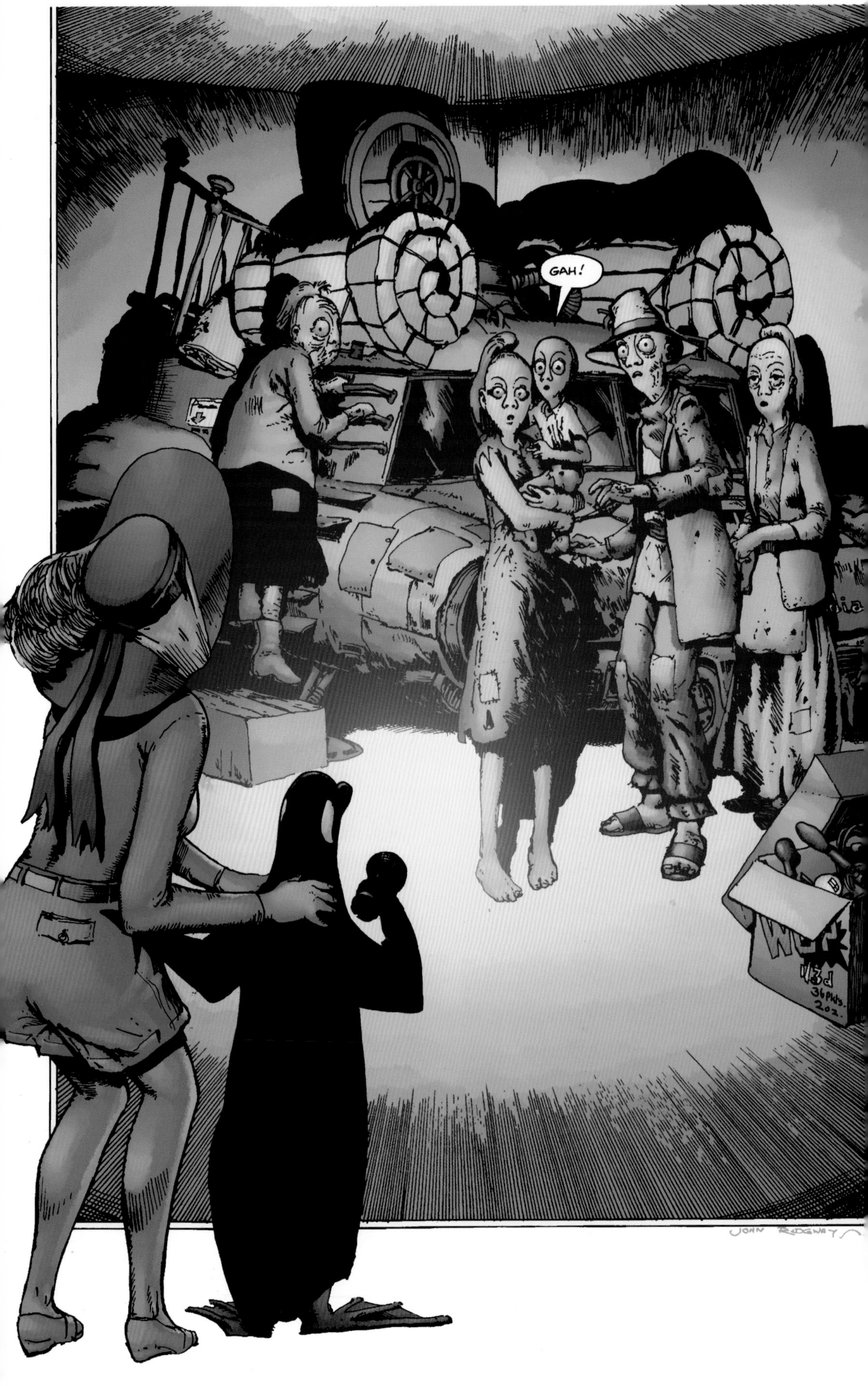
GAH!
1/3d
36 Pkts.
2oz.
JOHN RIDGWAY

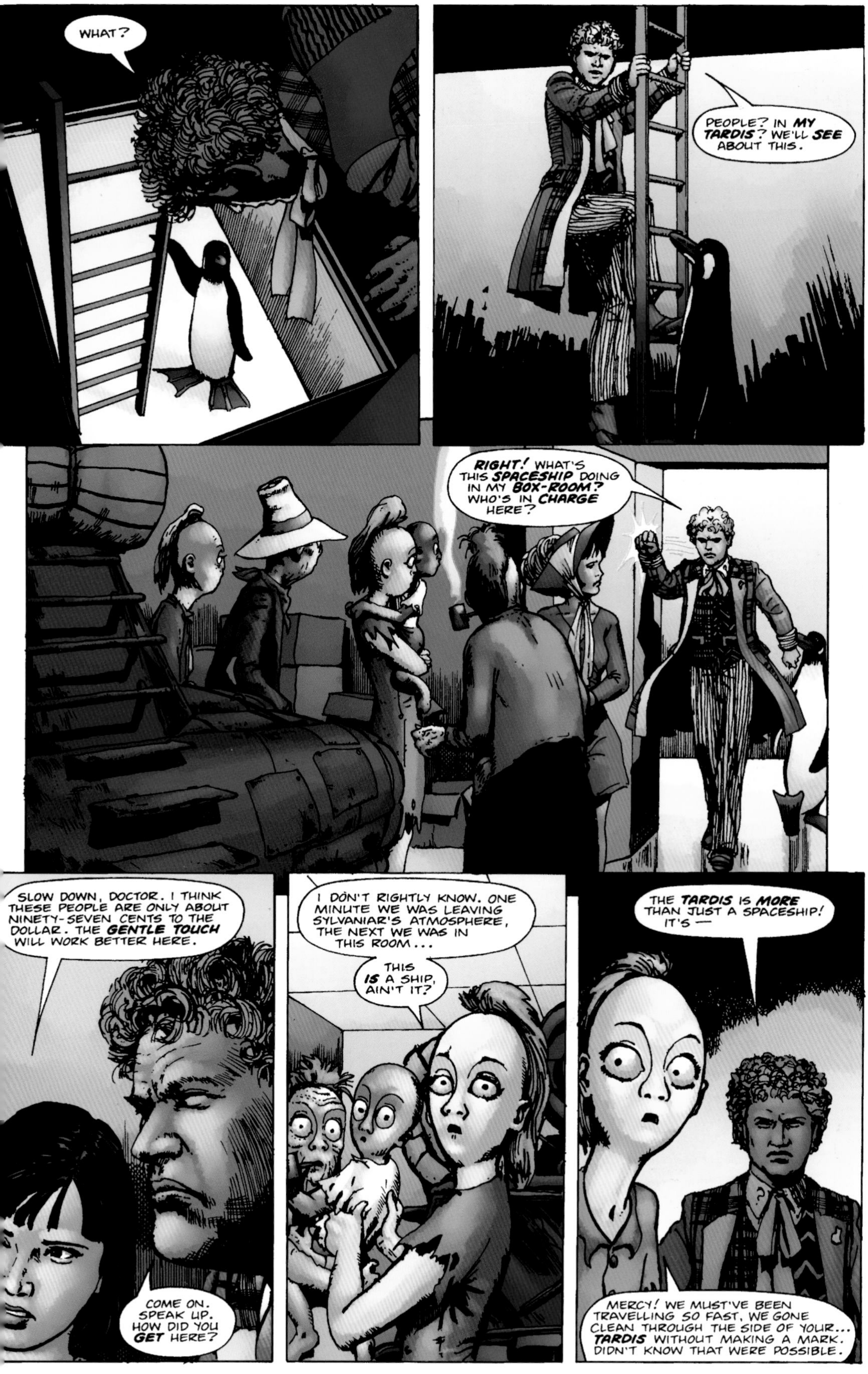
WHAT?
PEOPLE? IN MY TARDIS? WE'LL SEE ABOUT THIS.
RIGHT! WHAT'S THIS SPACESHIP DOING IN MY BOX-ROOM? WHO'S IN CHARGE HERE?
SLOW DOWN, DOCTOR. I THINK THESE PEOPLE ARE ONLY ABOUT NINETY-SEVEN CENTS TO THE DOLLAR. THE GENTLE TOUCH WILL WORK BETTER HERE.
COME ON. SPEAK UP. HOW DID YOU GET HERE?
I DON'T RIGHTLY KNOW. ONE MINUTE WE WAS LEAVING SYLVANIAR'S ATMOSPHERE, THE NEXT WE WAS IN THIS ROOM...
THIS IS A SHIP, AIN'T IT?
THE TARDIS IS MORE THAN JUST A SPACESHIP! IT'S —
MERCY! WE MUST'VE BEEN TRAVELLING SO FAST, WE GONE CLEAN THROUGH THE SIDE OF YOUR... TARDIS WITHOUT MAKING A MARK. DIDN'T KNOW THAT WERE POSSIBLE.

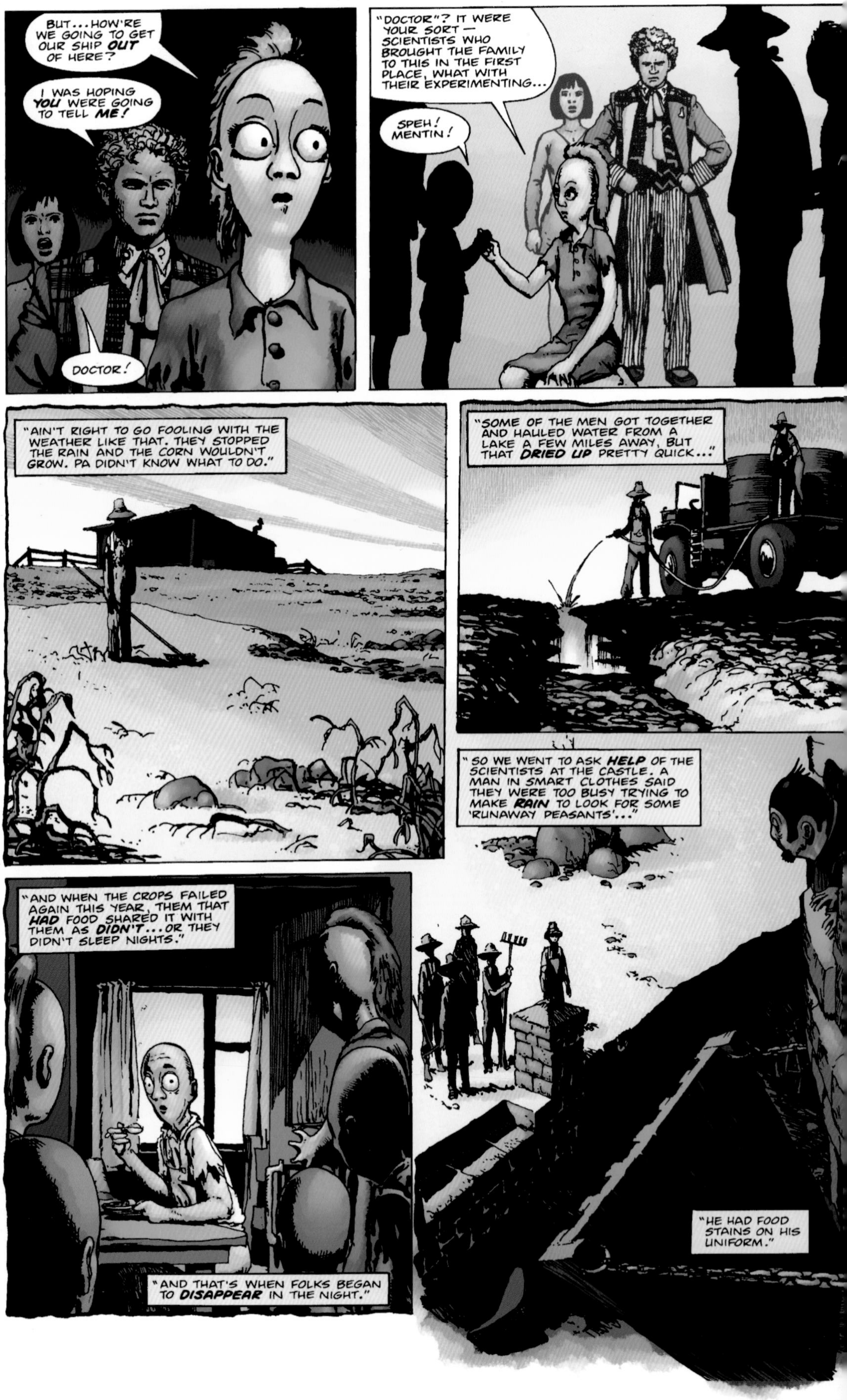

BUT... HOW'RE WE GOING TO GET OUR SHIP OUT OF HERE?
I WAS HOPING YOU WERE GOING TO TELL ME!
DOCTOR!
"DOCTOR"? IT WERE YOUR SORT — SCIENTISTS WHO BROUGHT THE FAMILY TO THIS IN THE FIRST PLACE, WHAT WITH THEIR EXPERIMENTING...
SPEH! MENTIN!
"AIN'T RIGHT TO GO FOOLING WITH THE WEATHER LIKE THAT. THEY STOPPED THE RAIN AND THE CORN WOULDN'T GROW. PA DIDN'T KNOW WHAT TO DO."
"SOME OF THE MEN GOT TOGETHER AND HAULED WATER FROM A LAKE A FEW MILES AWAY, BUT THAT DRIED UP PRETTY QUICK..."
"SO WE WENT TO ASK HELP OF THE SCIENTISTS AT THE CASTLE. A MAN IN SMART CLOTHES SAID THEY WERE TOO BUSY TRYING TO MAKE RAIN TO LOOK FOR SOME 'RUNAWAY PEASANTS'..."
"HE HAD FOOD STAINS ON HIS UNIFORM."
"AND WHEN THE CROPS FAILED AGAIN THIS YEAR, THEM THAT HAD FOOD SHARED IT WITH THEM AS DIDN'T... OR THEY DIDN'T SLEEP NIGHTS."
"AND THAT'S WHEN FOLKS BEGAN TO DISAPPEAR IN THE NIGHT."

ENOUGH! IT SEEMS TO ME THAT ALL I HAVE TO DO IS DEMATERIALISE THE TARDIS TO TURN YOU AND YOUR TRIBE LOOSE ON THE GALAXY ONCE MORE. SO IF YOU'LL KINDLY BOARD--

THAT DOES IT!

YOU KNOW, DOCTOR, I THOUGHT YOU HAD MORE CHARACTER THAN YOU SHOW. I WAS WRONG. YOU'RE A REAL COLD FISH.

I'VE HEARD YOU MAKE SPEECHES ABOUT NEVER TAKING AN INTELLIGENT LIFE AND MAKING THE GALAXY A SAFE DEMOCRACY. OKAY, LET'S SEE SOME OF THAT COMPASSION...

FOR HEAVEN'S SAKE, YOU DIDN'T EVEN OFFER THEM FOOD...

SHE DIDN'T ASK FOR FOOD!

SHE SHOULDN'T HAVE TO.

YOU'RE RIGHT... FROBISHER, HELP ME LOAD SOME FOOD ONTO THEIR SHIP. AND YOU, PERI, NOW HAVE A HOME FOR THOSE OLD CLOTHES.

AND LET'S HURRY IT UP... WE HAVE A WHOLE LOT OF WORK AHEAD OF US TODAY.

RIGHT YOU ARE, SKIPPER!

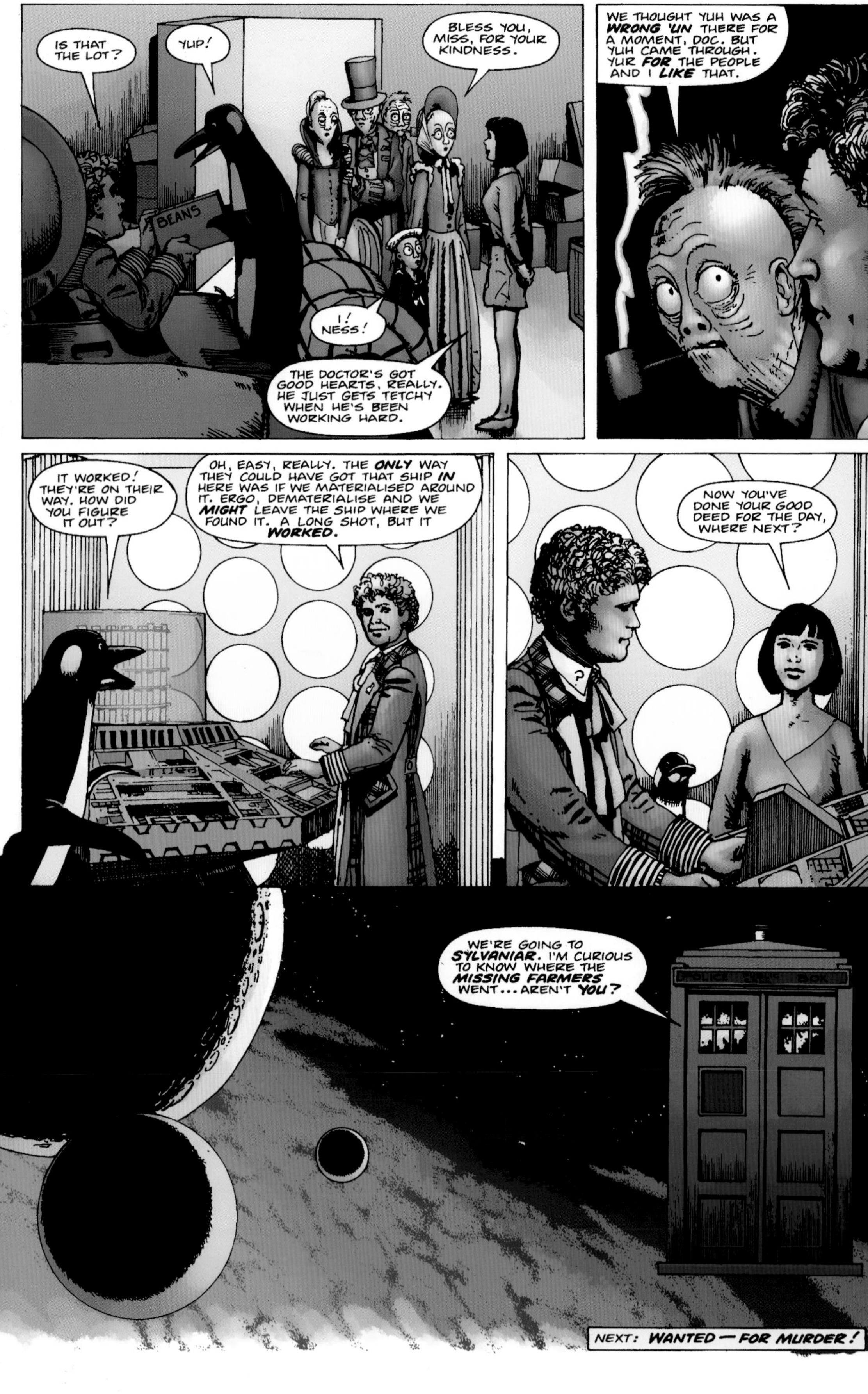

IS THAT THE LOT?
YUP!
BLESS YOU, MISS, FOR YOUR KINDNESS.
I! NESS!
THE DOCTOR'S GOT GOOD HEARTS, REALLY. HE JUST GETS TETCHY WHEN HE'S BEEN WORKING HARD.
BEANS
WE THOUGHT YUH WAS A WRONG 'UN THERE FOR A MOMENT, DOC. BUT YUH CAME THROUGH. YUR FOR THE PEOPLE AND I LIKE THAT.
IT WORKED! THEY'RE ON THEIR WAY. HOW DID YOU FIGURE IT OUT?
OH, EASY, REALLY. THE ONLY WAY THEY COULD HAVE GOT THAT SHIP IN HERE WAS IF WE MATERIALISED AROUND IT. ERGO, DEMATERIALISE AND WE MIGHT LEAVE THE SHIP WHERE WE FOUND IT. A LONG SHOT, BUT IT WORKED.
NOW YOU'VE DONE YOUR GOOD DEED FOR THE DAY, WHERE NEXT?
WE'RE GOING TO SYLVANIAR. I'M CURIOUS TO KNOW WHERE THE MISSING FARMERS WENT... AREN'T YOU?
NEXT: WANTED — FOR MURDER!

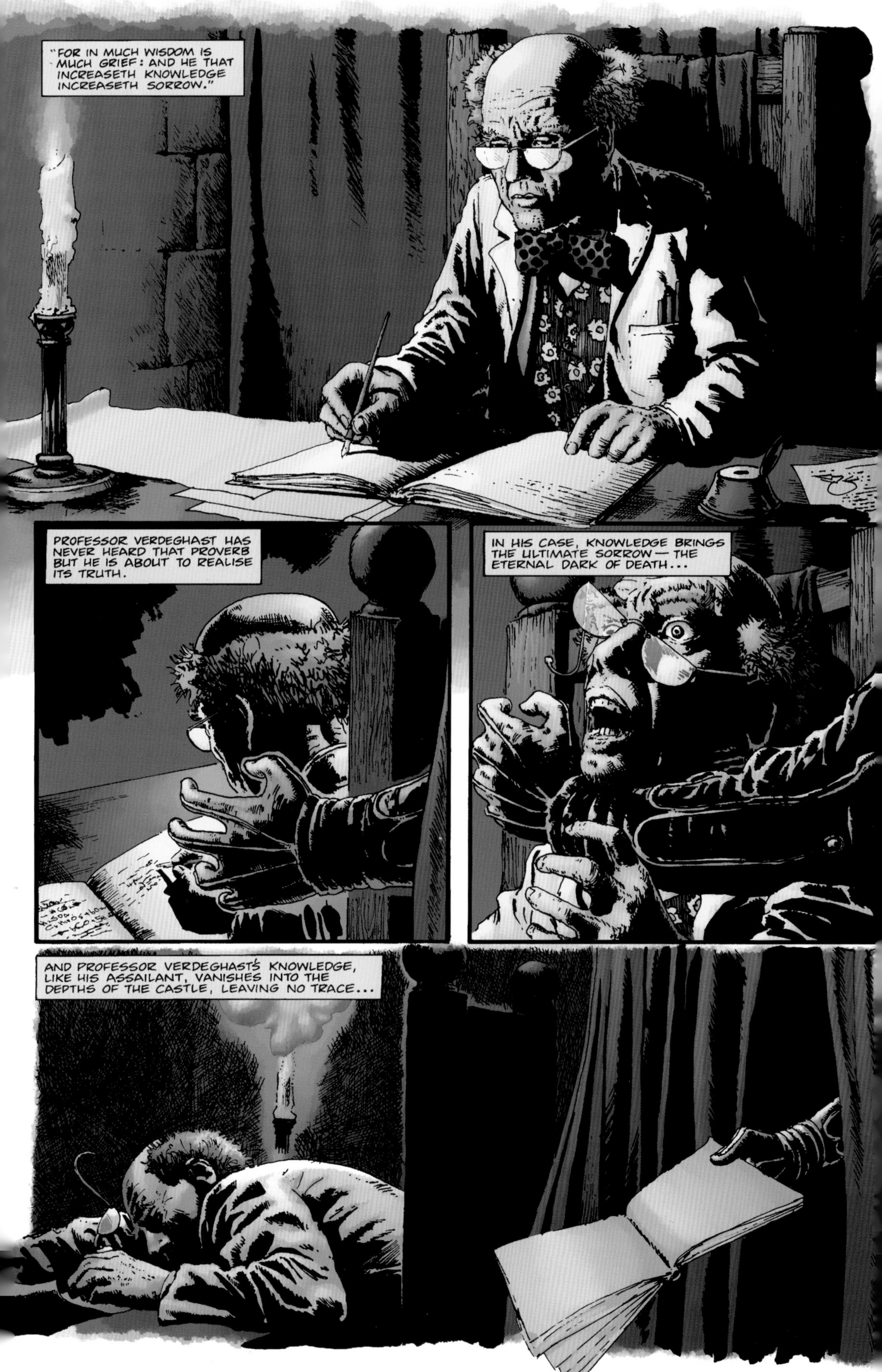
"FOR IN MUCH WISDOM IS MUCH GRIEF: AND HE THAT INCREASETH KNOWLEDGE INCREASETH SORROW."
PROFESSOR VERDEGHAST HAS NEVER HEARD THAT PROVERB BUT HE IS ABOUT TO REALISE ITS TRUTH.
IN HIS CASE, KNOWLEDGE BRINGS THE ULTIMATE SORROW — THE ETERNAL DARK OF DEATH...
AND PROFESSOR VERDEGHAST'S KNOWLEDGE, LIKE HIS ASSAILANT, VANISHES INTO THE DEPTHS OF THE CASTLE, LEAVING NO TRACE...

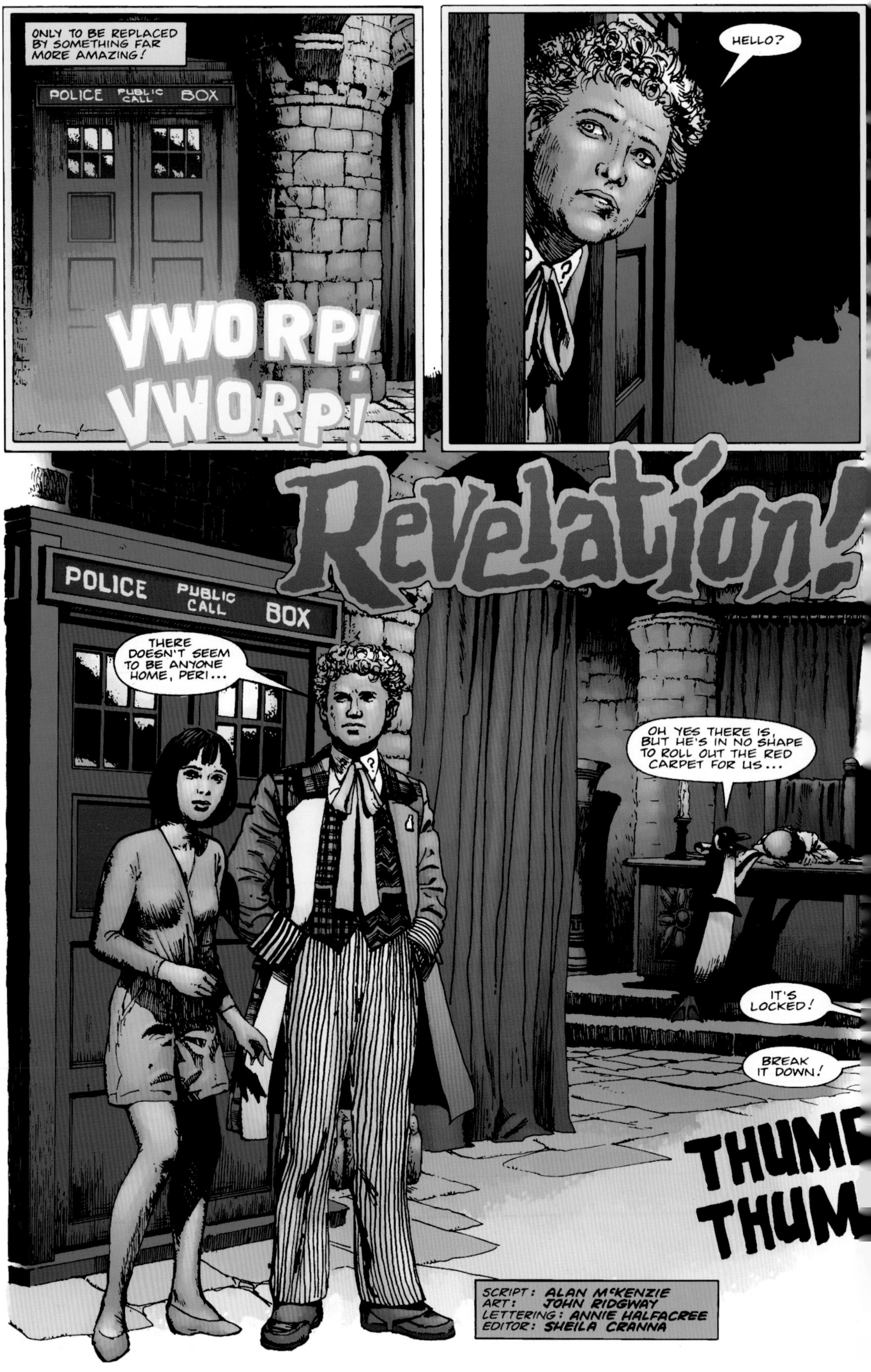

ONLY TO BE REPLACED BY SOMETHING FAR MORE AMAZING!
POLICE PUBLIC CALL BOX
VWORP! VWORP!
HELLO?
Revelation!
POLICE PUBLIC CALL BOX
THERE DOESN'T SEEM TO BE ANYONE HOME, PERI...
OH YES THERE IS, BUT HE'S IN NO SHAPE TO ROLL OUT THE RED CARPET FOR US...
IT'S LOCKED!
BREAK IT DOWN!
SCRIPT: ALAN McKENZIE
ART: JOHN RIDGWAY
LETTERING: ANNIE HALFACREE
EDITOR: SHEILA CRANNA

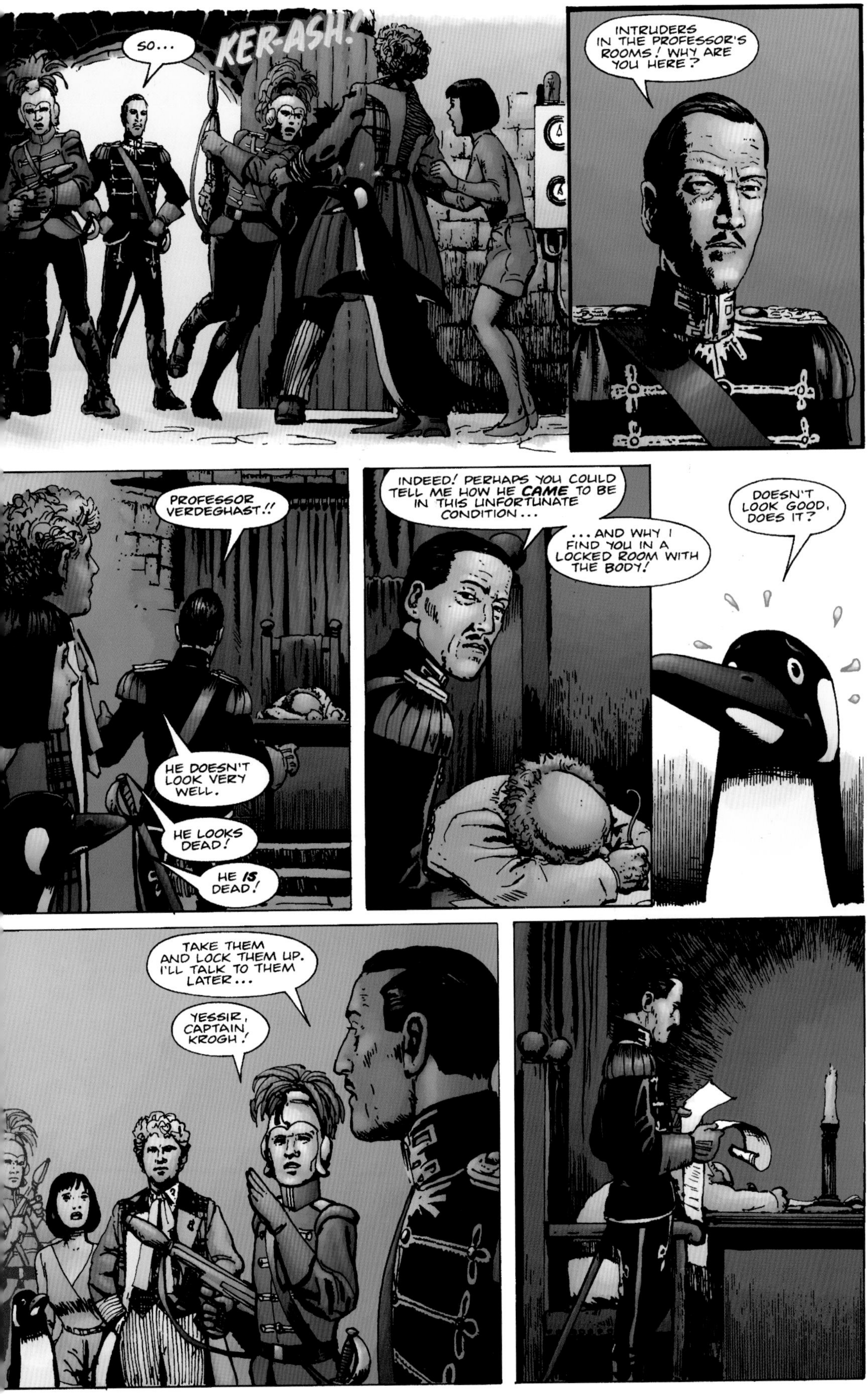
SO...
KER-ASH!
INTRUDERS IN THE PROFESSOR'S ROOMS! WHY ARE YOU HERE?
PROFESSOR VERDEGHAST!!
HE DOESN'T LOOK VERY WELL.
HE LOOKS DEAD!
HE IS, DEAD!
INDEED! PERHAPS YOU COULD TELL ME HOW HE CAME TO BE IN THIS UNFORTUNATE CONDITION...
...AND WHY I FIND YOU IN A LOCKED ROOM WITH THE BODY!
DOESN'T LOOK GOOD, DOES IT?
TAKE THEM AND LOCK THEM UP. I'LL TALK TO THEM LATER...
YESSIR, CAPTAIN KROGH!

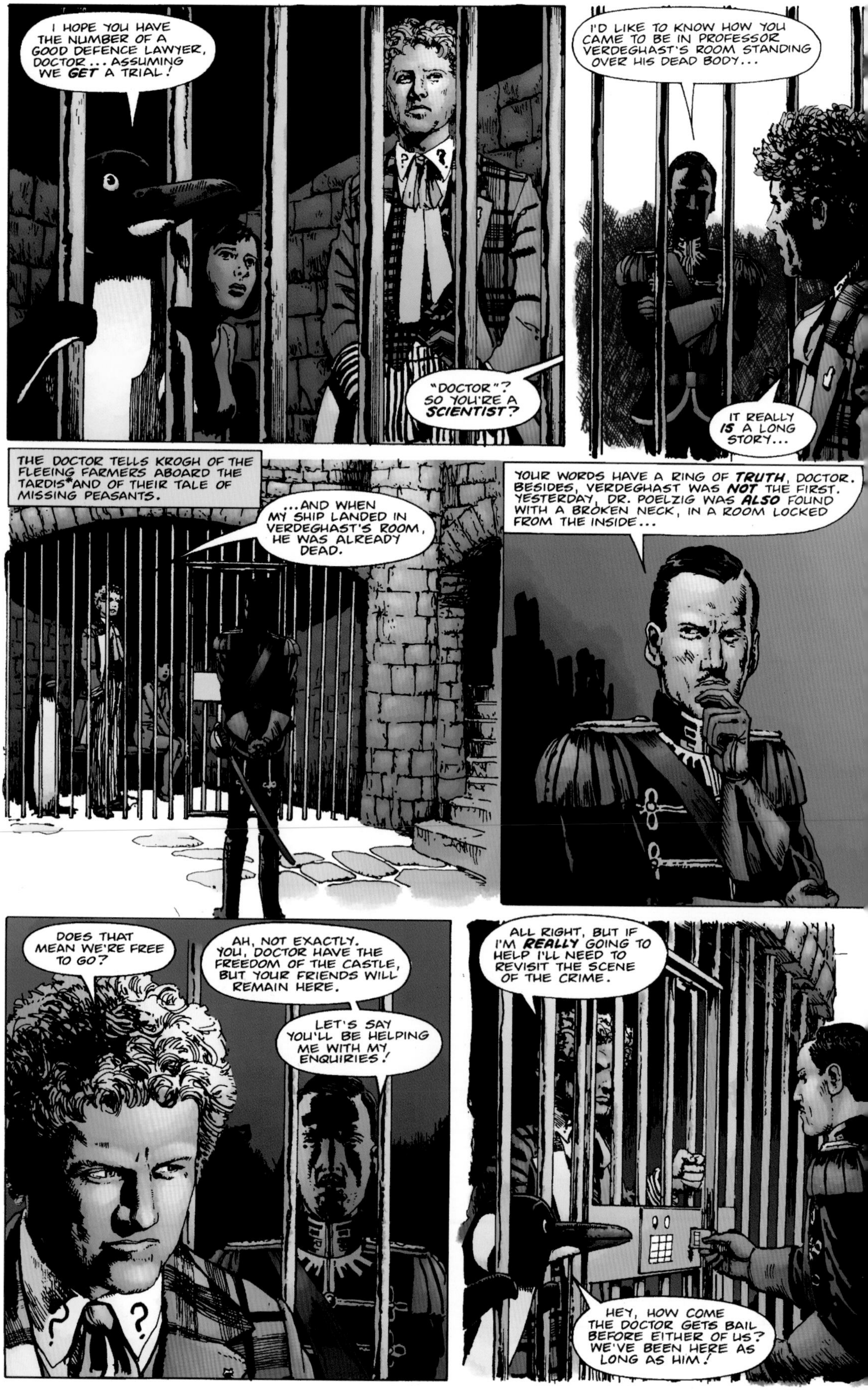

I HOPE YOU HAVE THE NUMBER OF A GOOD DEFENCE LAWYER, DOCTOR... ASSUMING WE GET A TRIAL!
"DOCTOR"? SO YOU'RE A SCIENTIST?
I'D LIKE TO KNOW HOW YOU CAME TO BE IN PROFESSOR VERDEGHAST'S ROOM STANDING OVER HIS DEAD BODY...
IT REALLY IS A LONG STORY...
THE DOCTOR TELLS KROGH OF THE FLEEING FARMERS ABOARD THE TARDIS* AND OF THEIR TALE OF MISSING PEASANTS.
...AND WHEN MY SHIP LANDED IN VERDEGHAST'S ROOM, HE WAS ALREADY DEAD.
YOUR WORDS HAVE A RING OF TRUTH, DOCTOR. BESIDES, VERDEGHAST WAS NOT THE FIRST. YESTERDAY, DR. POELZIG WAS ALSO FOUND WITH A BROKEN NECK, IN A ROOM LOCKED FROM THE INSIDE...
DOES THAT MEAN WE'RE FREE TO GO?
AH, NOT EXACTLY. YOU, DOCTOR HAVE THE FREEDOM OF THE CASTLE, BUT YOUR FRIENDS WILL REMAIN HERE.
LET'S SAY YOU'LL BE HELPING ME WITH MY ENQUIRIES!
ALL RIGHT, BUT IF I'M REALLY GOING TO HELP I'LL NEED TO REVISIT THE SCENE OF THE CRIME.
HEY, HOW COME THE DOCTOR GETS BAIL BEFORE EITHER OF US? WE'VE BEEN HERE AS LONG AS HIM!

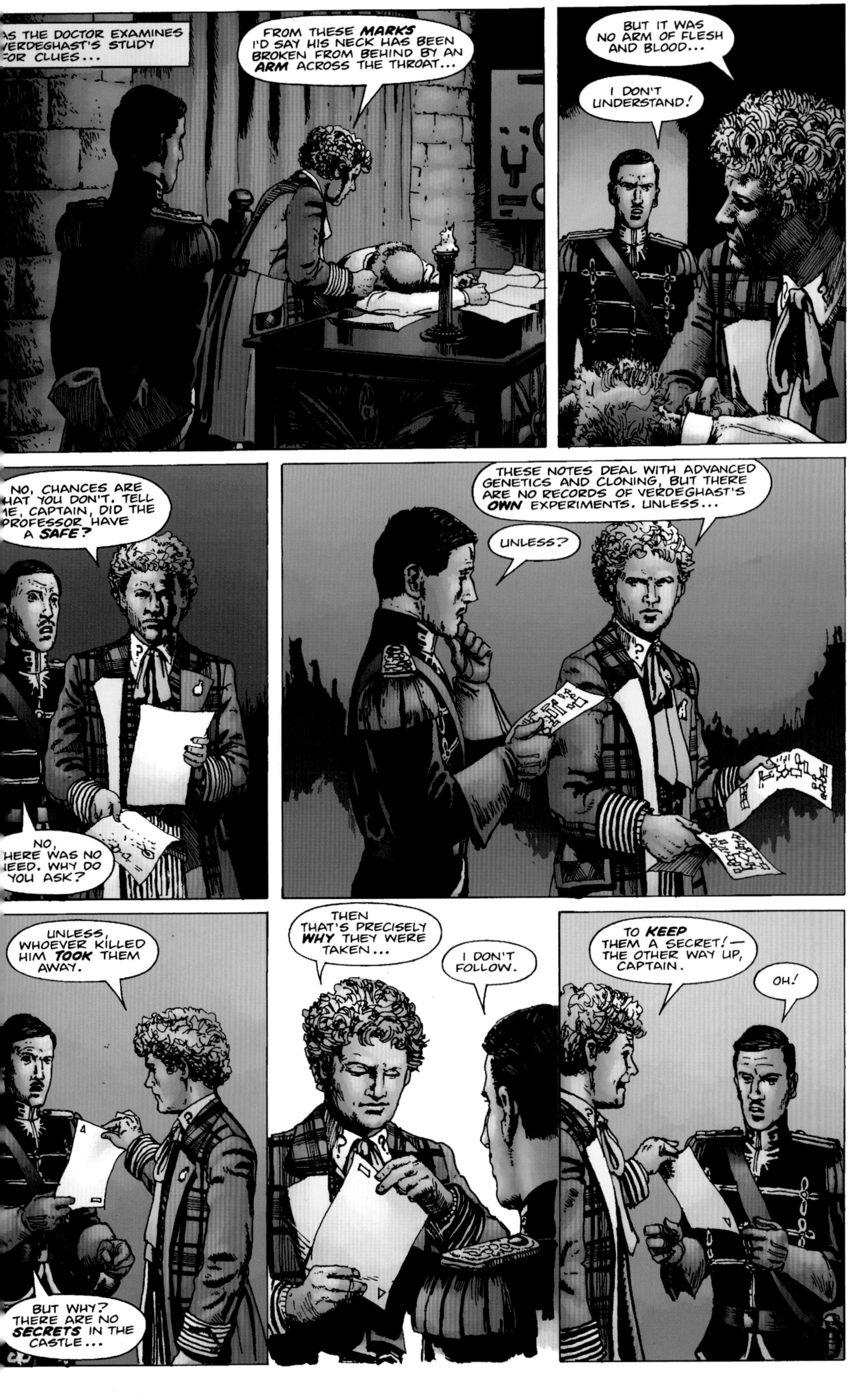

AS THE DOCTOR EXAMINES VERDEGHAST'S STUDY FOR CLUES...
FROM THESE **MARKS** I'D SAY HIS NECK HAS BEEN BROKEN FROM BEHIND BY AN **ARM** ACROSS THE THROAT...
BUT IT WAS NO ARM OF FLESH AND BLOOD...
I DON'T UNDERSTAND!
NO, CHANCES ARE THAT YOU DON'T. TELL ME, CAPTAIN, DID THE PROFESSOR HAVE A **SAFE?**
NO, THERE WAS NO NEED. WHY DO YOU ASK?
THESE NOTES DEAL WITH ADVANCED GENETICS AND CLONING, BUT THERE ARE NO RECORDS OF VERDEGHAST'S **OWN** EXPERIMENTS. UNLESS...
UNLESS?
UNLESS, WHOEVER KILLED HIM **TOOK** THEM AWAY.
BUT WHY? THERE ARE NO **SECRETS** IN THE CASTLE...
THEN THAT'S PRECISELY **WHY** THEY WERE TAKEN...
I DON'T FOLLOW.
TO **KEEP** THEM A SECRET! — THE OTHER WAY UP, CAPTAIN.
OH!

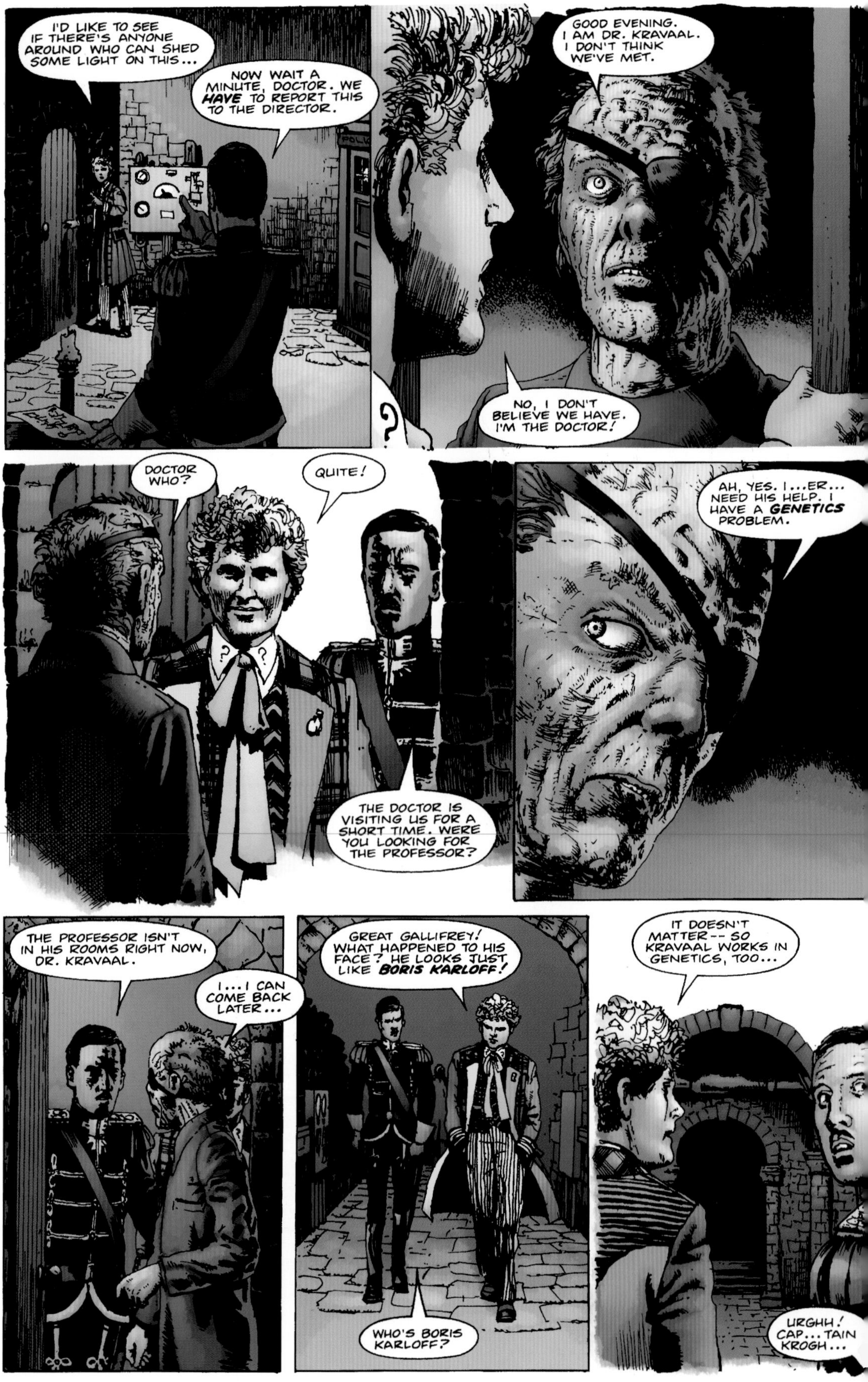
I'D LIKE TO SEE IF THERE'S ANYONE AROUND WHO CAN SHED SOME LIGHT ON THIS...
NOW WAIT A MINUTE, DOCTOR. WE **HAVE** TO REPORT THIS TO THE DIRECTOR.
GOOD EVENING. I AM DR. KRAVAAL. I DON'T THINK WE'VE MET.
NO, I DON'T BELIEVE WE HAVE. I'M THE DOCTOR!
DOCTOR WHO?
QUITE!
THE DOCTOR IS VISITING US FOR A SHORT TIME. WERE YOU LOOKING FOR THE PROFESSOR?
AH, YES. I...ER... NEED HIS HELP. I HAVE A **GENETICS** PROBLEM.
THE PROFESSOR ISN'T IN HIS ROOMS RIGHT NOW, DR. KRAVAAL.
I...I CAN COME BACK LATER...
GREAT GALLIFREY! WHAT HAPPENED TO HIS FACE? HE LOOKS JUST LIKE **BORIS KARLOFF**!
WHO'S BORIS KARLOFF?
IT DOESN'T MATTER-- SO KRAVAAL WORKS IN GENETICS, TOO...
URGHH! CAP...TAIN KROGH...

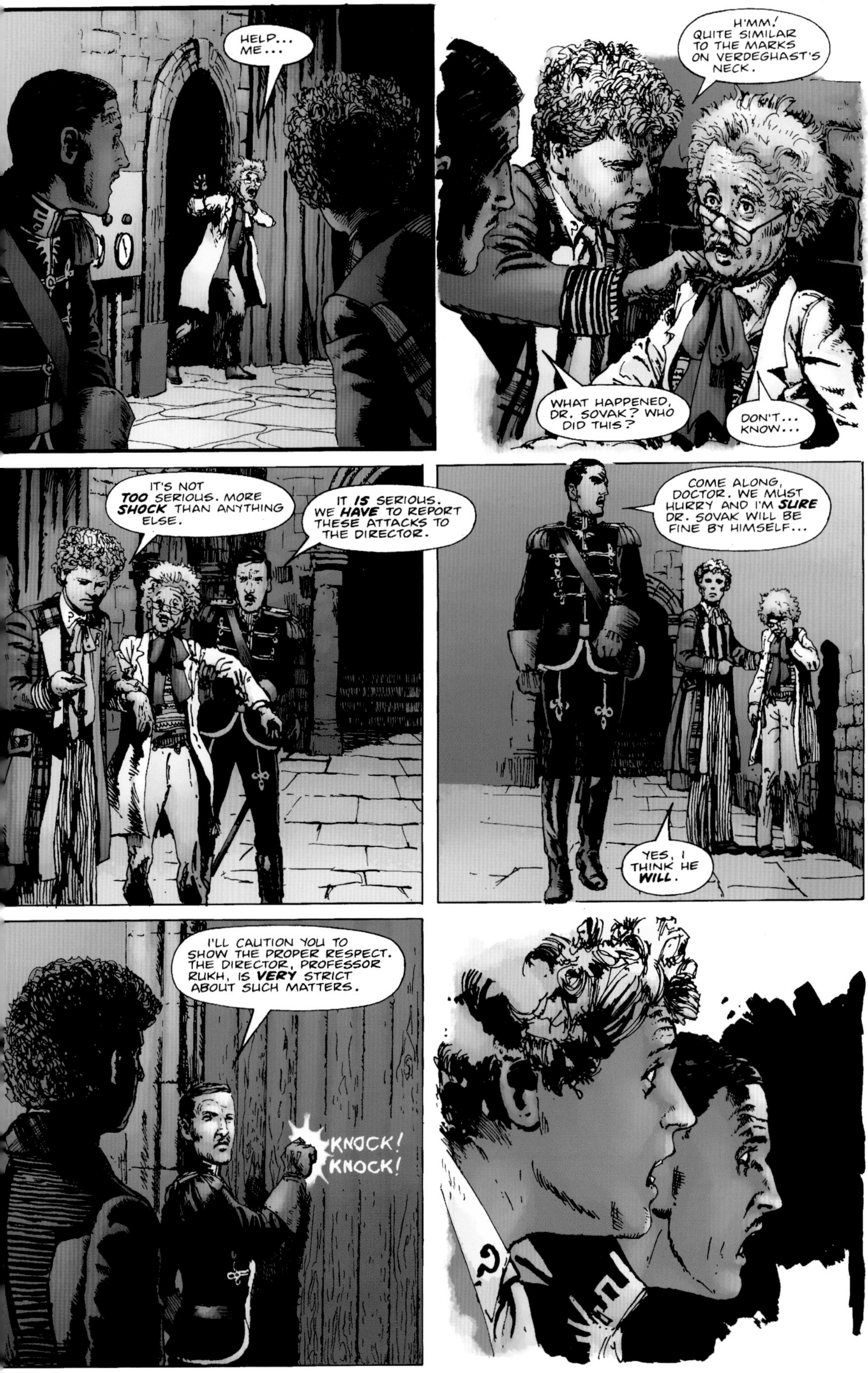
HELP... ME...
H'MM! QUITE SIMILAR TO THE MARKS ON VERDEGHAST'S NECK.
WHAT HAPPENED, DR. SOVAK? WHO DID THIS?
DON'T... KNOW...
IT'S NOT TOO SERIOUS. MORE SHOCK THAN ANYTHING ELSE.
IT IS SERIOUS. WE HAVE TO REPORT THESE ATTACKS TO THE DIRECTOR.
COME ALONG, DOCTOR. WE MUST HURRY AND I'M SURE DR. SOVAK WILL BE FINE BY HIMSELF...
YES, I THINK HE WILL.
I'LL CAUTION YOU TO SHOW THE PROPER RESPECT. THE DIRECTOR, PROFESSOR RUKH, IS VERY STRICT ABOUT SUCH MATTERS.
KNOCK! KNOCK!

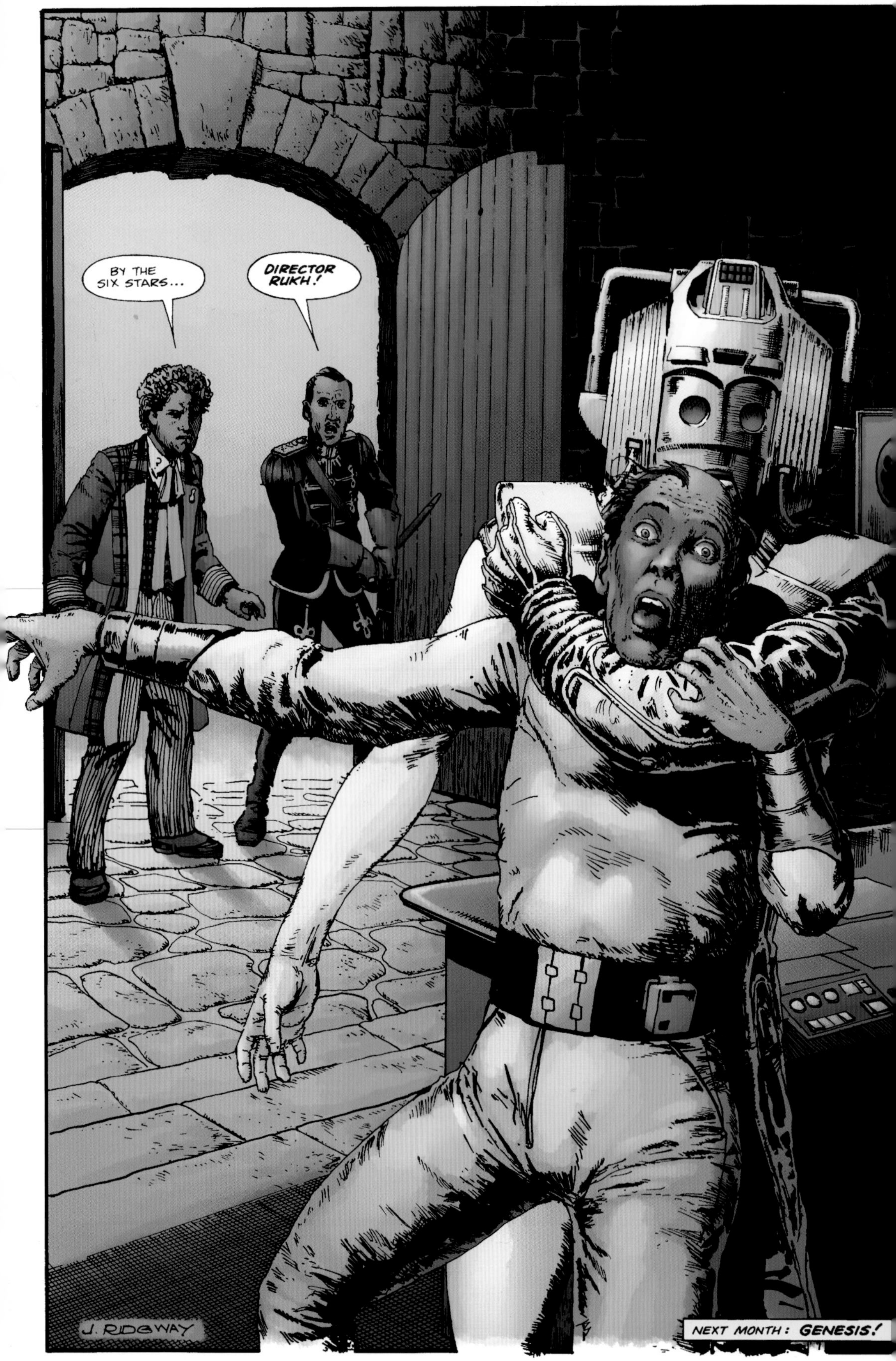
BY THE SIX STARS...
DIRECTOR RUKH!
J. RIDGWAY
NEXT MONTH: GENESIS!

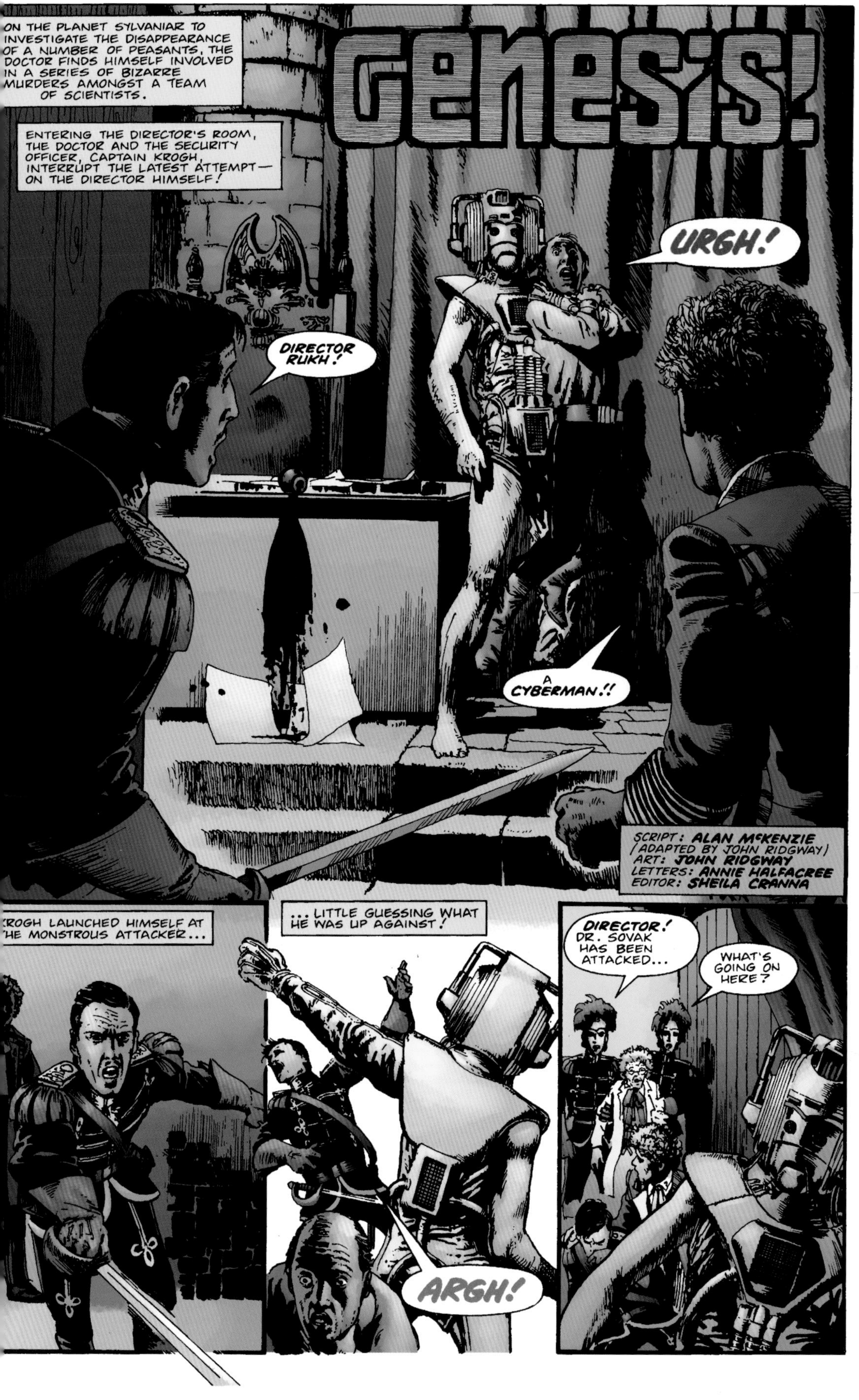

ON THE PLANET SYLVANIAR TO INVESTIGATE THE DISAPPEARANCE OF A NUMBER OF PEASANTS, THE DOCTOR FINDS HIMSELF INVOLVED IN A SERIES OF BIZARRE MURDERS AMONGST A TEAM OF SCIENTISTS.
GENESIS!
ENTERING THE DIRECTOR'S ROOM, THE DOCTOR AND THE SECURITY OFFICER, CAPTAIN KROGH, INTERRUPT THE LATEST ATTEMPT— ON THE DIRECTOR HIMSELF!
URGH!
DIRECTOR RUKH!
A CYBERMAN!!
SCRIPT: ALAN McKENZIE (ADAPTED BY JOHN RIDGWAY)
ART: JOHN RIDGWAY
LETTERS: ANNIE HALFACREE
EDITOR: SHEILA CRANNA
KROGH LAUNCHED HIMSELF AT THE MONSTROUS ATTACKER...
... LITTLE GUESSING WHAT HE WAS UP AGAINST!
ARGH!
DIRECTOR! DR. SOVAK HAS BEEN ATTACKED...
WHAT'S GOING ON HERE?

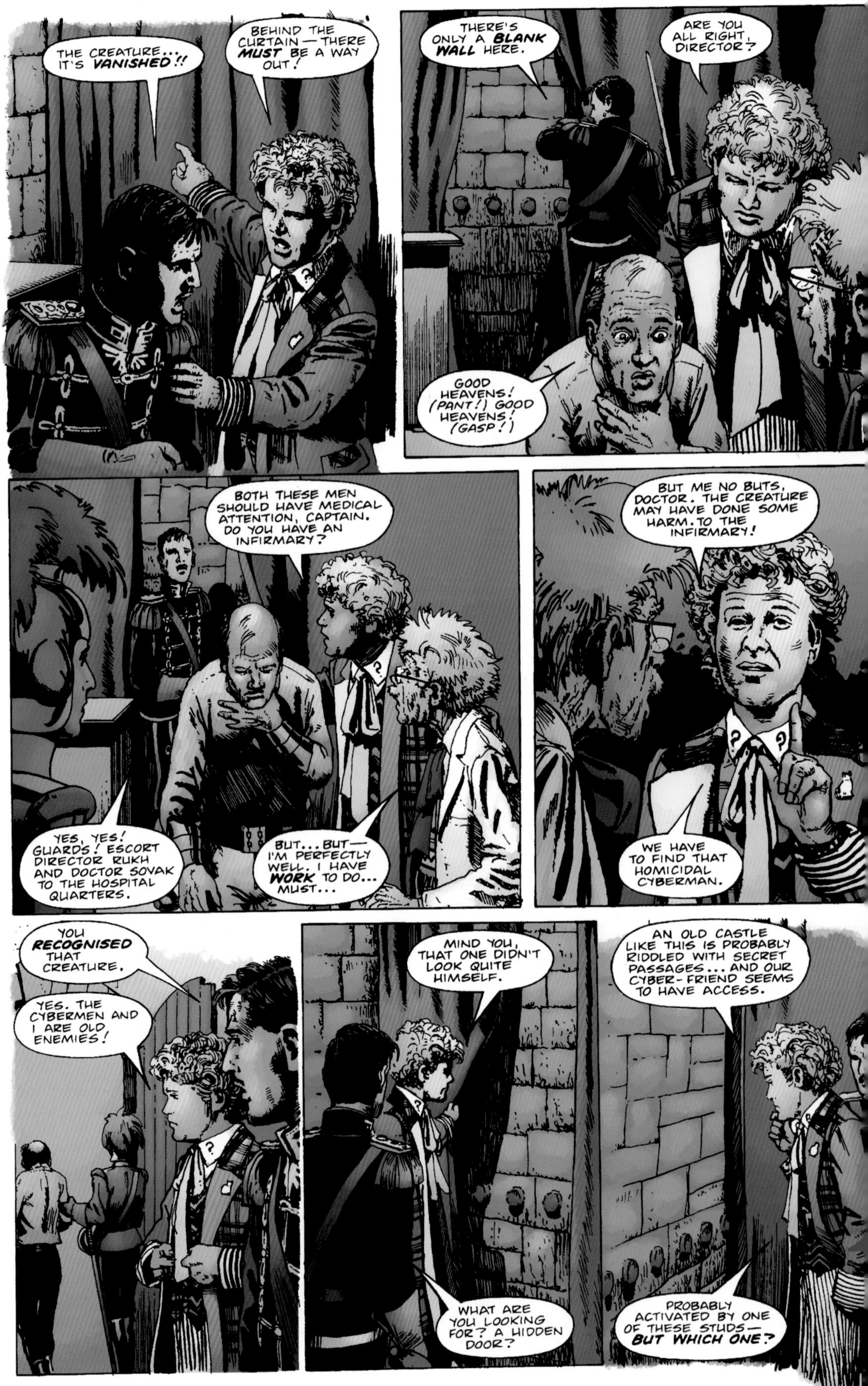
THE CREATURE... IT'S VANISHED!!
BEHIND THE CURTAIN — THERE MUST BE A WAY OUT!
THERE'S ONLY A BLANK WALL HERE.
ARE YOU ALL RIGHT, DIRECTOR?
GOOD HEAVENS! (PANT!) GOOD HEAVENS! (GASP!)
BOTH THESE MEN SHOULD HAVE MEDICAL ATTENTION, CAPTAIN. DO YOU HAVE AN INFIRMARY?
YES, YES! GUARDS! ESCORT DIRECTOR RUKH AND DOCTOR SOVAK TO THE HOSPITAL QUARTERS.
BUT...BUT— I'M PERFECTLY WELL. I HAVE WORK TO DO... MUST...
BUT ME NO BUTS, DOCTOR. THE CREATURE MAY HAVE DONE SOME HARM TO THE INFIRMARY!
WE HAVE TO FIND THAT HOMICIDAL CYBERMAN.
YOU RECOGNISED THAT CREATURE.
YES. THE CYBERMEN AND I ARE OLD ENEMIES!
MIND YOU, THAT ONE DIDN'T LOOK QUITE HIMSELF.
WHAT ARE YOU LOOKING FOR? A HIDDEN DOOR?
AN OLD CASTLE LIKE THIS IS PROBABLY RIDDLED WITH SECRET PASSAGES... AND OUR CYBER-FRIEND SEEMS TO HAVE ACCESS.
PROBABLY ACTIVATED BY ONE OF THESE STUDS— BUT WHICH ONE?

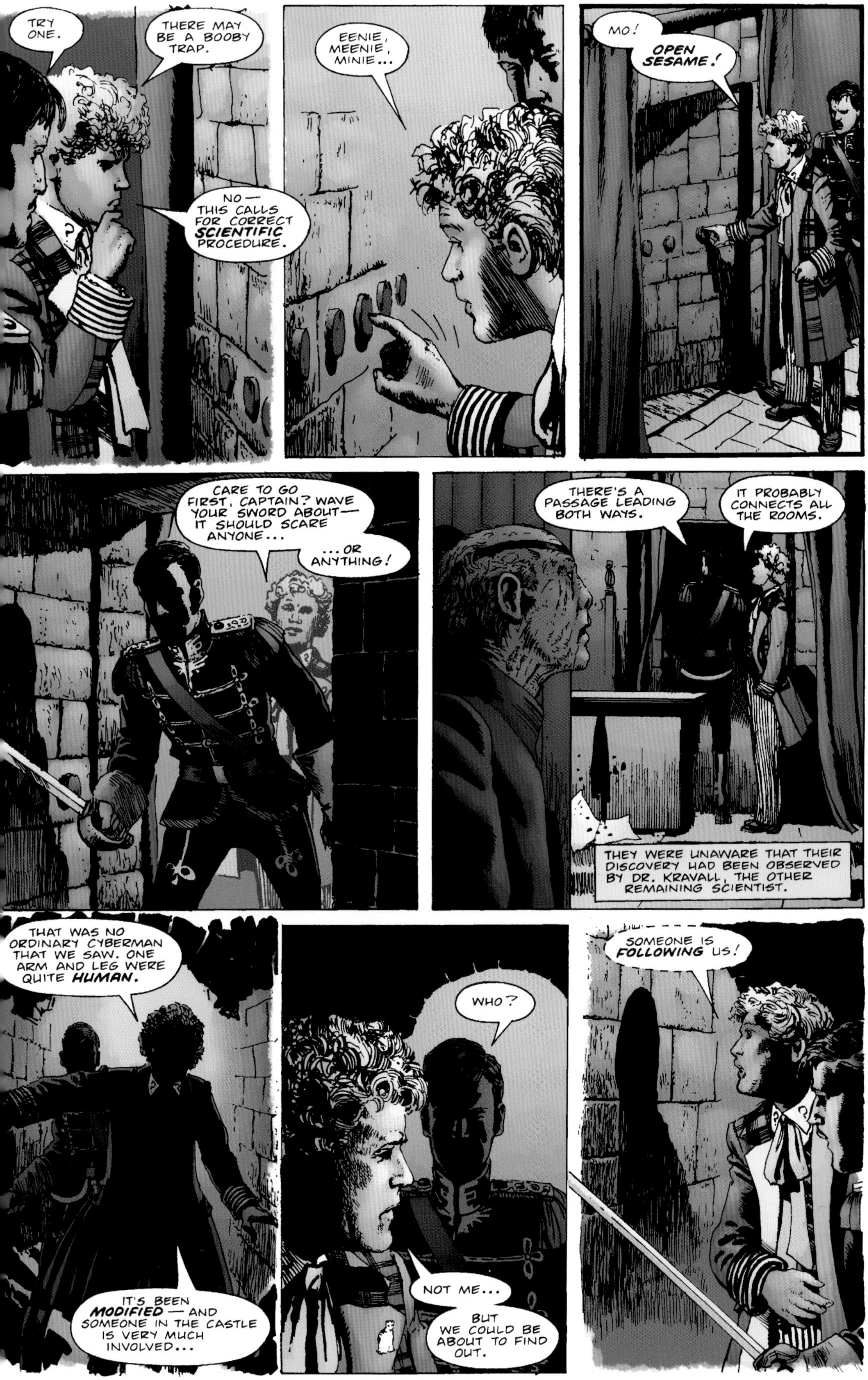
TRY ONE.
THERE MAY BE A BOOBY TRAP.
NO— THIS CALLS FOR CORRECT SCIENTIFIC PROCEDURE.
EENIE, MEENIE, MINIE...
MO! OPEN SESAME!
CARE TO GO FIRST, CAPTAIN? WAVE YOUR SWORD ABOUT— IT SHOULD SCARE ANYONE...
...OR ANYTHING!
THERE'S A PASSAGE LEADING BOTH WAYS.
IT PROBABLY CONNECTS ALL THE ROOMS.
THEY WERE UNAWARE THAT THEIR DISCOVERY HAD BEEN OBSERVED BY DR. KRAVALL, THE OTHER REMAINING SCIENTIST.
THAT WAS NO ORDINARY CYBERMAN THAT WE SAW. ONE ARM AND LEG WERE QUITE HUMAN.
IT'S BEEN MODIFIED — AND SOMEONE IN THE CASTLE IS VERY MUCH INVOLVED...
WHO?
NOT ME...
BUT WE COULD BE ABOUT TO FIND OUT.
SOMEONE IS FOLLOWING US!

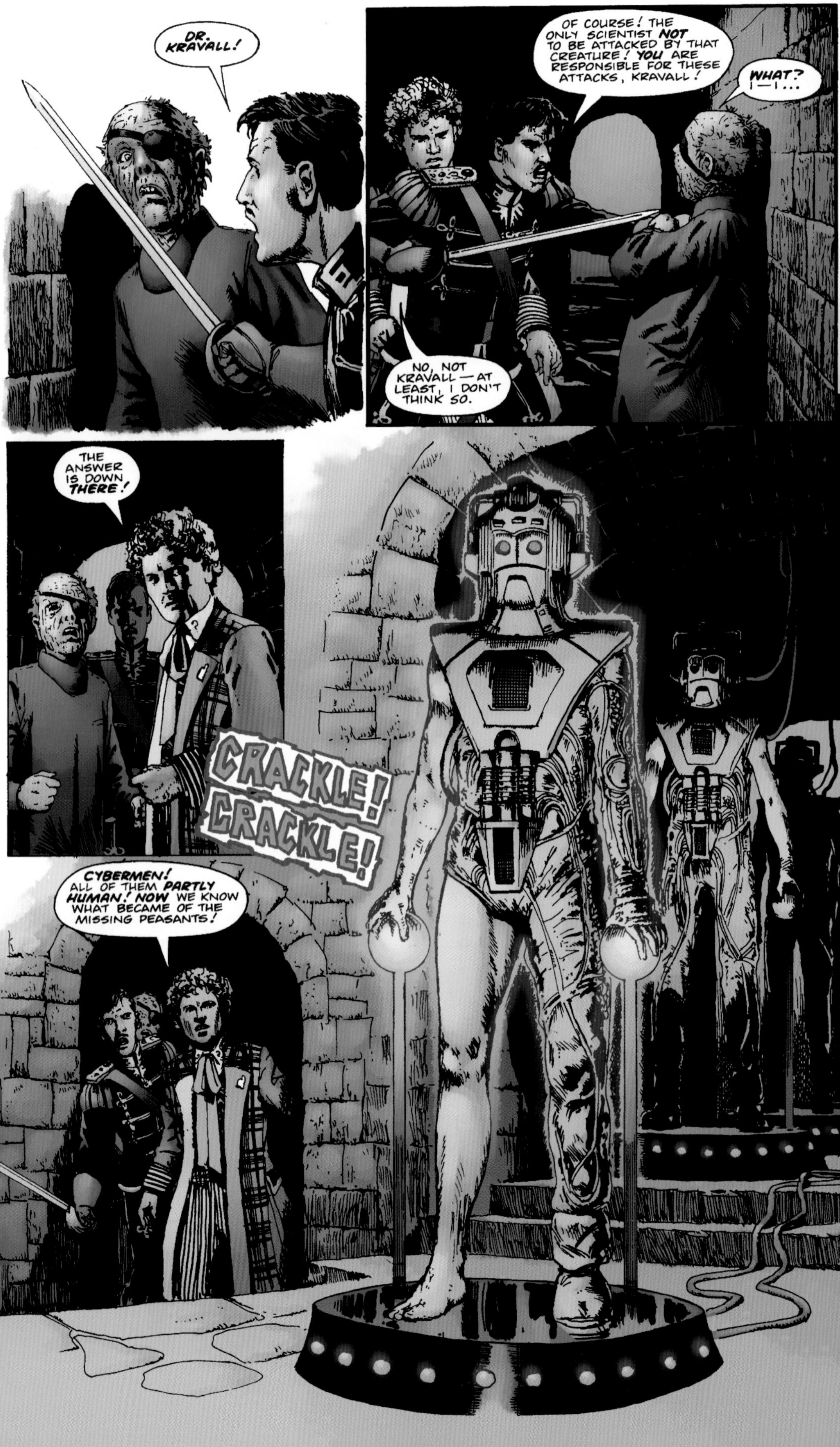
DR. KRAVALL!
OF COURSE! THE ONLY SCIENTIST NOT TO BE ATTACKED BY THAT CREATURE! YOU ARE RESPONSIBLE FOR THESE ATTACKS, KRAVALL!
WHAT? I—I...
NO, NOT KRAVALL—AT LEAST, I DON'T THINK SO.
THE ANSWER IS DOWN THERE!
CRACKLE! CRACKLE!
CYBERMEN! ALL OF THEM PARTLY HUMAN! NOW WE KNOW WHAT BECAME OF THE MISSING PEASANTS!

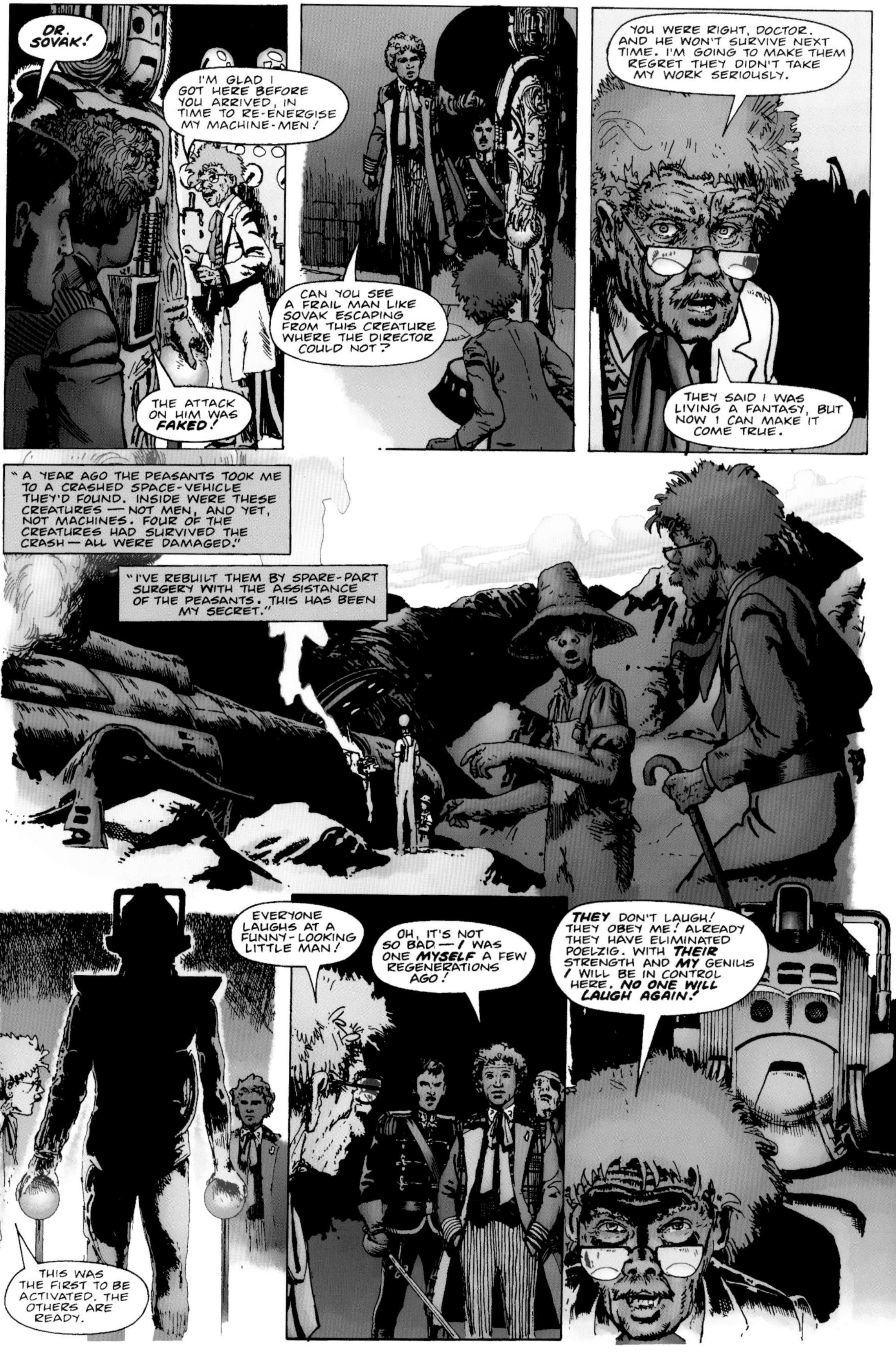
DR. SOVAK!
I'M GLAD I GOT HERE BEFORE YOU ARRIVED, IN TIME TO RE-ENERGISE MY MACHINE-MEN!
THE ATTACK ON HIM WAS FAKED!
CAN YOU SEE A FRAIL MAN LIKE SOVAK ESCAPING FROM THIS CREATURE WHERE THE DIRECTOR COULD NOT?
YOU WERE RIGHT, DOCTOR. AND HE WON'T SURVIVE NEXT TIME. I'M GOING TO MAKE THEM REGRET THEY DIDN'T TAKE MY WORK SERIOUSLY.
THEY SAID I WAS LIVING A FANTASY, BUT NOW I CAN MAKE IT COME TRUE.
"A YEAR AGO THE PEASANTS TOOK ME TO A CRASHED SPACE-VEHICLE THEY'D FOUND. INSIDE WERE THESE CREATURES — NOT MEN, AND YET, NOT MACHINES. FOUR OF THE CREATURES HAD SURVIVED THE CRASH — ALL WERE DAMAGED."
"I'VE REBUILT THEM BY SPARE-PART SURGERY WITH THE ASSISTANCE OF THE PEASANTS. THIS HAS BEEN MY SECRET."
THIS WAS THE FIRST TO BE ACTIVATED. THE OTHERS ARE READY.
EVERYONE LAUGHS AT A FUNNY-LOOKING LITTLE MAN!
OH, IT'S NOT SO BAD — I WAS ONE MYSELF A FEW REGENERATIONS AGO!
THEY DON'T LAUGH! THEY OBEY ME! ALREADY THEY HAVE ELIMINATED POELZIG. WITH THEIR STRENGTH AND MY GENIUS I WILL BE IN CONTROL HERE. NO ONE WILL LAUGH AGAIN!

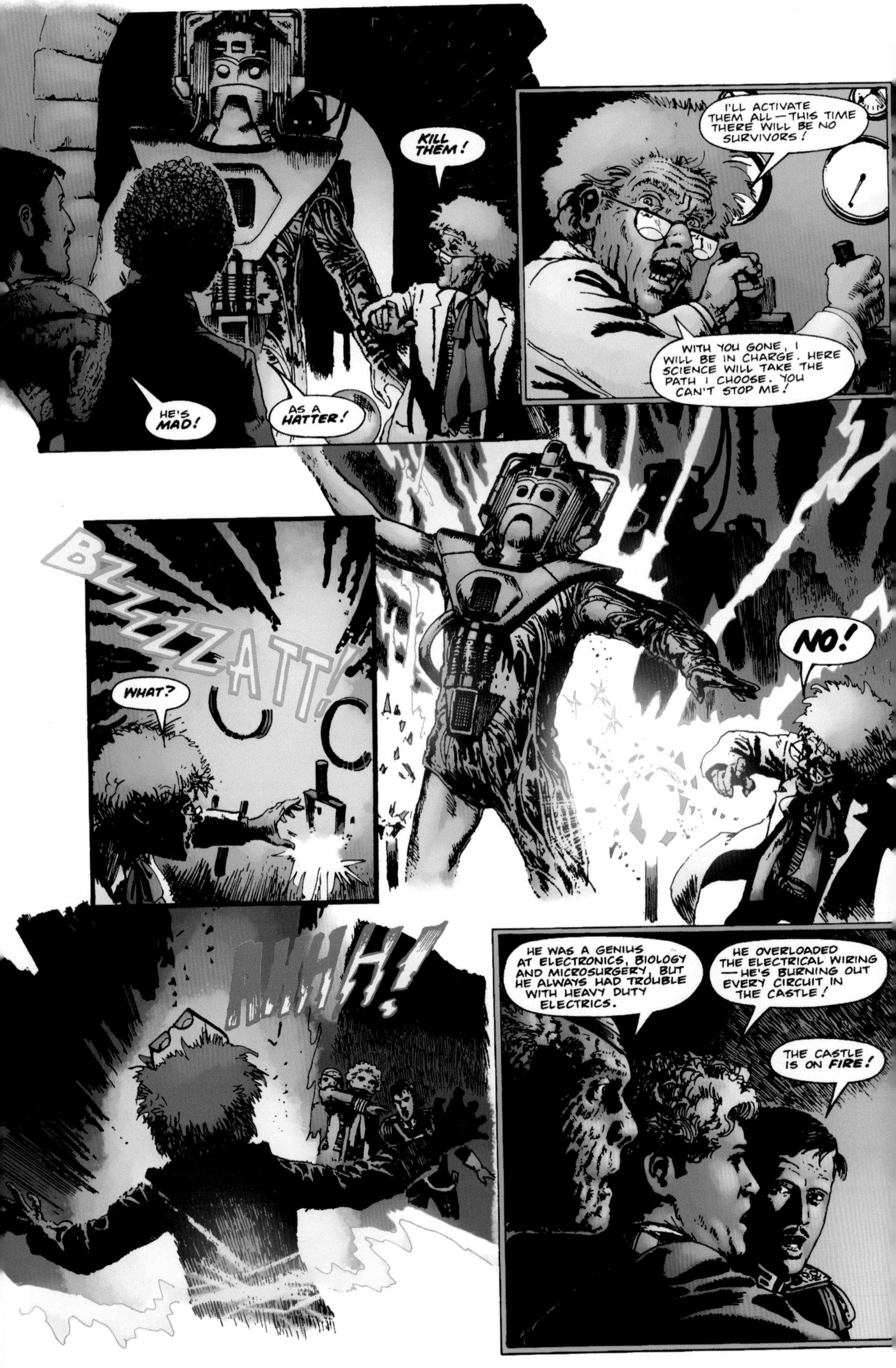
KILL THEM!
HE'S MAD!
AS A HATTER!
I'LL ACTIVATE THEM ALL—THIS TIME THERE WILL BE NO SURVIVORS!
WITH YOU GONE, I WILL BE IN CHARGE. HERE SCIENCE WILL TAKE THE PATH I CHOOSE. YOU CAN'T STOP ME!
BZZZZZATT!
WHAT?
NO!
AHHH!
HE WAS A GENIUS AT ELECTRONICS, BIOLOGY AND MICROSURGERY, BUT HE ALWAYS HAD TROUBLE WITH HEAVY DUTY ELECTRICS.
HE OVERLOADED THE ELECTRICAL WIRING—HE'S BURNING OUT EVERY CIRCUIT IN THE CASTLE!
THE CASTLE IS ON FIRE!

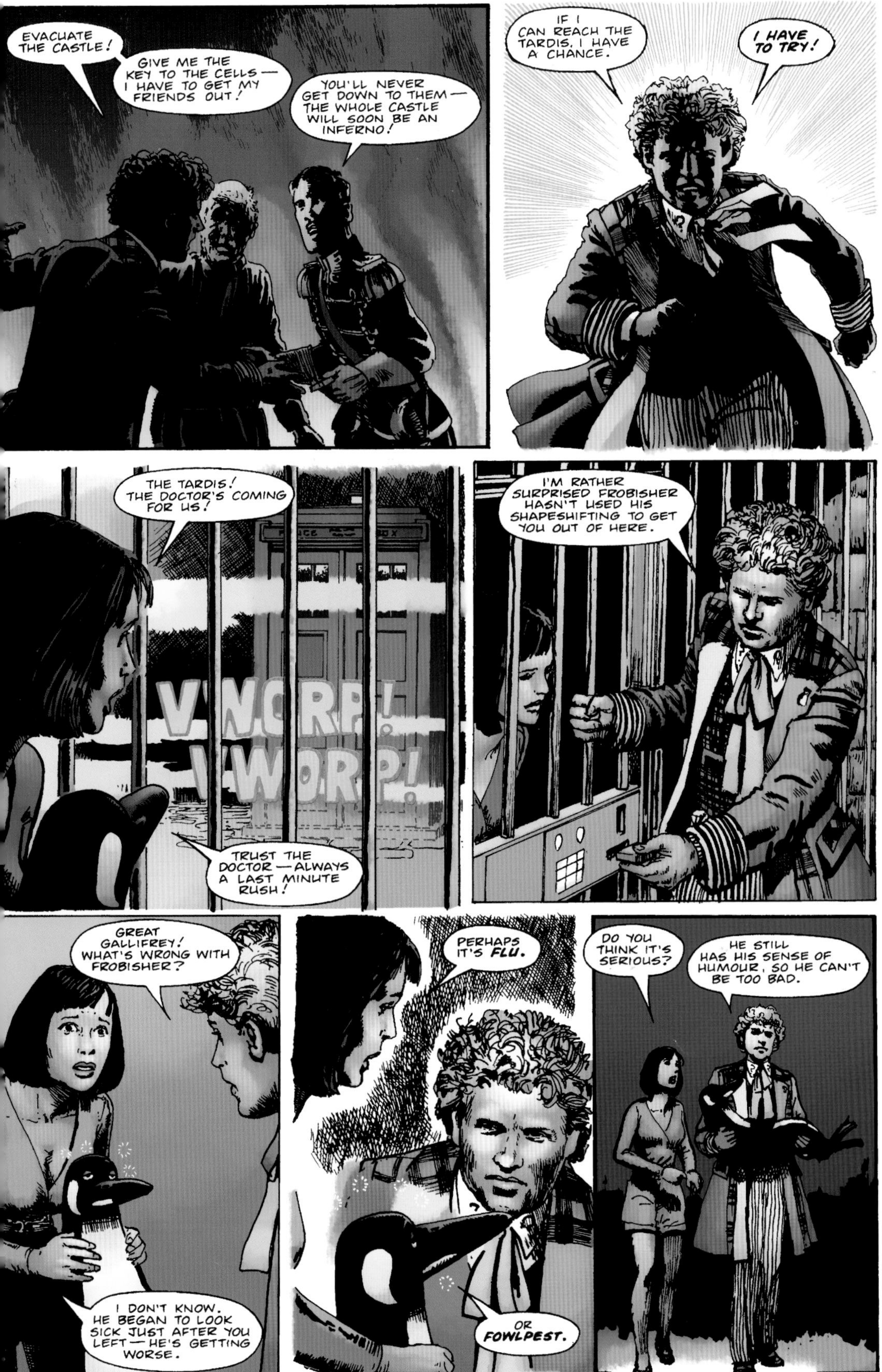
EVACUATE THE CASTLE!
GIVE ME THE KEY TO THE CELLS — I HAVE TO GET MY FRIENDS OUT!
YOU'LL NEVER GET DOWN TO THEM — THE WHOLE CASTLE WILL SOON BE AN INFERNO!
IF I CAN REACH THE TARDIS, I HAVE A CHANCE.
I HAVE TO TRY!
THE TARDIS! THE DOCTOR'S COMING FOR US!
VWORP! VWORP!
TRUST THE DOCTOR — ALWAYS A LAST MINUTE RUSH!
I'M RATHER SURPRISED FROBISHER HASN'T USED HIS SHAPESHIFTING TO GET YOU OUT OF HERE.
GREAT GALLIFREY! WHAT'S WRONG WITH FROBISHER?
I DON'T KNOW. HE BEGAN TO LOOK SICK JUST AFTER YOU LEFT — HE'S GETTING WORSE.
PERHAPS IT'S FLU.
OR FOWLPEST.
DO YOU THINK IT'S SERIOUS?
HE STILL HAS HIS SENSE OF HUMOUR, SO HE CAN'T BE TOO BAD.

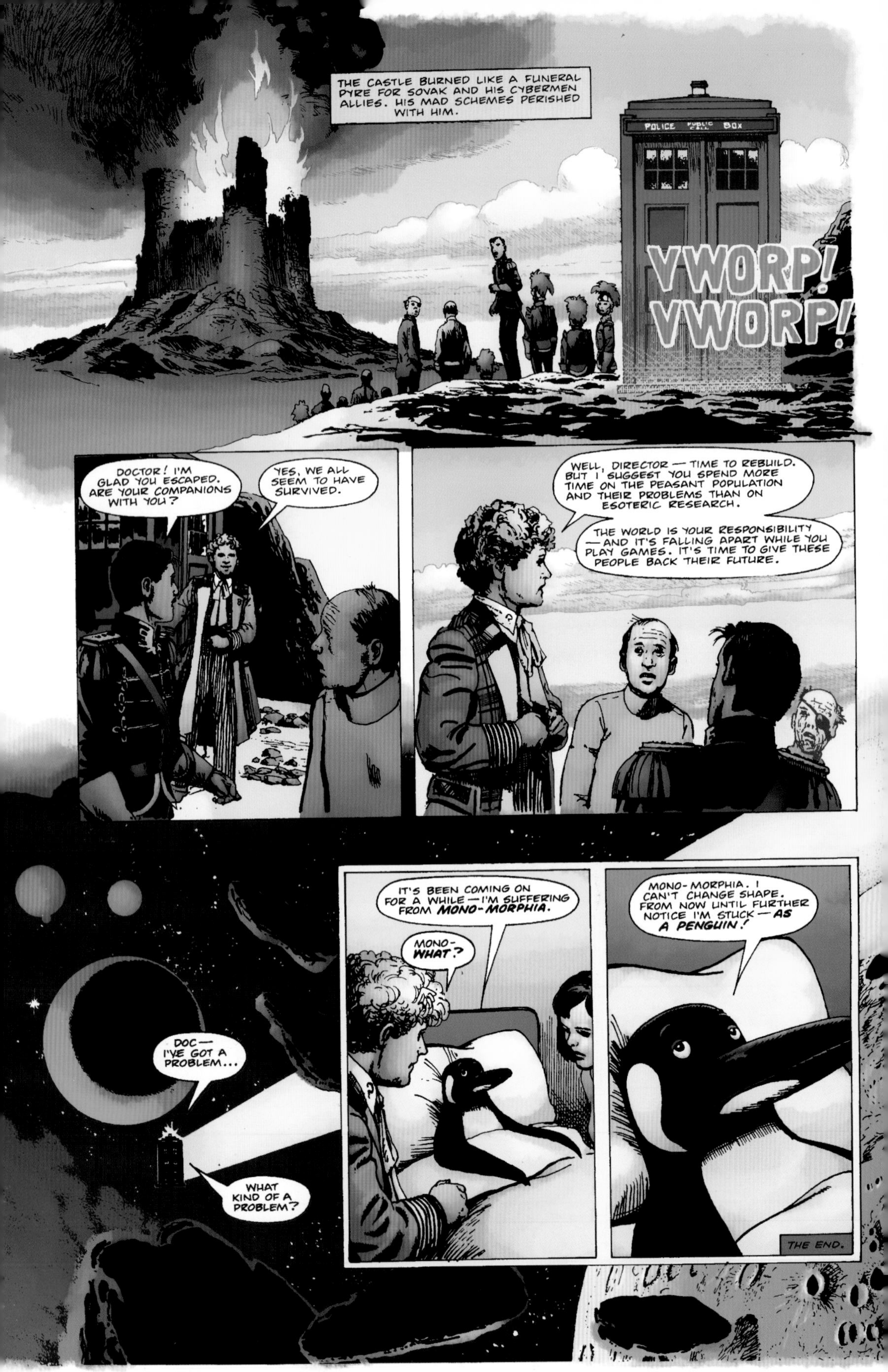
THE CASTLE BURNED LIKE A FUNERAL PYRE FOR SOVAK AND HIS CYBERMEN ALLIES. HIS MAD SCHEMES PERISHED WITH HIM.
POLICE PUBLIC CALL BOX
VWORP! VWORP!
DOCTOR! I'M GLAD YOU ESCAPED. ARE YOUR COMPANIONS WITH YOU?
YES, WE ALL SEEM TO HAVE SURVIVED.
WELL, DIRECTOR — TIME TO REBUILD. BUT I SUGGEST YOU SPEND MORE TIME ON THE PEASANT POPULATION AND THEIR PROBLEMS THAN ON ESOTERIC RESEARCH.
THE WORLD IS YOUR RESPONSIBILITY — AND IT'S FALLING APART WHILE YOU PLAY GAMES. IT'S TIME TO GIVE THESE PEOPLE BACK THEIR FUTURE.
DOC — I'VE GOT A PROBLEM...
WHAT KIND OF A PROBLEM?
IT'S BEEN COMING ON FOR A WHILE — I'M SUFFERING FROM MONO-MORPHIA.
MONO-WHAT?
MONO-MORPHIA. I CAN'T CHANGE SHAPE. FROM NOW UNTIL FURTHER NOTICE I'M STUCK — AS A PENGUIN!
THE END.

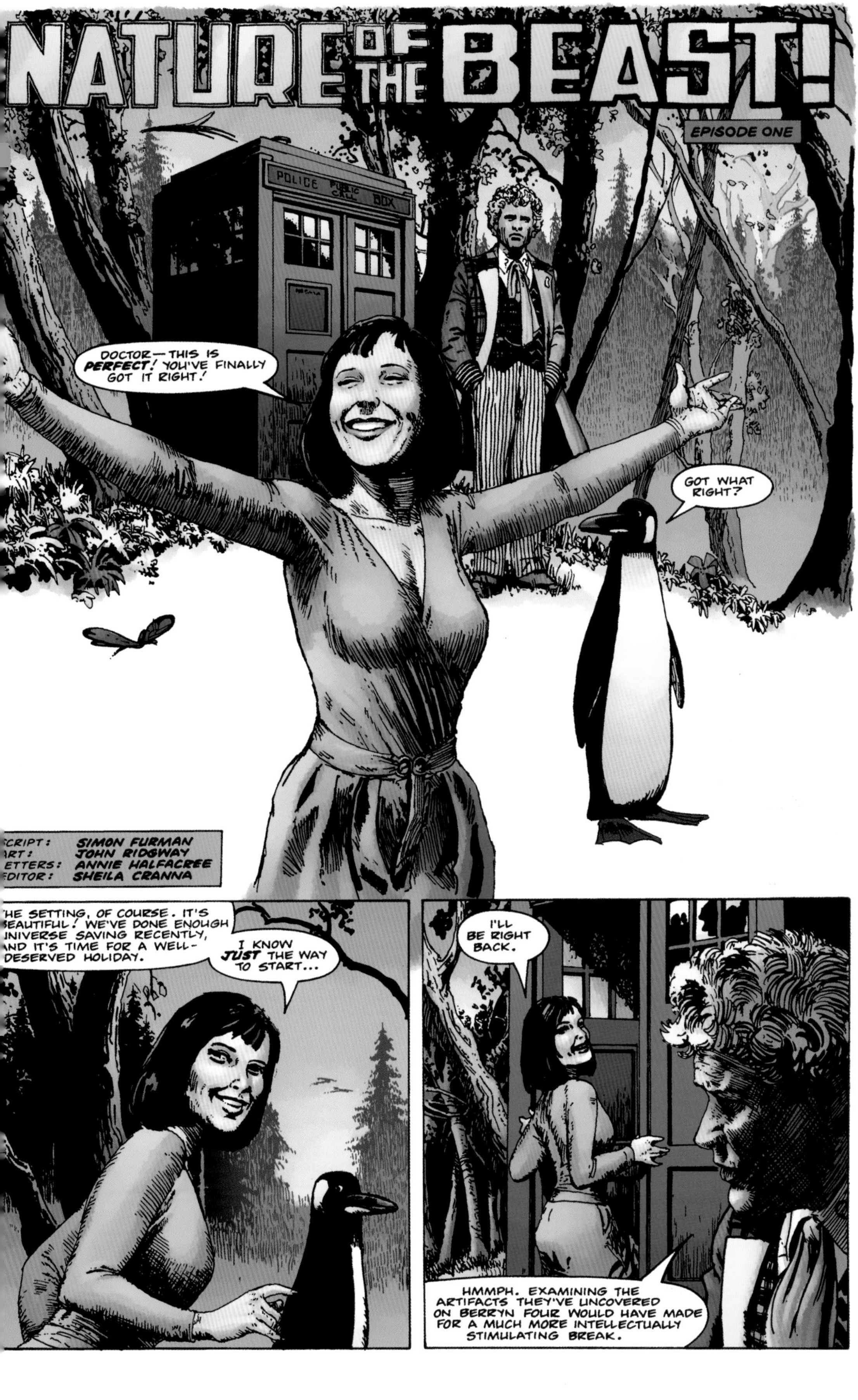
NATURE OF THE BEAST!
EPISODE ONE
POLICE PUBLIC CALL BOX
DOCTOR—THIS IS PERFECT! YOU'VE FINALLY GOT IT RIGHT!
GOT WHAT RIGHT?
CRIPT: SIMON FURMAN
RT: JOHN RIDGWAY
ETTERS: ANNIE HALFACREE
DITOR: SHEILA CRANNA
HE SETTING, OF COURSE. IT'S EAUTIFUL! WE'VE DONE ENOUGH NIVERSE SAVING RECENTLY, ND IT'S TIME FOR A WELL-DESERVED HOLIDAY.
I KNOW JUST THE WAY TO START...
I'LL BE RIGHT BACK.
HMMPH. EXAMINING THE ARTIFACTS THEY'VE UNCOVERED ON BERRYN FOUR WOULD HAVE MADE FOR A MUCH MORE INTELLECTUALLY STIMULATING BREAK.

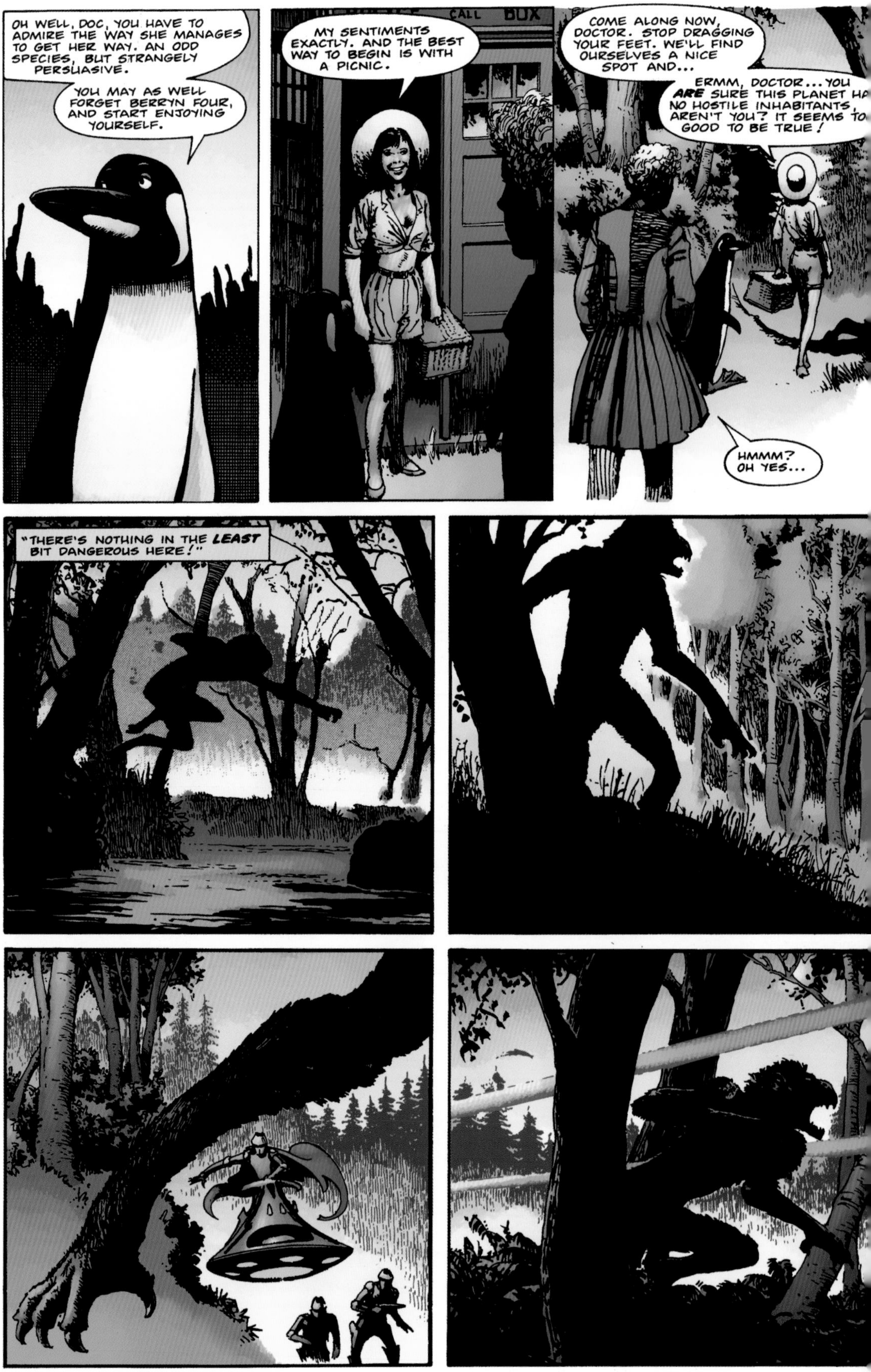
OH WELL, DOC, YOU HAVE TO ADMIRE THE WAY SHE MANAGES TO GET HER WAY. AN ODD SPECIES, BUT STRANGELY PERSUASIVE.
YOU MAY AS WELL FORGET BERRYN FOUR, AND START ENJOYING YOURSELF.
CALL BOX
MY SENTIMENTS EXACTLY. AND THE BEST WAY TO BEGIN IS WITH A PICNIC.
COME ALONG NOW, DOCTOR. STOP DRAGGING YOUR FEET. WE'LL FIND OURSELVES A NICE SPOT AND...
ERMM, DOCTOR... YOU ***ARE*** SURE THIS PLANET HA NO HOSTILE INHABITANTS, AREN'T YOU? IT SEEMS TO GOOD TO BE TRUE!
HMMM? OH YES...
"THERE'S NOTHING IN THE ***LEAST*** BIT DANGEROUS HERE!"

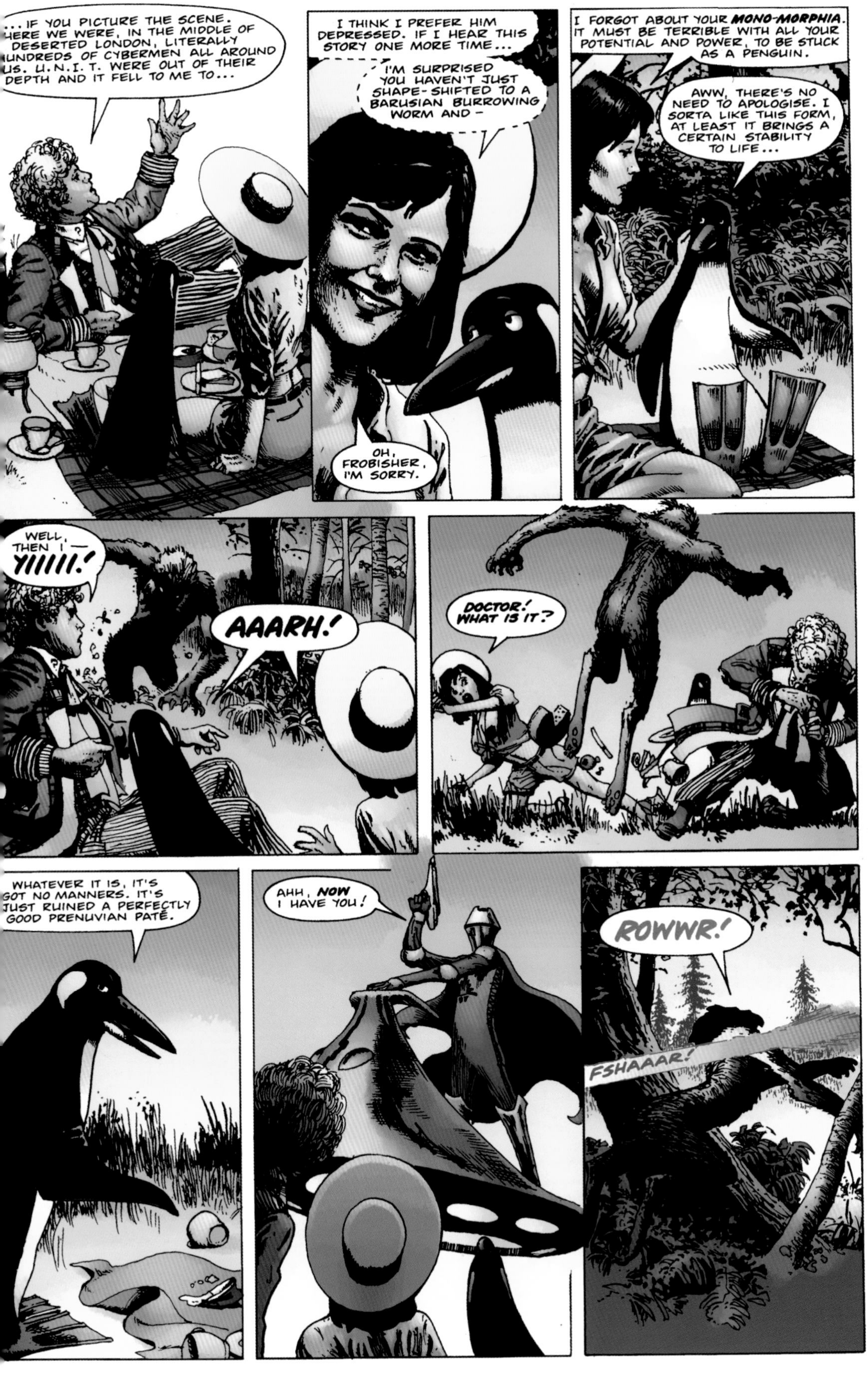

...IF YOU PICTURE THE SCENE. HERE WE WERE, IN THE MIDDLE OF DESERTED LONDON, LITERALLY HUNDREDS OF CYBERMEN ALL AROUND US. U.N.I.T. WERE OUT OF THEIR DEPTH AND IT FELL TO ME TO...
I THINK I PREFER HIM DEPRESSED. IF I HEAR THIS STORY ONE MORE TIME...
I'M SURPRISED YOU HAVEN'T JUST SHAPE-SHIFTED TO A BARUSIAN BURROWING WORM AND -
OH, FROBISHER, I'M SORRY.
I FORGOT ABOUT YOUR MONO-MORPHIA. IT MUST BE TERRIBLE WITH ALL YOUR POTENTIAL AND POWER, TO BE STUCK AS A PENGUIN.
AWW, THERE'S NO NEED TO APOLOGISE. I SORTA LIKE THIS FORM, AT LEAST IT BRINGS A CERTAIN STABILITY TO LIFE...
WELL, THEN I — YIIIII!
AAARH!
DOCTOR! WHAT IS IT?
WHATEVER IT IS, IT'S GOT NO MANNERS. IT'S JUST RUINED A PERFECTLY GOOD PRENUVIAN PATÉ.
AHH, NOW I HAVE YOU!
ROWWR!
FSHAAAR!

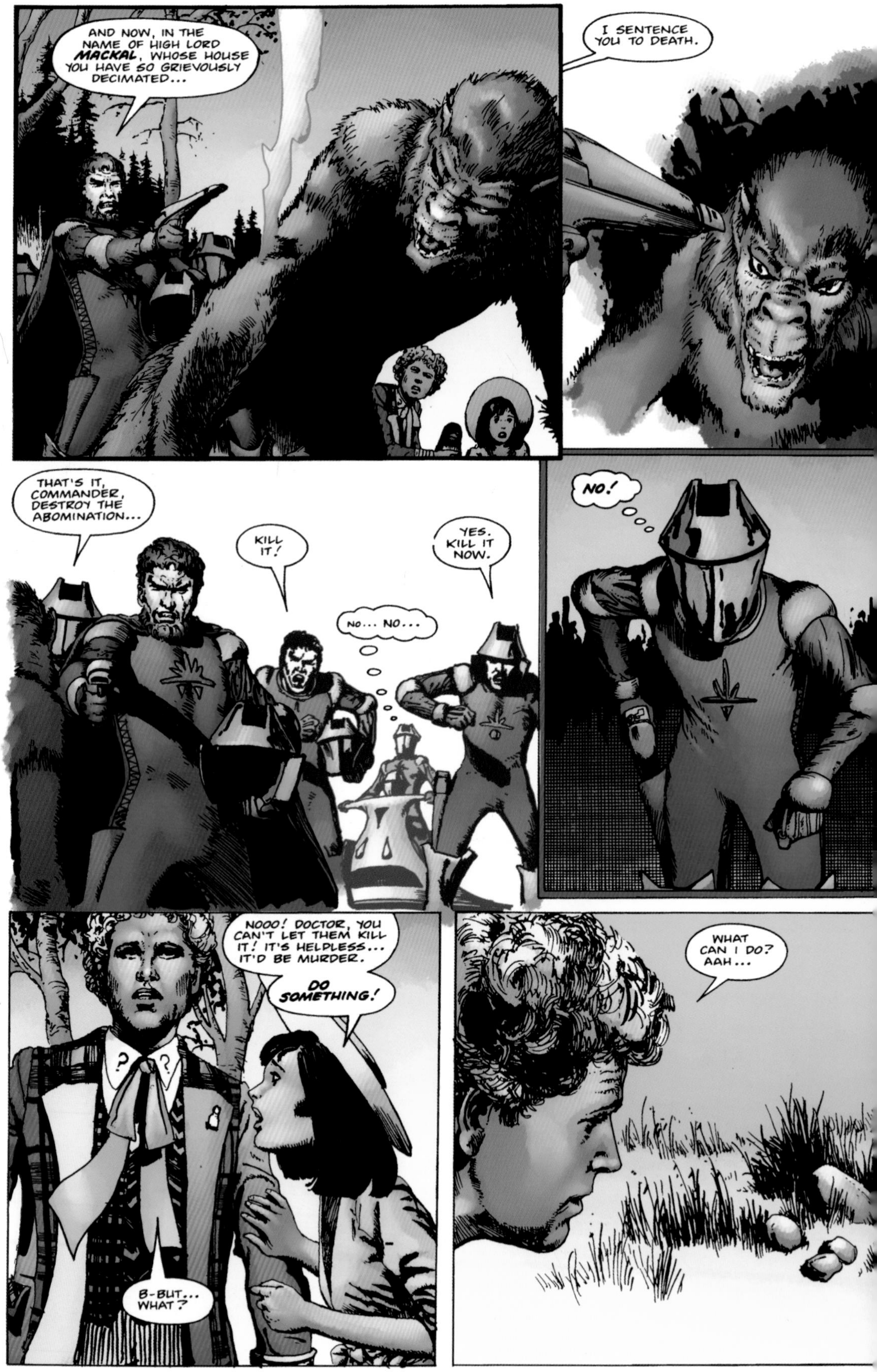
AND NOW, IN THE NAME OF HIGH LORD MACKAL, WHOSE HOUSE YOU HAVE SO GRIEVOUSLY DECIMATED...
I SENTENCE YOU TO DEATH.
THAT'S IT, COMMANDER, DESTROY THE ABOMINATION...
KILL IT!
YES. KILL IT NOW.
NO... NO...
NO!
NOOO! DOCTOR, YOU CAN'T LET THEM KILL IT! IT'S HELPLESS... IT'D BE MURDER.
DO SOMETHING!
B-BUT... WHAT?
WHAT CAN I DO? AAH...

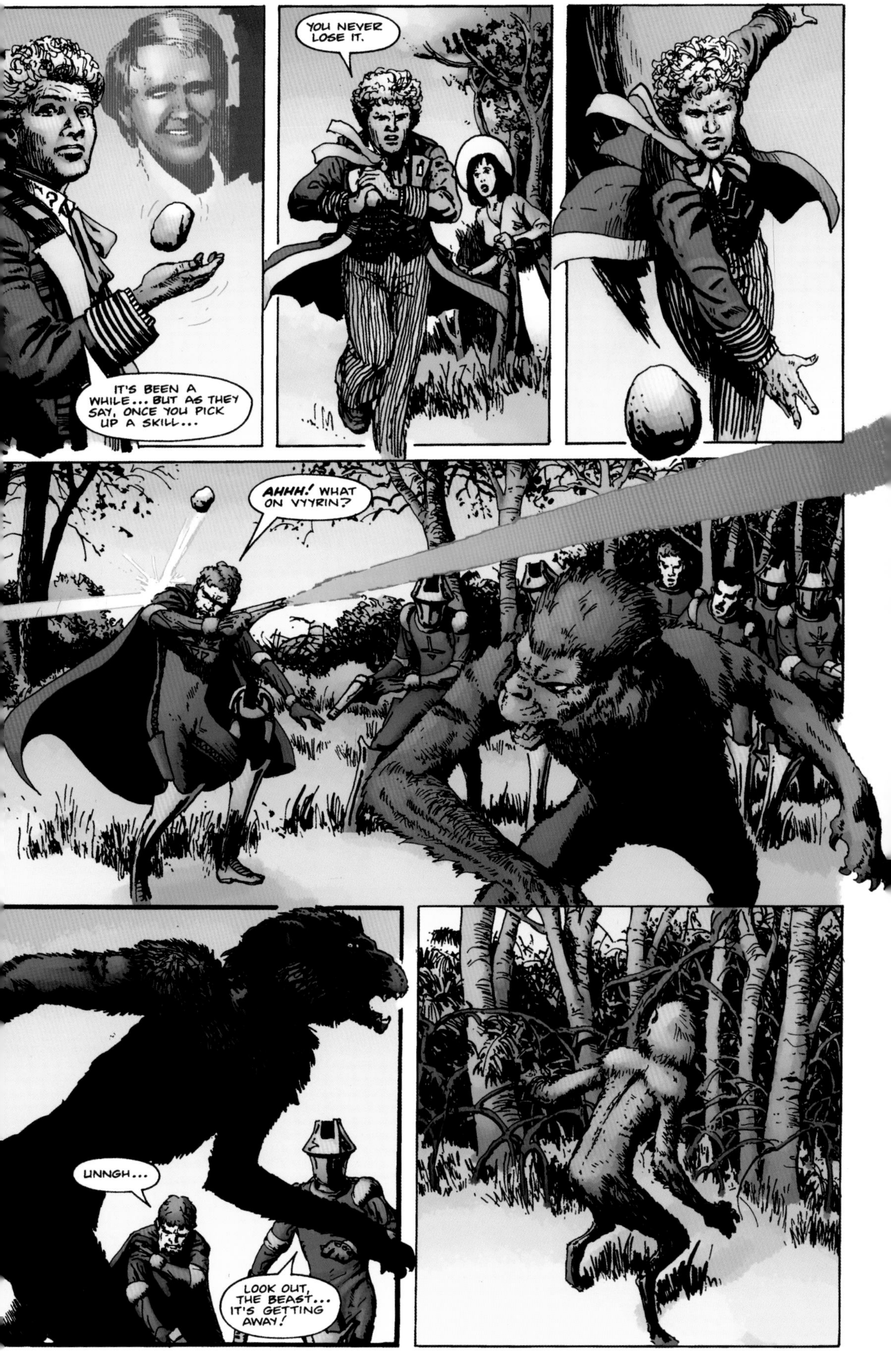

IT'S BEEN A WHILE... BUT AS THEY SAY, ONCE YOU PICK UP A SKILL...
YOU NEVER LOSE IT.
AHHH! WHAT ON VYYRIN?
UNNGH...
LOOK OUT, THE BEAST... IT'S GETTING AWAY!

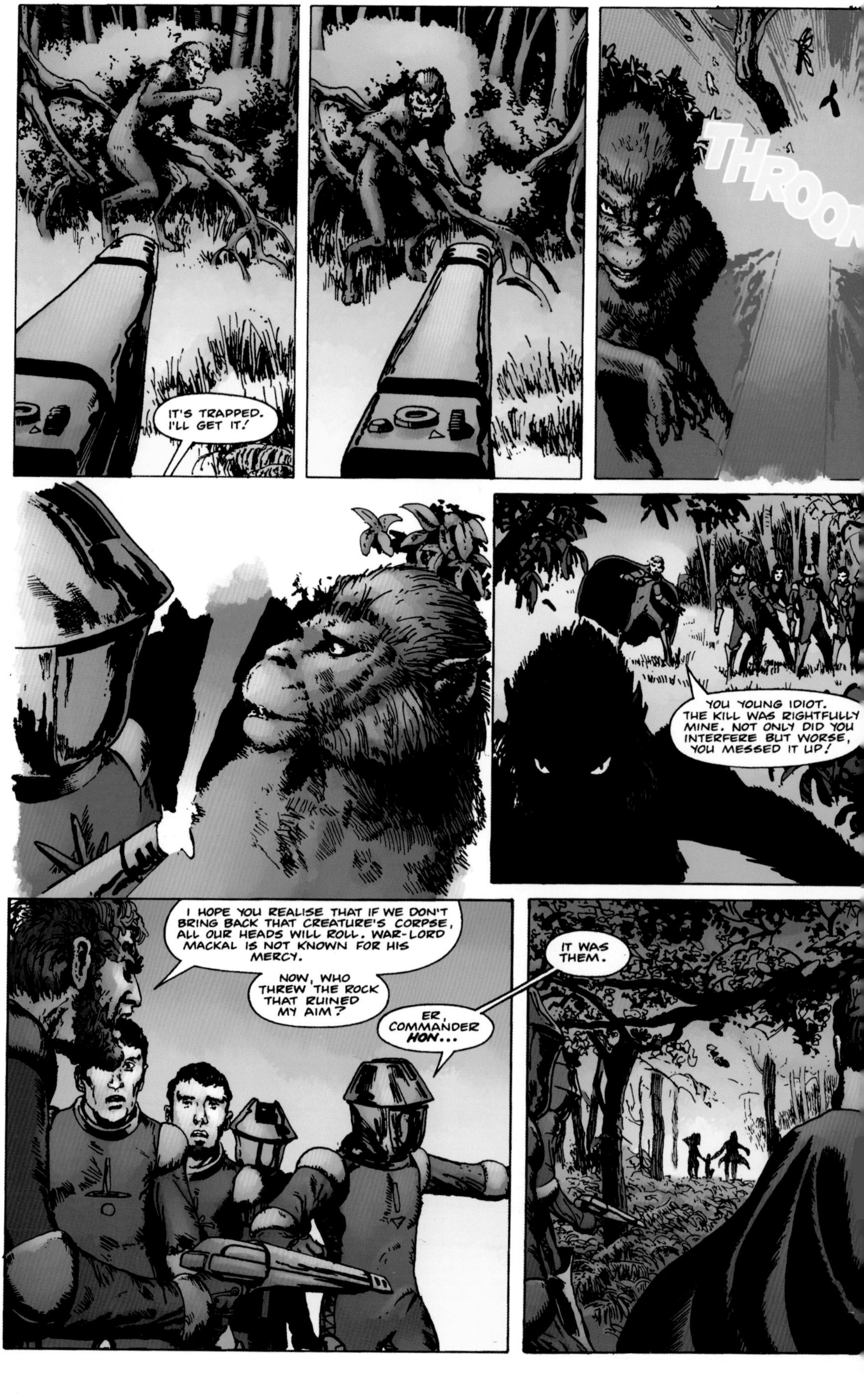
IT'S TRAPPED. I'LL GET IT!
THROOM
YOU YOUNG IDIOT. THE KILL WAS RIGHTFULLY MINE. NOT ONLY DID YOU INTERFERE BUT WORSE, YOU MESSED IT UP!
I HOPE YOU REALISE THAT IF WE DON'T BRING BACK THAT CREATURE'S CORPSE, ALL OUR HEADS WILL ROLL. WAR-LORD MACKAL IS NOT KNOWN FOR HIS MERCY.
NOW, WHO THREW THE ROCK THAT RUINED MY AIM?
ER, COMMANDER HON...
IT WAS THEM.

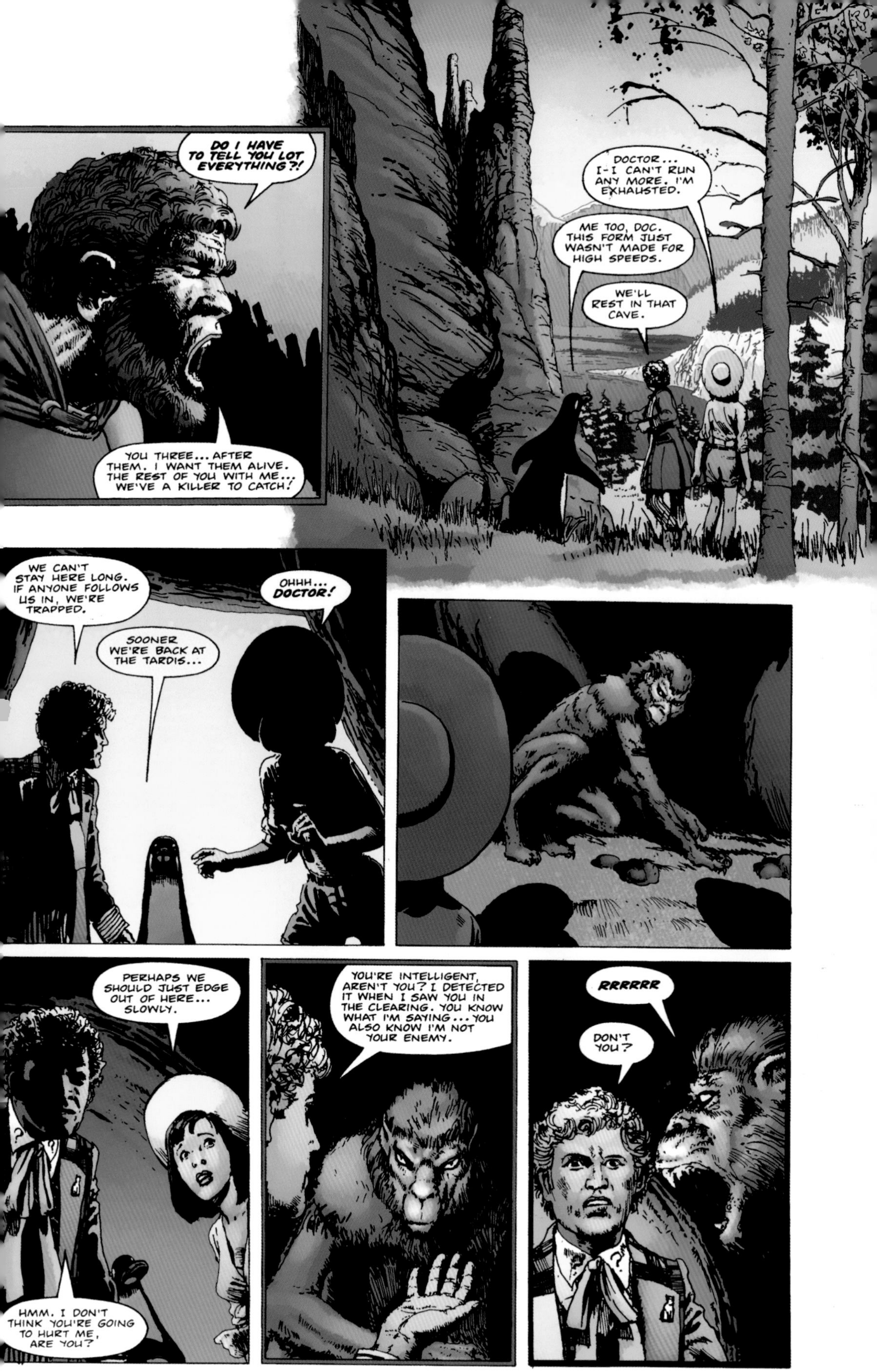

DO I HAVE TO TELL YOU LOT EVERYTHING?!
YOU THREE... AFTER THEM. I WANT THEM ALIVE. THE REST OF YOU WITH ME... WE'VE A KILLER TO CATCH!
DOCTOR... I-I CAN'T RUN ANY MORE. I'M EXHAUSTED.
ME TOO, DOC. THIS FORM JUST WASN'T MADE FOR HIGH SPEEDS.
WE'LL REST IN THAT CAVE.
WE CAN'T STAY HERE LONG. IF ANYONE FOLLOWS US IN, WE'RE TRAPPED.
SOONER WE'RE BACK AT THE TARDIS...
OHHH... DOCTOR!
PERHAPS WE SHOULD JUST EDGE OUT OF HERE... SLOWLY.
HMM. I DON'T THINK YOU'RE GOING TO HURT ME, ARE YOU?
YOU'RE INTELLIGENT, AREN'T YOU? I DETECTED IT WHEN I SAW YOU IN THE CLEARING. YOU KNOW WHAT I'M SAYING... YOU ALSO KNOW I'M NOT YOUR ENEMY.
RRRRRR
DON'T YOU?

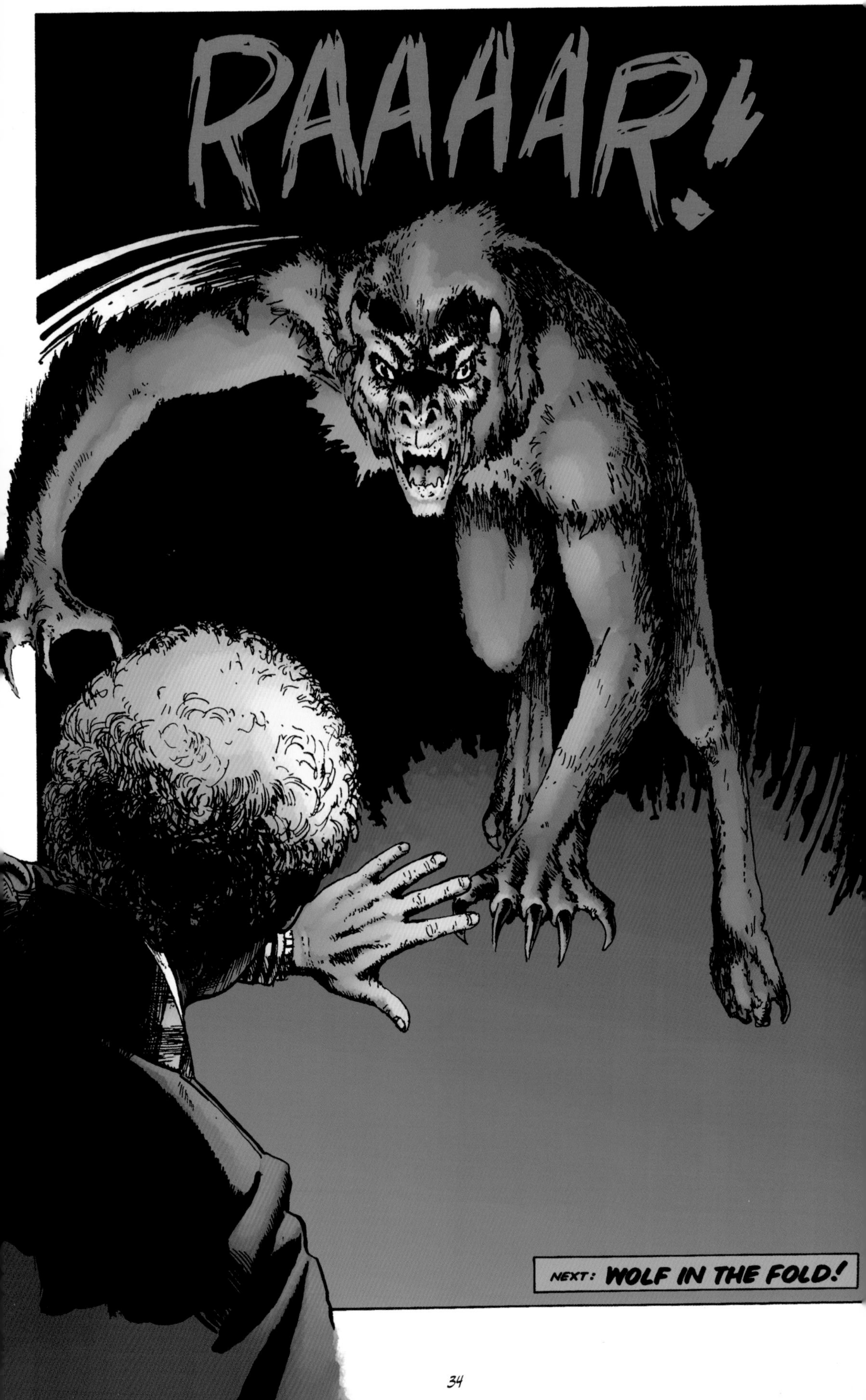
RAAAAR!
NEXT: WOLF IN THE FOLD!

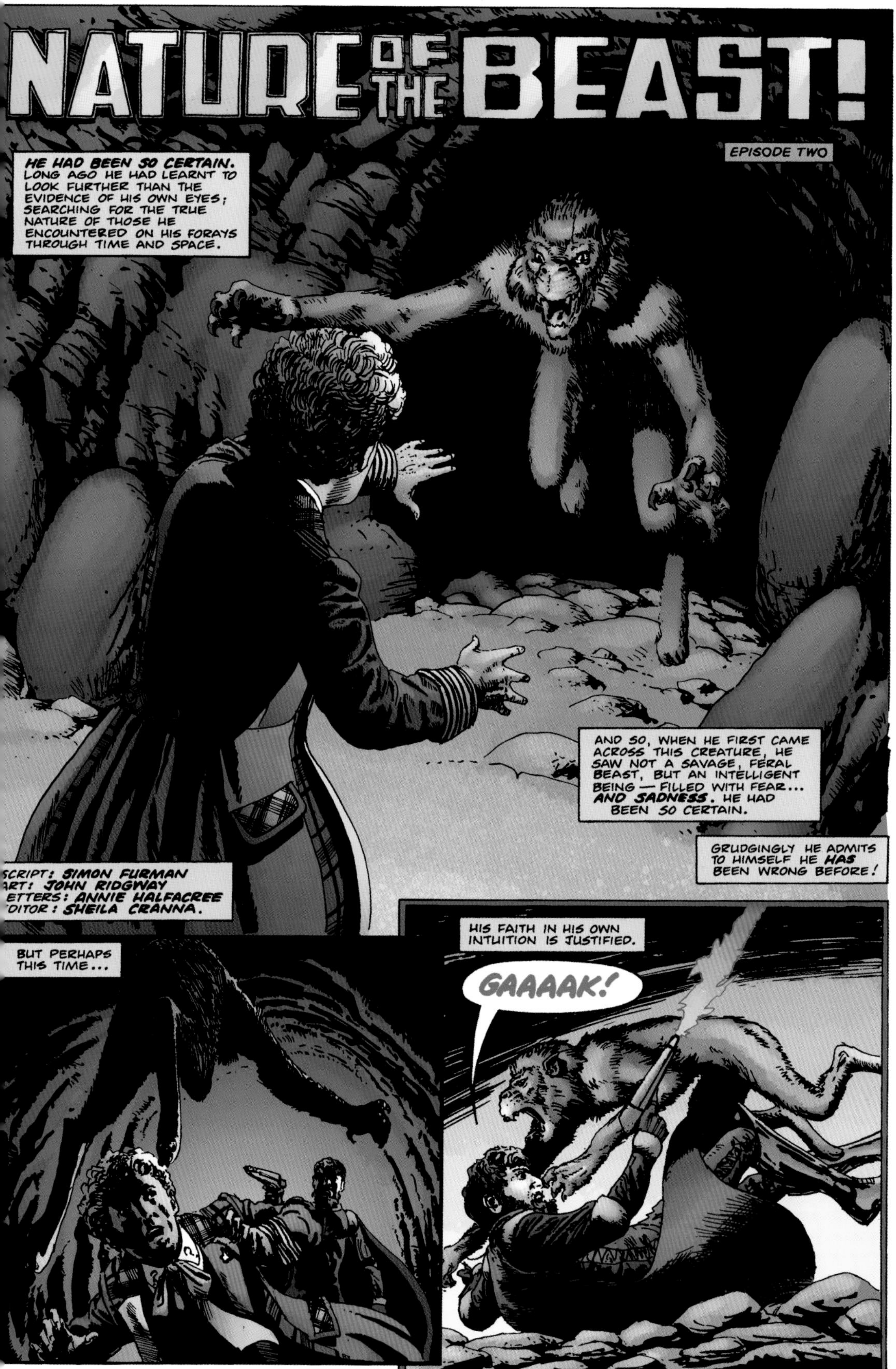
NATURE OF THE BEAST!
EPISODE TWO
HE HAD BEEN SO CERTAIN. LONG AGO HE HAD LEARNT TO LOOK FURTHER THAN THE EVIDENCE OF HIS OWN EYES; SEARCHING FOR THE TRUE NATURE OF THOSE HE ENCOUNTERED ON HIS FORAYS THROUGH TIME AND SPACE.
AND SO, WHEN HE FIRST CAME ACROSS THIS CREATURE, HE SAW NOT A SAVAGE, FERAL BEAST, BUT AN INTELLIGENT BEING — FILLED WITH FEAR... AND SADNESS. HE HAD BEEN SO CERTAIN.
GRUDGINGLY HE ADMITS TO HIMSELF HE HAS BEEN WRONG BEFORE!
SCRIPT: SIMON FURMAN
ART: JOHN RIDGWAY
LETTERS: ANNIE HALFACREE
EDITOR: SHEILA CRANNA.
BUT PERHAPS THIS TIME...
HIS FAITH IN HIS OWN INTUITION IS JUSTIFIED.
GAAAAK!

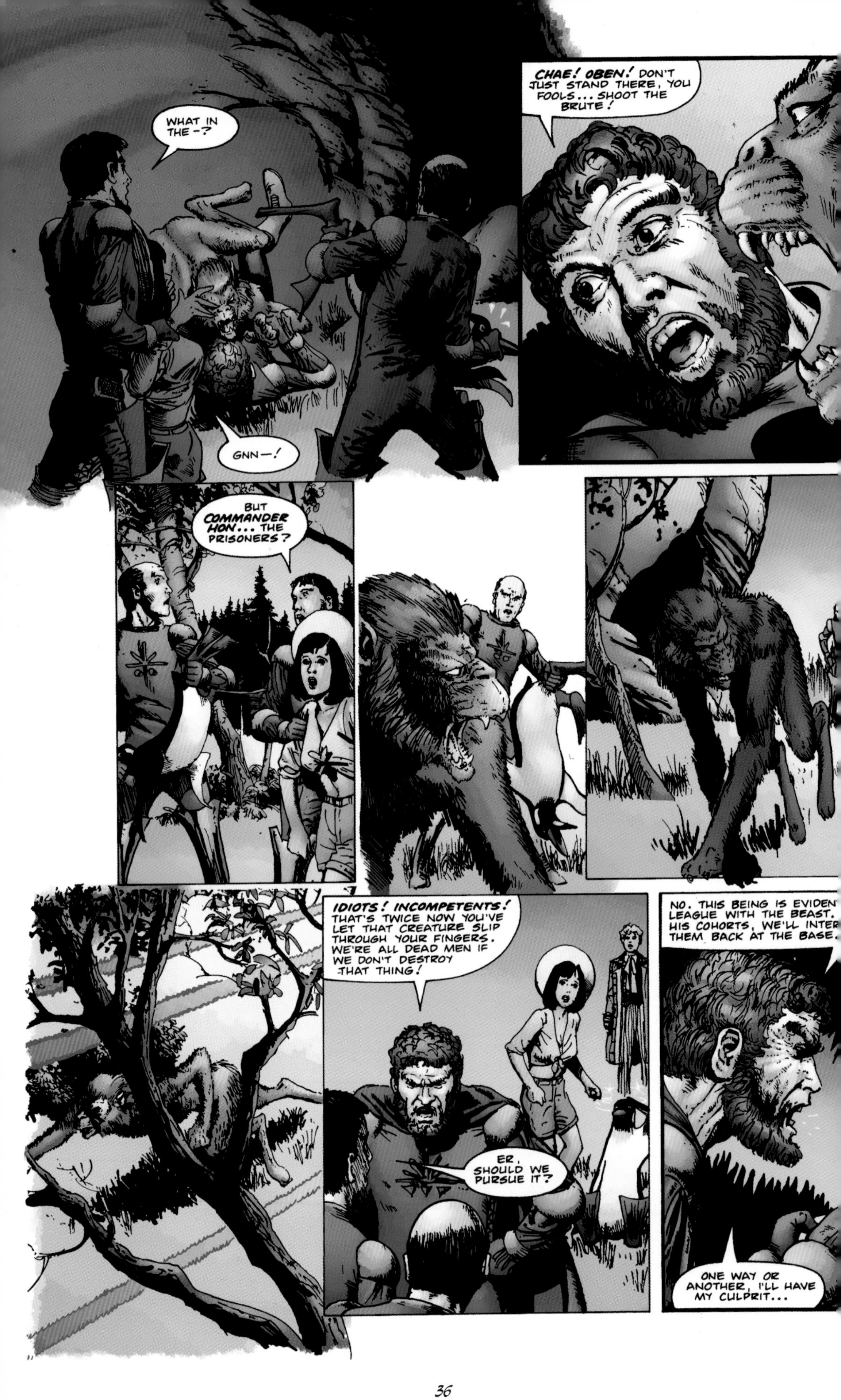
WHAT IN THE -?
GNN-!
CHAE! OBEN! DON'T JUST STAND THERE, YOU FOOLS... SHOOT THE BRUTE!
BUT COMMANDER HON... THE PRISONERS?
IDIOTS! INCOMPETENTS! THAT'S TWICE NOW YOU'VE LET THAT CREATURE SLIP THROUGH YOUR FINGERS. WE'RE ALL DEAD MEN IF WE DON'T DESTROY THAT THING!
ER, SHOULD WE PURSUE IT?
ONE WAY OR ANOTHER, I'LL HAVE MY CULPRIT...

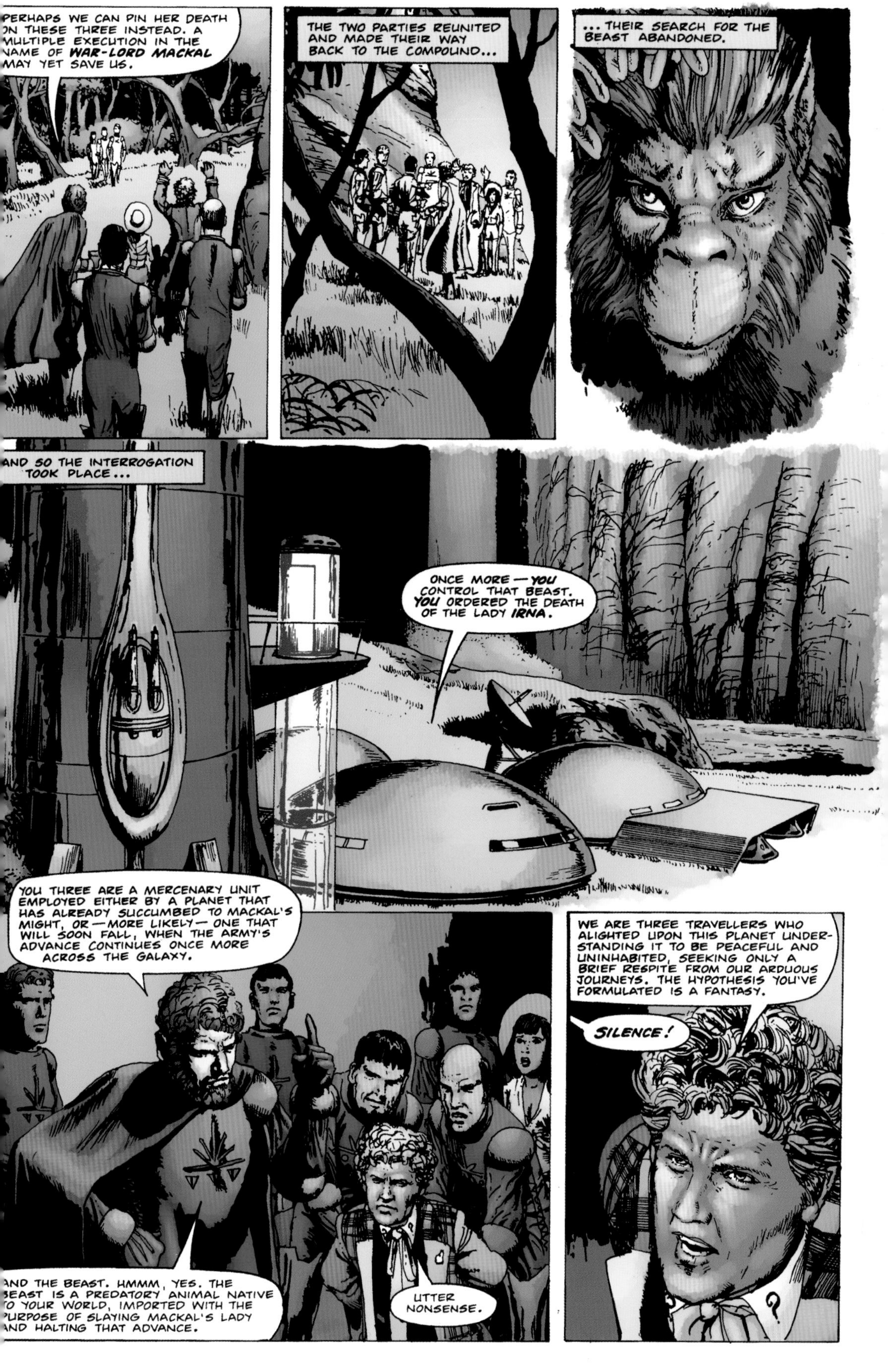

PERHAPS WE CAN PIN HER DEATH ON THESE THREE INSTEAD. A MULTIPLE EXECUTION IN THE NAME OF WAR-LORD MACKAL MAY YET SAVE US.
THE TWO PARTIES REUNITED AND MADE THEIR WAY BACK TO THE COMPOUND...
... THEIR SEARCH FOR THE BEAST ABANDONED.
AND SO THE INTERROGATION TOOK PLACE...
ONCE MORE — YOU CONTROL THAT BEAST. YOU ORDERED THE DEATH OF THE LADY IRNA.
YOU THREE ARE A MERCENARY UNIT EMPLOYED EITHER BY A PLANET THAT HAS ALREADY SUCCUMBED TO MACKAL'S MIGHT, OR — MORE LIKELY — ONE THAT WILL SOON FALL, WHEN THE ARMY'S ADVANCE CONTINUES ONCE MORE ACROSS THE GALAXY.
AND THE BEAST. HMMM, YES. THE BEAST IS A PREDATORY ANIMAL NATIVE TO YOUR WORLD, IMPORTED WITH THE PURPOSE OF SLAYING MACKAL'S LADY AND HALTING THAT ADVANCE.
UTTER NONSENSE.
WE ARE THREE TRAVELLERS WHO ALIGHTED UPON THIS PLANET UNDERSTANDING IT TO BE PEACEFUL AND UNINHABITED, SEEKING ONLY A BRIEF RESPITE FROM OUR ARDUOUS JOURNEYS. THE HYPOTHESIS YOU'VE FORMULATED IS A FANTASY.
SILENCE!

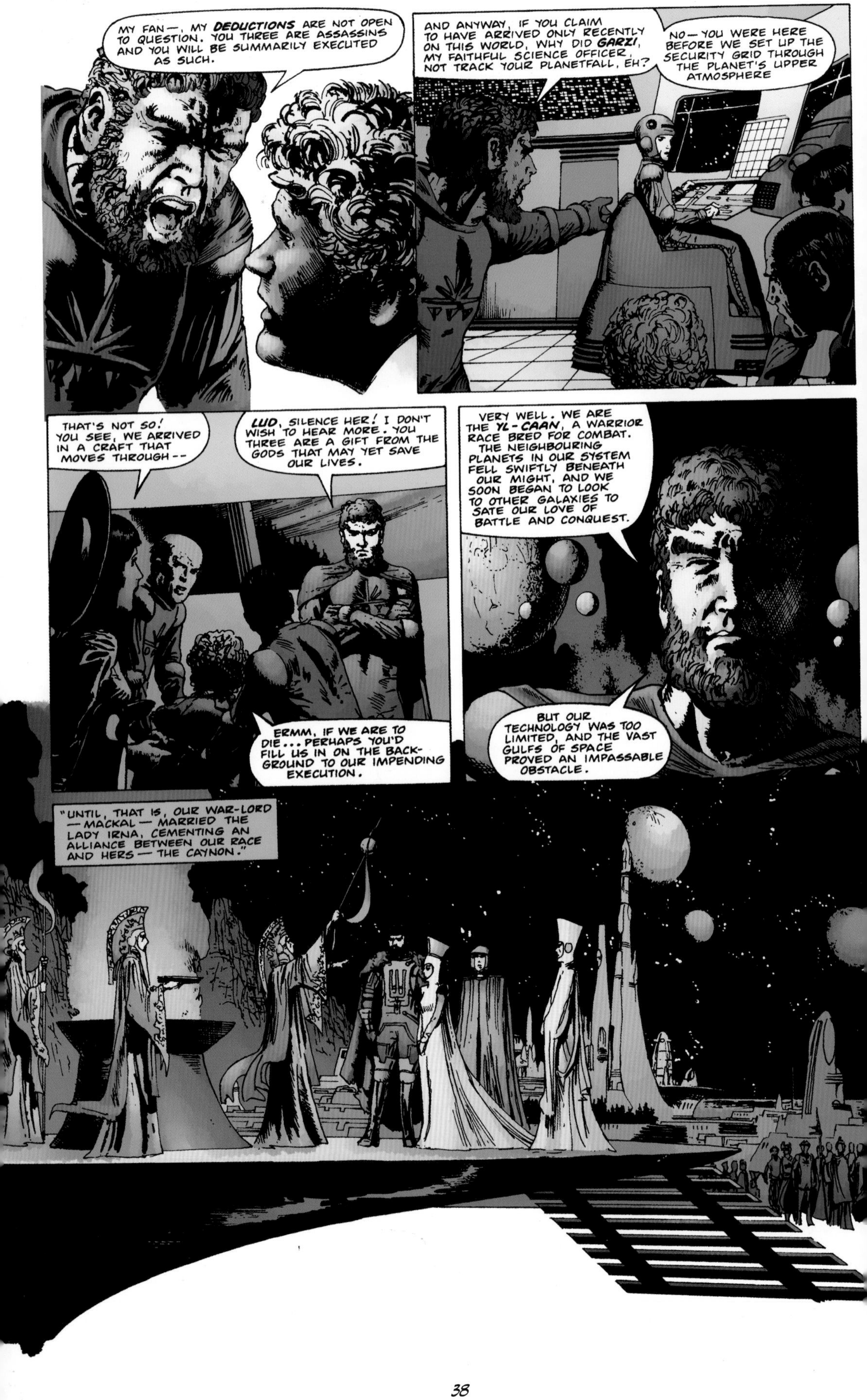
MY FAN—, MY DEDUCTIONS ARE NOT OPEN TO QUESTION. YOU THREE ARE ASSASSINS AND YOU WILL BE SUMMARILY EXECUTED AS SUCH.
AND ANYWAY, IF YOU CLAIM TO HAVE ARRIVED ONLY RECENTLY ON THIS WORLD, WHY DID GARZI, MY FAITHFUL SCIENCE OFFICER, NOT TRACK YOUR PLANETFALL, EH?
NO—YOU WERE HERE BEFORE WE SET UP THE SECURITY GRID THROUGH THE PLANET'S UPPER ATMOSPHERE
THAT'S NOT SO! YOU SEE, WE ARRIVED IN A CRAFT THAT MOVES THROUGH--
LUD, SILENCE HER! I DON'T WISH TO HEAR MORE. YOU THREE ARE A GIFT FROM THE GODS THAT MAY YET SAVE OUR LIVES.
ERMM, IF WE ARE TO DIE... PERHAPS YOU'D FILL US IN ON THE BACKGROUND TO OUR IMPENDING EXECUTION.
VERY WELL. WE ARE THE YL-CAAN, A WARRIOR RACE BRED FOR COMBAT. THE NEIGHBOURING PLANETS IN OUR SYSTEM FELL SWIFTLY BENEATH OUR MIGHT, AND WE SOON BEGAN TO LOOK TO OTHER GALAXIES TO SATE OUR LOVE OF BATTLE AND CONQUEST.
BUT OUR TECHNOLOGY WAS TOO LIMITED, AND THE VAST GULFS OF SPACE PROVED AN IMPASSABLE OBSTACLE.
"UNTIL, THAT IS, OUR WAR-LORD —MACKAL— MARRIED THE LADY IRNA, CEMENTING AN ALLIANCE BETWEEN OUR RACE AND HERS — THE CAYNON."

"THE CAYNON HAD MASTERED THE TECHNIQUES OF TRAVEL THROUGH WARP SPACE, COVERING VAST DISTANCES IN THE BLINK OF AN EYE. UNITING, OUR VAST ARMADAS CLEARED THE WAY TO THE CONQUEST OF WORLDS AND GALAXIES, NO MATTER HOW DISTANT."

"QUICKLY OUR EMPIRE SPREAD ACROSS KNOWN SPACE AND BEYOND. NO PLANET COULD STAND IN OUR WAY."

THERE WAS NO QUESTION OF DEFEAT FOR OUR FORCES. SHOULD A PLANET SUCCESSFULLY RESIST CONQUEST, EACH MILITARY FORCE CARRIED A NO-WIN DEVICE —TO BE DETONATED IN THE EVENT OF DEFEAT. IF WE COULDN'T HAVE THEIR PLANET, NEITHER WOULD THEY."

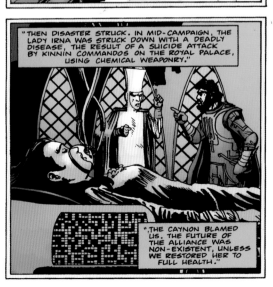

"THEN DISASTER STRUCK. IN MID-CAMPAIGN, THE LADY IRNA WAS STRUCK DOWN WITH A DEADLY DISEASE, THE RESULT OF A SUICIDE ATTACK BY KINNIN COMMANDOS ON THE ROYAL PALACE, USING CHEMICAL WEAPONRY."

".THE CAYNON BLAMED US. THE FUTURE OF THE ALLIANCE WAS NON-EXISTENT, UNLESS WE RESTORED HER TO FULL HEALTH."

"THE PROPERTIES OF A RARE PLANETARY ATMOSPHERE WERE DISCOVERED TO BE THE ONLY WAY TO COMBAT IRNA'S CONDITION. HOSTILITIES WERE HALTED WHILE TASK FORCES SEARCHED FOR SUCH A PLANET."

"UNFORTUNATELY, WE FOUND IT."

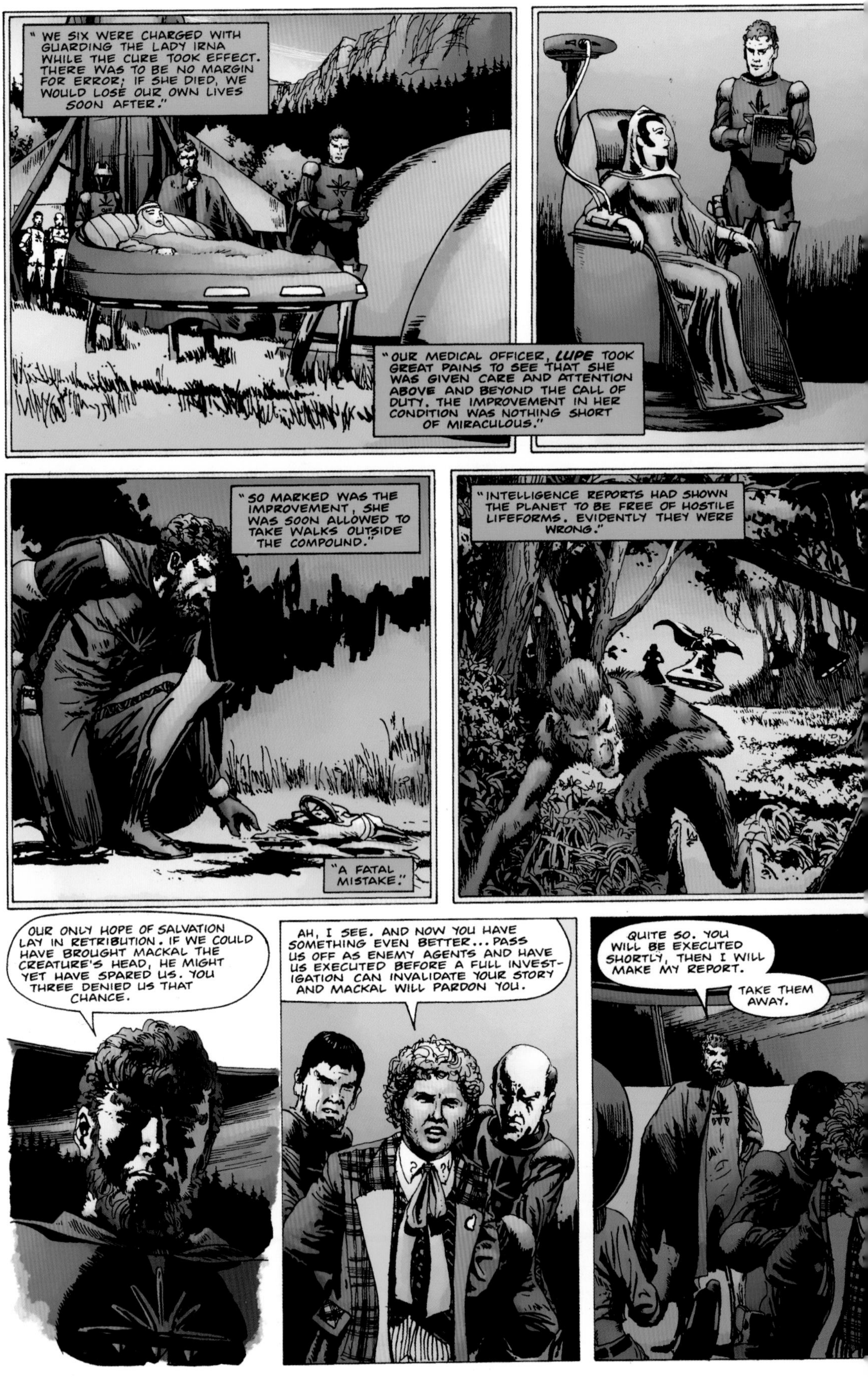
"WE SIX WERE CHARGED WITH GUARDING THE LADY IRNA WHILE THE CURE TOOK EFFECT. THERE WAS TO BE NO MARGIN FOR ERROR; IF SHE DIED, WE WOULD LOSE OUR OWN LIVES SOON AFTER."
"OUR MEDICAL OFFICER, LUPE TOOK GREAT PAINS TO SEE THAT SHE WAS GIVEN CARE AND ATTENTION ABOVE AND BEYOND THE CALL OF DUTY. THE IMPROVEMENT IN HER CONDITION WAS NOTHING SHORT OF MIRACULOUS."
"SO MARKED WAS THE IMPROVEMENT, SHE WAS SOON ALLOWED TO TAKE WALKS OUTSIDE THE COMPOUND."
"A FATAL MISTAKE."
"INTELLIGENCE REPORTS HAD SHOWN THE PLANET TO BE FREE OF HOSTILE LIFEFORMS. EVIDENTLY THEY WERE WRONG."
OUR ONLY HOPE OF SALVATION LAY IN RETRIBUTION. IF WE COULD HAVE BROUGHT MACKAL THE CREATURE'S HEAD, HE MIGHT YET HAVE SPARED US. YOU THREE DENIED US THAT CHANCE.
AH, I SEE. AND NOW YOU HAVE SOMETHING EVEN BETTER... PASS US OFF AS ENEMY AGENTS AND HAVE US EXECUTED BEFORE A FULL INVESTIGATION CAN INVALIDATE YOUR STORY AND MACKAL WILL PARDON YOU.
QUITE SO. YOU WILL BE EXECUTED SHORTLY, THEN I WILL MAKE MY REPORT.
TAKE THEM AWAY.

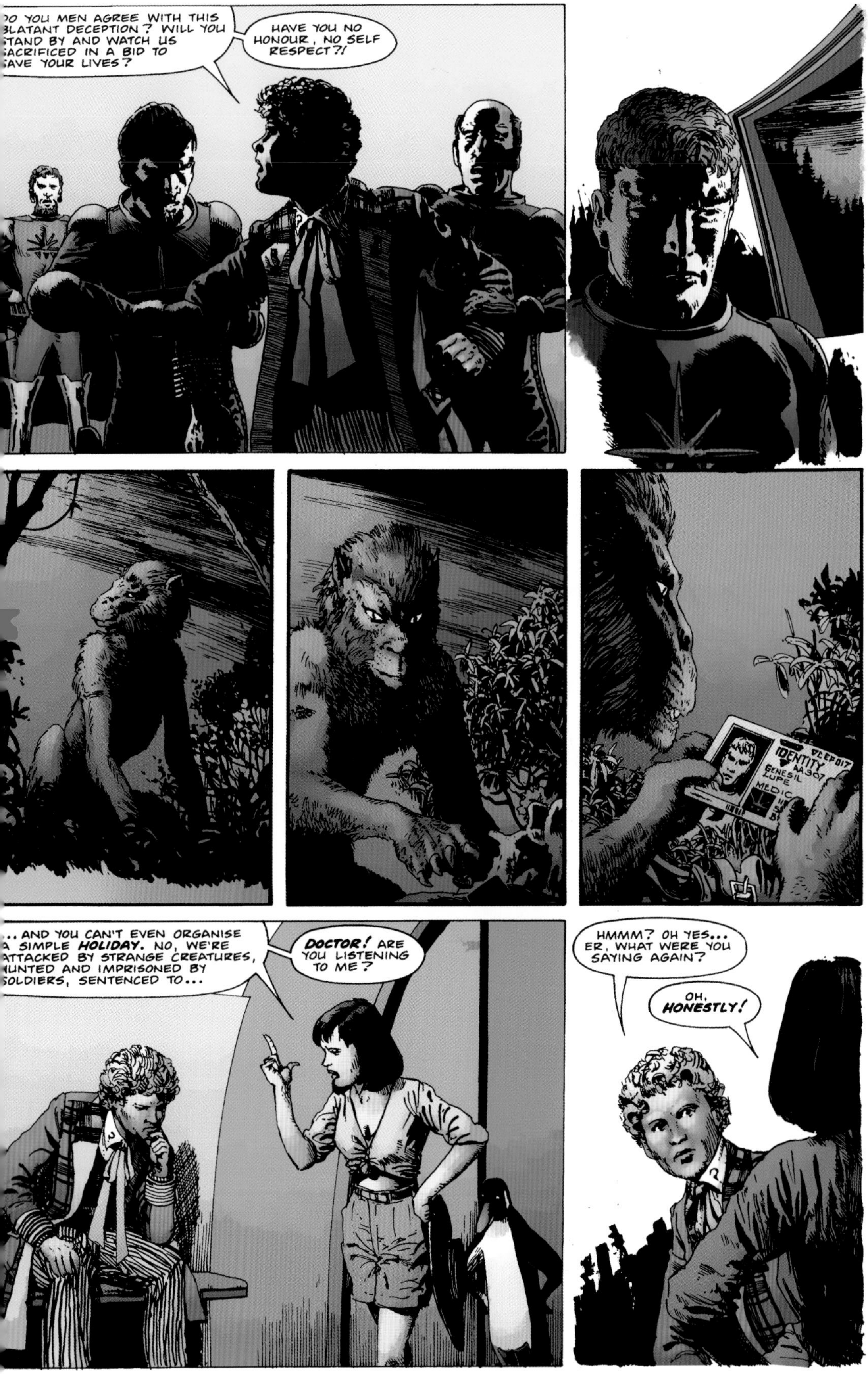
DO YOU MEN AGREE WITH THIS BLATANT DECEPTION? WILL YOU STAND BY AND WATCH US SACRIFICED IN A BID TO SAVE YOUR LIVES?
HAVE YOU NO HONOUR, NO SELF RESPECT?!
IDENTITY
GENESIL LUPE
MEDIC
...AND YOU CAN'T EVEN ORGANISE A SIMPLE HOLIDAY. NO, WE'RE ATTACKED BY STRANGE CREATURES, HUNTED AND IMPRISONED BY SOLDIERS, SENTENCED TO...
DOCTOR! ARE YOU LISTENING TO ME?
HMMM? OH YES... ER, WHAT WERE YOU SAYING AGAIN?
OH, HONESTLY!

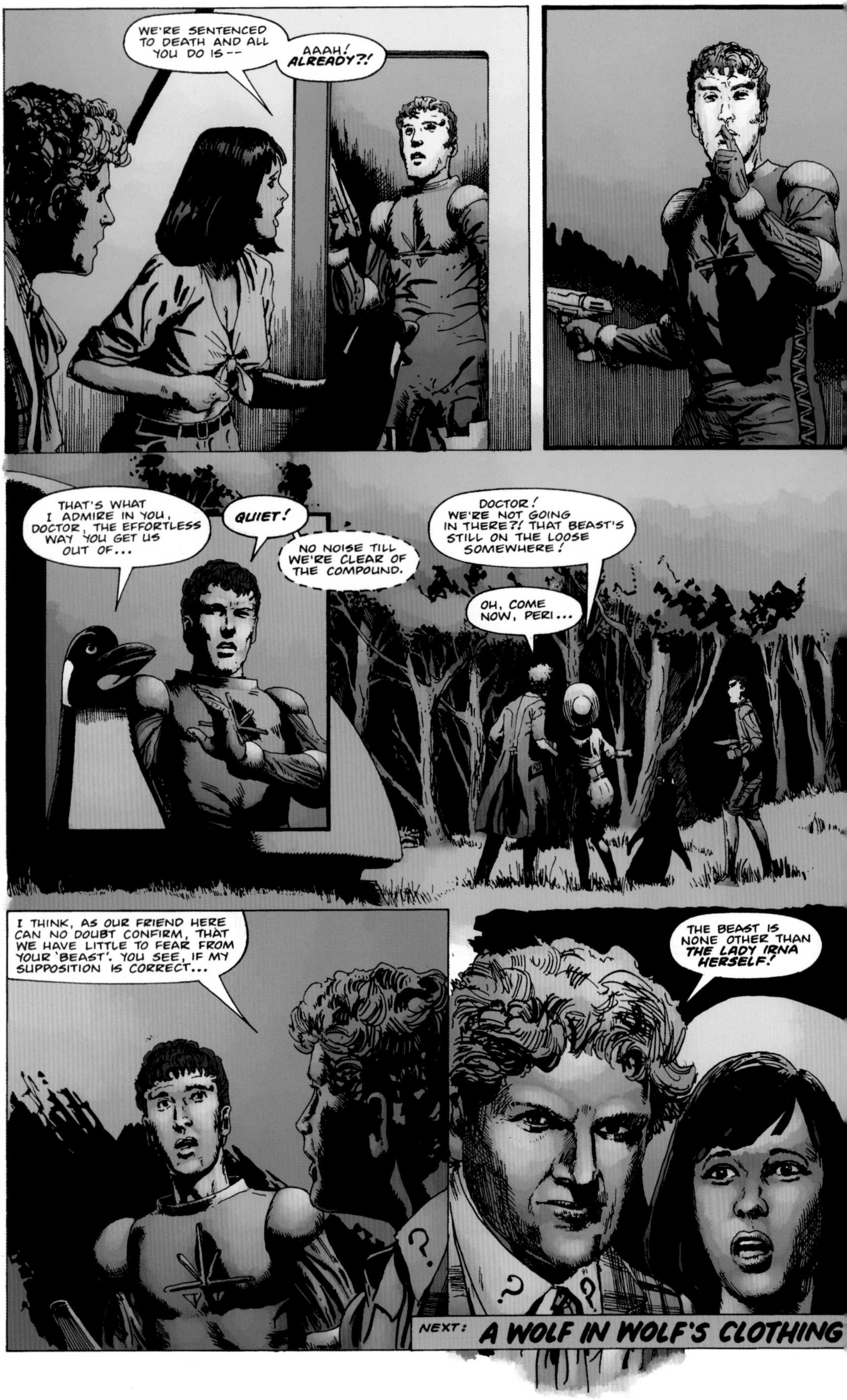
WE'RE SENTENCED TO DEATH AND ALL YOU DO IS --
AAAH! ALREADY?!
THAT'S WHAT I ADMIRE IN YOU, DOCTOR, THE EFFORTLESS WAY YOU GET US OUT OF...
QUIET!
NO NOISE TILL WE'RE CLEAR OF THE COMPOUND.
DOCTOR! WE'RE NOT GOING IN THERE?! THAT BEAST'S STILL ON THE LOOSE SOMEWHERE!
OH, COME NOW, PERI...
I THINK, AS OUR FRIEND HERE CAN NO DOUBT CONFIRM, THAT WE HAVE LITTLE TO FEAR FROM YOUR 'BEAST'. YOU SEE, IF MY SUPPOSITION IS CORRECT...
THE BEAST IS NONE OTHER THAN THE LADY IRNA HERSELF!
NEXT: A WOLF IN WOLF'S CLOTHING

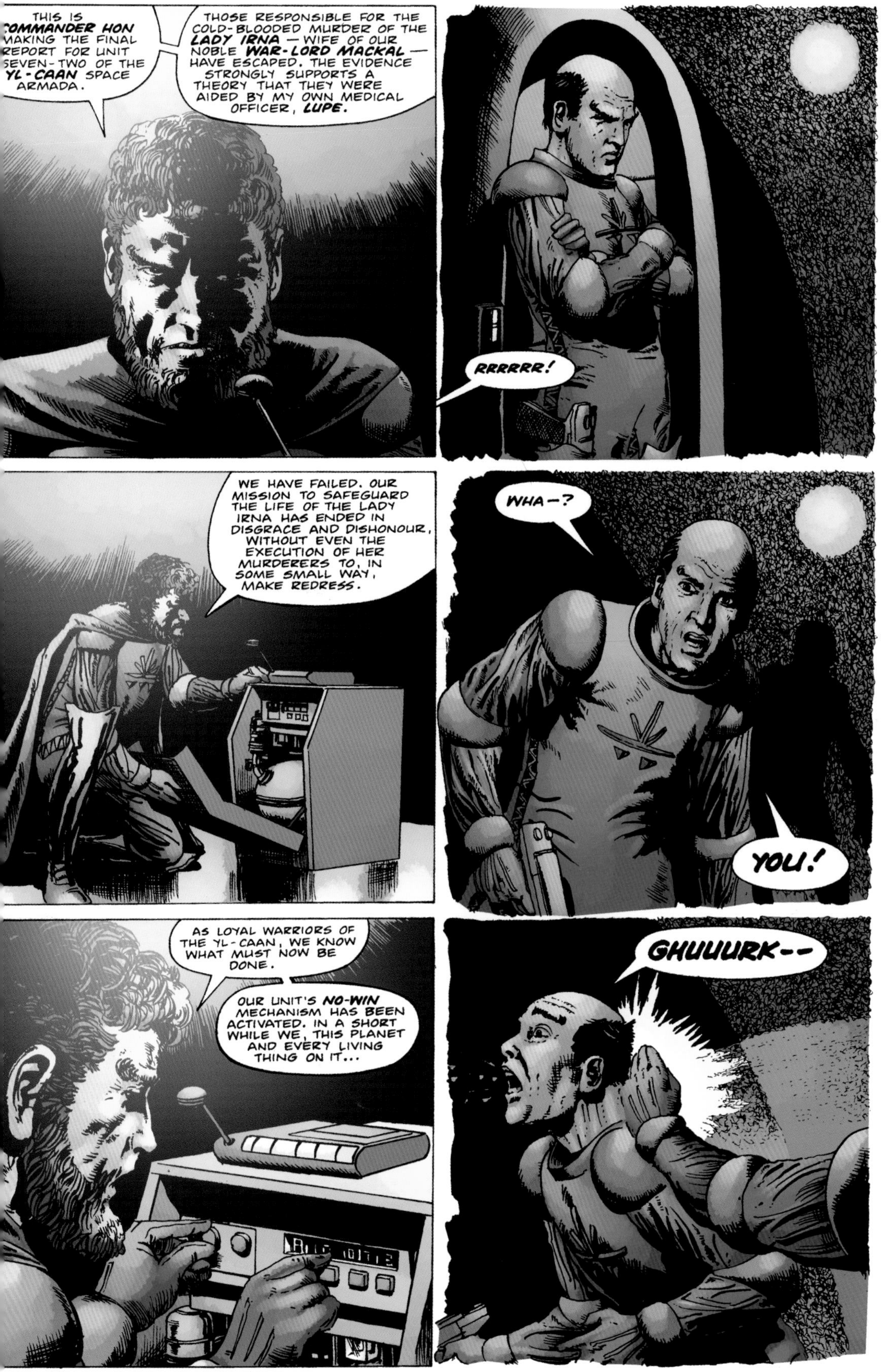
THIS IS COMMANDER HON MAKING THE FINAL REPORT FOR UNIT SEVEN-TWO OF THE YL-CAAN SPACE ARMADA.
THOSE RESPONSIBLE FOR THE COLD-BLOODED MURDER OF THE LADY IRNA — WIFE OF OUR NOBLE WAR-LORD MACKAL — HAVE ESCAPED. THE EVIDENCE STRONGLY SUPPORTS A THEORY THAT THEY WERE AIDED BY MY OWN MEDICAL OFFICER, LUPE.
RRRRRR!
WE HAVE FAILED. OUR MISSION TO SAFEGUARD THE LIFE OF THE LADY IRNA HAS ENDED IN DISGRACE AND DISHONOUR, WITHOUT EVEN THE EXECUTION OF HER MURDERERS TO, IN SOME SMALL WAY, MAKE REDRESS.
WHA-?
YOU!
AS LOYAL WARRIORS OF THE YL-CAAN, WE KNOW WHAT MUST NOW BE DONE.
OUR UNIT'S NO-WIN MECHANISM HAS BEEN ACTIVATED. IN A SHORT WHILE WE, THIS PLANET AND EVERY LIVING THING ON IT...
GHUUURK--

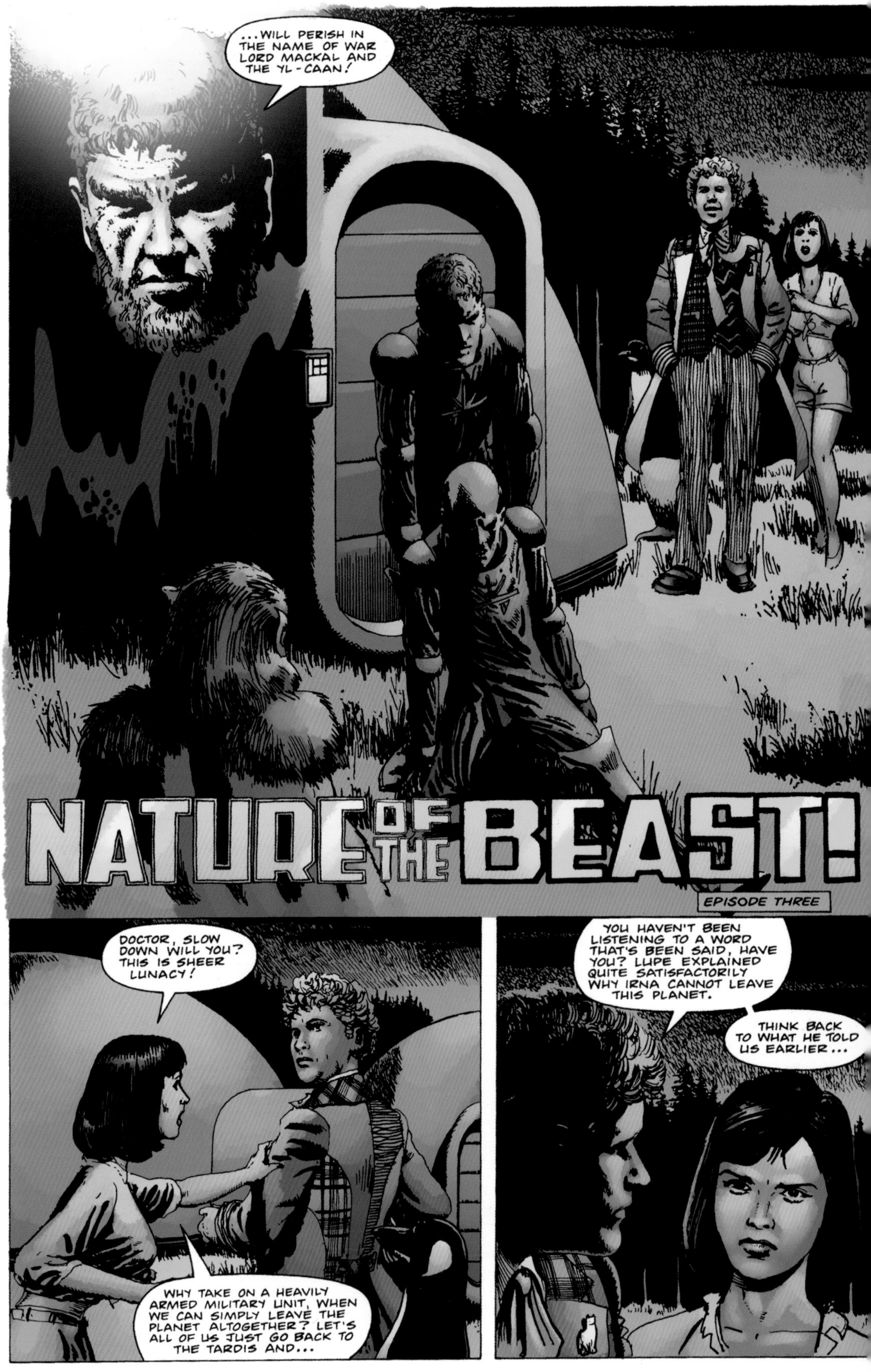
...WILL PERISH IN THE NAME OF WAR LORD MACKAL AND THE YL-CAAN!
NATURE OF THE BEAST!
EPISODE THREE
DOCTOR, SLOW DOWN WILL YOU? THIS IS SHEER LUNACY!
WHY TAKE ON A HEAVILY ARMED MILITARY UNIT, WHEN WE CAN SIMPLY LEAVE THE PLANET ALTOGETHER? LET'S ALL OF US JUST GO BACK TO THE TARDIS AND...
YOU HAVEN'T BEEN LISTENING TO A WORD THAT'S BEEN SAID, HAVE YOU? LUPE EXPLAINED QUITE SATISFACTORILY WHY IRNA CANNOT LEAVE THIS PLANET.
THINK BACK TO WHAT HE TOLD US EARLIER...

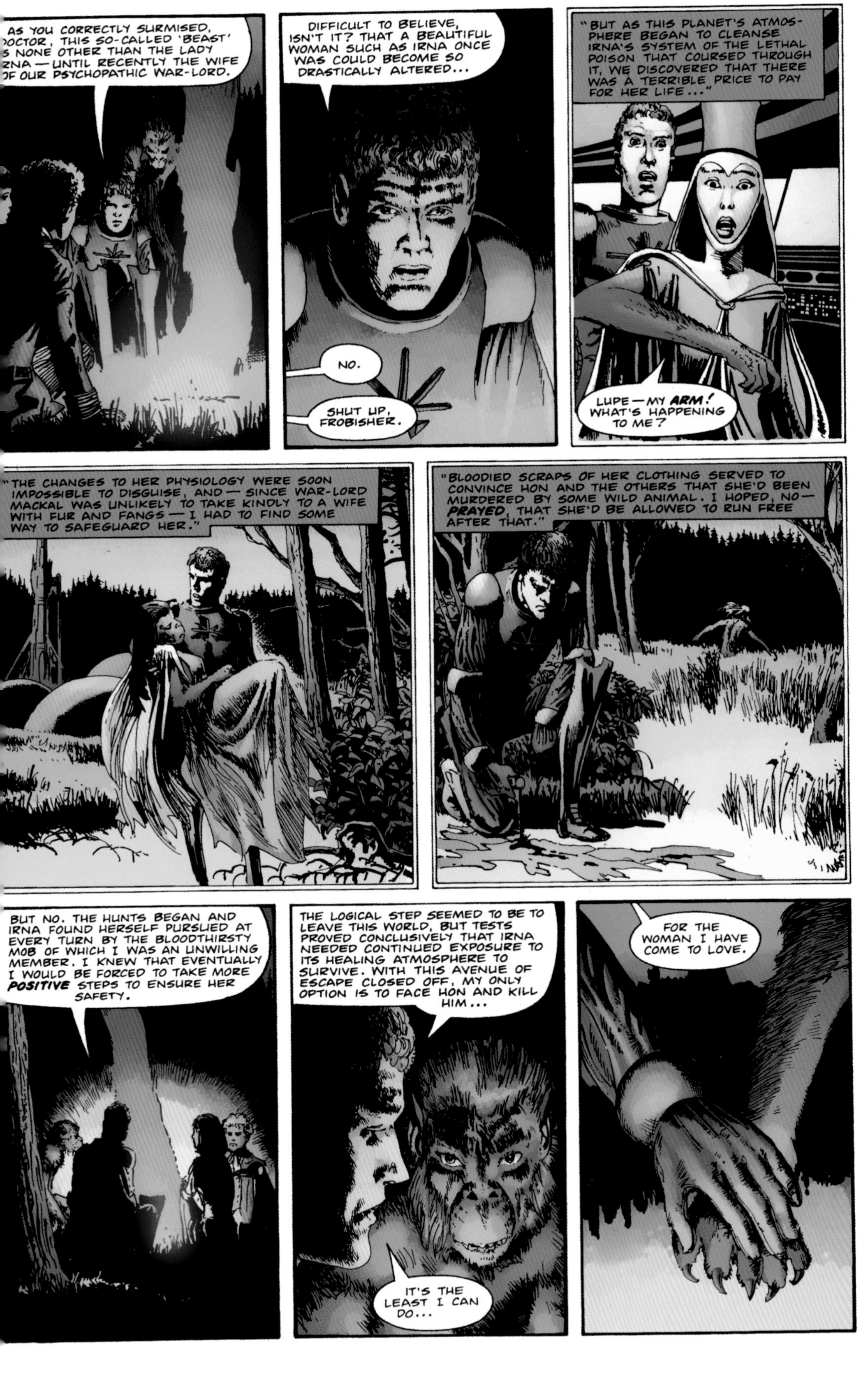
AS YOU CORRECTLY SURMISED, DOCTOR, THIS SO-CALLED 'BEAST' IS NONE OTHER THAN THE LADY IRNA — UNTIL RECENTLY THE WIFE OF OUR PSYCHOPATHIC WAR-LORD.
DIFFICULT TO BELIEVE, ISN'T IT? THAT A BEAUTIFUL WOMAN SUCH AS IRNA ONCE WAS COULD BECOME SO DRASTICALLY ALTERED...
NO.
SHUT UP, FROBISHER.
"BUT AS THIS PLANET'S ATMOSPHERE BEGAN TO CLEANSE IRNA'S SYSTEM OF THE LETHAL POISON THAT COURSED THROUGH IT, WE DISCOVERED THAT THERE WAS A TERRIBLE PRICE TO PAY FOR HER LIFE..."
LUPE — MY ARM! WHAT'S HAPPENING TO ME?
"THE CHANGES TO HER PHYSIOLOGY WERE SOON IMPOSSIBLE TO DISGUISE, AND — SINCE WAR-LORD MACKAL WAS UNLIKELY TO TAKE KINDLY TO A WIFE WITH FUR AND FANGS — I HAD TO FIND SOME WAY TO SAFEGUARD HER."
"BLOODIED SCRAPS OF HER CLOTHING SERVED TO CONVINCE HON AND THE OTHERS THAT SHE'D BEEN MURDERED BY SOME WILD ANIMAL. I HOPED, NO — PRAYED, THAT SHE'D BE ALLOWED TO RUN FREE AFTER THAT."
BUT NO. THE HUNTS BEGAN AND IRNA FOUND HERSELF PURSUED AT EVERY TURN BY THE BLOODTHIRSTY MOB OF WHICH I WAS AN UNWILLING MEMBER. I KNEW THAT EVENTUALLY I WOULD BE FORCED TO TAKE MORE POSITIVE STEPS TO ENSURE HER SAFETY.
THE LOGICAL STEP SEEMED TO BE TO LEAVE THIS WORLD, BUT TESTS PROVED CONCLUSIVELY THAT IRNA NEEDED CONTINUED EXPOSURE TO ITS HEALING ATMOSPHERE TO SURVIVE. WITH THIS AVENUE OF ESCAPE CLOSED OFF, MY ONLY OPTION IS TO FACE HON AND KILL HIM...
IT'S THE LEAST I CAN DO...
FOR THE WOMAN I HAVE COME TO LOVE.

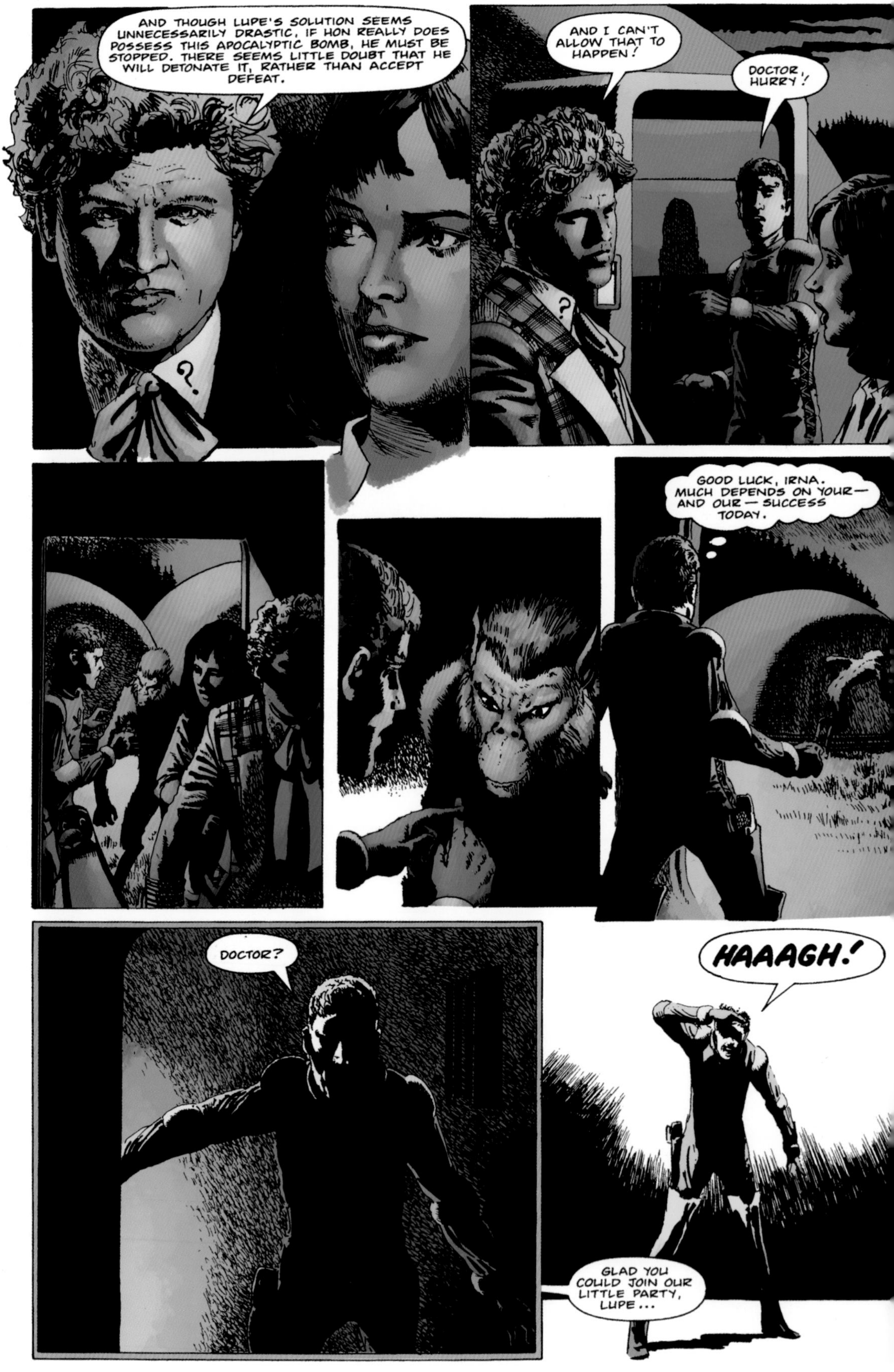
AND THOUGH LUPE'S SOLUTION SEEMS UNNECESSARILY DRASTIC, IF HON REALLY DOES POSSESS THIS APOCALYPTIC BOMB, HE MUST BE STOPPED. THERE SEEMS LITTLE DOUBT THAT HE WILL DETONATE IT, RATHER THAN ACCEPT DEFEAT.
AND I CAN'T ALLOW THAT TO HAPPEN!
DOCTOR, HURRY!
GOOD LUCK, IRNA. MUCH DEPENDS ON YOUR— AND OUR— SUCCESS TODAY.
DOCTOR?
HAAAGH!
GLAD YOU COULD JOIN OUR LITTLE PARTY, LUPE...

I FEARED FOR A MOMENT YOU WOULD MISS THIS PLEASANT REUNION.

CHAE — RELIEVE OUR GUEST OF THAT CUMBERSOME WEAPON.

BIND THEM SECURELY AND THEN LEAVE US.

LEAVE YOU? ARE YOU SURE?

QUITE SURE. I WISH TO HAVE WORDS WITH OUR TRAITOROUS MEDICAL OFFICER AND HIS ALLIES *ALONE.*

I'M PUZZLED, HON. SURELY OUR CAPTURE CAN MEAN NO REPRIEVE FOR YOU AT THIS LATE STAGE? I'M INTERESTED TO KNOW WHY YOU'RE SO HAPPY.

I'M JUST INTERESTED TO KNOW WHY THIS LOT SEEM TO THINK I BELONG UPSIDE-DOWN.

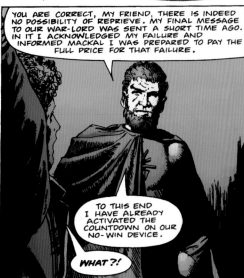

YOU ARE CORRECT, MY FRIEND, THERE IS INDEED NO POSSIBILITY OF REPRIEVE. MY FINAL MESSAGE TO OUR WAR-LORD WAS SENT A SHORT TIME AGO. IN IT I ACKNOWLEDGED MY FAILURE AND INFORMED MACKAL I WAS PREPARED TO PAY THE FULL PRICE FOR THAT FAILURE.

TO THIS END I HAVE ALREADY ACTIVATED THE COUNTDOWN ON OUR NO-WIN DEVICE.

WHAT ?!

WHEN THIS PLANET DIES I, AND I ALONE, WILL BE SAFELY ENSCONCED IN MY SHUTTLE-CRAFT, HUNDREDS OF THOUSANDS OF MILES ABOVE THIS DOOMED MUDBALL. MACKAL WILL ASSUME I PERISHED WITH THE OTHERS AND INSTIGATE NO SEARCH.

AT A ROUGH ESTIMATE, I'D SAY THAT THIS PLANET HAS ABOUT FIFTEEN MINUTES LEFT.

YOU'RE INSANE! I CAN'T BELIEVE YOU'RE WILLING TO SACRIFICE YOURSELF AND THIS WHOLE PLANET, JUST TO SAVE FACE.

OH NO, NOTHING SO DRASTIC.

I HAVE MY EYE ON A NICE LITTLE PLANET IN THE HYDRUS SYSTEM FOR MY RETIREMENT.

KAAROOOM

WELL, THERE HE GOES. I SUPPOSE THERE'S NO CHANCE OF CONVINCING THE OTHERS OF HIS TREACHERY?

NO POINT. EVEN IF YOU SUCCEEDED, HON WAS THE ONLY ONE WHO COULD HAVE DEACTIVATED THE BOMB. FOR THAT MATTER, HON WAS THE ONLY ONE WHO KNEW WHAT IT LOOKED LIKE.

HOW CAN YOU TWO DISCUSS THIS SO RATIONALLY?! WE'RE GOING TO DIE. *DON'T YOU UNDERSTAND?*

THERE IS LITTLE WE CAN D—

IRNA!

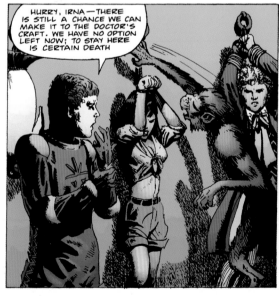

HURRY, IRNA—THERE IS STILL A CHANCE WE CAN MAKE IT TO THE DOCTOR'S CRAFT. WE HAVE NO OPTION LEFT NOW; TO STAY HERE IS CERTAIN DEATH

COME ALONG, MAN... THERE'S NOT A MOMENT TO LOSE.

YES, HURRY— *PLEASE.*

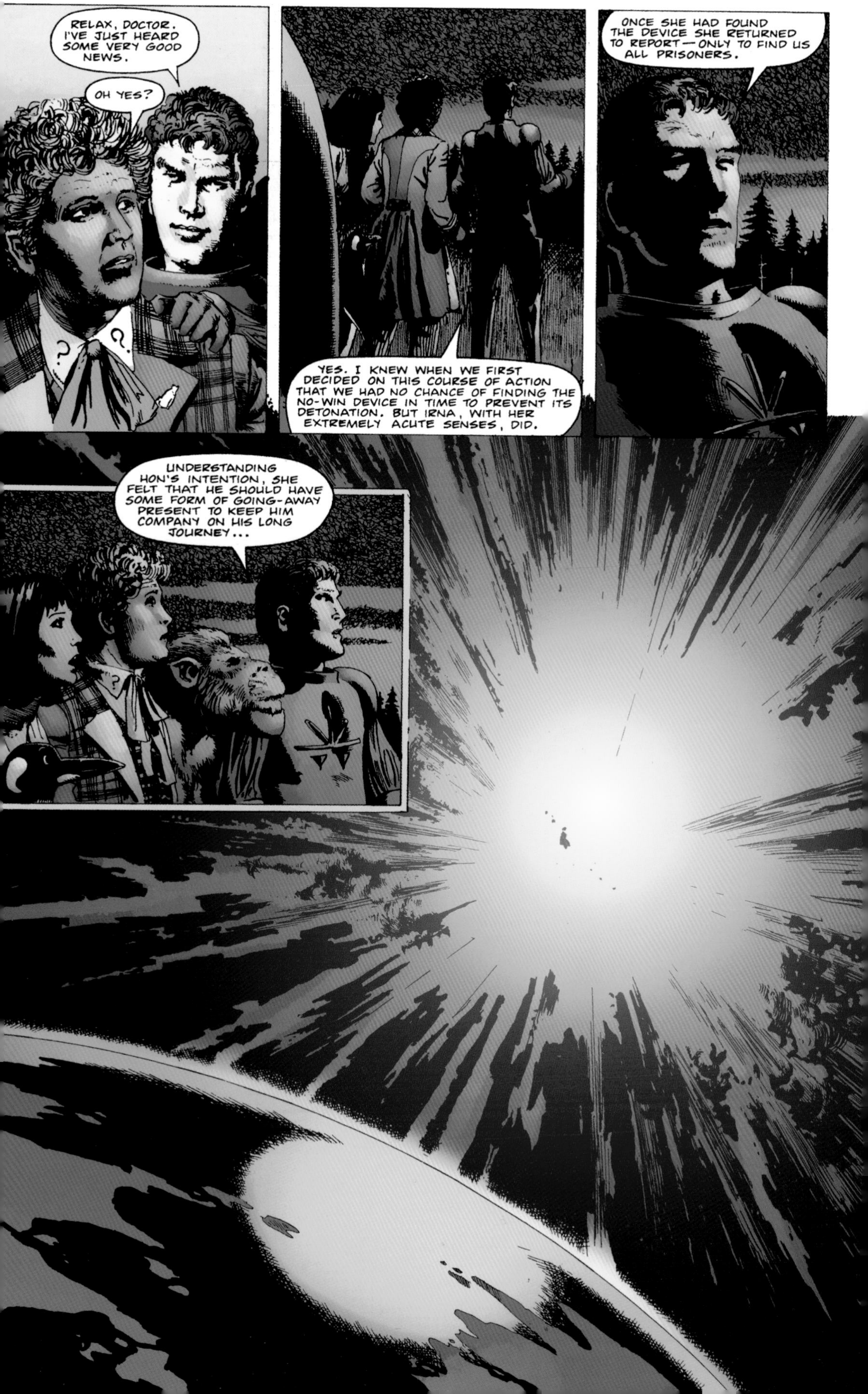
RELAX, DOCTOR. I'VE JUST HEARD SOME VERY GOOD NEWS.
OH YES?
YES. I KNEW WHEN WE FIRST DECIDED ON THIS COURSE OF ACTION THAT WE HAD NO CHANCE OF FINDING THE NO-WIN DEVICE IN TIME TO PREVENT ITS DETONATION. BUT IRNA, WITH HER EXTREMELY ACUTE SENSES, DID.
ONCE SHE HAD FOUND THE DEVICE SHE RETURNED TO REPORT—ONLY TO FIND US ALL PRISONERS.
UNDERSTANDING HON'S INTENTION, SHE FELT THAT HE SHOULD HAVE SOME FORM OF GOING-AWAY PRESENT TO KEEP HIM COMPANY ON HIS LONG JOURNEY...

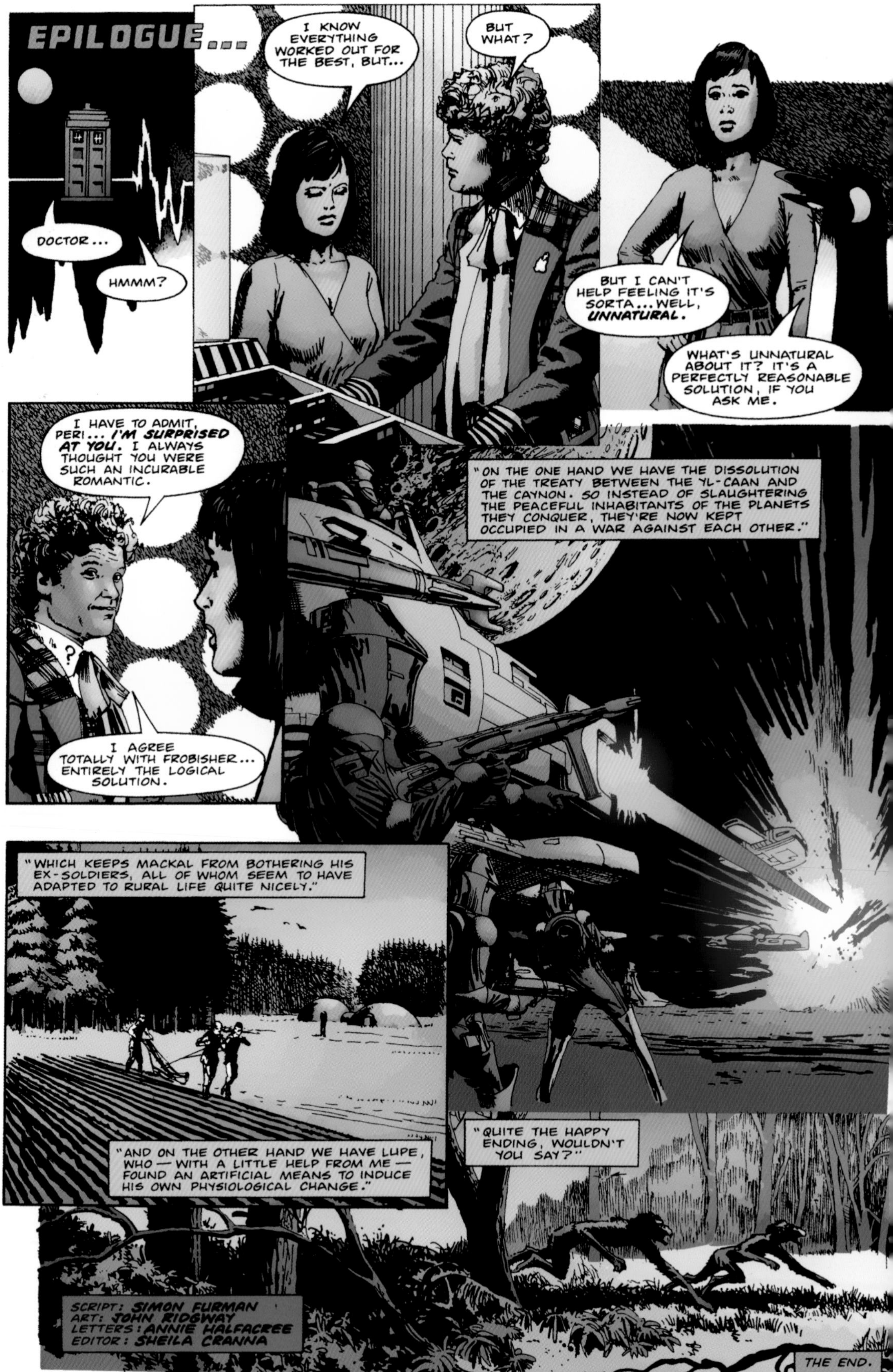
EPILOGUE...
DOCTOR...
HMMM?
I KNOW EVERYTHING WORKED OUT FOR THE BEST, BUT...
BUT WHAT?
BUT I CAN'T HELP FEELING IT'S SORTA... WELL, UNNATURAL.
WHAT'S UNNATURAL ABOUT IT? IT'S A PERFECTLY REASONABLE SOLUTION, IF YOU ASK ME.
I HAVE TO ADMIT, PERI!... I'M SURPRISED AT YOU. I ALWAYS THOUGHT YOU WERE SUCH AN INCURABLE ROMANTIC.
I AGREE TOTALLY WITH FROBISHER... ENTIRELY THE LOGICAL SOLUTION.
"ON THE ONE HAND WE HAVE THE DISSOLUTION OF THE TREATY BETWEEN THE YL-CAAN AND THE CAYNON. SO INSTEAD OF SLAUGHTERING THE PEACEFUL INHABITANTS OF THE PLANETS THEY CONQUER, THEY'RE NOW KEPT OCCUPIED IN A WAR AGAINST EACH OTHER."
"WHICH KEEPS MACKAL FROM BOTHERING HIS EX-SOLDIERS, ALL OF WHOM SEEM TO HAVE ADAPTED TO RURAL LIFE QUITE NICELY."
"AND ON THE OTHER HAND WE HAVE LUPE, WHO — WITH A LITTLE HELP FROM ME — FOUND AN ARTIFICIAL MEANS TO INDUCE HIS OWN PHYSIOLOGICAL CHANGE."
"QUITE THE HAPPY ENDING, WOULDN'T YOU SAY?"
SCRIPT: SIMON FURMAN
ART: JOHN RIDGWAY
LETTERS: ANNIE HALFACREE
EDITOR: SHEILA CRANNA
THE END.

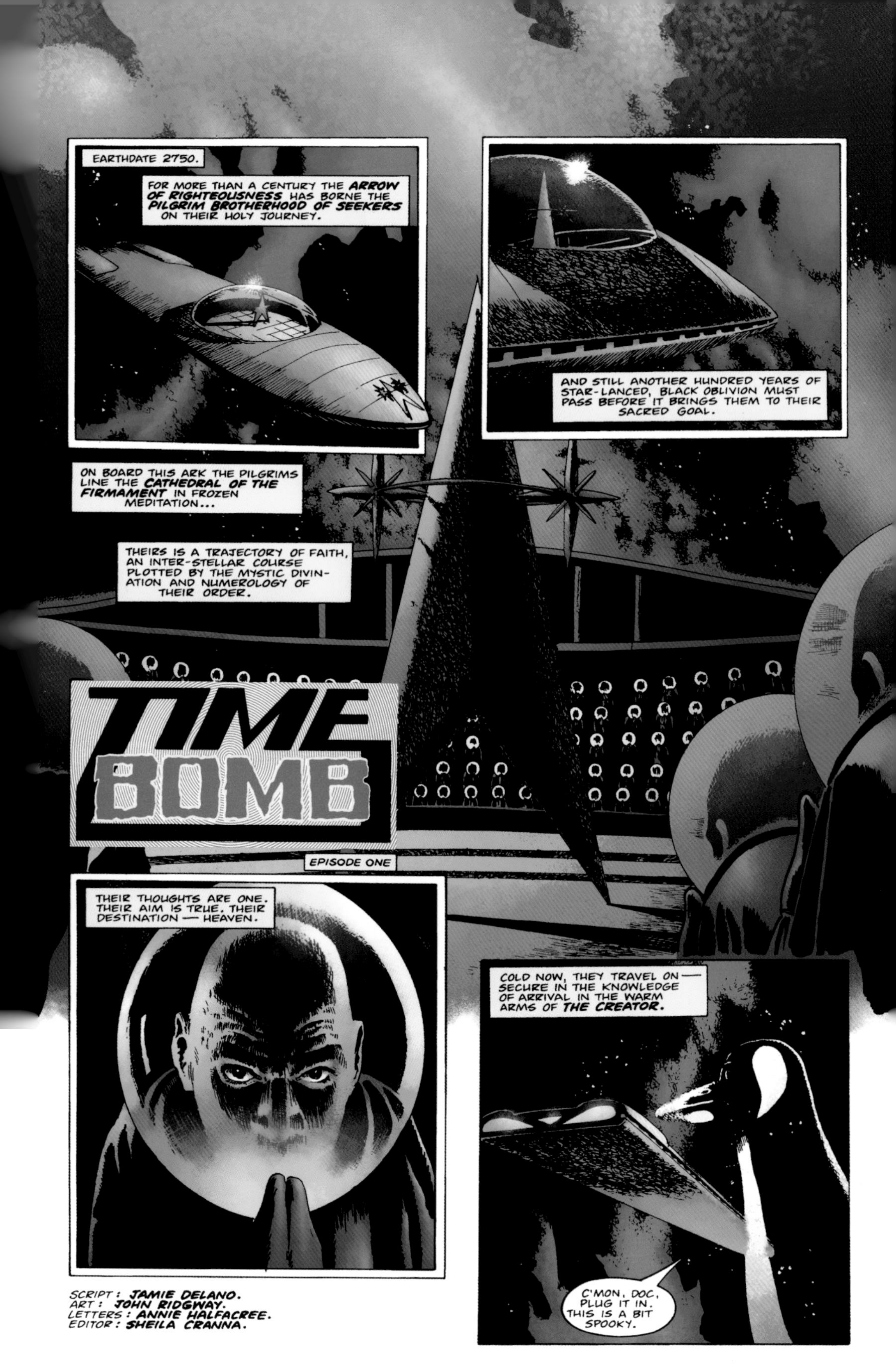
EARTHDATE 2750.
FOR MORE THAN A CENTURY THE ARROW OF RIGHTEOUSNESS HAS BORNE THE PILGRIM BROTHERHOOD OF SEEKERS ON THEIR HOLY JOURNEY.
AND STILL ANOTHER HUNDRED YEARS OF STAR-LANCED, BLACK OBLIVION MUST PASS BEFORE IT BRINGS THEM TO THEIR SACRED GOAL.
ON BOARD THIS ARK THE PILGRIMS LINE THE CATHEDRAL OF THE FIRMAMENT IN FROZEN MEDITATION...
THEIRS IS A TRAJECTORY OF FAITH, AN INTER-STELLAR COURSE PLOTTED BY THE MYSTIC DIVINATION AND NUMEROLOGY OF THEIR ORDER.
TIME BOMB
EPISODE ONE
THEIR THOUGHTS ARE ONE. THEIR AIM IS TRUE. THEIR DESTINATION — HEAVEN.
COLD NOW, THEY TRAVEL ON — SECURE IN THE KNOWLEDGE OF ARRIVAL IN THE WARM ARMS OF THE CREATOR.
C'MON, DOC, PLUG IT IN. THIS IS A BIT SPOOKY.

SCRIPT: **JAMIE DELANO.**
ART: **JOHN RIDGWAY.**
LETTERS: **ANNIE HALFACREE.**
EDITOR: **SHEILA CRANNA.**

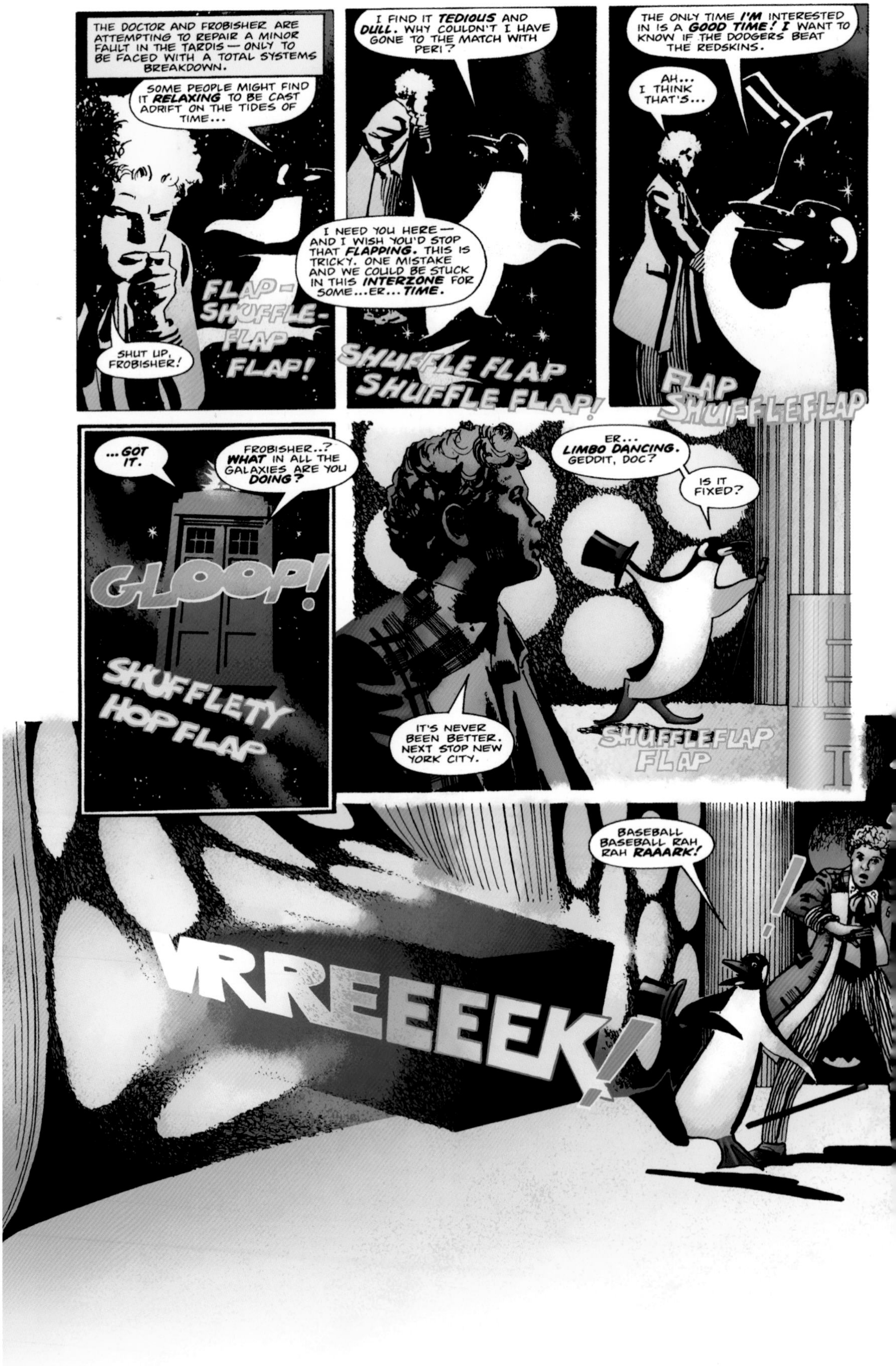

THE DOCTOR AND FROBISHER ARE ATTEMPTING TO REPAIR A MINOR FAULT IN THE TARDIS — ONLY TO BE FACED WITH A TOTAL SYSTEMS BREAKDOWN.
SOME PEOPLE MIGHT FIND IT RELAXING TO BE CAST ADRIFT ON THE TIDES OF TIME...
FLAP-SHUFFLE-FLAP FLAP!
SHUT UP, FROBISHER!
I FIND IT TEDIOUS AND DULL. WHY COULDN'T I HAVE GONE TO THE MATCH WITH PERI?
I NEED YOU HERE — AND I WISH YOU'D STOP THAT FLAPPING. THIS IS TRICKY. ONE MISTAKE AND WE COULD BE STUCK IN THIS INTERZONE FOR SOME...ER...TIME.
SHUFFLE FLAP SHUFFLE FLAP!
THE ONLY TIME I'M INTERESTED IN IS A GOOD TIME! I WANT TO KNOW IF THE DODGERS BEAT THE REDSKINS.
AH... I THINK THAT'S...
FLAP SHUFFLEFLAP
...GOT IT.
FROBISHER..? WHAT IN ALL THE GALAXIES ARE YOU DOING?
GLOOP!
SHUFFLETY HOP FLAP
ER... LIMBO DANCING. GEDDIT, DOC?
IS IT FIXED?
IT'S NEVER BEEN BETTER. NEXT STOP NEW YORK CITY.
SHUFFLEFLAP FLAP
VRREEEEK!
BASEBALL BASEBALL RAH RAH RAAARK!
!

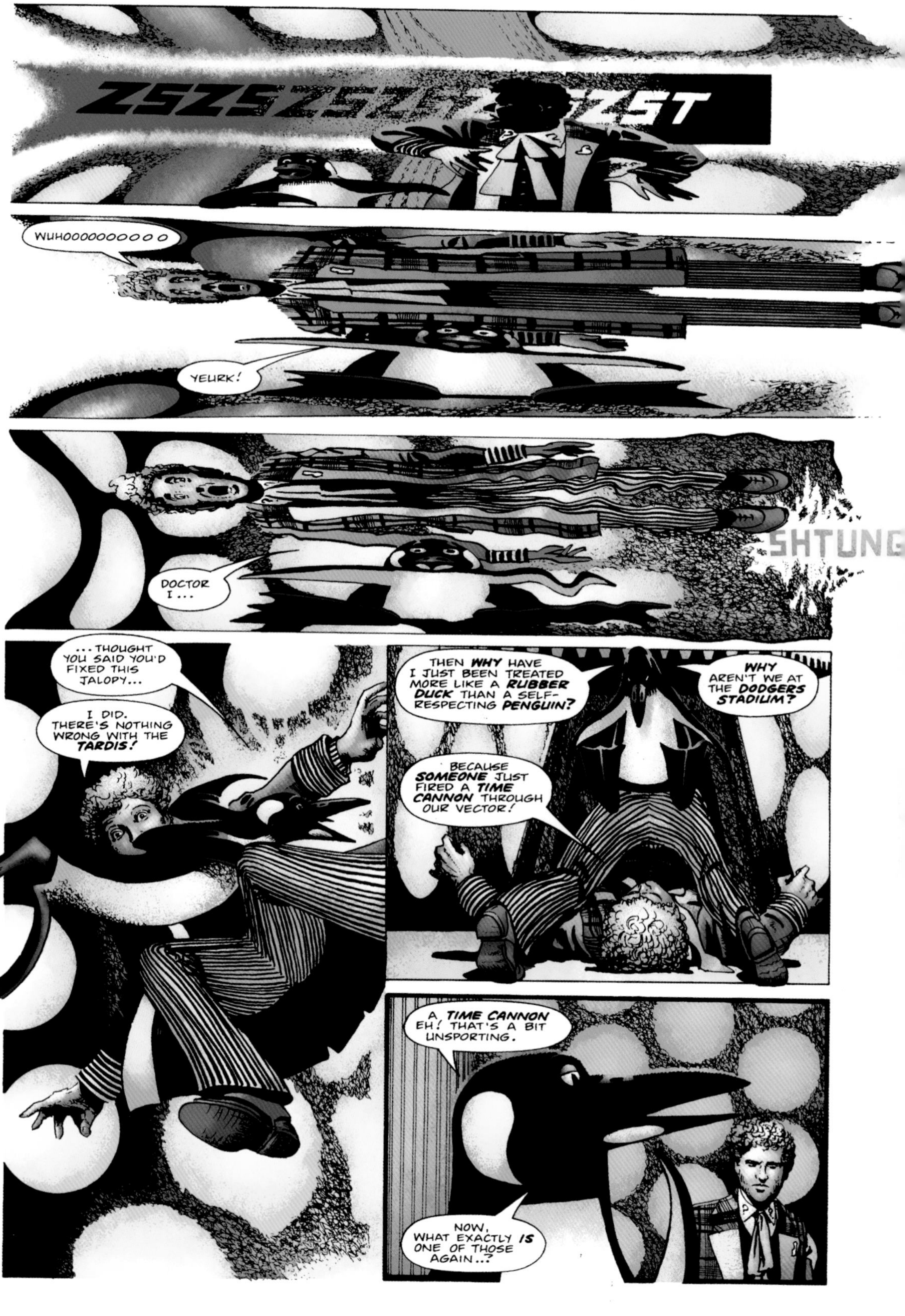
ZSZSZSZS ZST
WUHOOOOOOOOOO O
YEURK!
DOCTOR I...
SHTUNG
...THOUGHT YOU SAID YOU'D FIXED THIS JALOPY...
I DID. THERE'S NOTHING WRONG WITH THE TARDIS!
THEN WHY HAVE I JUST BEEN TREATED MORE LIKE A RUBBER DUCK THAN A SELF-RESPECTING PENGUIN?
WHY AREN'T WE AT THE DODGERS STADIUM?
BECAUSE SOMEONE JUST FIRED A TIME CANNON THROUGH OUR VECTOR!
A TIME CANNON EH! THAT'S A BIT UNSPORTING.
NOW, WHAT EXACTLY IS ONE OF THOSE AGAIN..?

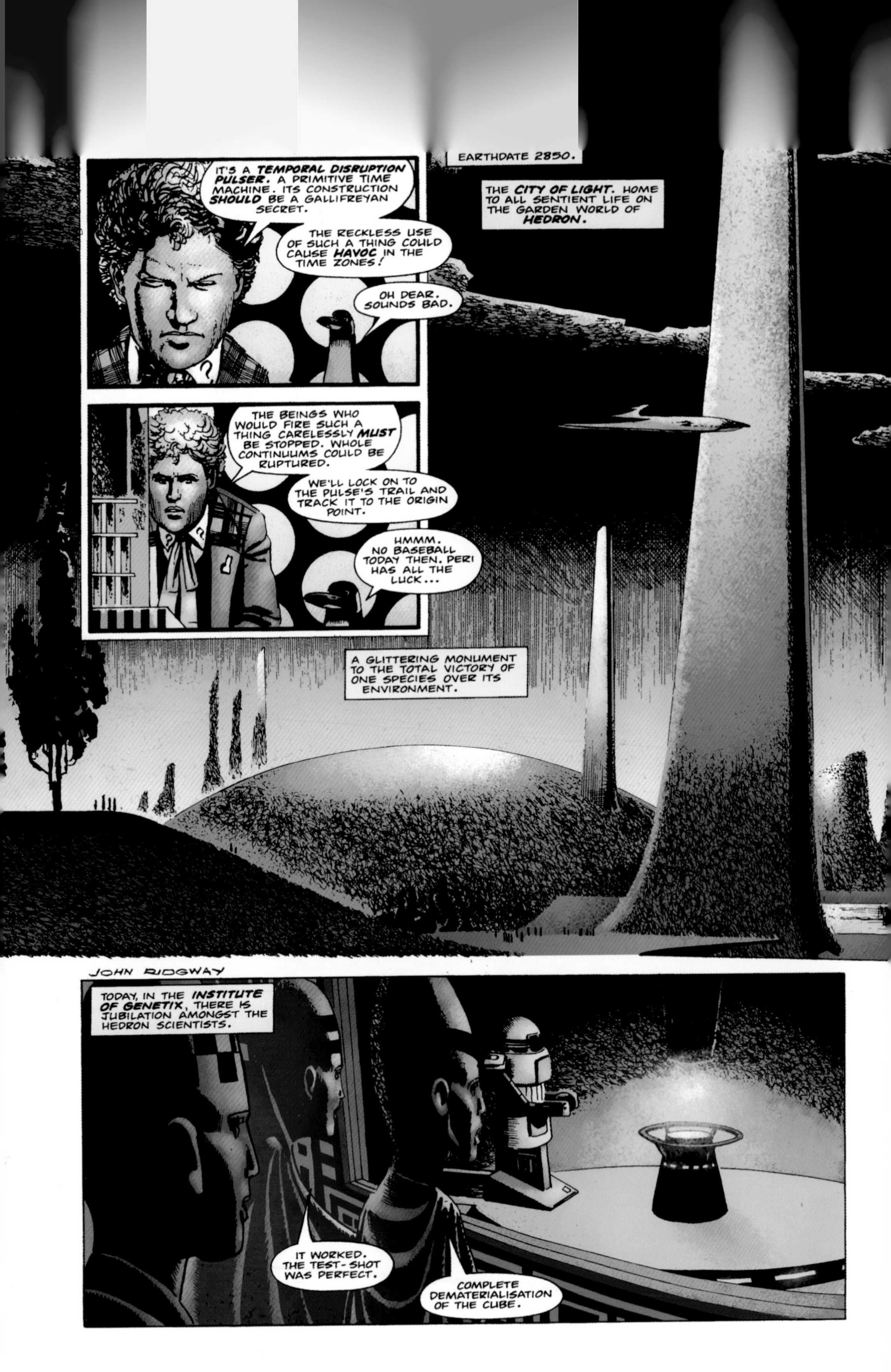
EARTHDATE 2850.
THE CITY OF LIGHT. HOME TO ALL SENTIENT LIFE ON THE GARDEN WORLD OF HEDRON.
IT'S A TEMPORAL DISRUPTION PULSER. A PRIMITIVE TIME MACHINE. ITS CONSTRUCTION SHOULD BE A GALLIFREYAN SECRET.
THE RECKLESS USE OF SUCH A THING COULD CAUSE HAVOC IN THE TIME ZONES!
OH DEAR. SOUNDS BAD.
THE BEINGS WHO WOULD FIRE SUCH A THING CARELESSLY MUST BE STOPPED. WHOLE CONTINUUMS COULD BE RUPTURED.
WE'LL LOCK ON TO THE PULSE'S TRAIL AND TRACK IT TO THE ORIGIN POINT.
HMMM. NO BASEBALL TODAY THEN. PERI HAS ALL THE LUCK...
A GLITTERING MONUMENT TO THE TOTAL VICTORY OF ONE SPECIES OVER ITS ENVIRONMENT.
JOHN RIDGWAY
TODAY, IN THE INSTITUTE OF GENETIX, THERE IS JUBILATION AMONGST THE HEDRON SCIENTISTS.
IT WORKED. THE TEST-SHOT WAS PERFECT.
COMPLETE DEMATERIALISATION OF THE CUBE.

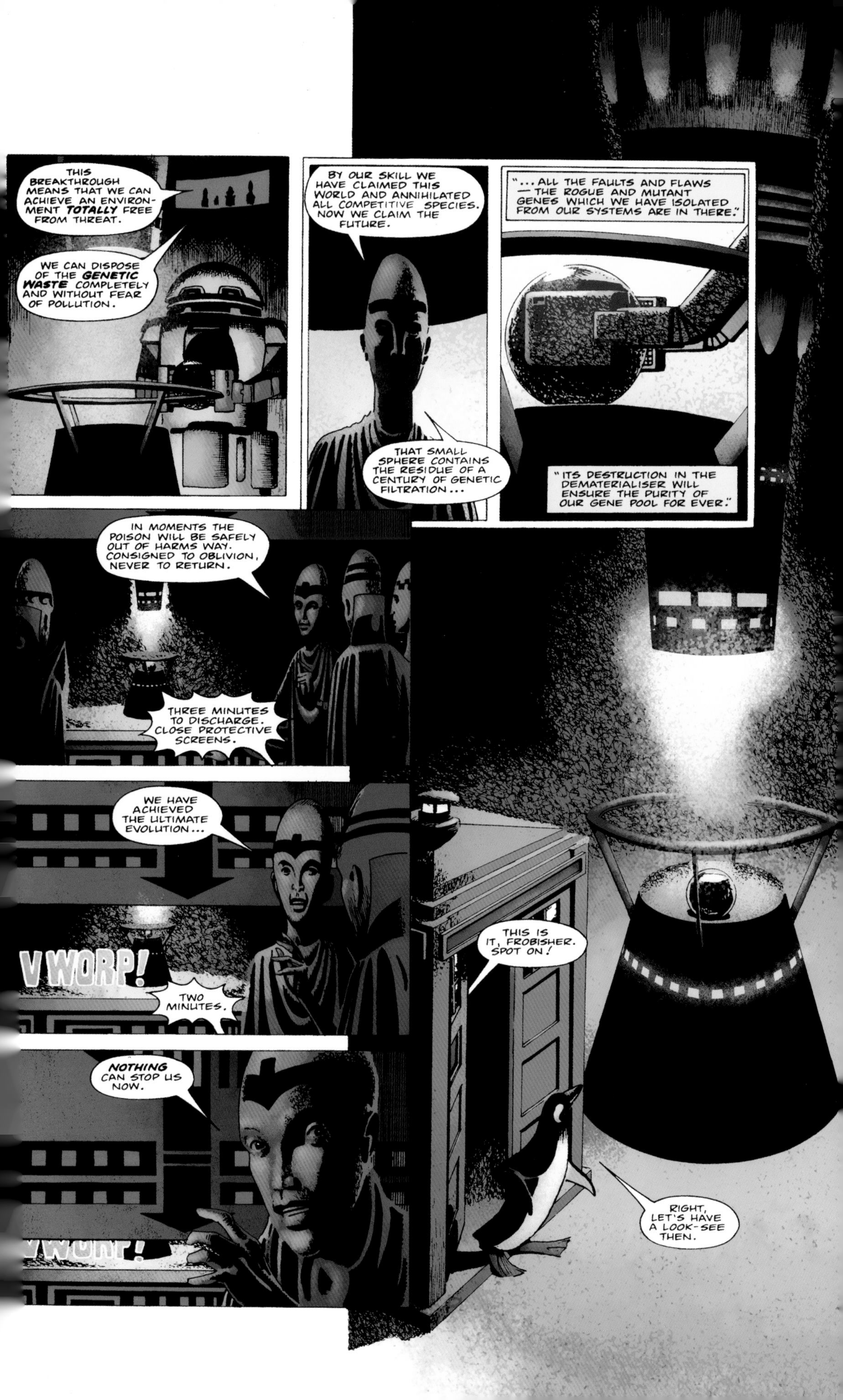
THIS BREAKTHROUGH MEANS THAT WE CAN ACHIEVE AN ENVIRONMENT TOTALLY FREE FROM THREAT.
WE CAN DISPOSE OF THE GENETIC WASTE COMPLETELY AND WITHOUT FEAR OF POLLUTION.
BY OUR SKILL WE HAVE CLAIMED THIS WORLD AND ANNIHILATED ALL COMPETITIVE SPECIES. NOW WE CLAIM THE FUTURE.
THAT SMALL SPHERE CONTAINS THE RESIDUE OF A CENTURY OF GENETIC FILTRATION...
"...ALL THE FAULTS AND FLAWS — THE ROGUE AND MUTANT GENES WHICH WE HAVE ISOLATED FROM OUR SYSTEMS ARE IN THERE."
"ITS DESTRUCTION IN THE DEMATERIALISER WILL ENSURE THE PURITY OF OUR GENE POOL FOR EVER."
IN MOMENTS THE POISON WILL BE SAFELY OUT OF HARMS WAY. CONSIGNED TO OBLIVION, NEVER TO RETURN.
THREE MINUTES TO DISCHARGE. CLOSE PROTECTIVE SCREENS.
WE HAVE ACHIEVED THE ULTIMATE EVOLUTION...
VWORP!
TWO MINUTES.
NOTHING CAN STOP US NOW.
THIS IS IT, FROBISHER. SPOT ON!
RIGHT, LET'S HAVE A LOOK-SEE THEN.

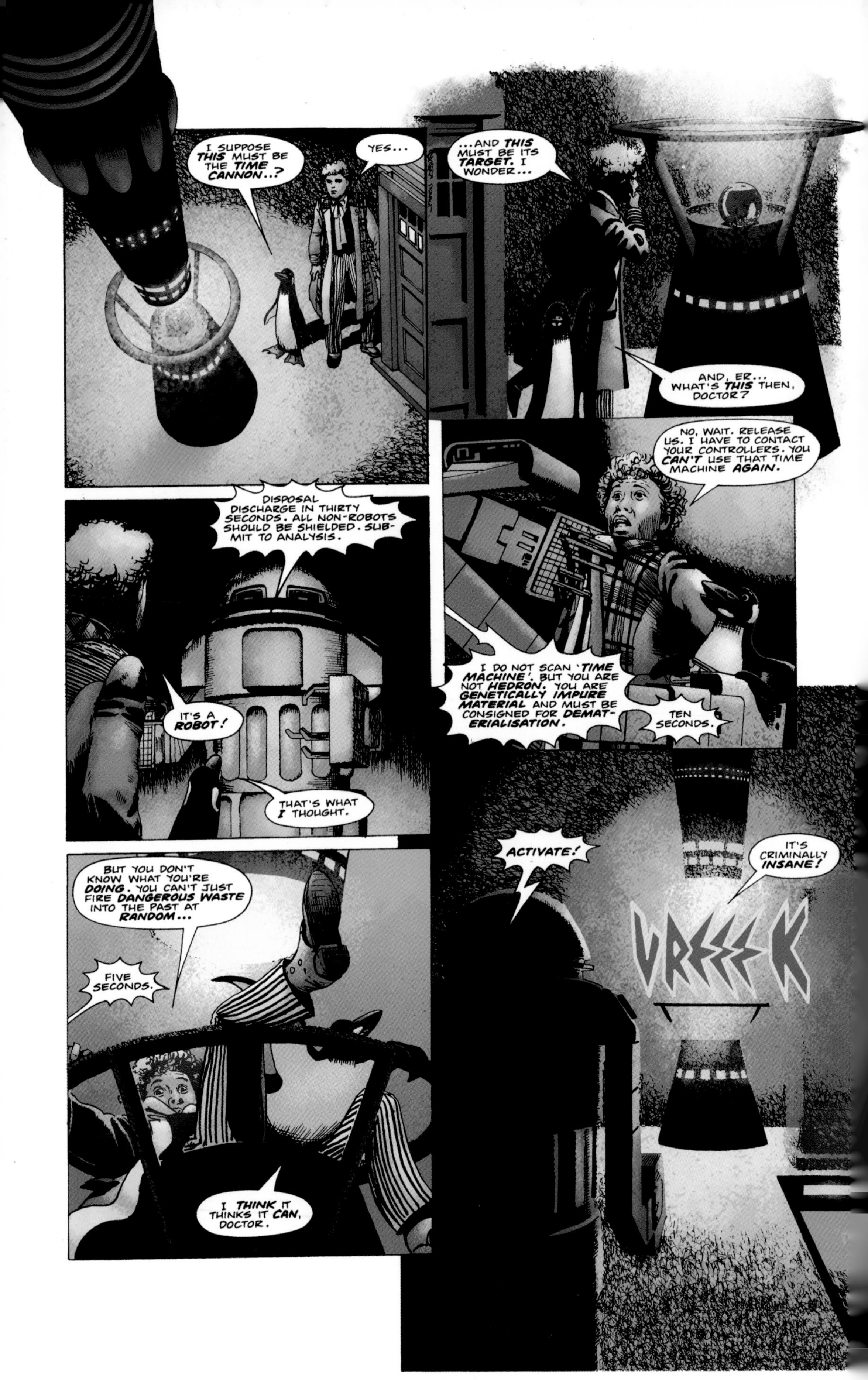

I SUPPOSE THIS MUST BE THE TIME CANNON..?
YES...
...AND THIS MUST BE ITS TARGET. I WONDER...
AND, ER... WHAT'S THIS THEN, DOCTOR?
DISPOSAL DISCHARGE IN THIRTY SECONDS. ALL NON-ROBOTS SHOULD BE SHIELDED. SUBMIT TO ANALYSIS.
IT'S A ROBOT!
THAT'S WHAT I THOUGHT.
NO, WAIT. RELEASE US. I HAVE TO CONTACT YOUR CONTROLLERS. YOU CAN'T USE THAT TIME MACHINE AGAIN.
I DO NOT SCAN 'TIME MACHINE'. BUT YOU ARE NOT HEDRON. YOU ARE GENETICALLY IMPURE MATERIAL AND MUST BE CONSIGNED FOR DEMATERIALISATION.
TEN SECONDS.
BUT YOU DON'T KNOW WHAT YOU'RE DOING. YOU CAN'T JUST FIRE DANGEROUS WASTE INTO THE PAST AT RANDOM...
FIVE SECONDS.
I THINK IT THINKS IT CAN, DOCTOR.
ACTIVATE!
IT'S CRIMINALLY INSANE!
VREEEK

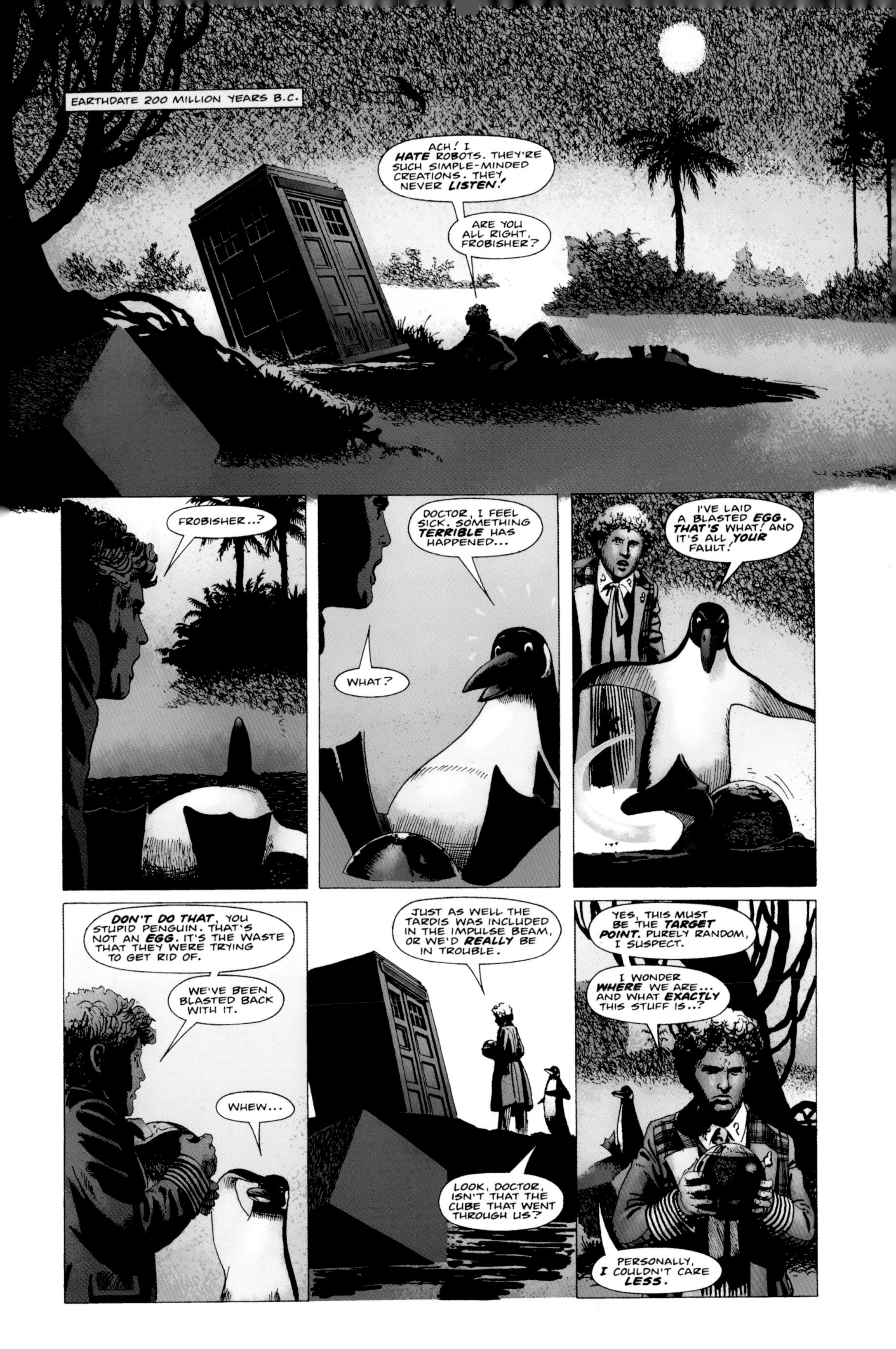
EARTHDATE 200 MILLION YEARS B.C.
ACH! I HATE ROBOTS. THEY'RE SUCH SIMPLE-MINDED CREATIONS. THEY NEVER LISTEN!
ARE YOU ALL RIGHT, FROBISHER?
FROBISHER..?
DOCTOR, I FEEL SICK. SOMETHING TERRIBLE HAS HAPPENED...
WHAT?
I'VE LAID A BLASTED EGG. THAT'S WHAT! AND IT'S ALL YOUR FAULT!
DON'T DO THAT, YOU STUPID PENGUIN. THAT'S NOT AN EGG. IT'S THE WASTE THAT THEY WERE TRYING TO GET RID OF.
WE'VE BEEN BLASTED BACK WITH IT.
WHEW...
JUST AS WELL THE TARDIS WAS INCLUDED IN THE IMPULSE BEAM, OR WE'D REALLY BE IN TROUBLE.
LOOK, DOCTOR, ISN'T THAT THE CUBE THAT WENT THROUGH US?
YES, THIS MUST BE THE TARGET POINT. PURELY RANDOM, I SUSPECT.
I WONDER WHERE WE ARE... AND WHAT EXACTLY THIS STUFF IS..?
PERSONALLY, I COULDN'T CARE LESS.

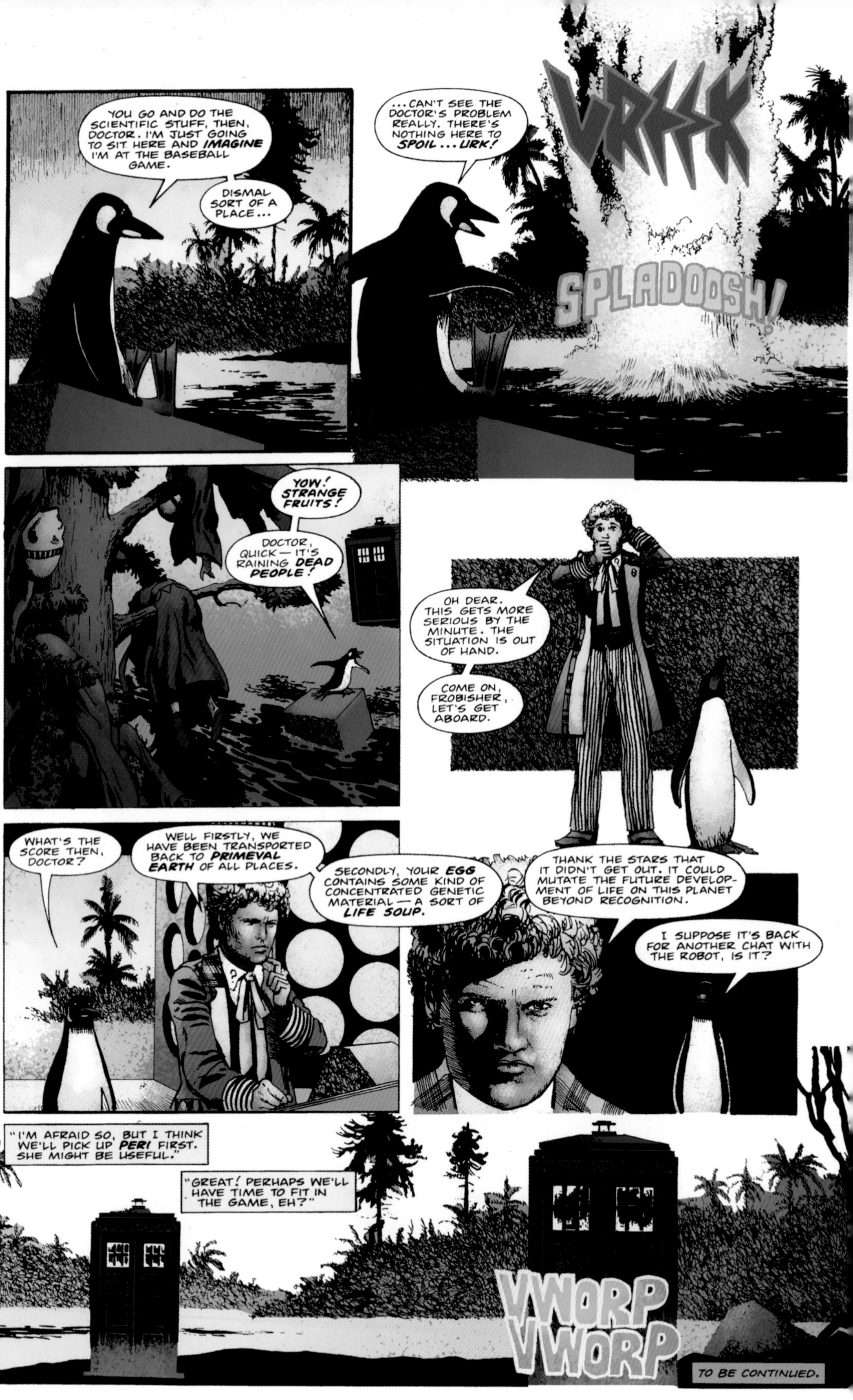

YOU GO AND DO THE SCIENTIFIC STUFF, THEN, DOCTOR. I'M JUST GOING TO SIT HERE AND IMAGINE I'M AT THE BASEBALL GAME.
DISMAL SORT OF A PLACE...
...CAN'T SEE THE DOCTOR'S PROBLEM REALLY. THERE'S NOTHING HERE TO SPOIL... URK!
SPLADOOSH!
YOW! STRANGE FRUITS!
DOCTOR, QUICK — IT'S RAINING DEAD PEOPLE!
OH DEAR. THIS GETS MORE SERIOUS BY THE MINUTE. THE SITUATION IS OUT OF HAND.
COME ON, FROBISHER, LET'S GET ABOARD.
WHAT'S THE SCORE THEN, DOCTOR?
WELL FIRSTLY, WE HAVE BEEN TRANSPORTED BACK TO PRIMEVAL EARTH OF ALL PLACES.
SECONDLY, YOUR EGG CONTAINS SOME KIND OF CONCENTRATED GENETIC MATERIAL — A SORT OF LIFE SOUP.
THANK THE STARS THAT IT DIDN'T GET OUT. IT COULD MUTATE THE FUTURE DEVELOPMENT OF LIFE ON THIS PLANET BEYOND RECOGNITION.
I SUPPOSE IT'S BACK FOR ANOTHER CHAT WITH THE ROBOT, IS IT?
"I'M AFRAID SO, BUT I THINK WE'LL PICK UP PERI FIRST. SHE MIGHT BE USEFUL."
"GREAT! PERHAPS WE'LL HAVE TIME TO FIT IN THE GAME, EH?"
VWORP VWORP
TO BE CONTINUED.

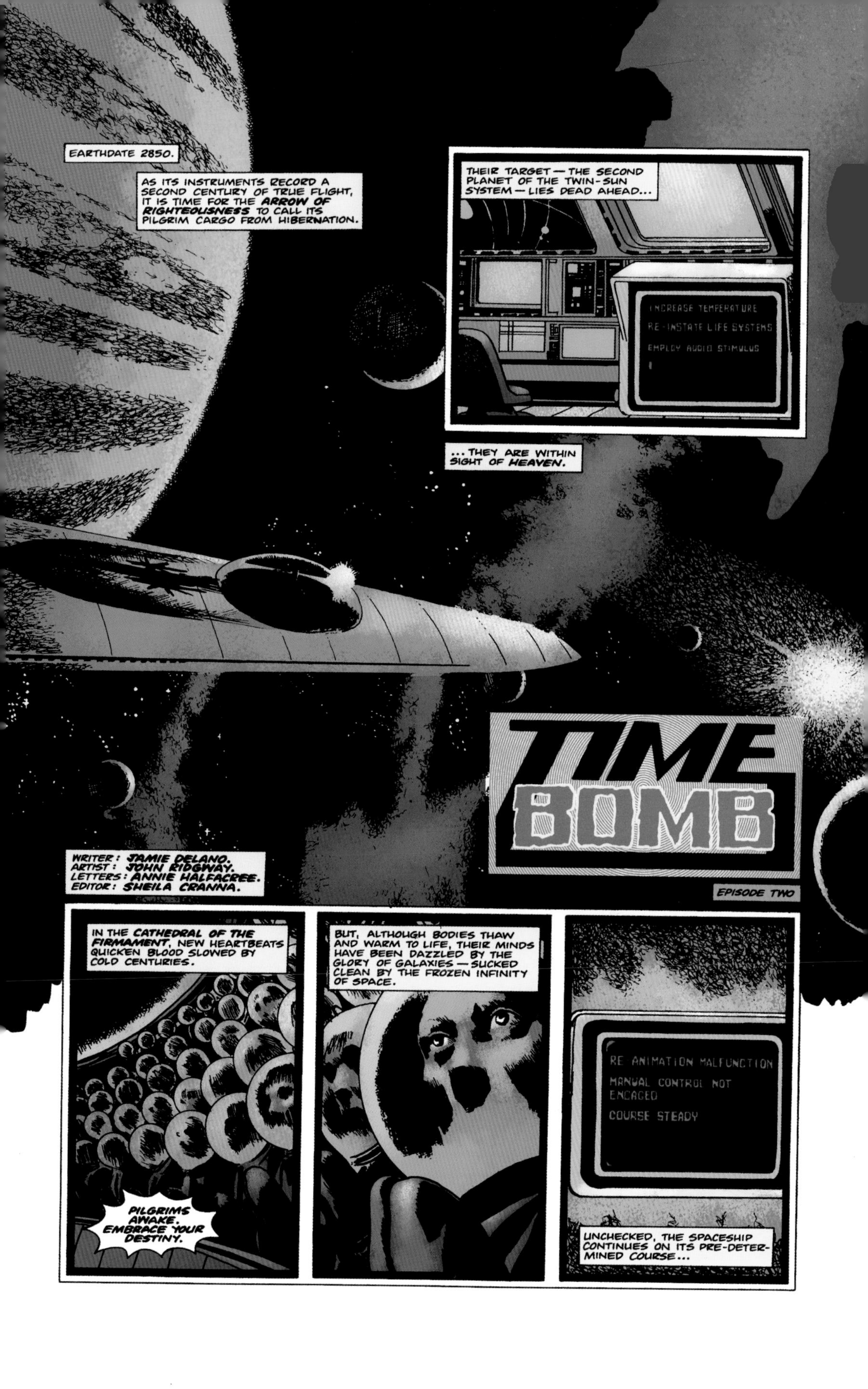
EARTHDATE 2850.
AS ITS INSTRUMENTS RECORD A SECOND CENTURY OF TRUE FLIGHT, IT IS TIME FOR THE ARROW OF RIGHTEOUSNESS TO CALL ITS PILGRIM CARGO FROM HIBERNATION.
THEIR TARGET — THE SECOND PLANET OF THE TWIN-SUN SYSTEM — LIES DEAD AHEAD...
INCREASE TEMPERATURE
RE-INSTATE LIFE SYSTEMS
EMPLOY AUDIO STIMULUS
... THEY ARE WITHIN SIGHT OF HEAVEN.
TIME BOMB
WRITER: JAMIE DELANO.
ARTIST: JOHN RIDGWAY.
LETTERS: ANNIE HALFACREE.
EDITOR: SHEILA CRANNA.
EPISODE TWO
IN THE CATHEDRAL OF THE FIRMAMENT, NEW HEARTBEATS QUICKEN BLOOD SLOWED BY COLD CENTURIES.
PILGRIMS AWAKE. EMBRACE YOUR DESTINY.
BUT, ALTHOUGH BODIES THAW AND WARM TO LIFE, THEIR MINDS HAVE BEEN DAZZLED BY THE GLORY OF GALAXIES — SUCKED CLEAN BY THE FROZEN INFINITY OF SPACE.
RE ANIMATION MALFUNCTION
MANUAL CONTROL NOT ENGAGED
COURSE STEADY
UNCHECKED, THE SPACESHIP CONTINUES ON ITS PRE-DETERMINED COURSE...

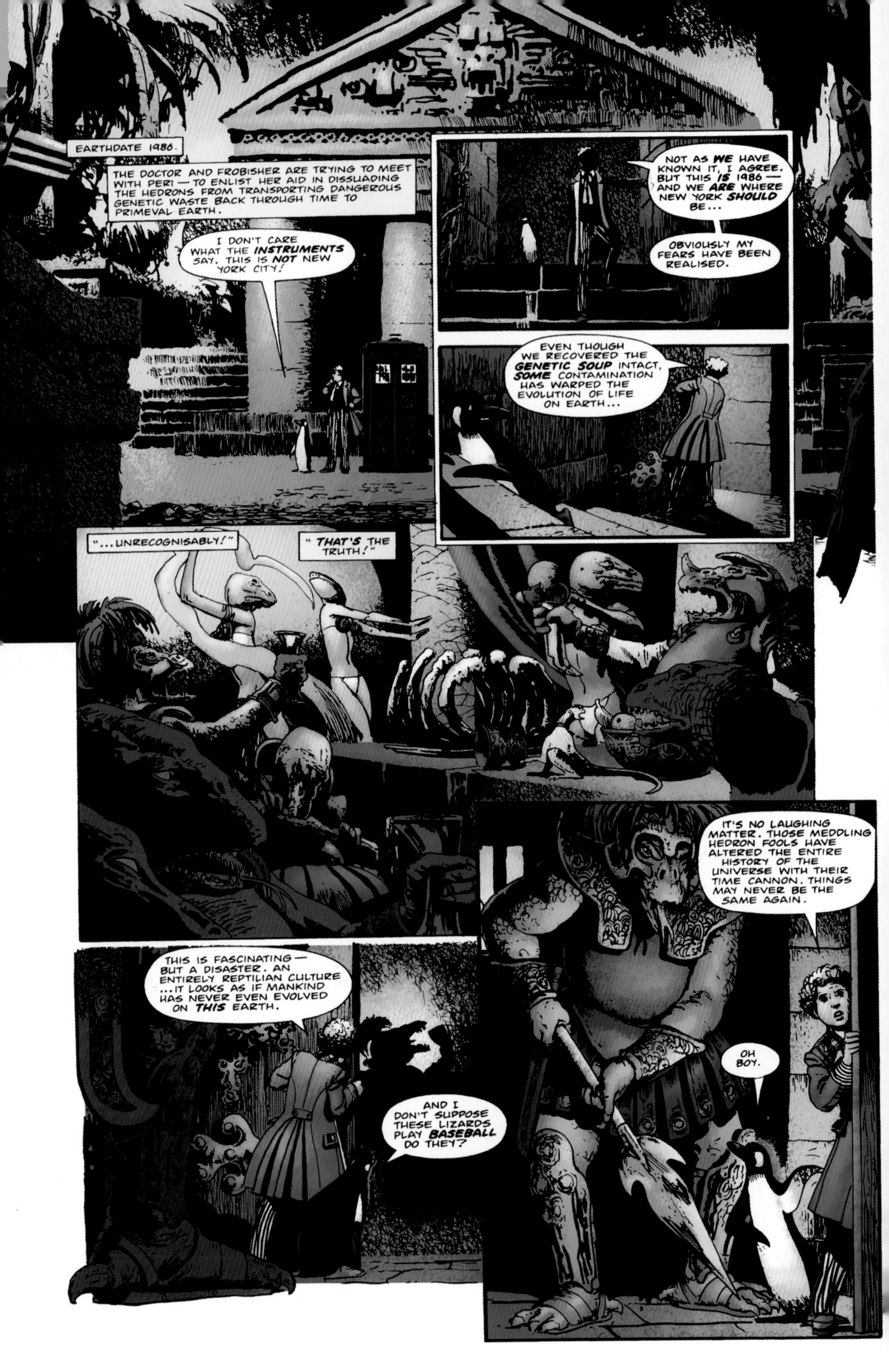
EARTHDATE 1986.
THE DOCTOR AND FROBISHER ARE TRYING TO MEET WITH PERI — TO ENLIST HER AID IN DISSUADING THE HEDRONS FROM TRANSPORTING DANGEROUS GENETIC WASTE BACK THROUGH TIME TO PRIMEVAL EARTH.
I DON'T CARE WHAT THE INSTRUMENTS SAY. THIS IS NOT NEW YORK CITY!
NOT AS WE HAVE KNOWN IT, I AGREE. BUT THIS IS 1986 — AND WE ARE WHERE NEW YORK SHOULD BE...
OBVIOUSLY MY FEARS HAVE BEEN REALISED.
EVEN THOUGH WE RECOVERED THE GENETIC SOUP INTACT, SOME CONTAMINATION HAS WARPED THE EVOLUTION OF LIFE ON EARTH...
"...UNRECOGNISABLY!"
"THAT'S THE TRUTH!"
THIS IS FASCINATING — BUT A DISASTER. AN ENTIRELY REPTILIAN CULTURE ...IT LOOKS AS IF MANKIND HAS NEVER EVEN EVOLVED ON THIS EARTH.
AND I DON'T SUPPOSE THESE LIZARDS PLAY BASEBALL DO THEY?
IT'S NO LAUGHING MATTER. THOSE MEDDLING HEDRON FOOLS HAVE ALTERED THE ENTIRE HISTORY OF THE UNIVERSE WITH THEIR TIME CANNON. THINGS MAY NEVER BE THE SAME AGAIN.
OH BOY.

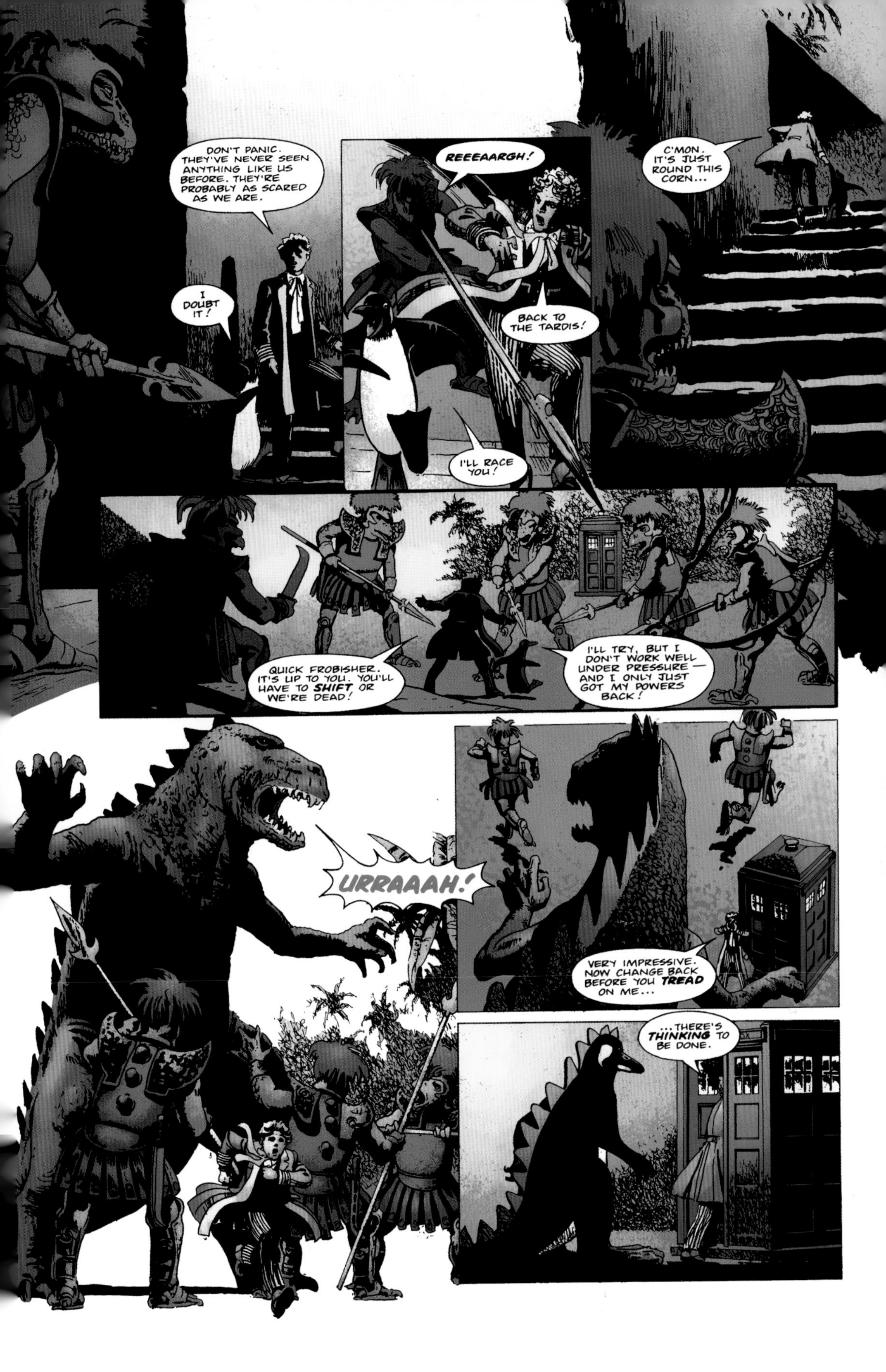

DON'T PANIC. THEY'VE NEVER SEEN ANYTHING LIKE US BEFORE. THEY'RE PROBABLY AS SCARED AS WE ARE.
I DOUBT IT!
REEEAARGH!
BACK TO THE TARDIS!
I'LL RACE YOU!
C'MON. IT'S JUST ROUND THIS CORN...
QUICK FROBISHER. IT'S UP TO YOU. YOU'LL HAVE TO SHIFT OR WE'RE DEAD!
I'LL TRY, BUT I DON'T WORK WELL UNDER PRESSURE — AND I ONLY JUST GOT MY POWERS BACK!
URRAAAH!
VERY IMPRESSIVE. NOW CHANGE BACK BEFORE YOU TREAD ON ME...
...THERE'S THINKING TO BE DONE.

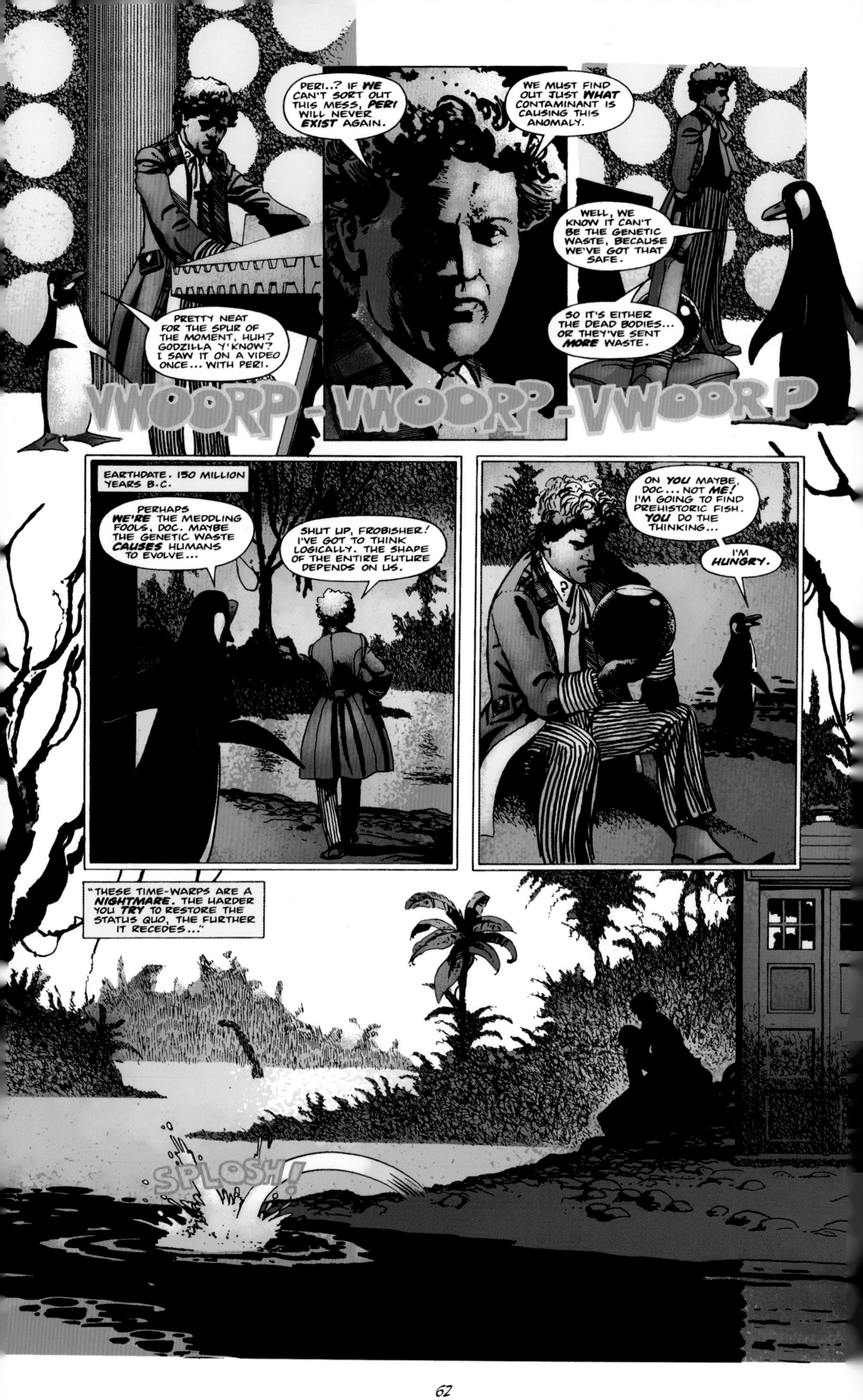

PRETTY NEAT FOR THE SPUR OF THE MOMENT, HUH? GODZILLA Y'KNOW? I SAW IT ON A VIDEO ONCE... WITH PERI.
PERI..? IF WE CAN'T SORT OUT THIS MESS, PERI WILL NEVER EXIST AGAIN.
WE MUST FIND OUT JUST WHAT CONTAMINANT IS CAUSING THIS ANOMALY.
WELL, WE KNOW IT CAN'T BE THE GENETIC WASTE, BECAUSE WE'VE GOT THAT SAFE.
SO IT'S EITHER THE DEAD BODIES... OR THEY'VE SENT MORE WASTE.
VWOORP - VWOORP - VWOORP
EARTHDATE. 150 MILLION YEARS B.C.
PERHAPS WE'RE THE MEDDLING FOOLS, DOC. MAYBE THE GENETIC WASTE CAUSES HUMANS TO EVOLVE...
SHUT UP, FROBISHER! I'VE GOT TO THINK LOGICALLY. THE SHAPE OF THE ENTIRE FUTURE DEPENDS ON US.
ON YOU MAYBE, DOC... NOT ME! I'M GOING TO FIND PREHISTORIC FISH. YOU DO THE THINKING...
I'M HUNGRY.
"THESE TIME-WARPS ARE A NIGHTMARE. THE HARDER YOU TRY TO RESTORE THE STATUS QUO, THE FURTHER IT RECEDES..."
SPLOSH!

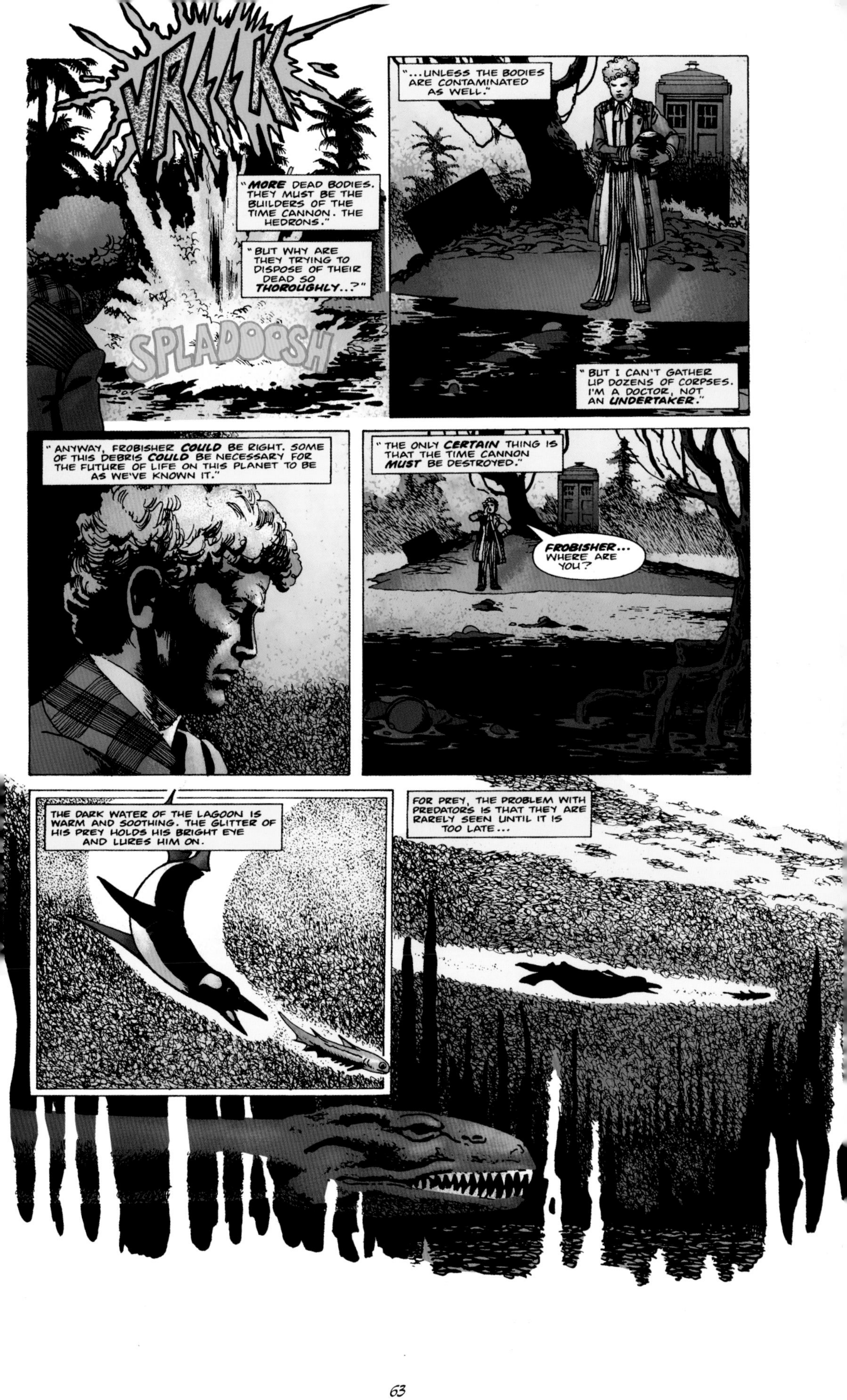
VRKK
"MORE DEAD BODIES. THEY MUST BE THE BUILDERS OF THE TIME CANNON. THE HEDRONS."
"BUT WHY ARE THEY TRYING TO DISPOSE OF THEIR DEAD SO THOROUGHLY..?"
SPLADOOSH
"...UNLESS THE BODIES ARE CONTAMINATED AS WELL."
"BUT I CAN'T GATHER UP DOZENS OF CORPSES. I'M A DOCTOR, NOT AN UNDERTAKER."
"ANYWAY, FROBISHER COULD BE RIGHT. SOME OF THIS DEBRIS COULD BE NECESSARY FOR THE FUTURE OF LIFE ON THIS PLANET TO BE AS WE'VE KNOWN IT."
"THE ONLY CERTAIN THING IS THAT THE TIME CANNON MUST BE DESTROYED."
FROBISHER... WHERE ARE YOU?
THE DARK WATER OF THE LAGOON IS WARM AND SOOTHING. THE GLITTER OF HIS PREY HOLDS HIS BRIGHT EYE AND LURES HIM ON.
FOR PREY, THE PROBLEM WITH PREDATORS IS THAT THEY ARE RARELY SEEN UNTIL IT IS TOO LATE...

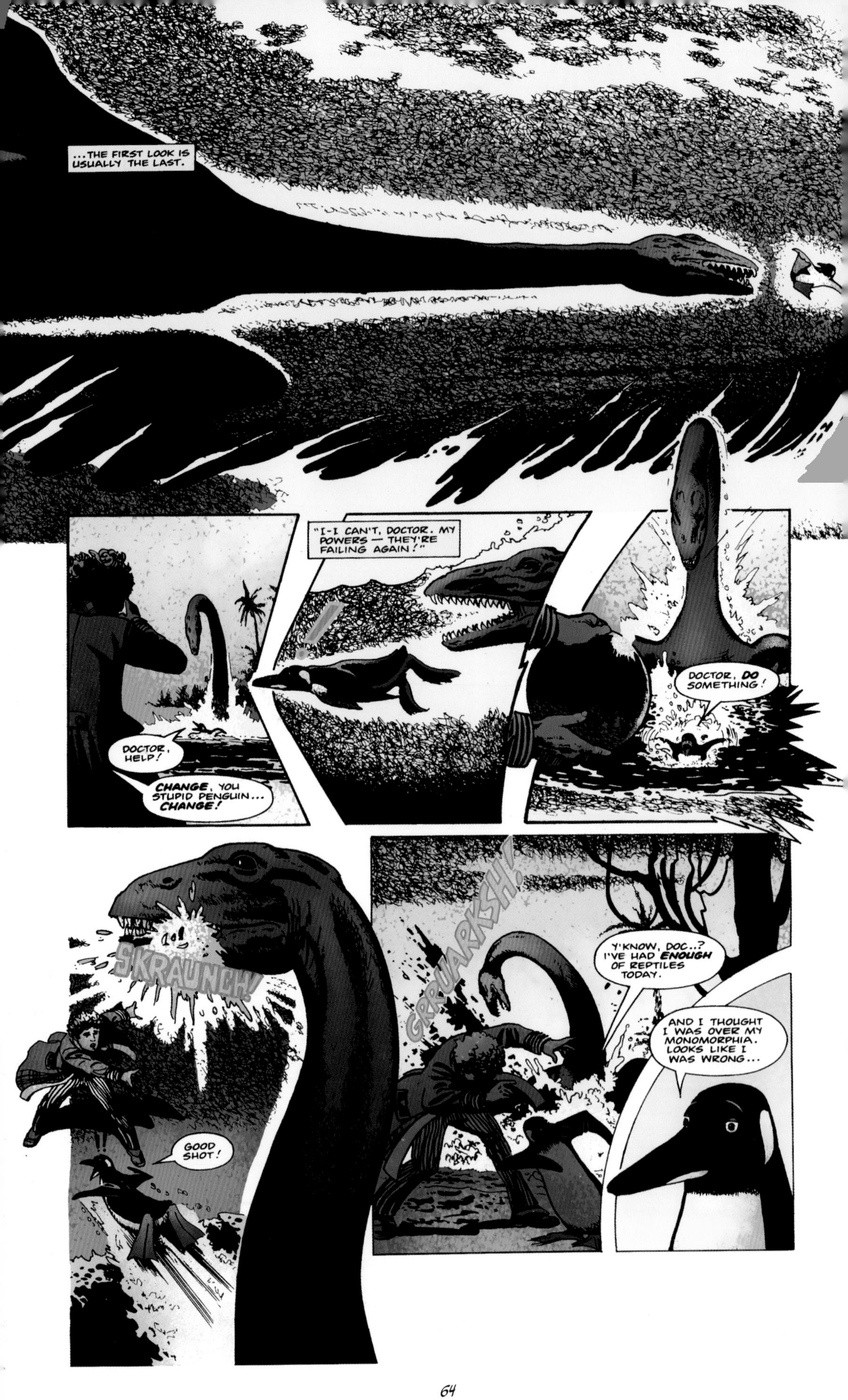
...THE FIRST LOOK IS USUALLY THE LAST.
DOCTOR, HELP!
CHANGE, YOU STUPID PENGUIN... CHANGE!
"I-I CAN'T, DOCTOR. MY POWERS — THEY'RE FAILING AGAIN!"
DOCTOR, DO SOMETHING!
SKRAUNCH!
GOOD SHOT!
GRRUARKSH!
Y'KNOW, DOC..? I'VE HAD ENOUGH OF REPTILES TODAY.
AND I THOUGHT I WAS OVER MY MONOMORPHIA. LOOKS LIKE I WAS WRONG...

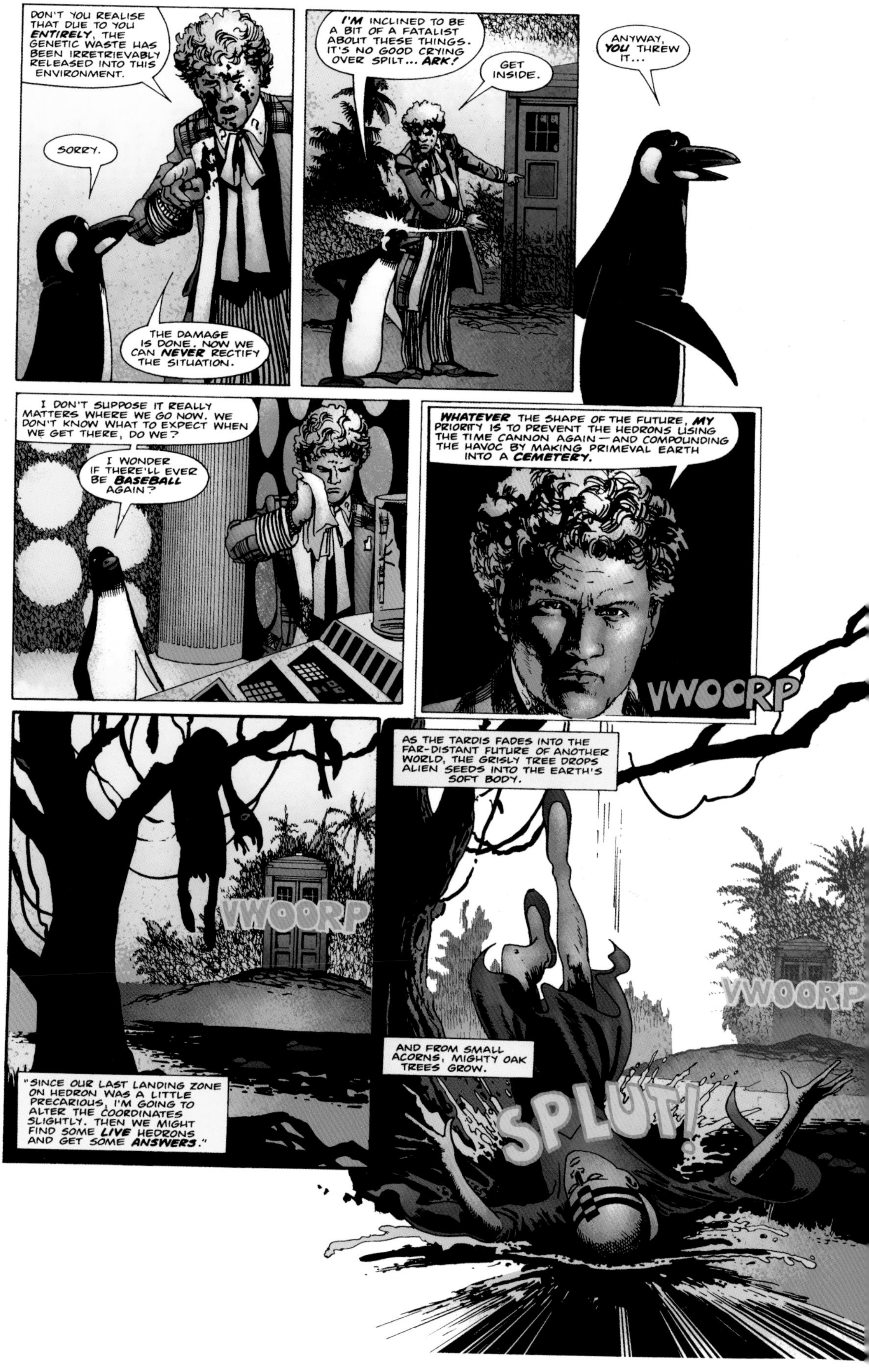
DON'T YOU REALISE THAT DUE TO YOU ENTIRELY, THE GENETIC WASTE HAS BEEN IRRETRIEVABLY RELEASED INTO THIS ENVIRONMENT.
SORRY.
THE DAMAGE IS DONE. NOW WE CAN NEVER RECTIFY THE SITUATION.
I'M INCLINED TO BE A BIT OF A FATALIST ABOUT THESE THINGS. IT'S NO GOOD CRYING OVER SPILT... ARK!
GET INSIDE.
ANYWAY, YOU THREW IT...
I DON'T SUPPOSE IT REALLY MATTERS WHERE WE GO NOW. WE DON'T KNOW WHAT TO EXPECT WHEN WE GET THERE, DO WE?
I WONDER IF THERE'LL EVER BE BASEBALL AGAIN?
WHATEVER THE SHAPE OF THE FUTURE, MY PRIORITY IS TO PREVENT THE HEDRONS USING THE TIME CANNON AGAIN — AND COMPOUNDING THE HAVOC BY MAKING PRIMEVAL EARTH INTO A CEMETERY.
VWOORP
VWOORP
"SINCE OUR LAST LANDING ZONE ON HEDRON WAS A LITTLE PRECARIOUS, I'M GOING TO ALTER THE COORDINATES SLIGHTLY. THEN WE MIGHT FIND SOME LIVE HEDRONS AND GET SOME ANSWERS."
AS THE TARDIS FADES INTO THE FAR-DISTANT FUTURE OF ANOTHER WORLD, THE GRISLY TREE DROPS ALIEN SEEDS INTO THE EARTH'S SOFT BODY.
VWOORP
AND FROM SMALL ACORNS, MIGHTY OAK TREES GROW.
SPLUT!

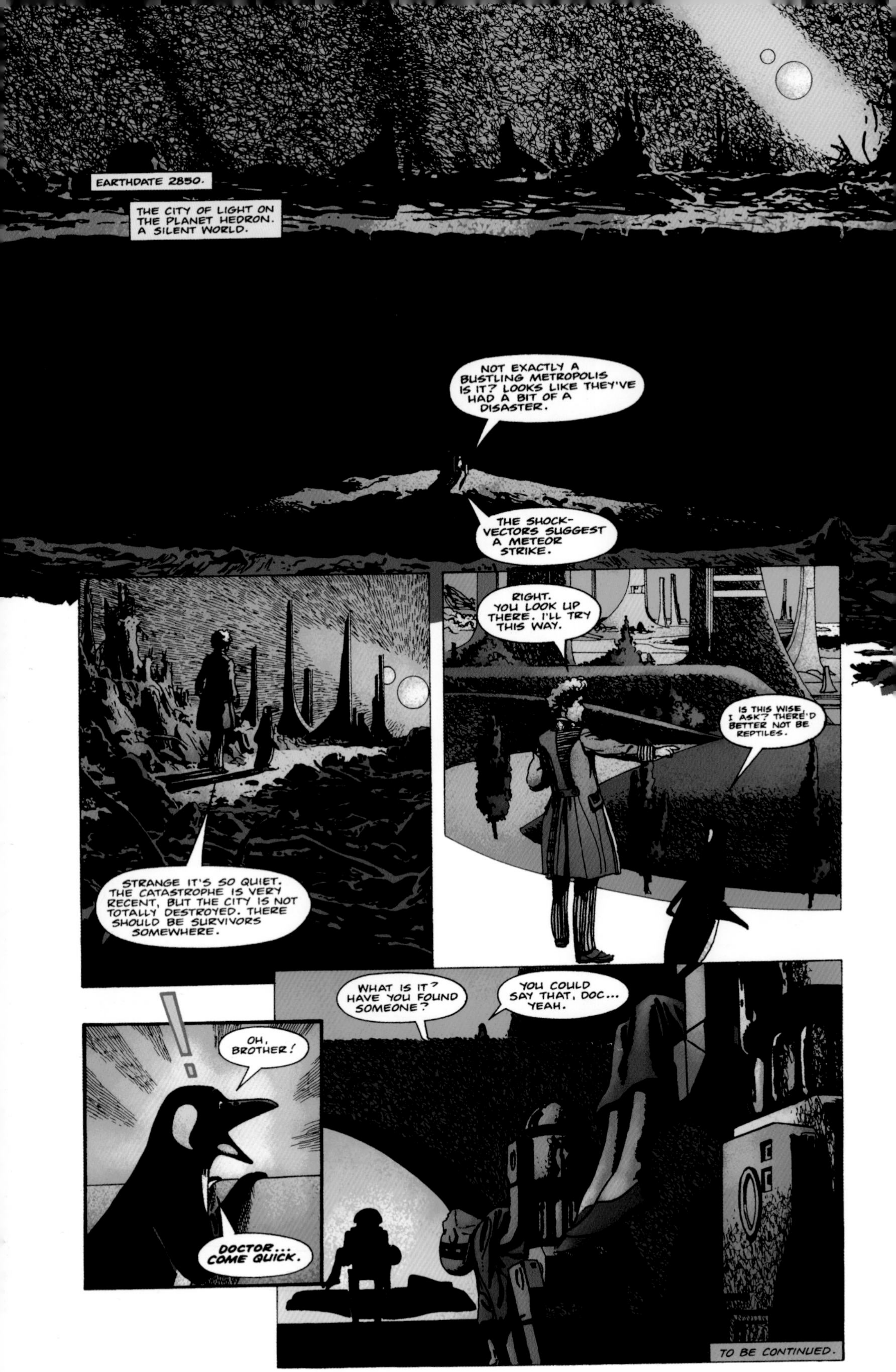
EARTHDATE 2850.
THE CITY OF LIGHT ON THE PLANET HEDRON. A SILENT WORLD.
NOT EXACTLY A BUSTLING METROPOLIS IS IT? LOOKS LIKE THEY'VE HAD A BIT OF A DISASTER.
THE SHOCK-VECTORS SUGGEST A METEOR STRIKE.
STRANGE IT'S SO QUIET. THE CATASTROPHE IS VERY RECENT, BUT THE CITY IS NOT TOTALLY DESTROYED. THERE SHOULD BE SURVIVORS SOMEWHERE.
RIGHT. YOU LOOK UP THERE. I'LL TRY THIS WAY.
IS THIS WISE, I ASK? THERE'D BETTER NOT BE REPTILES.
OH, BROTHER!
DOCTOR... COME QUICK.
WHAT IS IT? HAVE YOU FOUND SOMEONE?
YOU COULD SAY THAT, DOC... YEAH.
TO BE CONTINUED.

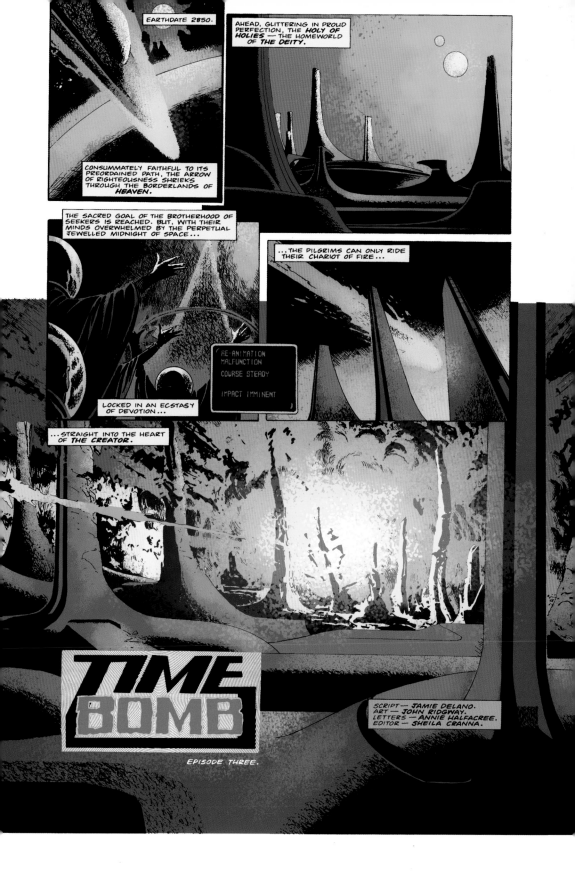

EARTHDATE 2850.

CONSUMMATELY FAITHFUL TO ITS PREORDAINED PATH, THE ARROW OF RIGHTEOUSNESS SHRIEKS THROUGH THE BORDERLANDS OF *HEAVEN*.

AHEAD, GLITTERING IN PROUD PERFECTION, THE *HOLY OF HOLIES* — THE HOMEWORLD OF *THE DEITY*.

THE SACRED GOAL OF THE BROTHERHOOD OF SEEKERS IS REACHED. BUT, WITH THEIR MINDS OVERWHELMED BY THE PERPETUAL JEWELLED MIDNIGHT OF SPACE...

...THE PILGRIMS CAN ONLY RIDE THEIR CHARIOT OF FIRE...

RE-ANIMATION MALFUNCTION

COURSE STEADY

IMPACT IMMINENT

LOCKED IN AN ECSTASY OF DEVOTION...

...STRAIGHT INTO THE HEART OF *THE CREATOR*.

TIME BOMB

EPISODE THREE.

SCRIPT — JAMIE DELANO.
ART — JOHN RIDGWAY.
LETTERS — ANNIE HALFACREE.
EDITOR — SHEILA CRANNA.

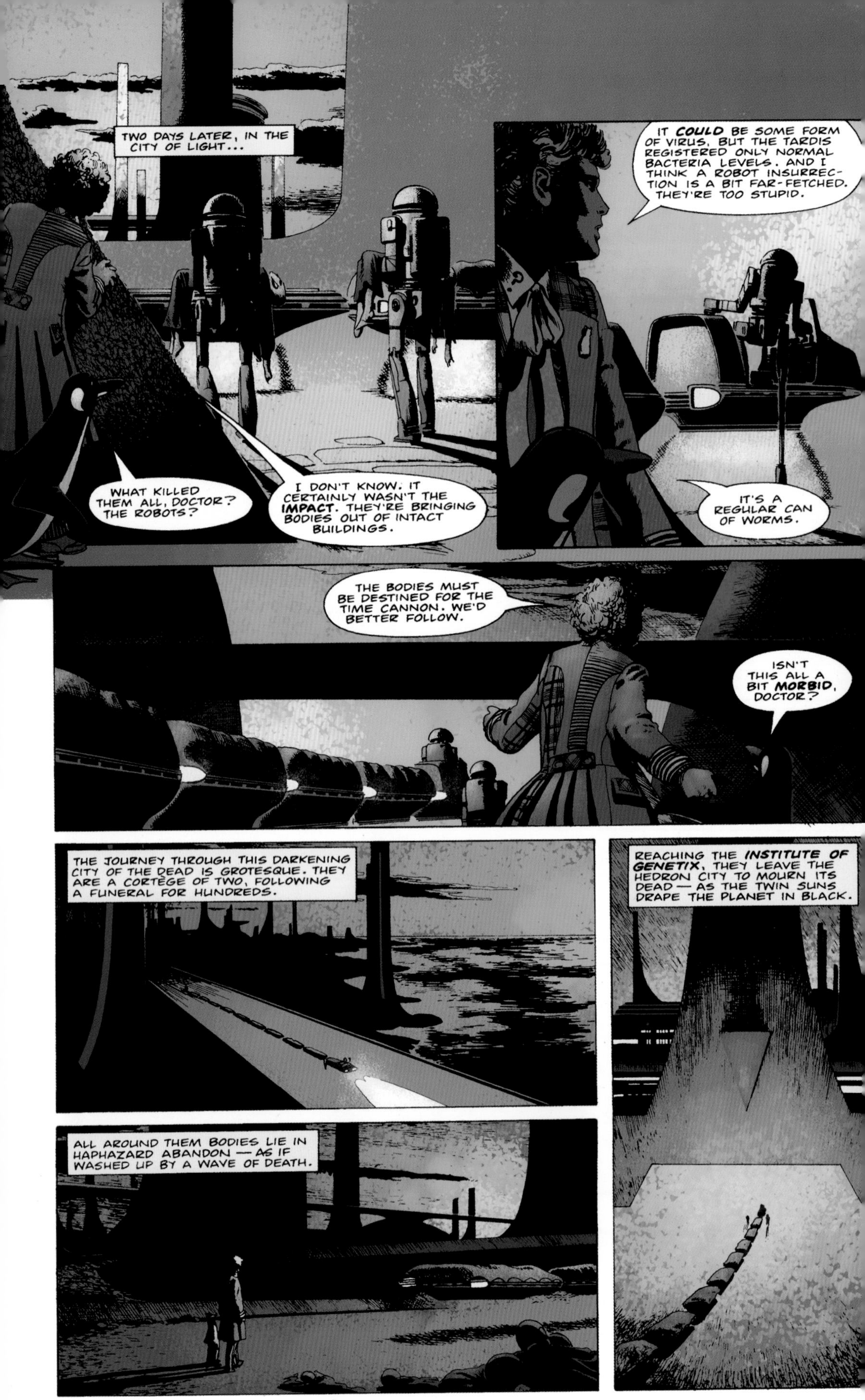
TWO DAYS LATER, IN THE CITY OF LIGHT...
WHAT KILLED THEM ALL, DOCTOR? THE ROBOTS?
I DON'T KNOW. IT CERTAINLY WASN'T THE IMPACT. THEY'RE BRINGING BODIES OUT OF INTACT BUILDINGS.
IT COULD BE SOME FORM OF VIRUS, BUT THE TARDIS REGISTERED ONLY NORMAL BACTERIA LEVELS. AND I THINK A ROBOT INSURRECTION IS A BIT FAR-FETCHED. THEY'RE TOO STUPID.
IT'S A REGULAR CAN OF WORMS.
THE BODIES MUST BE DESTINED FOR THE TIME CANNON. WE'D BETTER FOLLOW.
ISN'T THIS ALL A BIT MORBID, DOCTOR?
THE JOURNEY THROUGH THIS DARKENING CITY OF THE DEAD IS GROTESQUE. THEY ARE A CORTEGE OF TWO, FOLLOWING A FUNERAL FOR HUNDREDS.
ALL AROUND THEM BODIES LIE IN HAPHAZARD ABANDON — AS IF WASHED UP BY A WAVE OF DEATH.
REACHING THE INSTITUTE OF GENETIX, THEY LEAVE THE HEDRON CITY TO MOURN ITS DEAD — AS THE TWIN SUNS DRAPE THE PLANET IN BLACK.

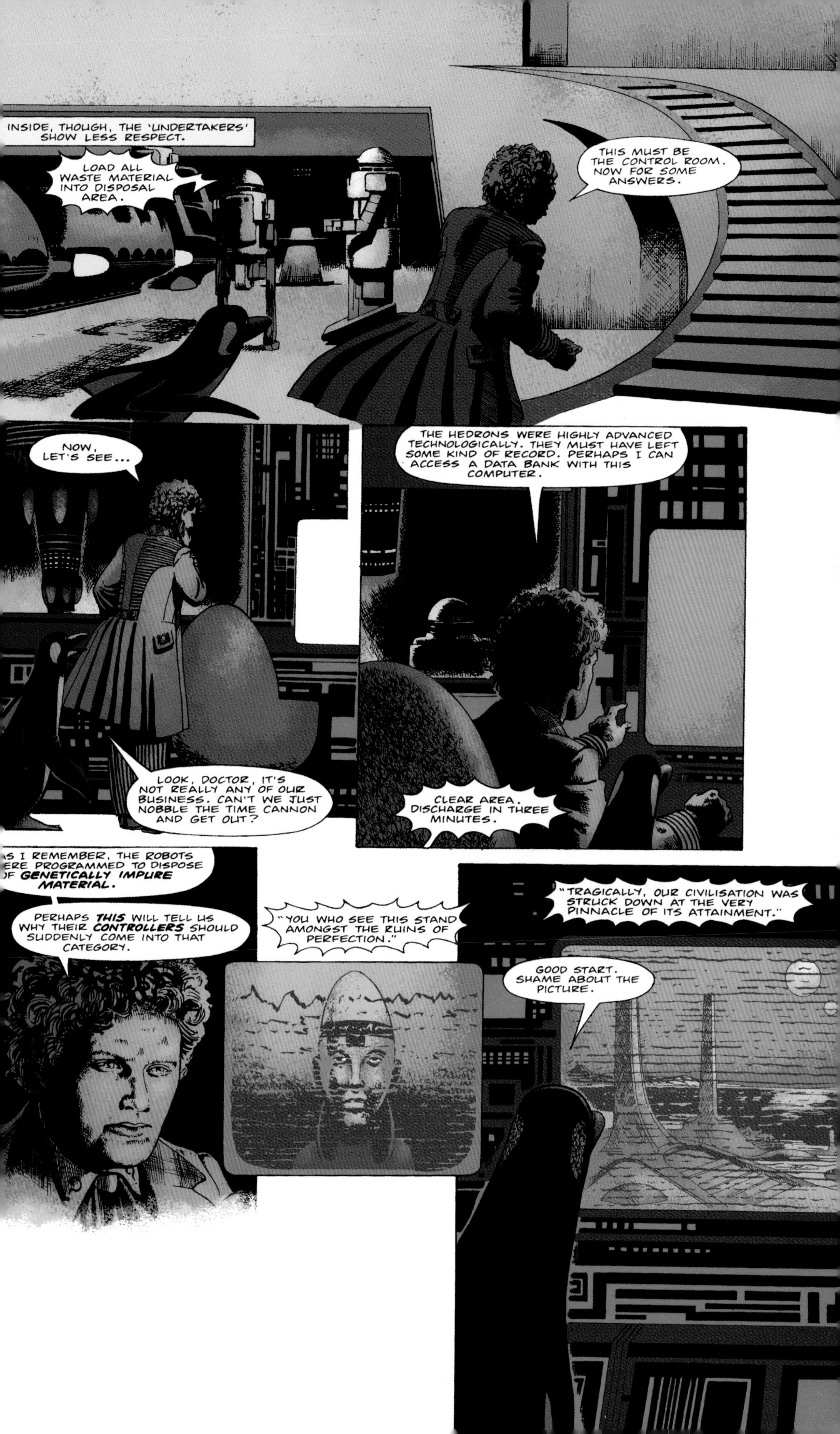
INSIDE, THOUGH, THE 'UNDERTAKERS' SHOW LESS RESPECT.
LOAD ALL WASTE MATERIAL INTO DISPOSAL AREA.
THIS MUST BE THE CONTROL ROOM. NOW FOR SOME ANSWERS.
NOW, LET'S SEE...
LOOK, DOCTOR, IT'S NOT REALLY ANY OF OUR BUSINESS. CAN'T WE JUST NOBBLE THE TIME CANNON AND GET OUT?
THE HEDRONS WERE HIGHLY ADVANCED TECHNOLOGICALLY. THEY MUST HAVE LEFT SOME KIND OF RECORD. PERHAPS I CAN ACCESS A DATA BANK WITH THIS COMPUTER.
CLEAR AREA. DISCHARGE IN THREE MINUTES.
AS I REMEMBER, THE ROBOTS WERE PROGRAMMED TO DISPOSE OF GENETICALLY IMPURE MATERIAL.
PERHAPS THIS WILL TELL US WHY THEIR CONTROLLERS SHOULD SUDDENLY COME INTO THAT CATEGORY.
"YOU WHO SEE THIS STAND AMONGST THE RUINS OF PERFECTION."
"TRAGICALLY, OUR CIVILISATION WAS STRUCK DOWN AT THE VERY PINNACLE OF ITS ATTAINMENT."
GOOD START. SHAME ABOUT THE PICTURE.

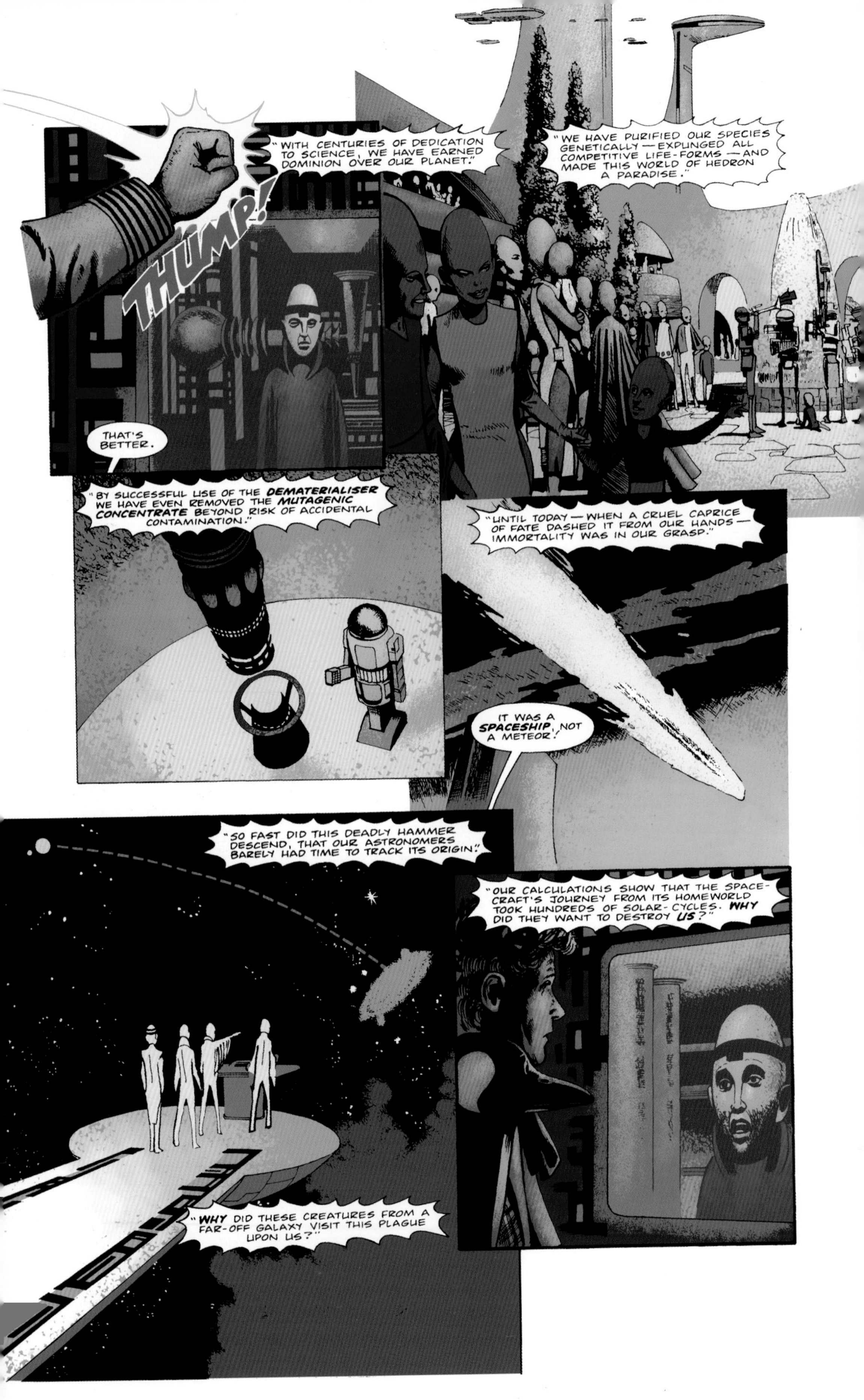
THUMP!
"WITH CENTURIES OF DEDICATION TO SCIENCE, WE HAVE EARNED DOMINION OVER OUR PLANET."
"WE HAVE PURIFIED OUR SPECIES GENETICALLY — EXPUNGED ALL COMPETITIVE LIFE-FORMS — AND MADE THIS WORLD OF HEDRON A PARADISE."
THAT'S BETTER.
"BY SUCCESSFUL USE OF THE DEMATERIALISER WE HAVE EVEN REMOVED THE MUTAGENIC CONCENTRATE BEYOND RISK OF ACCIDENTAL CONTAMINATION."
"UNTIL TODAY — WHEN A CRUEL CAPRICE OF FATE DASHED IT FROM OUR HANDS — IMMORTALITY WAS IN OUR GRASP."
IT WAS A SPACESHIP, NOT A METEOR!
"SO FAST DID THIS DEADLY HAMMER DESCEND, THAT OUR ASTRONOMERS BARELY HAD TIME TO TRACK ITS ORIGIN."
"WHY DID THESE CREATURES FROM A FAR-OFF GALAXY VISIT THIS PLAGUE UPON US?"
"OUR CALCULATIONS SHOW THAT THE SPACE-CRAFT'S JOURNEY FROM ITS HOMEWORLD TOOK HUNDREDS OF SOLAR-CYCLES. WHY DID THEY WANT TO DESTROY US?"

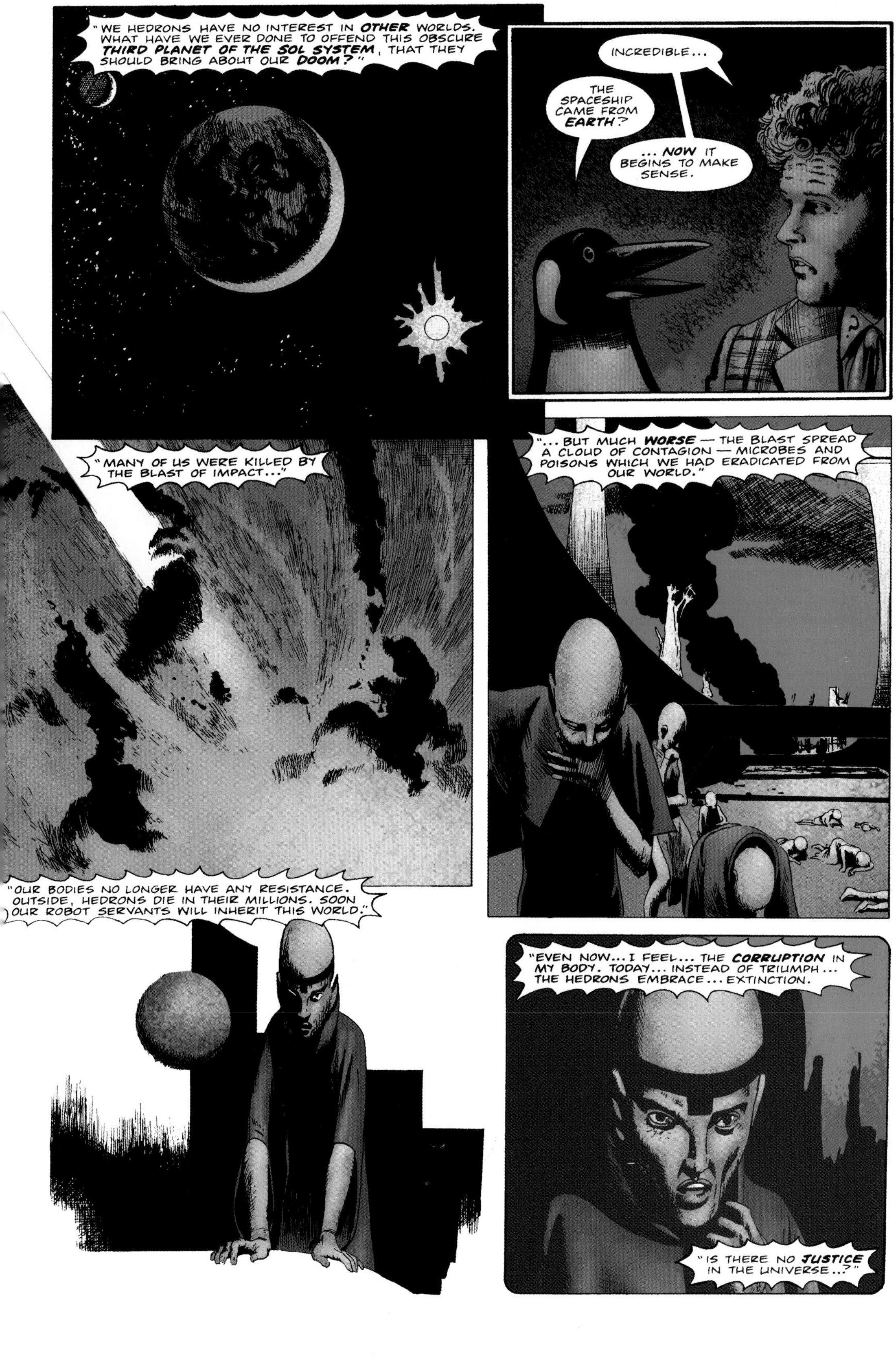
"WE HEDRONS HAVE NO INTEREST IN OTHER WORLDS. WHAT HAVE WE EVER DONE TO OFFEND THIS OBSCURE THIRD PLANET OF THE SOL SYSTEM, THAT THEY SHOULD BRING ABOUT OUR DOOM?"
INCREDIBLE...
THE SPACESHIP CAME FROM EARTH?
...NOW IT BEGINS TO MAKE SENSE.
"MANY OF US WERE KILLED BY THE BLAST OF IMPACT..."
"...BUT MUCH WORSE — THE BLAST SPREAD A CLOUD OF CONTAGION — MICROBES AND POISONS WHICH WE HAD ERADICATED FROM OUR WORLD."
"OUR BODIES NO LONGER HAVE ANY RESISTANCE. OUTSIDE, HEDRONS DIE IN THEIR MILLIONS. SOON OUR ROBOT SERVANTS WILL INHERIT THIS WORLD."
"EVEN NOW... I FEEL... THE CORRUPTION IN MY BODY. TODAY... INSTEAD OF TRIUMPH... THE HEDRONS EMBRACE... EXTINCTION.
"IS THERE NO JUSTICE IN THE UNIVERSE..?"

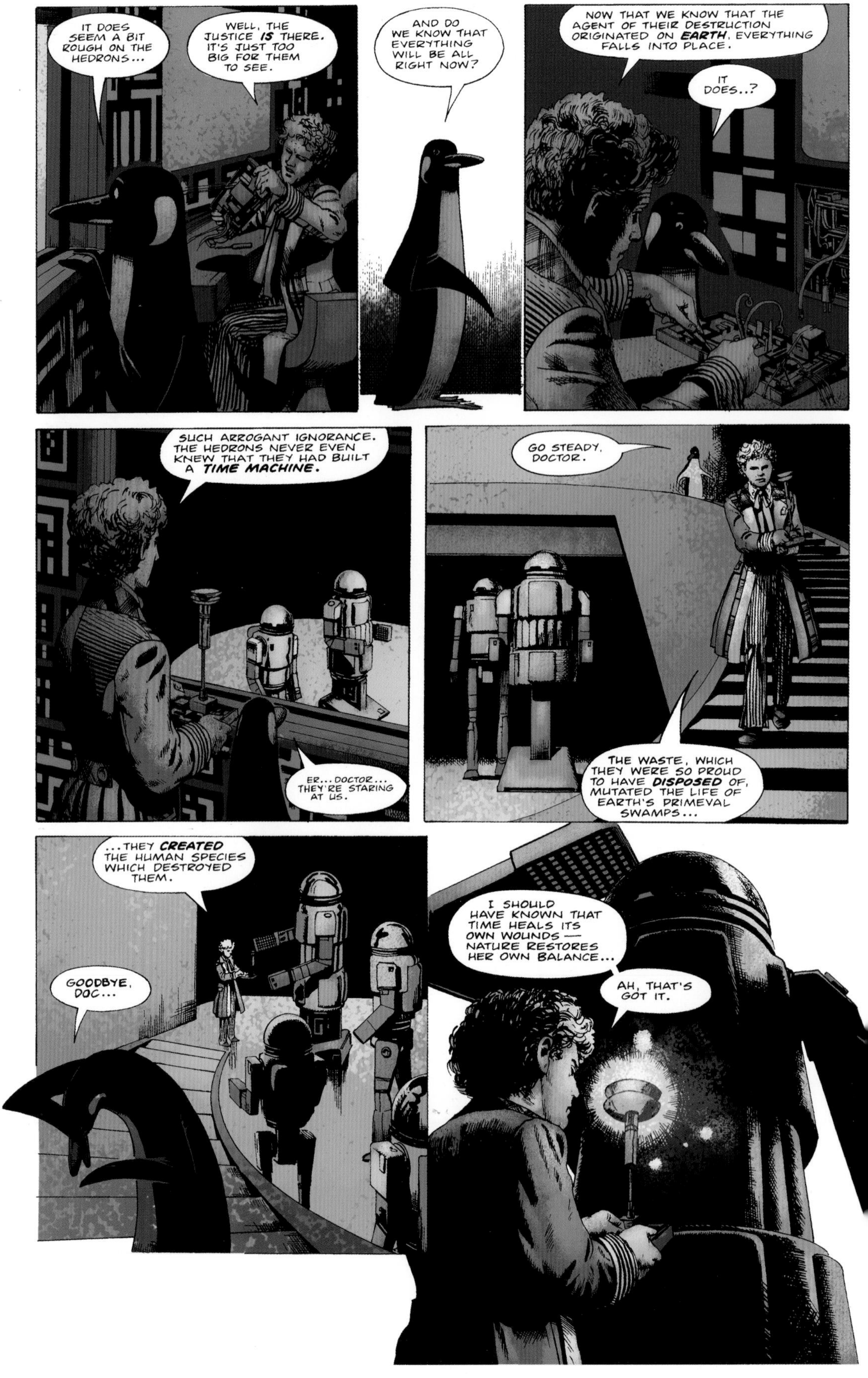
IT DOES SEEM A BIT ROUGH ON THE HEDRONS...
WELL, THE JUSTICE IS THERE. IT'S JUST TOO BIG FOR THEM TO SEE.
AND DO WE KNOW THAT EVERYTHING WILL BE ALL RIGHT NOW?
NOW THAT WE KNOW THAT THE AGENT OF THEIR DESTRUCTION ORIGINATED ON EARTH, EVERYTHING FALLS INTO PLACE.
IT DOES..?
SUCH ARROGANT IGNORANCE. THE HEDRONS NEVER EVEN KNEW THAT THEY HAD BUILT A TIME MACHINE.
ER...DOCTOR... THEY'RE STARING AT US.
GO STEADY, DOCTOR.
THE WASTE, WHICH THEY WERE SO PROUD TO HAVE DISPOSED OF, MUTATED THE LIFE OF EARTH'S PRIMEVAL SWAMPS...
...THEY CREATED THE HUMAN SPECIES WHICH DESTROYED THEM.
GOODBYE, DOC...
I SHOULD HAVE KNOWN THAT TIME HEALS ITS OWN WOUNDS — NATURE RESTORES HER OWN BALANCE...
AH, THAT'S GOT IT.

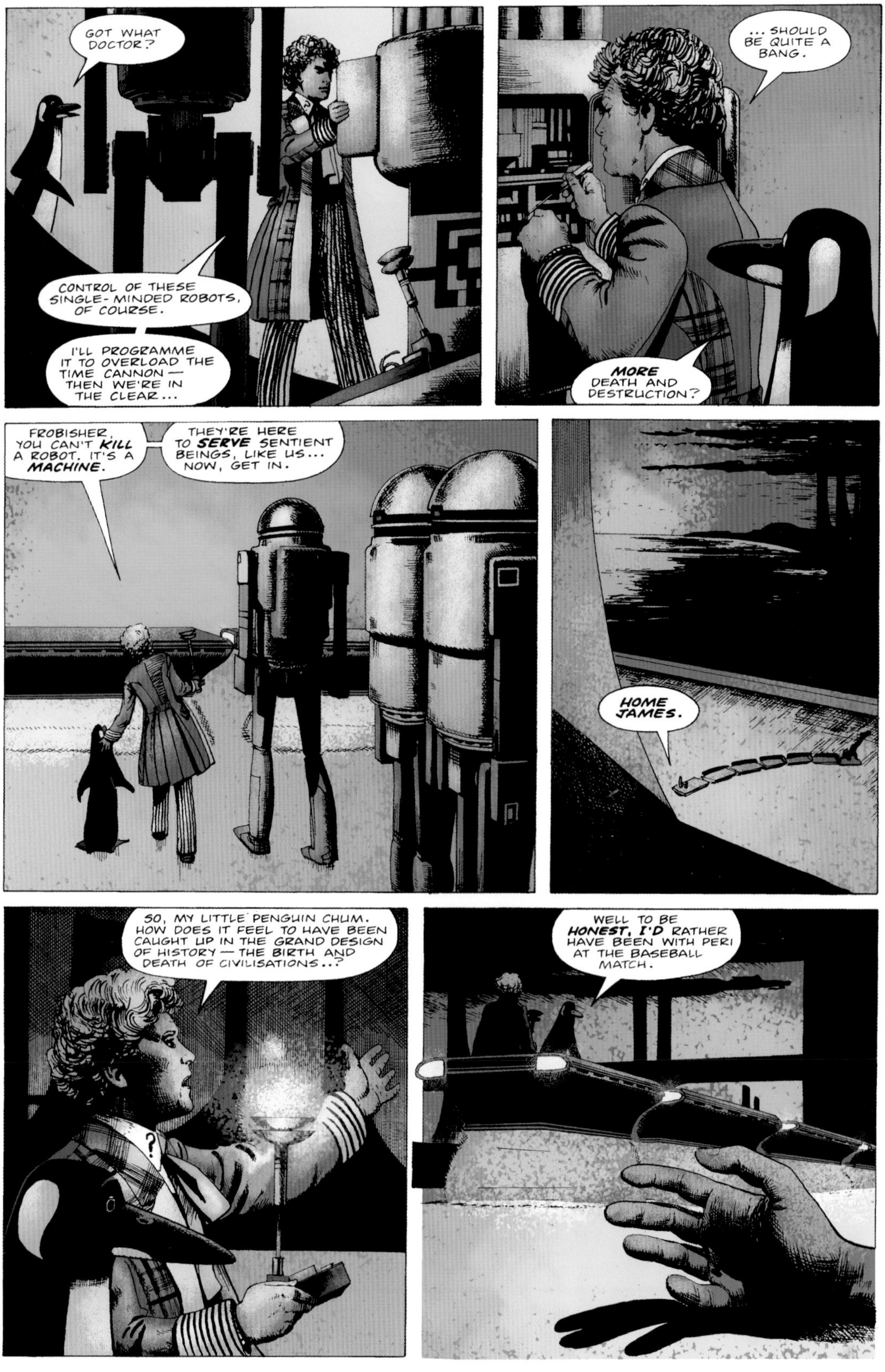

GOT WHAT DOCTOR?
CONTROL OF THESE SINGLE-MINDED ROBOTS, OF COURSE.
I'LL PROGRAMME IT TO OVERLOAD THE TIME CANNON — THEN WE'RE IN THE CLEAR...
... SHOULD BE QUITE A BANG.
MORE DEATH AND DESTRUCTION?
FROBISHER, YOU CAN'T KILL A ROBOT. IT'S A MACHINE.
THEY'RE HERE TO SERVE SENTIENT BEINGS, LIKE US... NOW, GET IN.
HOME JAMES.
SO, MY LITTLE PENGUIN CHUM. HOW DOES IT FEEL TO HAVE BEEN CAUGHT UP IN THE GRAND DESIGN OF HISTORY — THE BIRTH AND DEATH OF CIVILISATIONS..?
WELL TO BE HONEST, I'D RATHER HAVE BEEN WITH PERI AT THE BASEBALL MATCH.

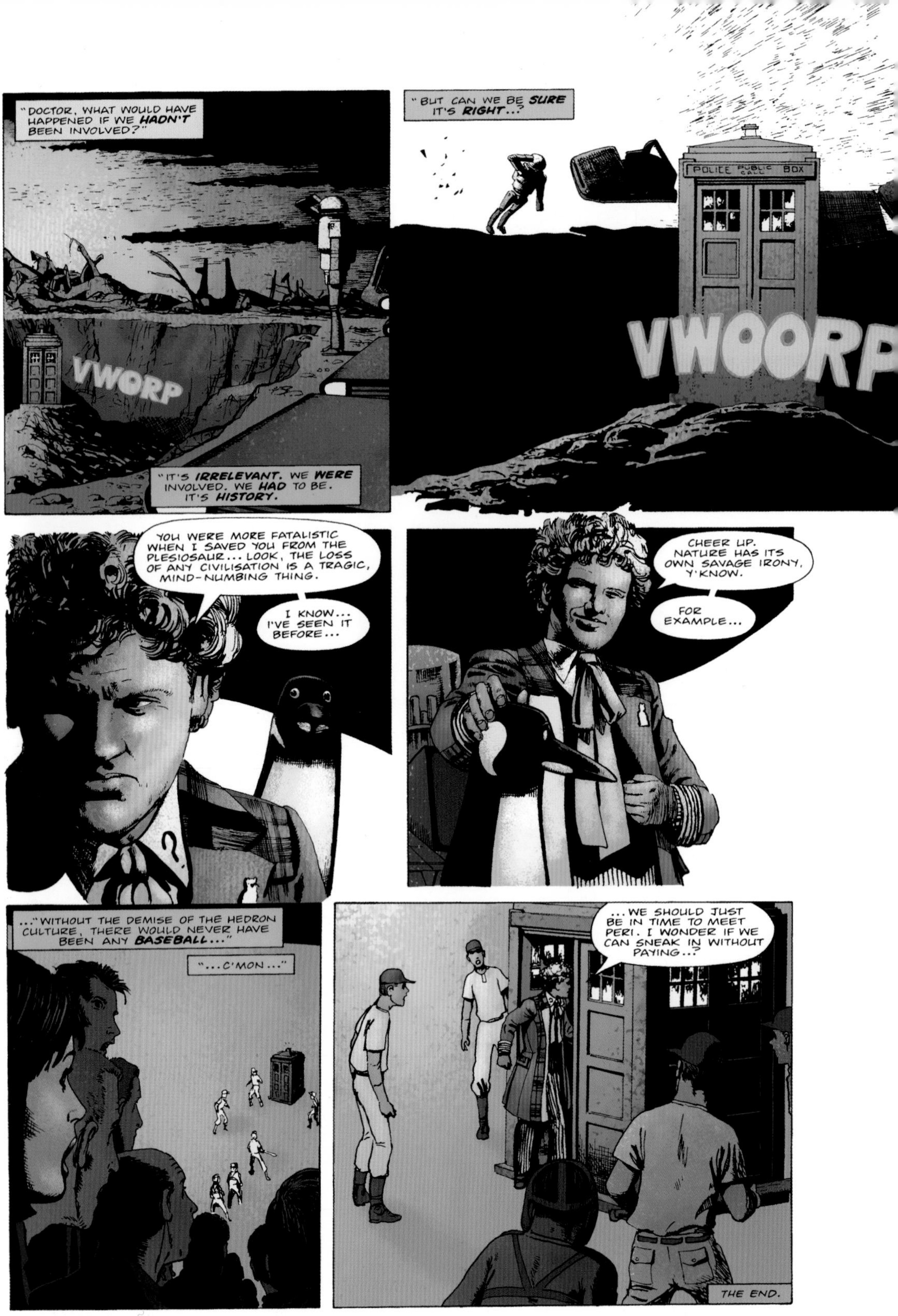
"DOCTOR, WHAT WOULD HAVE HAPPENED IF WE HADN'T BEEN INVOLVED?"
VWORP
"IT'S IRRELEVANT. WE WERE INVOLVED. WE HAD TO BE. IT'S HISTORY.
"BUT CAN WE BE SURE IT'S RIGHT..?
POLICE PUBLIC CALL BOX
VWOORP
YOU WERE MORE FATALISTIC WHEN I SAVED YOU FROM THE PLESIOSAUR... LOOK, THE LOSS OF ANY CIVILISATION IS A TRAGIC, MIND-NUMBING THING.
I KNOW... I'VE SEEN IT BEFORE...
CHEER UP. NATURE HAS ITS OWN SAVAGE IRONY, Y'KNOW.
FOR EXAMPLE...
..."WITHOUT THE DEMISE OF THE HEDRON CULTURE, THERE WOULD NEVER HAVE BEEN ANY BASEBALL..."
"...C'MON..."
...WE SHOULD JUST BE IN TIME TO MEET PERI. I WONDER IF WE CAN SNEAK IN WITHOUT PAYING..?
THE END.

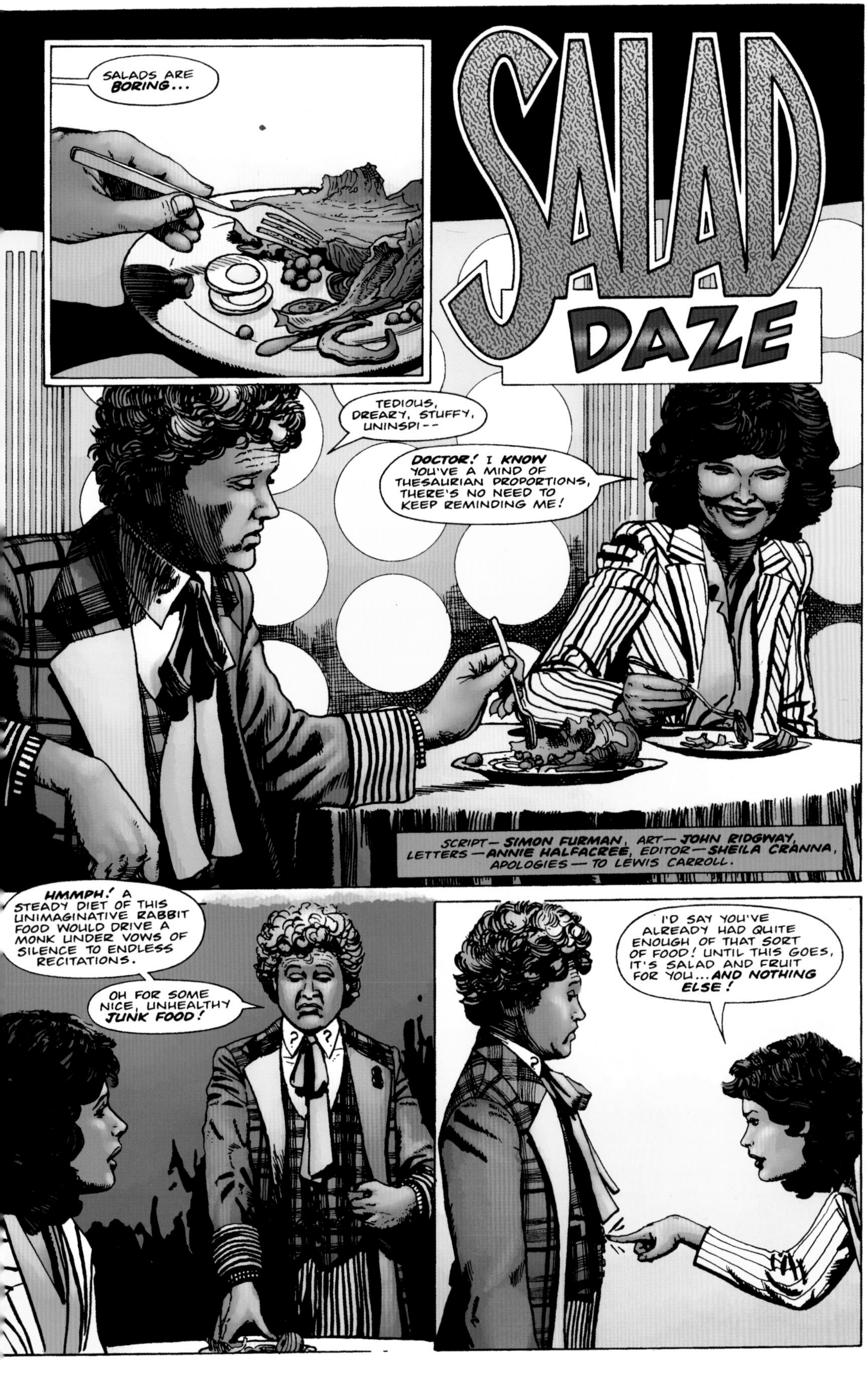

SALAD DAZE
SALADS ARE BORING...
TEDIOUS, DREARY, STUFFY, UNINSPI--
DOCTOR! I KNOW YOU'VE A MIND OF THESAURIAN PROPORTIONS, THERE'S NO NEED TO KEEP REMINDING ME!
SCRIPT— SIMON FURMAN, ART— JOHN RIDGWAY, LETTERS—ANNIE HALFACREE, EDITOR—SHEILA CRANNA, APOLOGIES — TO LEWIS CARROLL.
HMMPH! A STEADY DIET OF THIS UNIMAGINATIVE RABBIT FOOD WOULD DRIVE A MONK UNDER VOWS OF SILENCE TO ENDLESS RECITATIONS.
OH FOR SOME NICE, UNHEALTHY JUNK FOOD!
I'D SAY YOU'VE ALREADY HAD QUITE ENOUGH OF THAT SORT OF FOOD! UNTIL THIS GOES, IT'S SALAD AND FRUIT FOR YOU... AND NOTHING ELSE!

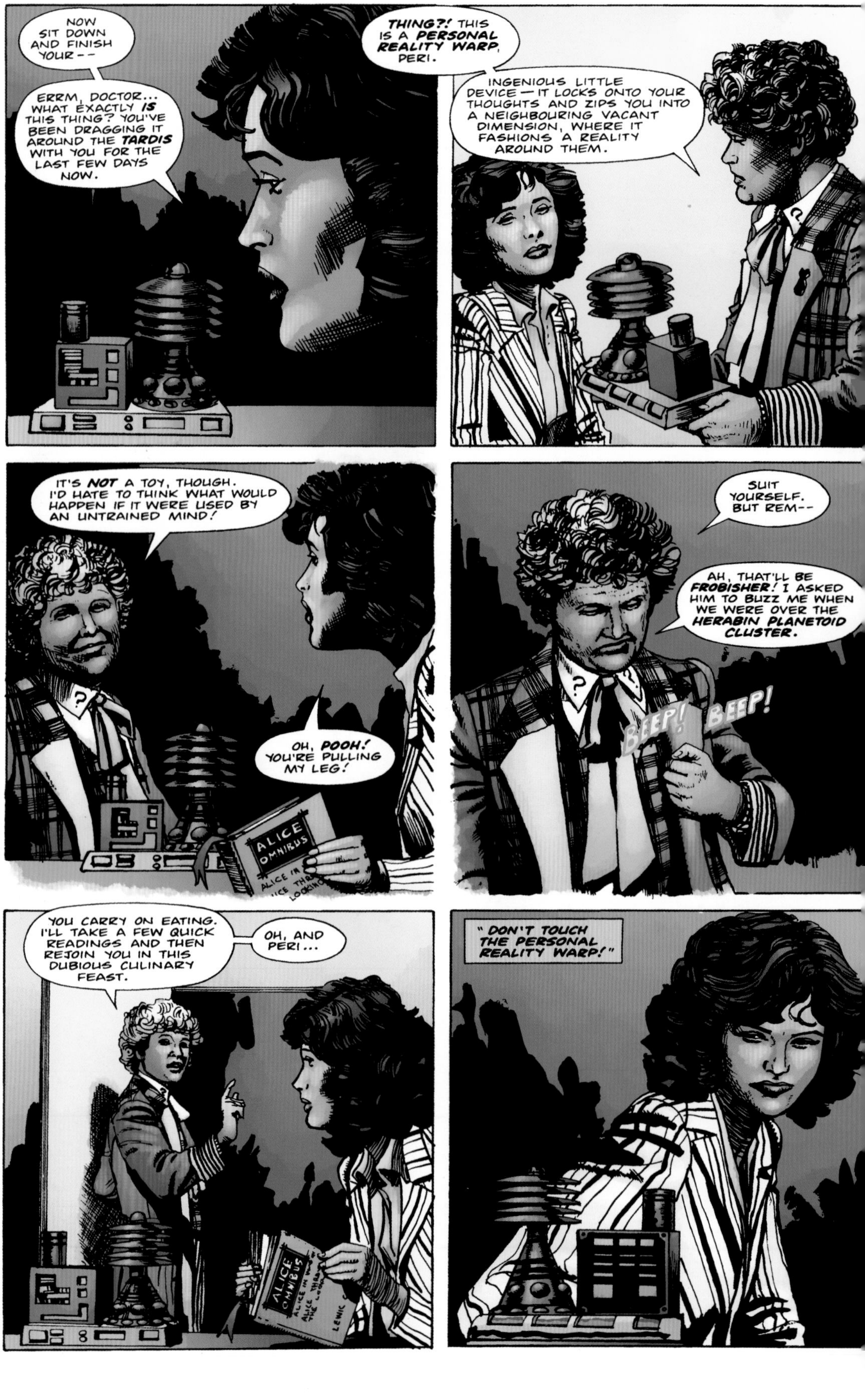
NOW SIT DOWN AND FINISH YOUR--
ERRM, DOCTOR... WHAT EXACTLY IS THIS THING? YOU'VE BEEN DRAGGING IT AROUND THE TARDIS WITH YOU FOR THE LAST FEW DAYS NOW.
THING?! THIS IS A PERSONAL REALITY WARP, PERI.
INGENIOUS LITTLE DEVICE — IT LOCKS ONTO YOUR THOUGHTS AND ZIPS YOU INTO A NEIGHBOURING VACANT DIMENSION, WHERE IT FASHIONS A REALITY AROUND THEM.
IT'S NOT A TOY, THOUGH. I'D HATE TO THINK WHAT WOULD HAPPEN IF IT WERE USED BY AN UNTRAINED MIND!
OH, POOH! YOU'RE PULLING MY LEG!
ALICE OMNIBUS
SUIT YOURSELF. BUT REM--
BEEP! BEEP!
AH, THAT'LL BE FROBISHER! I ASKED HIM TO BUZZ ME WHEN WE WERE OVER THE HERABIN PLANETOID CLUSTER.
YOU CARRY ON EATING. I'LL TAKE A FEW QUICK READINGS AND THEN REJOIN YOU IN THIS DUBIOUS CULINARY FEAST.
OH, AND PERI...
ALICE OMNIBUS
"DON'T TOUCH THE PERSONAL REALITY WARP!"

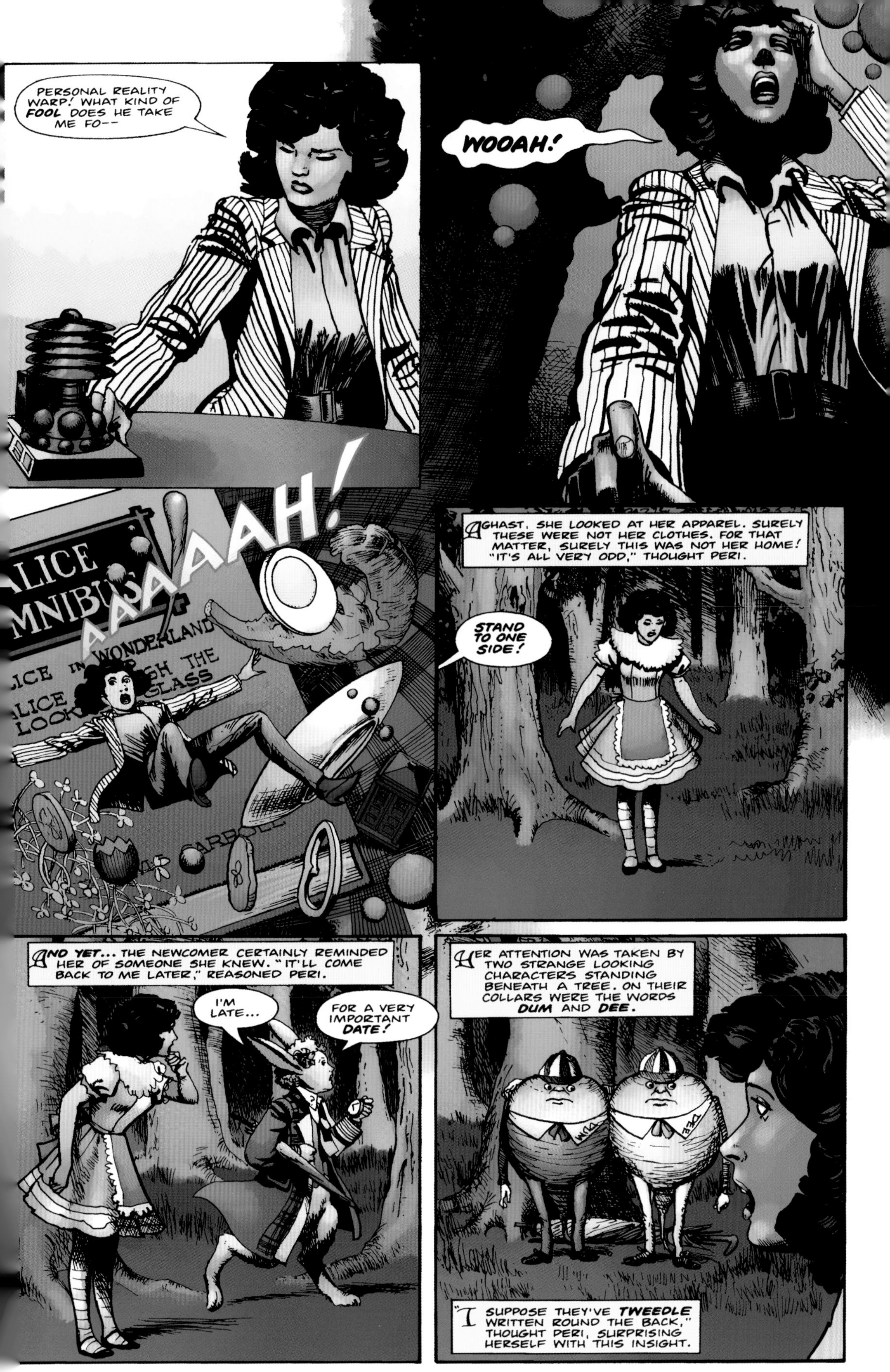

PERSONAL REALITY WARP! WHAT KIND OF FOOL DOES HE TAKE ME FO--
WOOAH!
AAAAAAH!
ALICE OMNIBUS
ALICE IN WONDERLAND
AGHAST, SHE LOOKED AT HER APPAREL. SURELY THESE WERE NOT HER CLOTHES. FOR THAT MATTER, SURELY THIS WAS NOT HER HOME! "IT'S ALL VERY ODD," THOUGHT PERI.
STAND TO ONE SIDE!
AND YET... THE NEWCOMER CERTAINLY REMINDED HER OF SOMEONE SHE KNEW. "IT'LL COME BACK TO ME LATER," REASONED PERI.
I'M LATE...
FOR A VERY IMPORTANT DATE!
HER ATTENTION WAS TAKEN BY TWO STRANGE LOOKING CHARACTERS STANDING BENEATH A TREE. ON THEIR COLLARS WERE THE WORDS DUM AND DEE.
DUM
DEE
"I SUPPOSE THEY'VE TWEEDLE WRITTEN ROUND THE BACK," THOUGHT PERI, SURPRISING HERSELF WITH THIS INSIGHT.

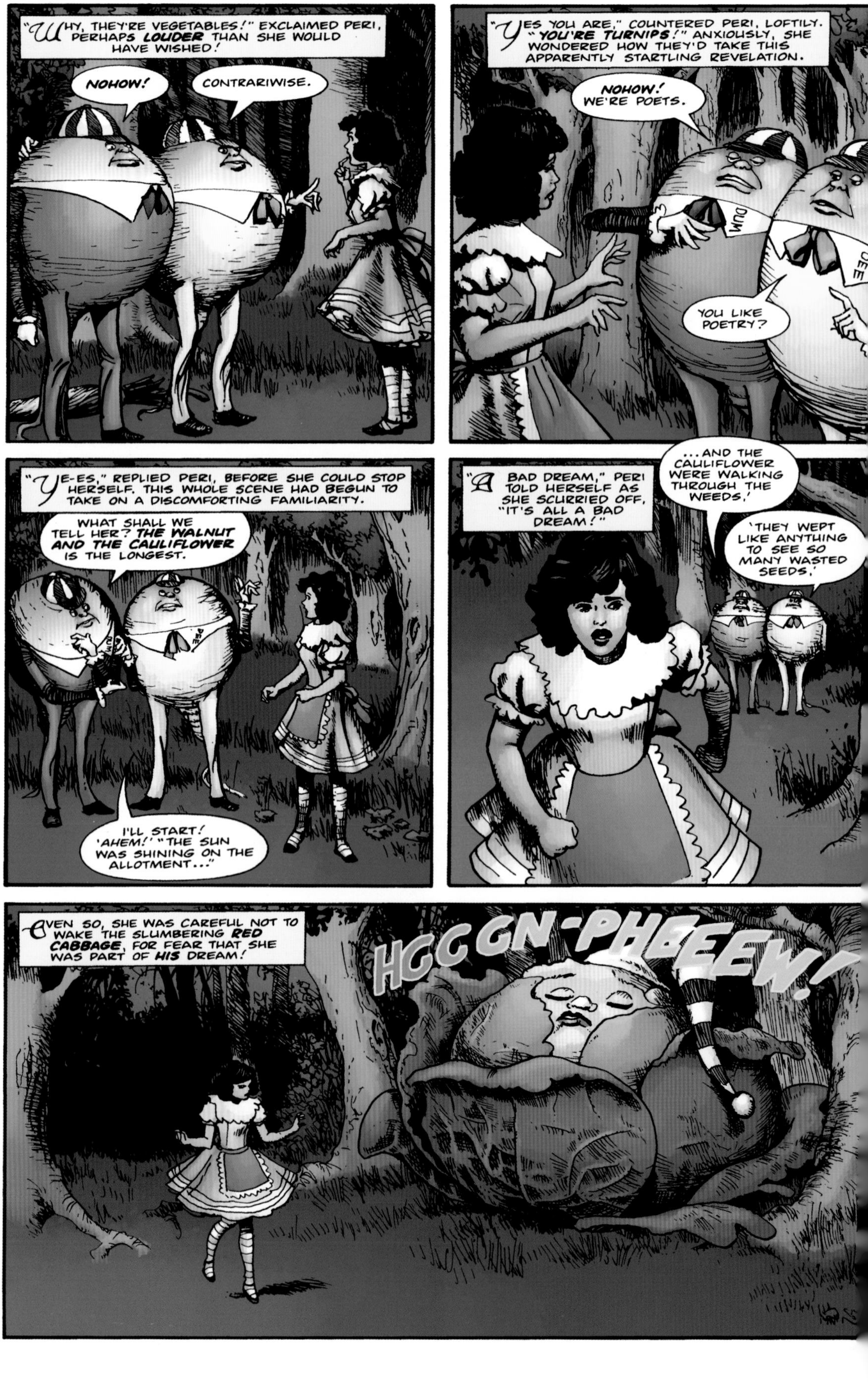
"WHY, THEY'RE VEGETABLES!" EXCLAIMED PERI, PERHAPS **LOUDER** THAN SHE WOULD HAVE WISHED!
NOHOW!
CONTRARIWISE.
"YES YOU ARE," COUNTERED PERI, LOFTILY. "**YOU'RE TURNIPS!**" ANXIOUSLY, SHE WONDERED HOW THEY'D TAKE THIS APPARENTLY STARTLING REVELATION.
NOHOW! WE'RE POETS.
DUM
YOU LIKE POETRY?
"YE-ES," REPLIED PERI, BEFORE SHE COULD STOP HERSELF. THIS WHOLE SCENE HAD BEGUN TO TAKE ON A DISCOMFORTING FAMILIARITY.
WHAT SHALL WE TELL HER? **THE WALNUT AND THE CAULIFLOWER** IS THE LONGEST.
I'LL START! 'AHEM!' "THE SUN WAS SHINING ON THE ALLOTMENT..."
"A BAD DREAM," PERI TOLD HERSELF AS SHE SCURRIED OFF, "IT'S ALL A BAD DREAM!"
...AND THE CAULIFLOWER WERE WALKING THROUGH THE WEEDS,'
'THEY WEPT LIKE ANYTHING TO SEE SO MANY WASTED SEEDS,'
EVEN SO, SHE WAS CAREFUL NOT TO WAKE THE SLUMBERING **RED CABBAGE**, FOR FEAR THAT SHE WAS PART OF **HIS** DREAM!
HGGGN-PHEEEW!

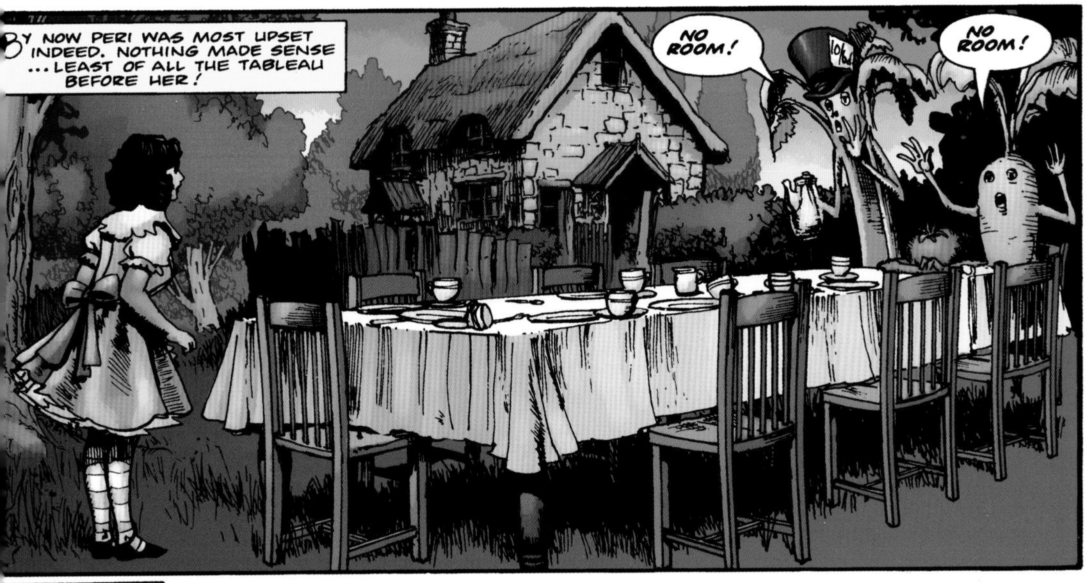
BY NOW PERI WAS MOST UPSET INDEED. NOTHING MADE SENSE ...LEAST OF ALL THE TABLEAU BEFORE HER!
NO ROOM!
NO ROOM!

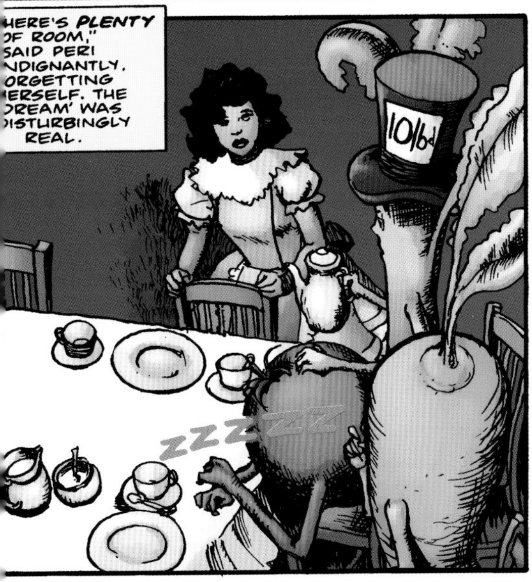
"THERE'S PLENTY OF ROOM," SAID PERI INDIGNANTLY, FORGETTING HERSELF. THE 'DREAM' WAS DISTURBINGLY REAL.
ZZZZZ

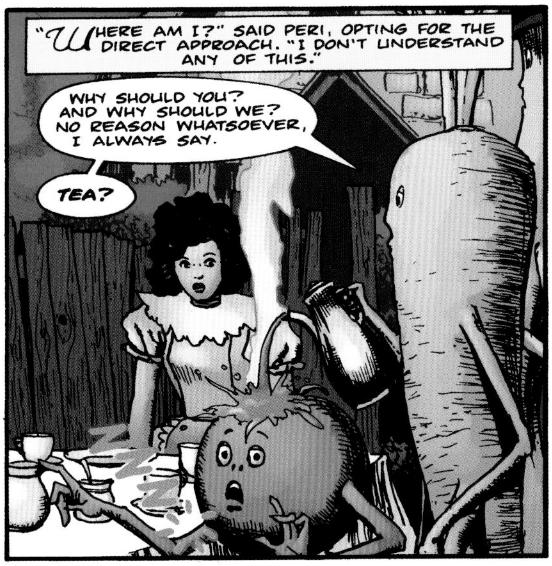
"WHERE AM I?" SAID PERI, OPTING FOR THE DIRECT APPROACH. "I DON'T UNDERSTAND ANY OF THIS."
WHY SHOULD YOU? AND WHY SHOULD WE? NO REASON WHATSOEVER, I ALWAYS SAY.
TEA?

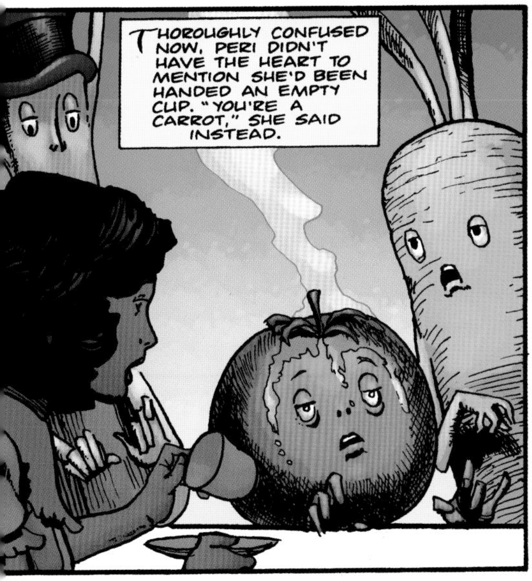
THOROUGHLY CONFUSED NOW, PERI DIDN'T HAVE THE HEART TO MENTION SHE'D BEEN HANDED AN EMPTY CUP. "YOU'RE A CARROT," SHE SAID INSTEAD.

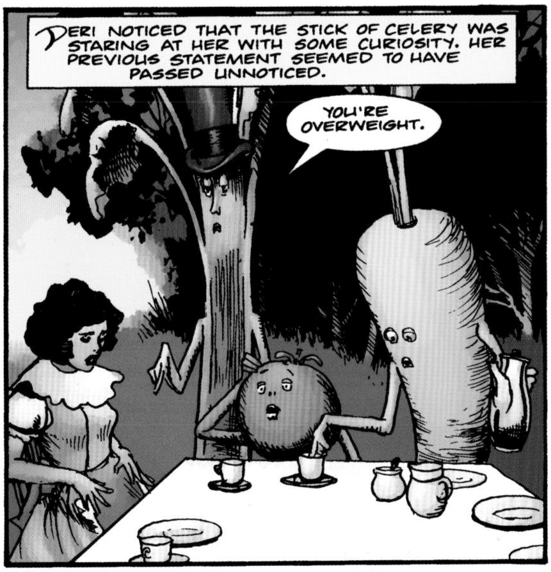
PERI NOTICED THAT THE STICK OF CELERY WAS STARING AT HER WITH SOME CURIOSITY. HER PREVIOUS STATEMENT SEEMED TO HAVE PASSED UNNOTICED.
YOU'RE OVERWEIGHT.

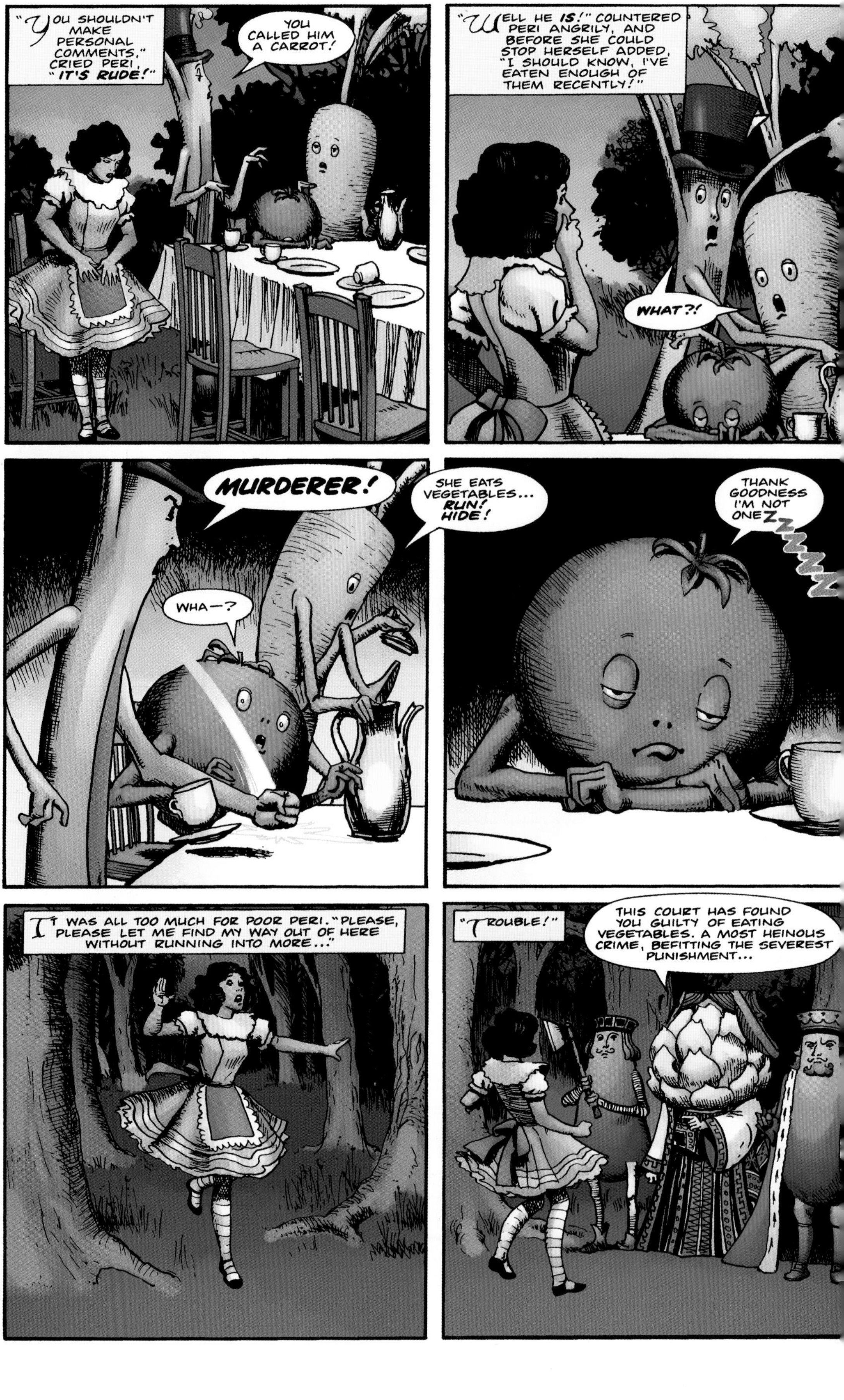
"You shouldn't make personal comments," cried Peri, "It's rude!"
You called him a carrot!
"Well he is!" countered Peri angrily, and before she could stop herself added, "I should know, I've eaten enough of them recently!"
What?!
Murderer!
She eats vegetables... Run! Hide!
Wha—?
Thank goodness I'm not one
ZZZZZ
It was all too much for poor Peri. "Please, please let me find my way out of here without running into more..."
"Trouble!"
This court has found you guilty of eating vegetables. A most heinous crime, befitting the severest punishment...

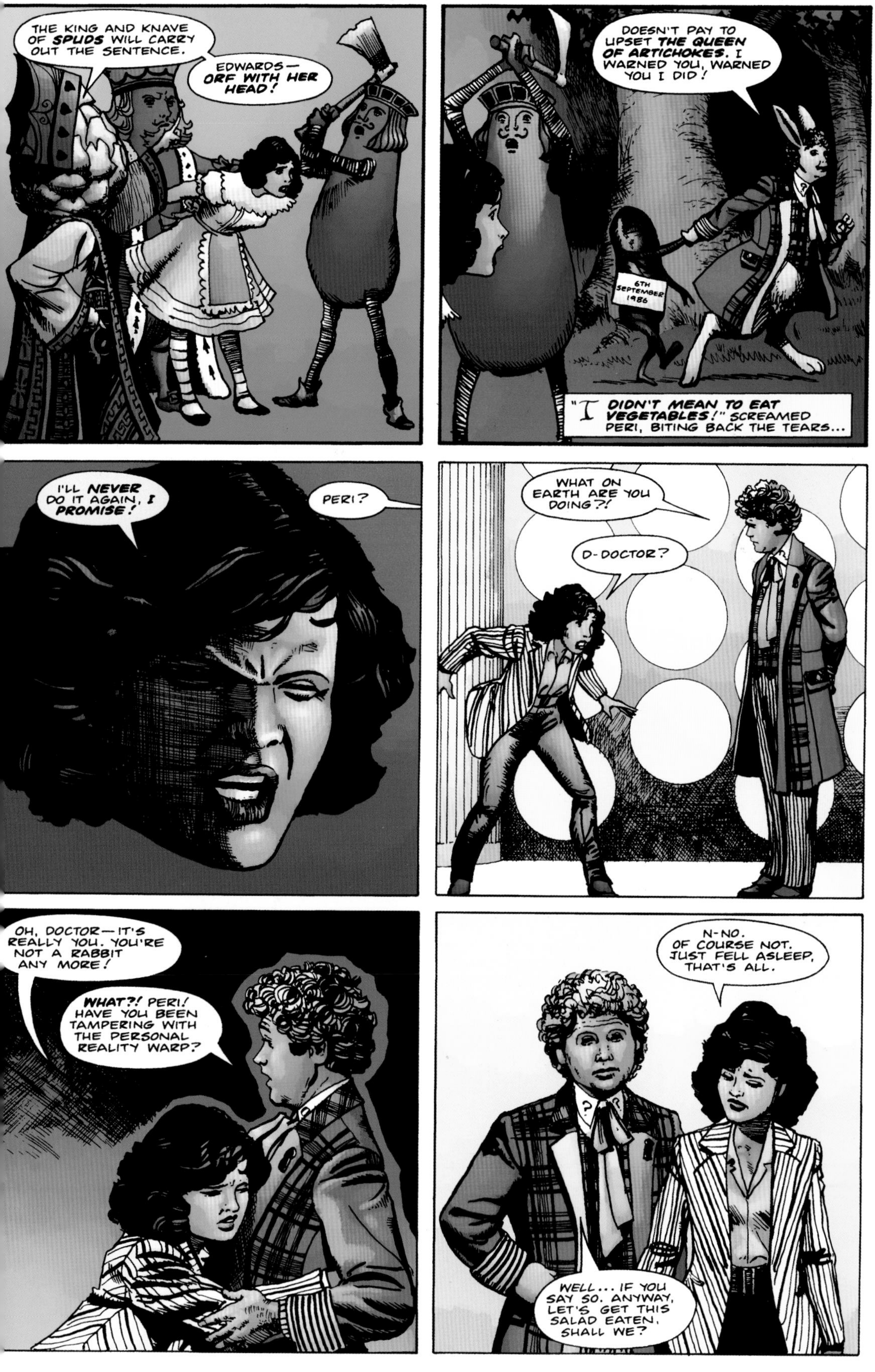
THE KING AND KNAVE OF SPUDS WILL CARRY OUT THE SENTENCE.
EDWARDS— ORF WITH HER HEAD!
DOESN'T PAY TO UPSET THE QUEEN OF ARTICHOKES. I WARNED YOU, WARNED YOU I DID!
6TH SEPTEMBER 1986
"I DIDN'T MEAN TO EAT VEGETABLES!" SCREAMED PERI, BITING BACK THE TEARS...
I'LL NEVER DO IT AGAIN, I PROMISE!
PERI?
WHAT ON EARTH ARE YOU DOING?!
D-DOCTOR?
OH, DOCTOR— IT'S REALLY YOU. YOU'RE NOT A RABBIT ANY MORE!
WHAT?! PERI! HAVE YOU BEEN TAMPERING WITH THE PERSONAL REALITY WARP?
N-NO. OF COURSE NOT. JUST FELL ASLEEP, THAT'S ALL.
WELL... IF YOU SAY SO. ANYWAY, LET'S GET THIS SALAD EATEN, SHALL WE?

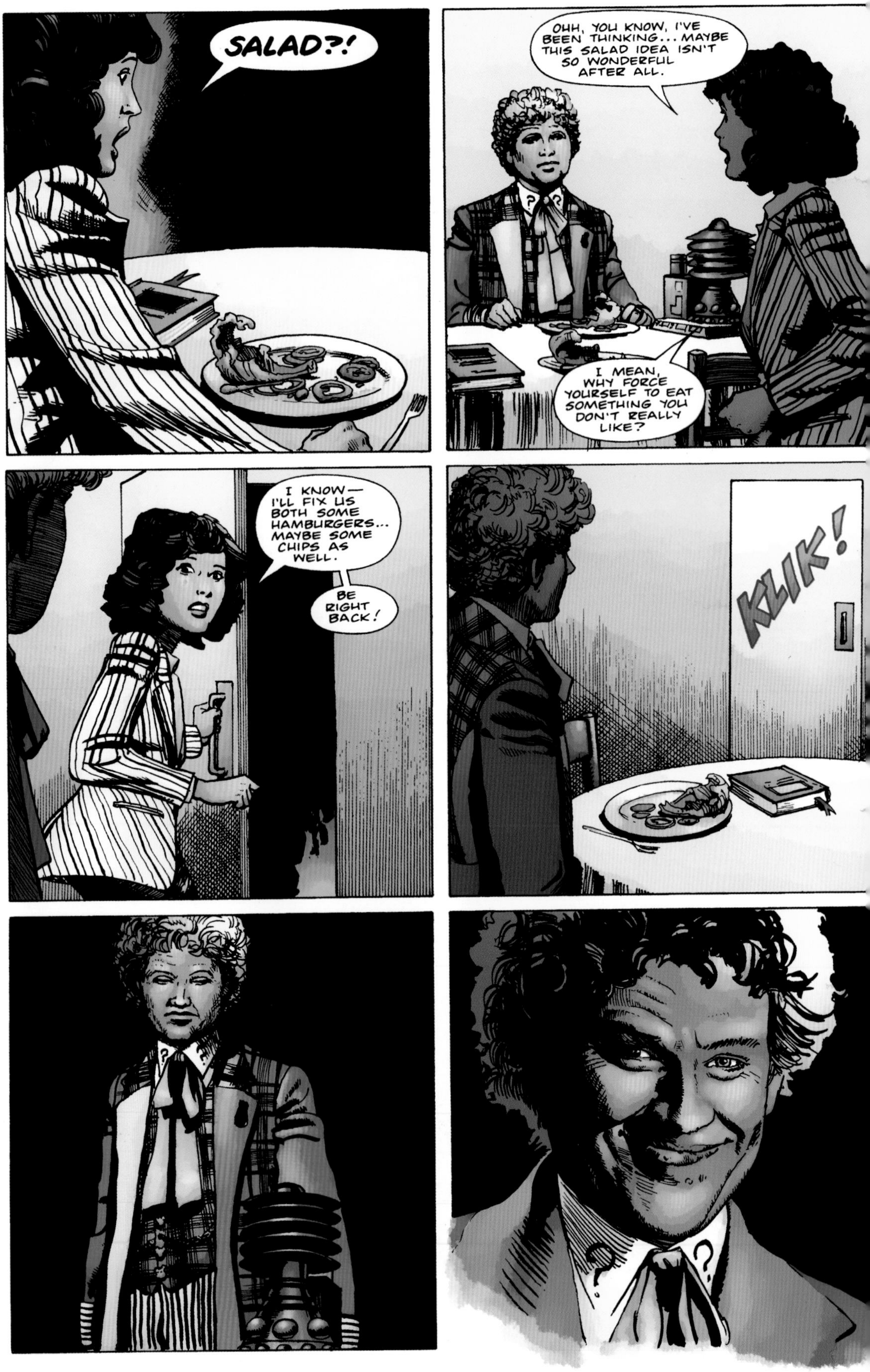
SALAD?!
OHH, YOU KNOW, I'VE BEEN THINKING... MAYBE THIS SALAD IDEA ISN'T SO WONDERFUL AFTER ALL.
I MEAN, WHY FORCE YOURSELF TO EAT SOMETHING YOU DON'T REALLY LIKE?
I KNOW— I'LL FIX US BOTH SOME HAMBURGERS... MAYBE SOME CHIPS AS WELL.
BE RIGHT BACK!
KLIK!

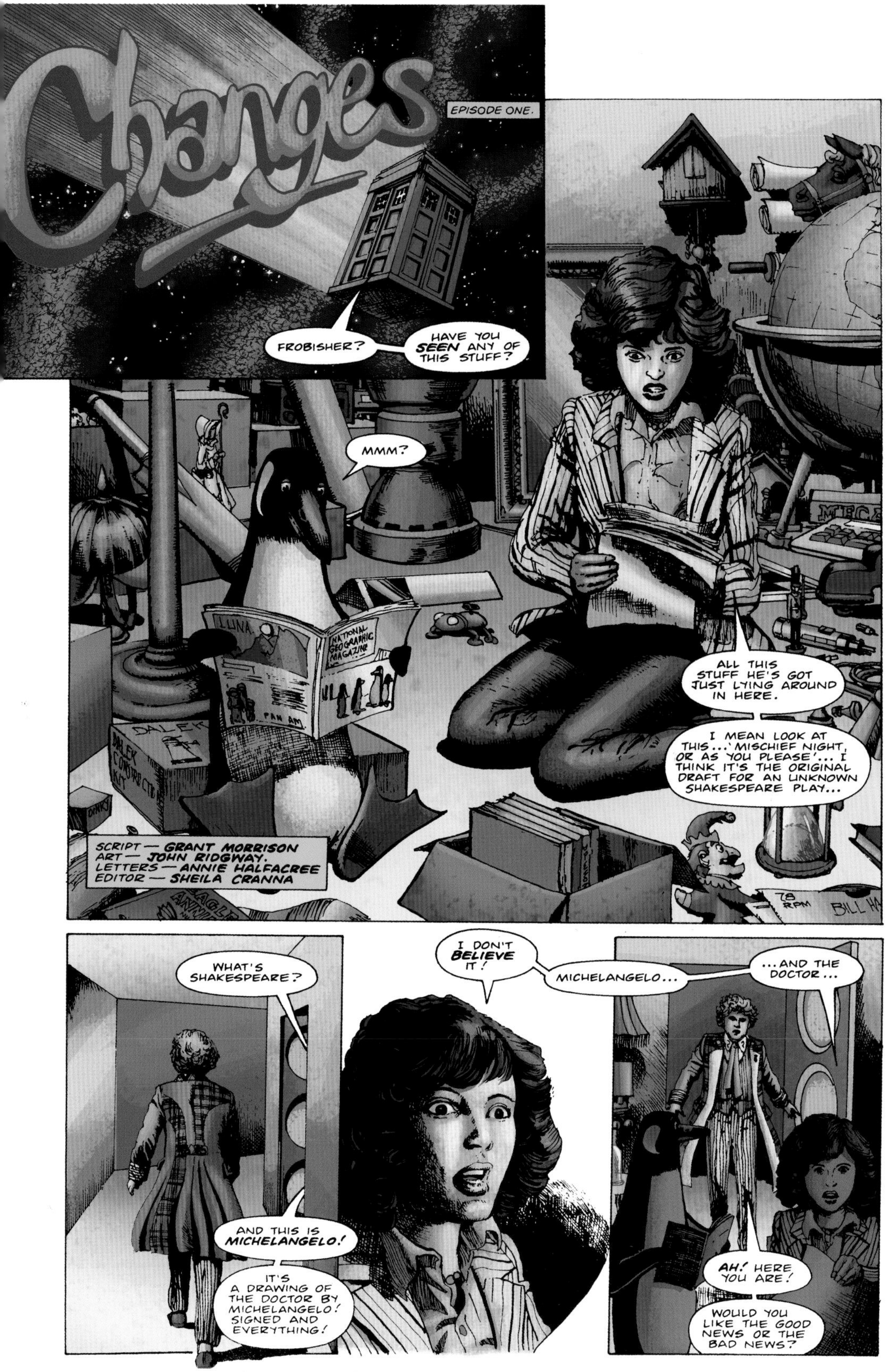
Changes
EPISODE ONE.
FROBISHER?
HAVE YOU SEEN ANY OF THIS STUFF?
MMM?
ALL THIS STUFF HE'S GOT JUST LYING AROUND IN HERE.
I MEAN LOOK AT THIS...'MISCHIEF NIGHT, OR AS YOU PLEASE'... I THINK IT'S THE ORIGINAL DRAFT FOR AN UNKNOWN SHAKESPEARE PLAY...
SCRIPT — GRANT MORRISON
ART — JOHN RIDGWAY.
LETTERS — ANNIE HALFACREE
EDITOR — SHEILA CRANNA
WHAT'S SHAKESPEARE?
I DON'T BELIEVE IT!
MICHELANGELO...
...AND THE DOCTOR...
AND THIS IS MICHELANGELO!
IT'S A DRAWING OF THE DOCTOR BY MICHELANGELO! SIGNED AND EVERYTHING!
AH! HERE YOU ARE!
WOULD YOU LIKE THE GOOD NEWS OR THE BAD NEWS?

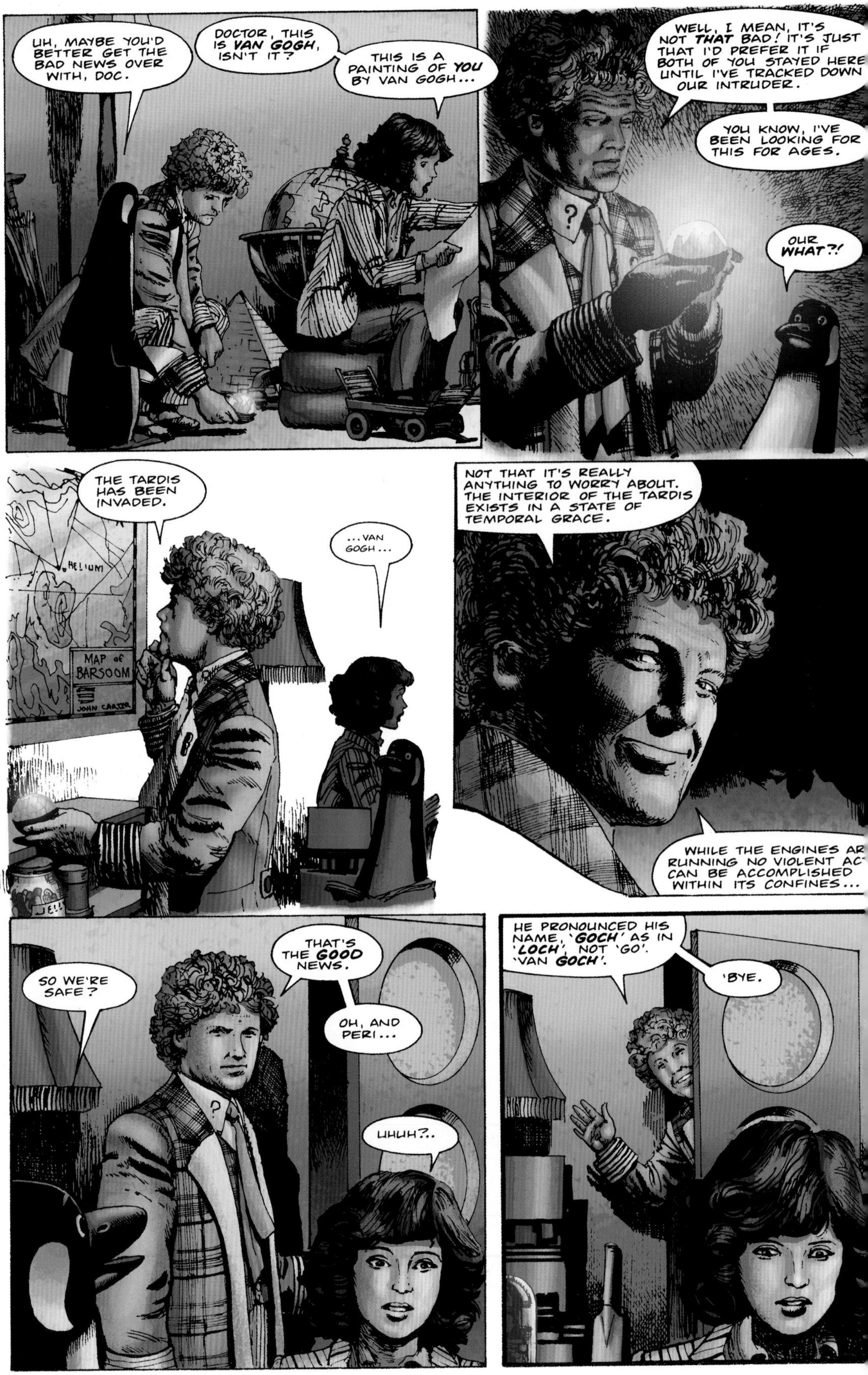
UH, MAYBE YOU'D BETTER GET THE BAD NEWS OVER WITH, DOC.
DOCTOR, THIS IS VAN GOGH, ISN'T IT?
THIS IS A PAINTING OF YOU BY VAN GOGH...
WELL, I MEAN, IT'S NOT THAT BAD! IT'S JUST THAT I'D PREFER IT IF BOTH OF YOU STAYED HERE UNTIL I'VE TRACKED DOWN OUR INTRUDER.
YOU KNOW, I'VE BEEN LOOKING FOR THIS FOR AGES.
OUR WHAT?!
THE TARDIS HAS BEEN INVADED.
...VAN GOGH...
HELIUM
MAP of BARSOOM
JOHN CARTER
NOT THAT IT'S REALLY ANYTHING TO WORRY ABOUT. THE INTERIOR OF THE TARDIS EXISTS IN A STATE OF TEMPORAL GRACE.
WHILE THE ENGINES AR RUNNING NO VIOLENT AC CAN BE ACCOMPLISHED WITHIN ITS CONFINES...
SO WE'RE SAFE?
THAT'S THE GOOD NEWS.
OH, AND PERI...
UHUH?..
HE PRONOUNCED HIS NAME, 'GOCH' AS IN 'LOCH', NOT 'GO'. 'VAN GOCH'.
'BYE.

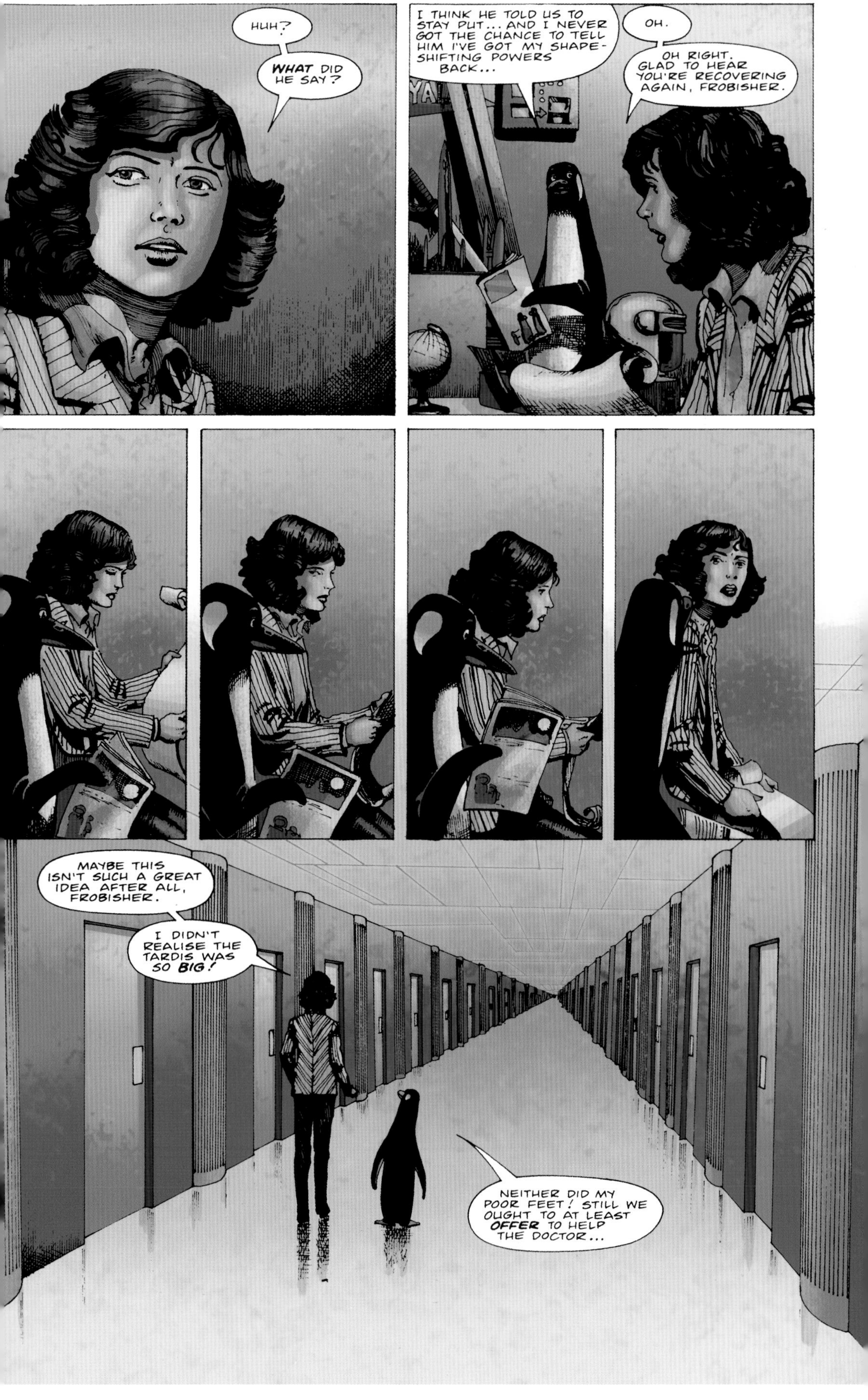
HUH?
WHAT DID HE SAY?
I THINK HE TOLD US TO STAY PUT... AND I NEVER GOT THE CHANCE TO TELL HIM I'VE GOT MY SHAPE-SHIFTING POWERS BACK...
OH.
OH RIGHT. GLAD TO HEAR YOU'RE RECOVERING AGAIN, FROBISHER.
MAYBE THIS ISN'T SUCH A GREAT IDEA AFTER ALL, FROBISHER.
I DIDN'T REALISE THE TARDIS WAS SO BIG!
NEITHER DID MY POOR FEET! STILL WE OUGHT TO AT LEAST OFFER TO HELP THE DOCTOR...

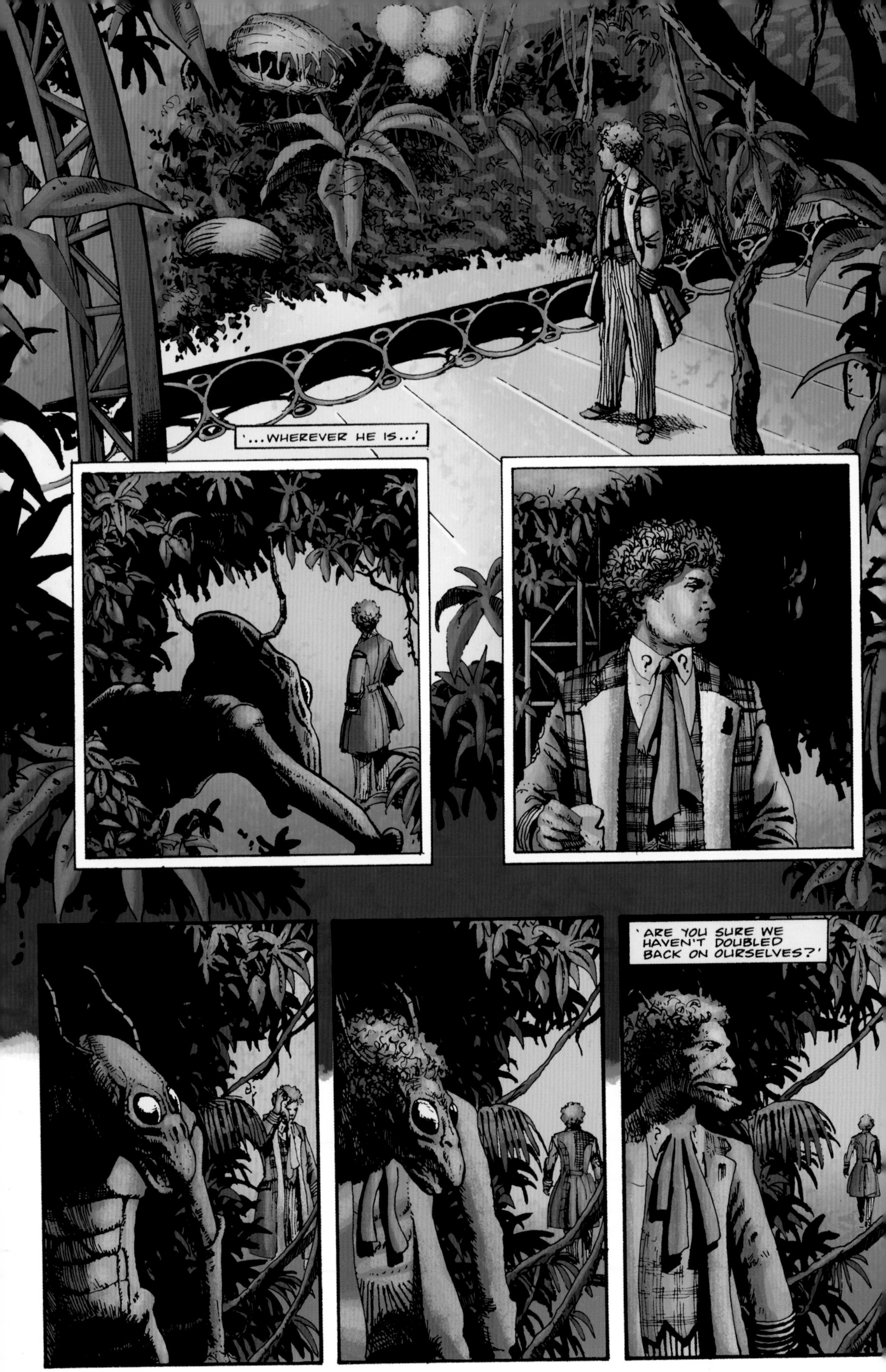
'...WHEREVER HE IS...'
'ARE YOU SURE WE HAVEN'T DOUBLED BACK ON OURSELVES?'

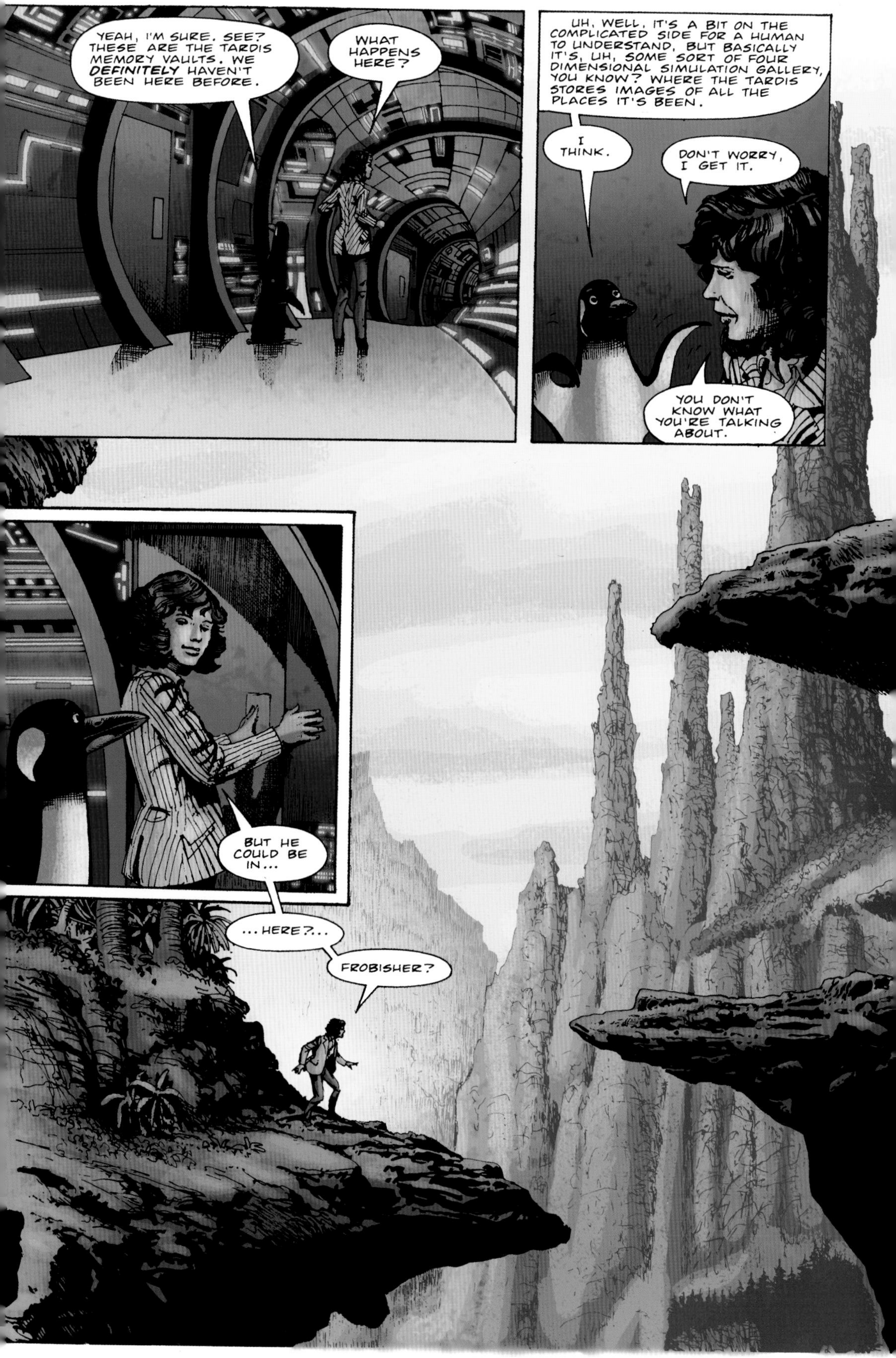

YEAH, I'M SURE. SEE? THESE ARE THE TARDIS MEMORY VAULTS. WE **DEFINITELY** HAVEN'T BEEN HERE BEFORE.
WHAT HAPPENS HERE?
UH, WELL, IT'S A BIT ON THE COMPLICATED SIDE FOR A HUMAN TO UNDERSTAND, BUT BASICALLY IT'S, UH, SOME SORT OF FOUR DIMENSIONAL SIMULATION GALLERY, YOU KNOW? WHERE THE TARDIS STORES IMAGES OF ALL THE PLACES IT'S BEEN.
I THINK.
DON'T WORRY, I GET IT.
YOU DON'T KNOW WHAT YOU'RE TALKING ABOUT.
BUT HE COULD BE IN...
...HERE?...
FROBISHER?

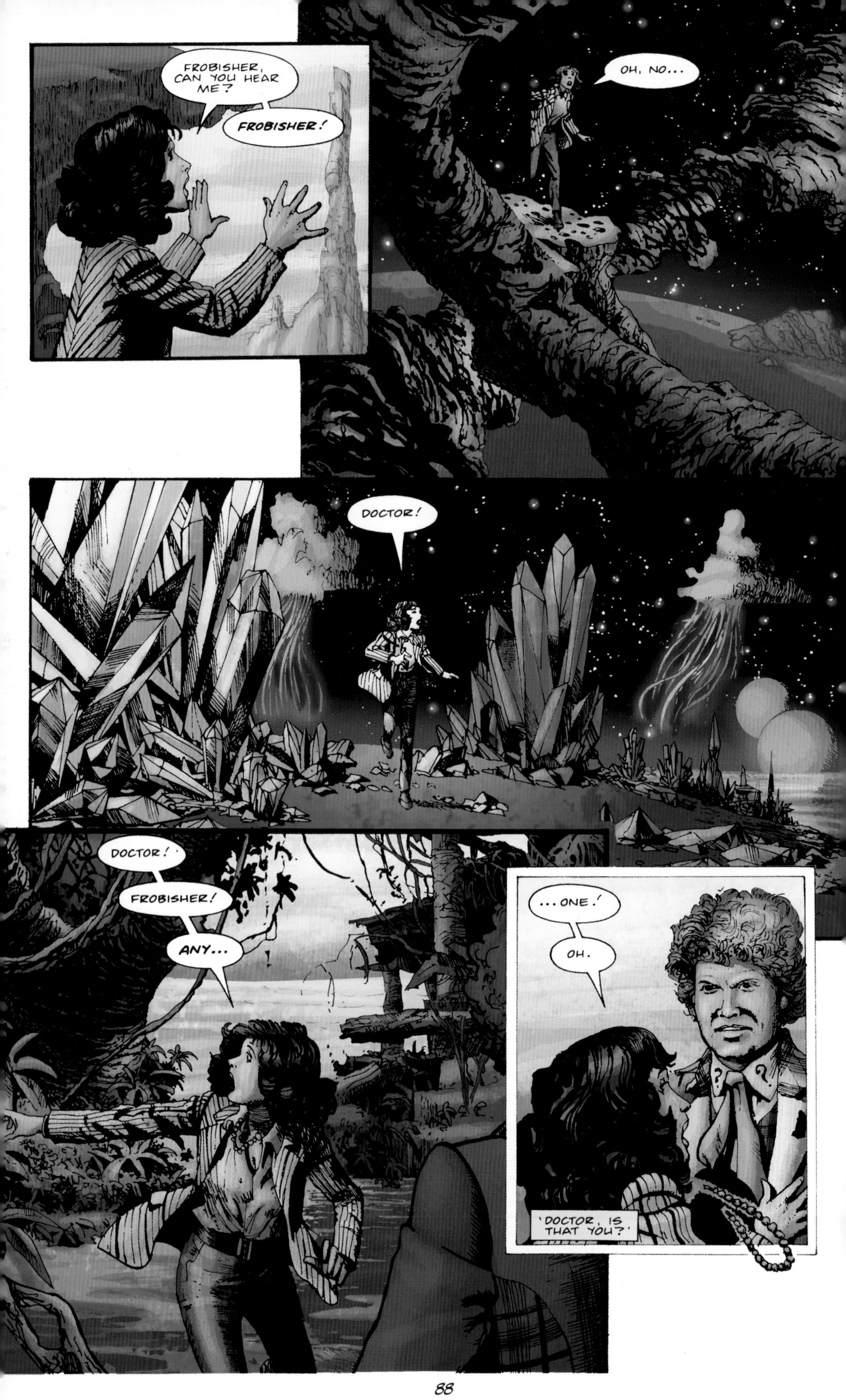
FROBISHER, CAN YOU HEAR ME?
FROBISHER!
OH, NO...
DOCTOR!
DOCTOR!
FROBISHER!
ANY...
...ONE!
OH.
'DOCTOR, IS THAT YOU?'

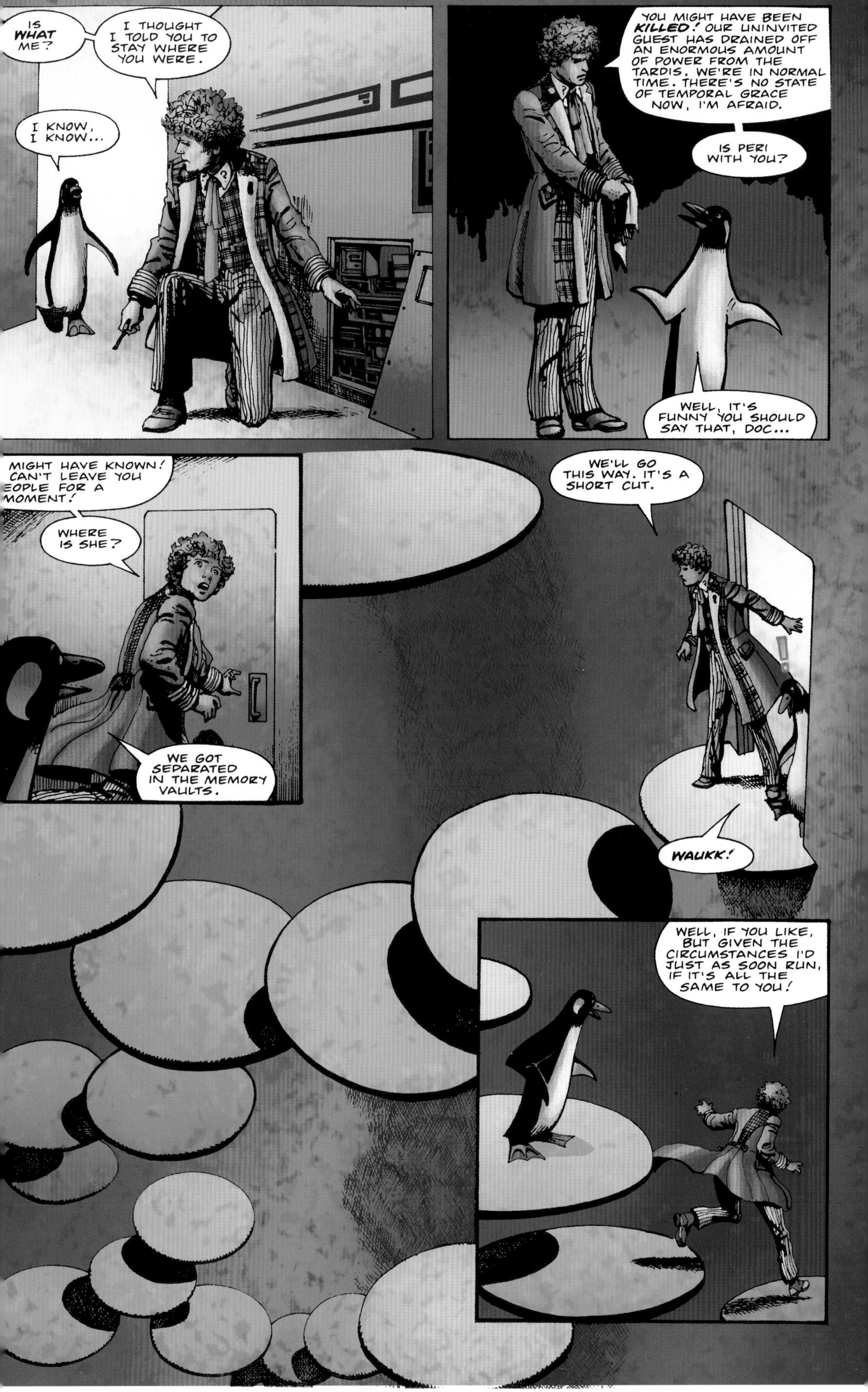
IS *WHAT* ME?
I THOUGHT I TOLD YOU TO STAY WHERE YOU WERE.
I KNOW, I KNOW...
YOU MIGHT HAVE BEEN *KILLED!* OUR UNINVITED GUEST HAS DRAINED OFF AN ENORMOUS AMOUNT OF POWER FROM THE TARDIS. WE'RE IN NORMAL TIME. THERE'S NO STATE OF TEMPORAL GRACE NOW, I'M AFRAID.
IS PERI WITH YOU?
WELL, IT'S FUNNY YOU SHOULD SAY THAT, DOC...
MIGHT HAVE KNOWN! CAN'T LEAVE YOU EOPLE FOR A MOMENT!
WHERE IS SHE?
WE GOT SEPARATED IN THE MEMORY VAULTS.
WE'LL GO THIS WAY. IT'S A SHORT CUT.
WAUKK!
WELL, IF YOU LIKE, BUT GIVEN THE CIRCUMSTANCES I'D JUST AS SOON RUN, IF IT'S ALL THE SAME TO YOU!

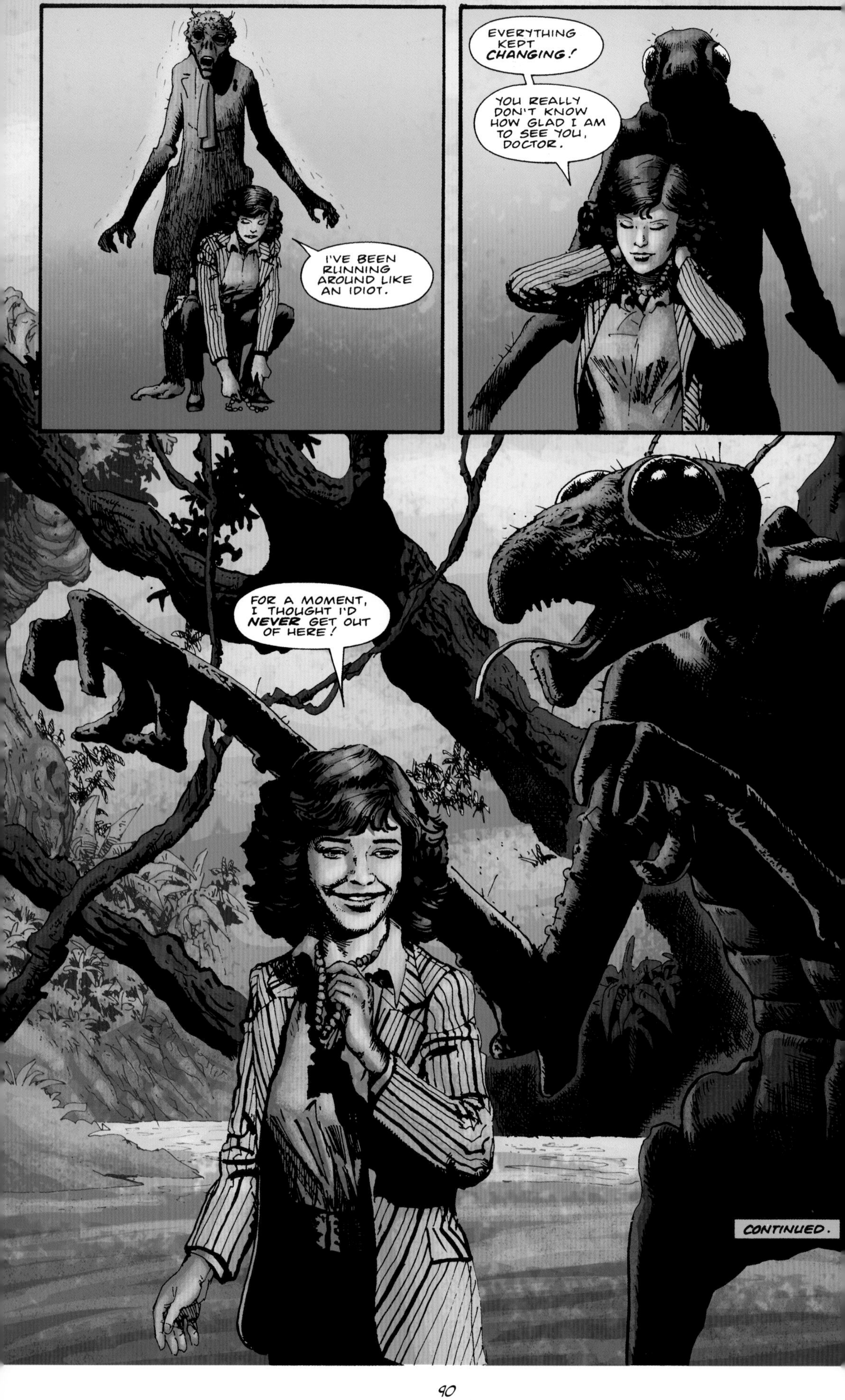
I'VE BEEN RUNNING AROUND LIKE AN IDIOT.
EVERYTHING KEPT **CHANGING**!
YOU REALLY DON'T KNOW HOW GLAD I AM TO SEE YOU, DOCTOR.
FOR A MOMENT, I THOUGHT I'D **NEVER** GET OUT OF HERE!
CONTINUED.

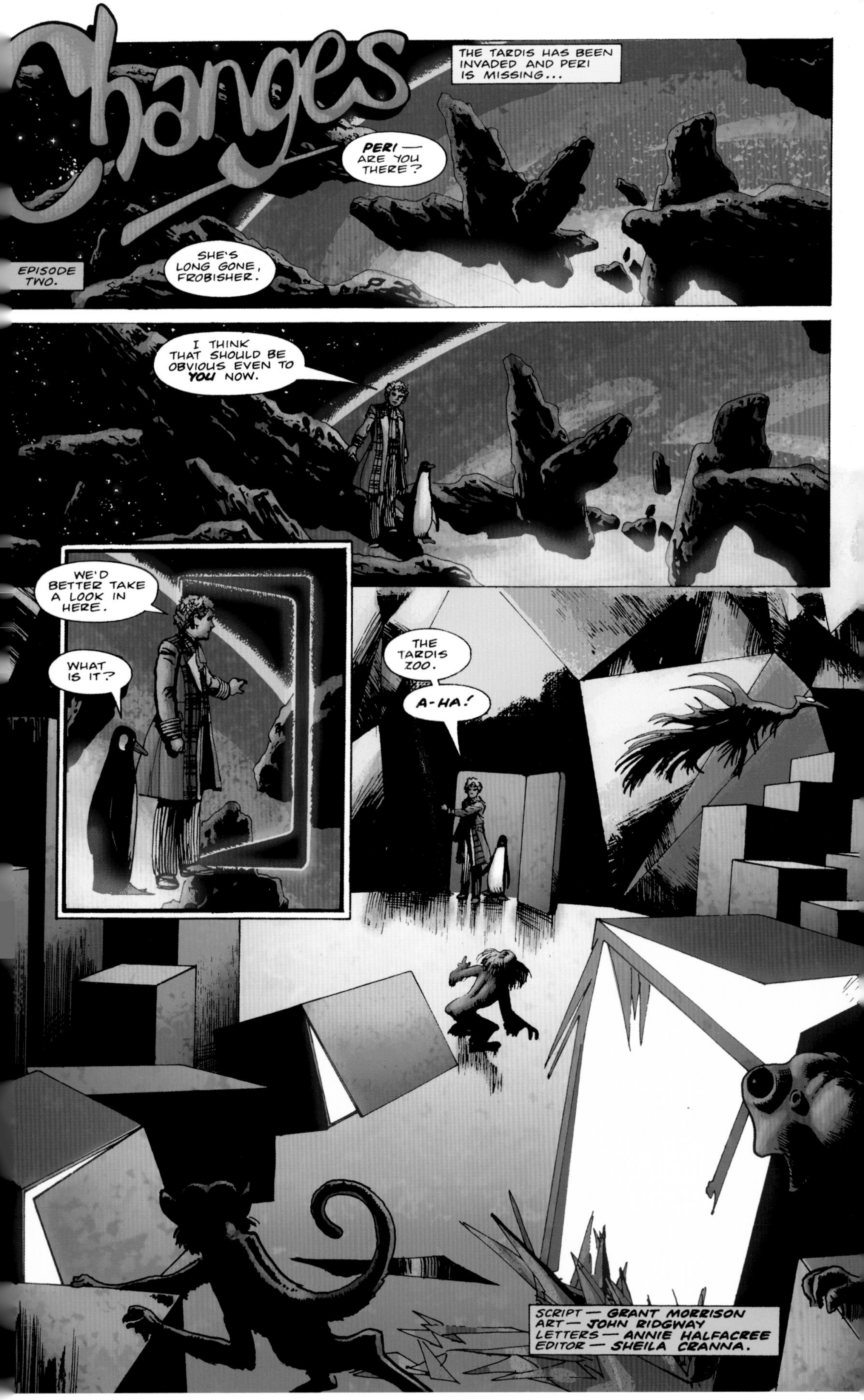

Changes
THE TARDIS HAS BEEN INVADED AND PERI IS MISSING...
PERI — ARE YOU THERE?
EPISODE TWO.
SHE'S LONG GONE, FROBISHER.
I THINK THAT SHOULD BE OBVIOUS EVEN TO YOU NOW.
WE'D BETTER TAKE A LOOK IN HERE.
WHAT IS IT?
THE TARDIS ZOO.
A-HA!
SCRIPT — GRANT MORRISON
ART — JOHN RIDGWAY
LETTERS — ANNIE HALFACREE
EDITOR — SHEILA CRANNA.

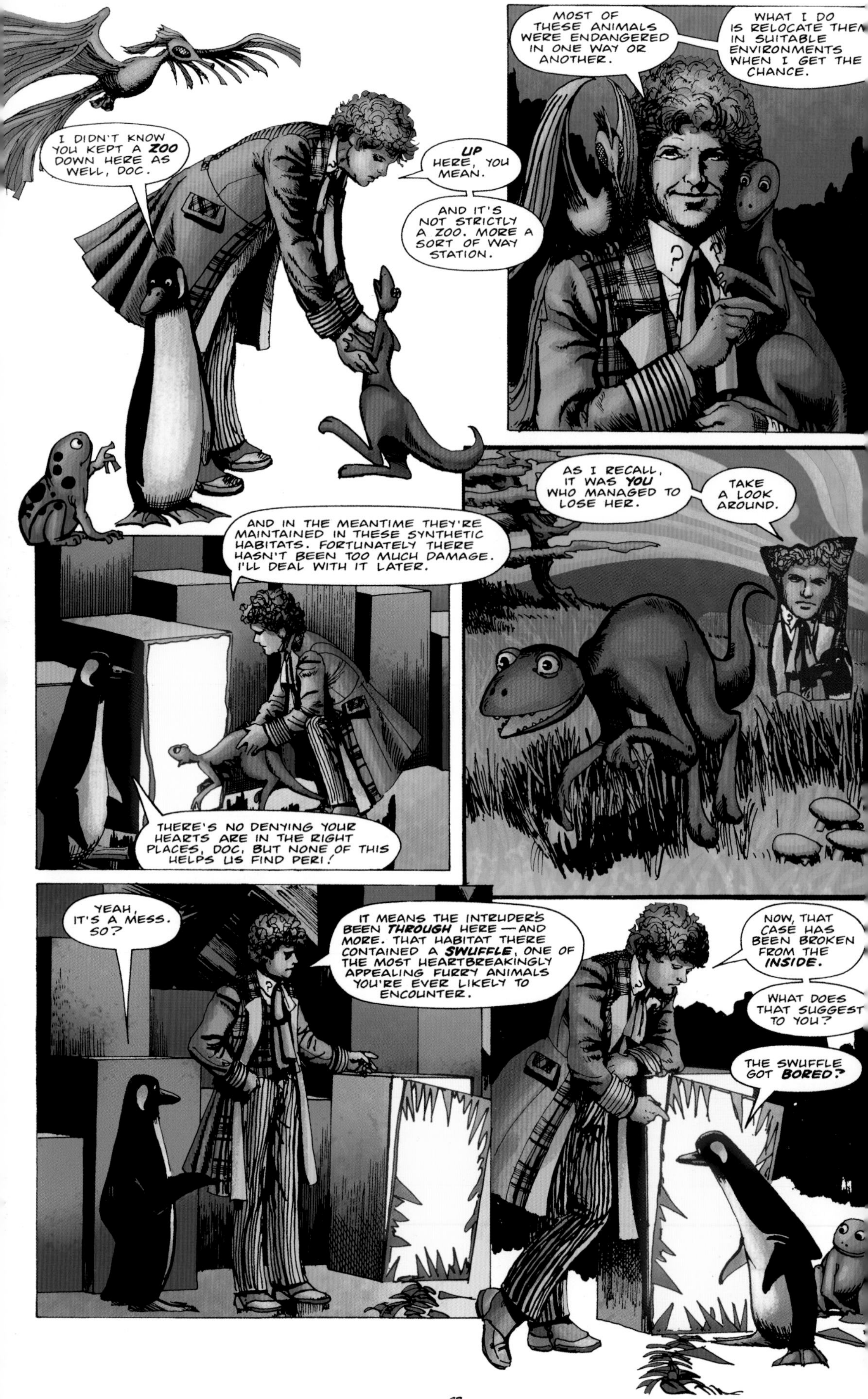

I DIDN'T KNOW YOU KEPT A ZOO DOWN HERE AS WELL, DOC.
UP HERE, YOU MEAN.
AND IT'S NOT STRICTLY A ZOO. MORE A SORT OF WAY STATION.
MOST OF THESE ANIMALS WERE ENDANGERED IN ONE WAY OR ANOTHER.
WHAT I DO IS RELOCATE THEM IN SUITABLE ENVIRONMENTS WHEN I GET THE CHANCE.
AND IN THE MEANTIME THEY'RE MAINTAINED IN THESE SYNTHETIC HABITATS. FORTUNATELY THERE HASN'T BEEN TOO MUCH DAMAGE. I'LL DEAL WITH IT LATER.
THERE'S NO DENYING YOUR HEARTS ARE IN THE RIGHT PLACES, DOC, BUT NONE OF THIS HELPS US FIND PERI!
AS I RECALL, IT WAS YOU WHO MANAGED TO LOSE HER.
TAKE A LOOK AROUND.
YEAH, IT'S A MESS. SO?
IT MEANS THE INTRUDER'S BEEN THROUGH HERE — AND MORE. THAT HABITAT THERE CONTAINED A SWUFFLE, ONE OF THE MOST HEARTBREAKINGLY APPEALING FURRY ANIMALS YOU'RE EVER LIKELY TO ENCOUNTER.
NOW, THAT CASE HAS BEEN BROKEN FROM THE INSIDE.
WHAT DOES THAT SUGGEST TO YOU?
THE SWUFFLE GOT BORED?

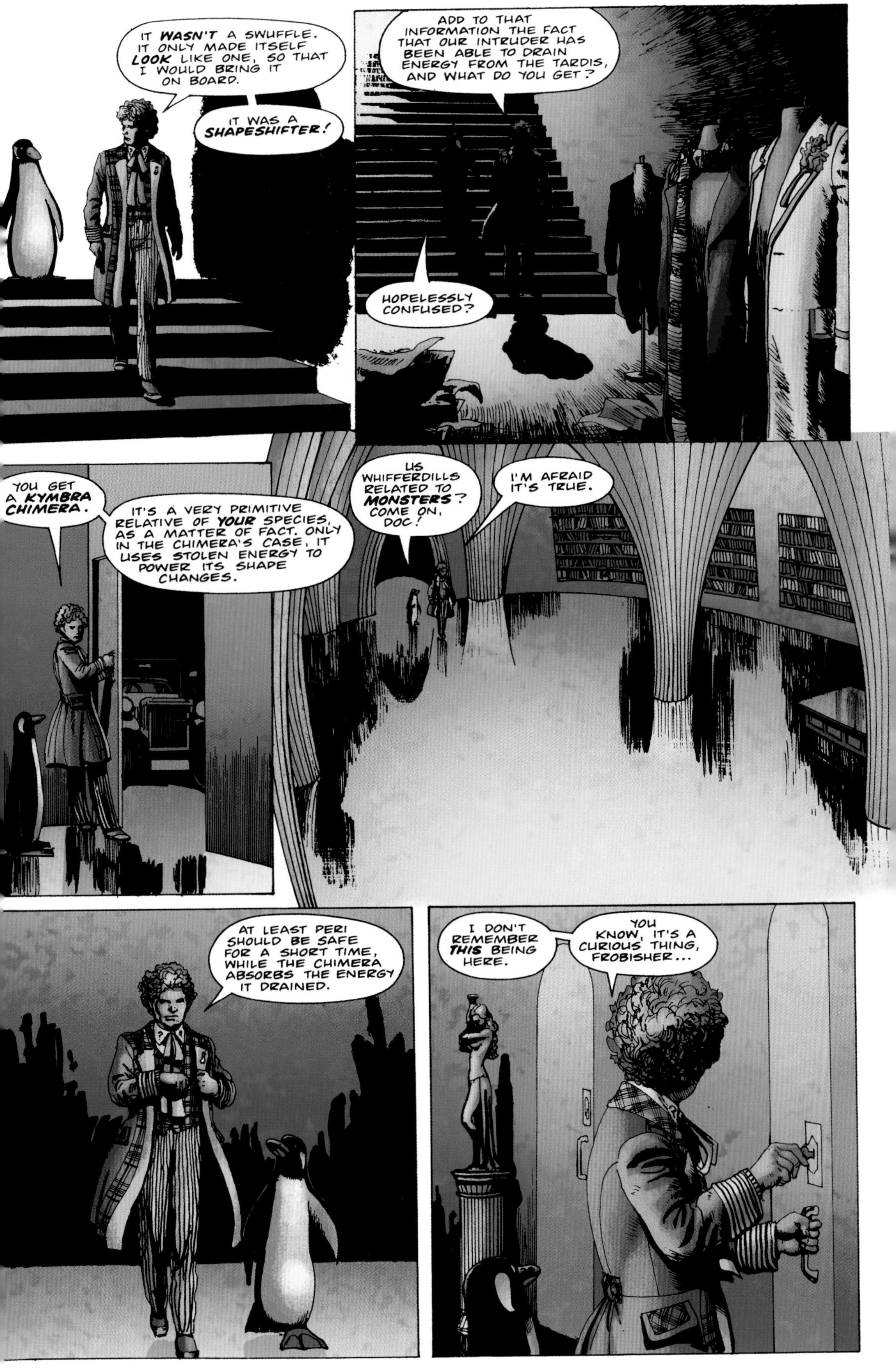
IT WASN'T A SWUFFLE. IT ONLY MADE ITSELF LOOK LIKE ONE, SO THAT I WOULD BRING IT ON BOARD.
IT WAS A SHAPESHIFTER!
ADD TO THAT INFORMATION THE FACT THAT OUR INTRUDER HAS BEEN ABLE TO DRAIN ENERGY FROM THE TARDIS, AND WHAT DO YOU GET?
HOPELESSLY CONFUSED?
YOU GET A KYMBRA CHIMERA.
IT'S A VERY PRIMITIVE RELATIVE OF YOUR SPECIES, AS A MATTER OF FACT. ONLY IN THE CHIMERA'S CASE, IT USES STOLEN ENERGY TO POWER ITS SHAPE CHANGES.
US WHIFFERDILLS RELATED TO MONSTERS? COME ON, DOC!
I'M AFRAID IT'S TRUE.
AT LEAST PERI SHOULD BE SAFE FOR A SHORT TIME, WHILE THE CHIMERA ABSORBS THE ENERGY IT DRAINED.
I DON'T REMEMBER THIS BEING HERE.
YOU KNOW, IT'S A CURIOUS THING, FROBISHER...

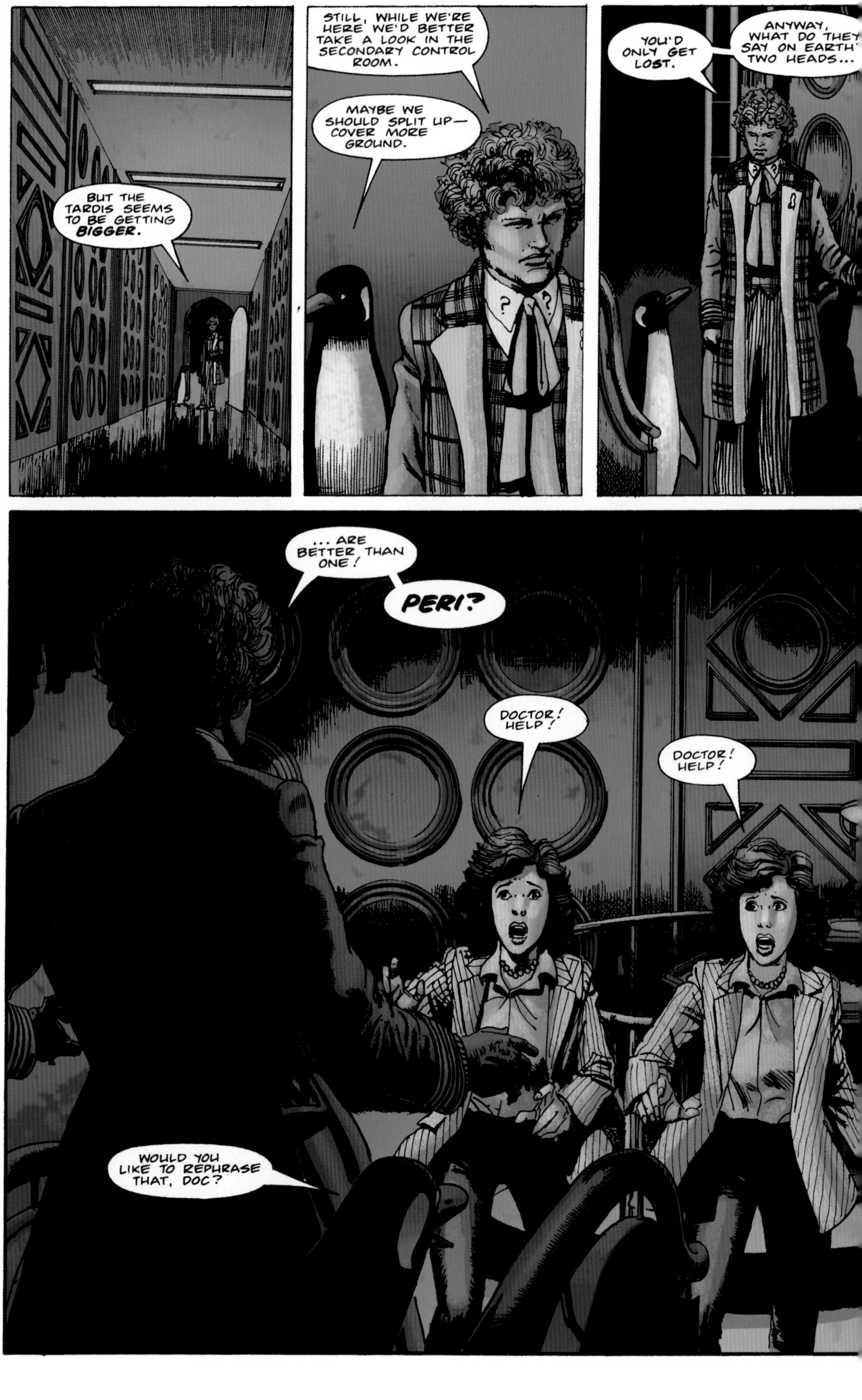
BUT THE TARDIS SEEMS TO BE GETTING BIGGER.
STILL, WHILE WE'RE HERE WE'D BETTER TAKE A LOOK IN THE SECONDARY CONTROL ROOM.
MAYBE WE SHOULD SPLIT UP— COVER MORE GROUND.
YOU'D ONLY GET LOST.
ANYWAY, WHAT DO THEY SAY ON EARTH? TWO HEADS...
... ARE BETTER THAN ONE!
PERI?
DOCTOR! HELP!
DOCTOR! HELP!
WOULD YOU LIKE TO REPHRASE THAT, DOC?

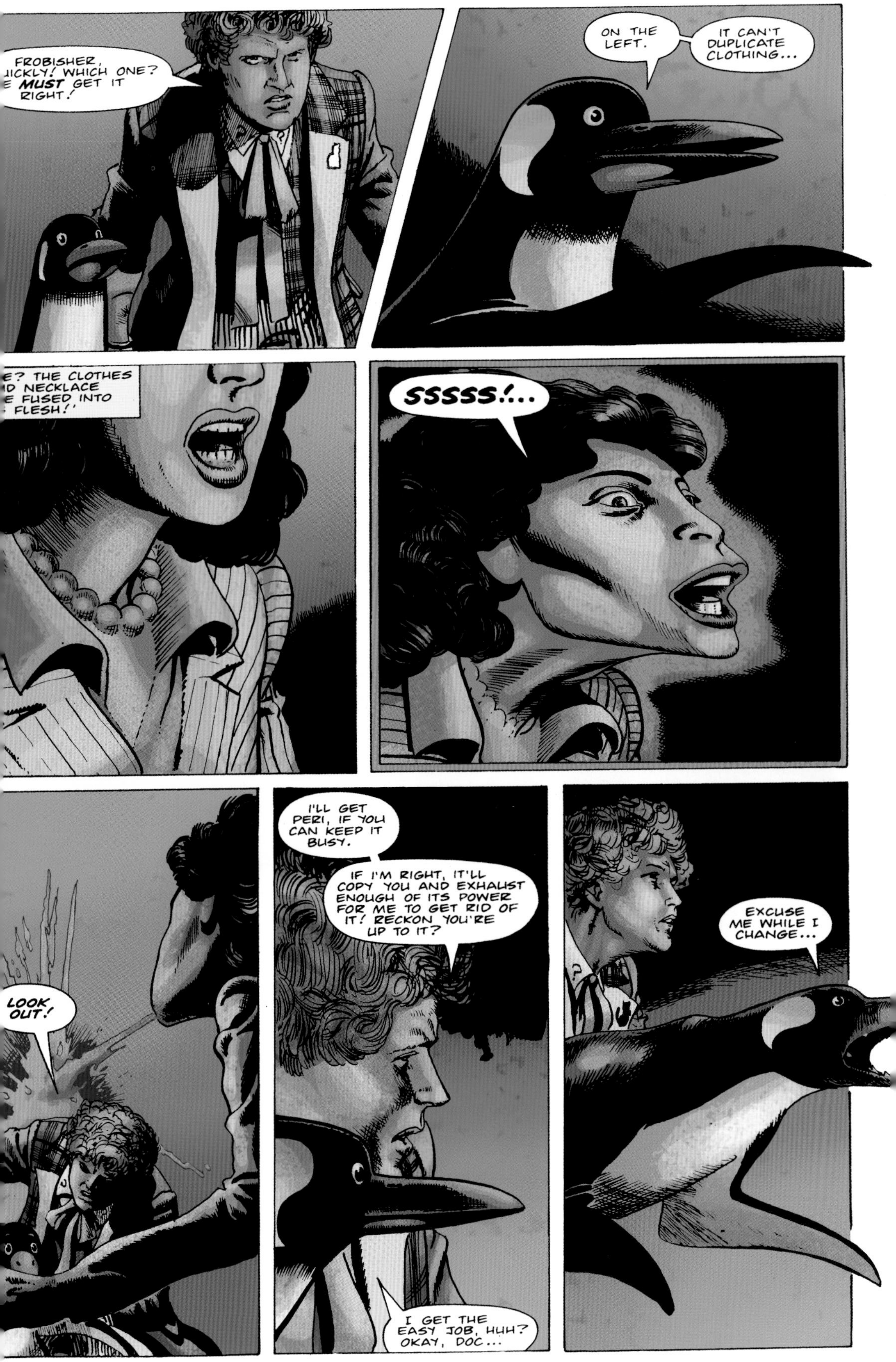
FROBISHER, UICKLY! WHICH ONE? E MUST GET IT RIGHT!
ON THE LEFT.
IT CAN'T DUPLICATE CLOTHING...
E? THE CLOTHES D NECKLACE E FUSED INTO FLESH!'
SSSSS!...
LOOK OUT!
I'LL GET PERI, IF YOU CAN KEEP IT BUSY.
IF I'M RIGHT, IT'LL COPY YOU AND EXHAUST ENOUGH OF ITS POWER FOR ME TO GET RID OF IT! RECKON YOU'RE UP TO IT?
I GET THE EASY JOB, HUH? OKAY, DOC...
EXCUSE ME WHILE I CHANGE...

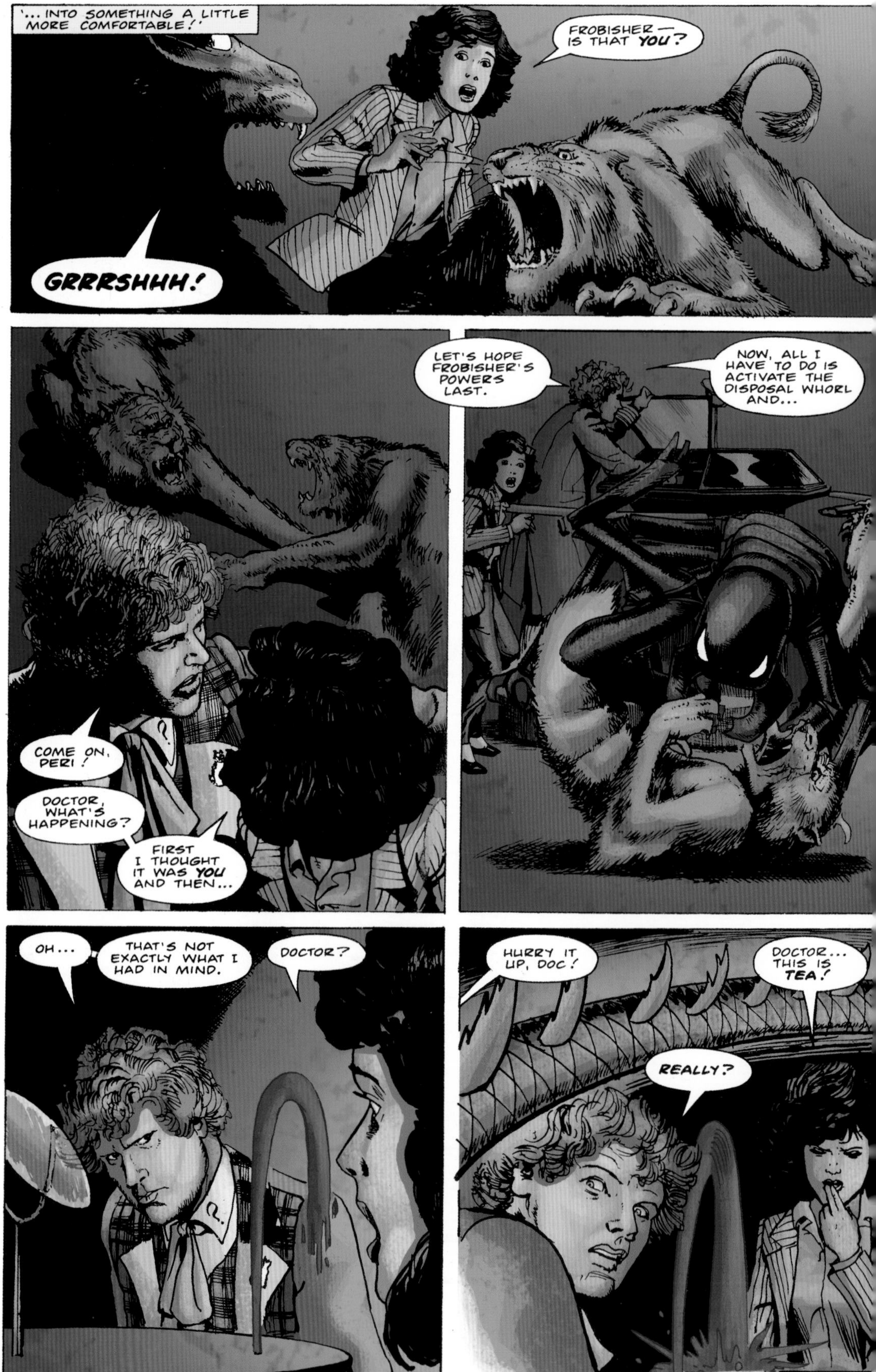
'... INTO SOMETHING A LITTLE MORE COMFORTABLE!'
FROBISHER — IS THAT YOU?
GRRRSHHH!
COME ON, PERI!
DOCTOR, WHAT'S HAPPENING?
FIRST I THOUGHT IT WAS YOU AND THEN...
LET'S HOPE FROBISHER'S POWERS LAST.
NOW, ALL I HAVE TO DO IS ACTIVATE THE DISPOSAL WHORL AND...
OH...
THAT'S NOT EXACTLY WHAT I HAD IN MIND.
DOCTOR?
HURRY IT UP, DOC!
DOCTOR... THIS IS TEA!
REALLY?

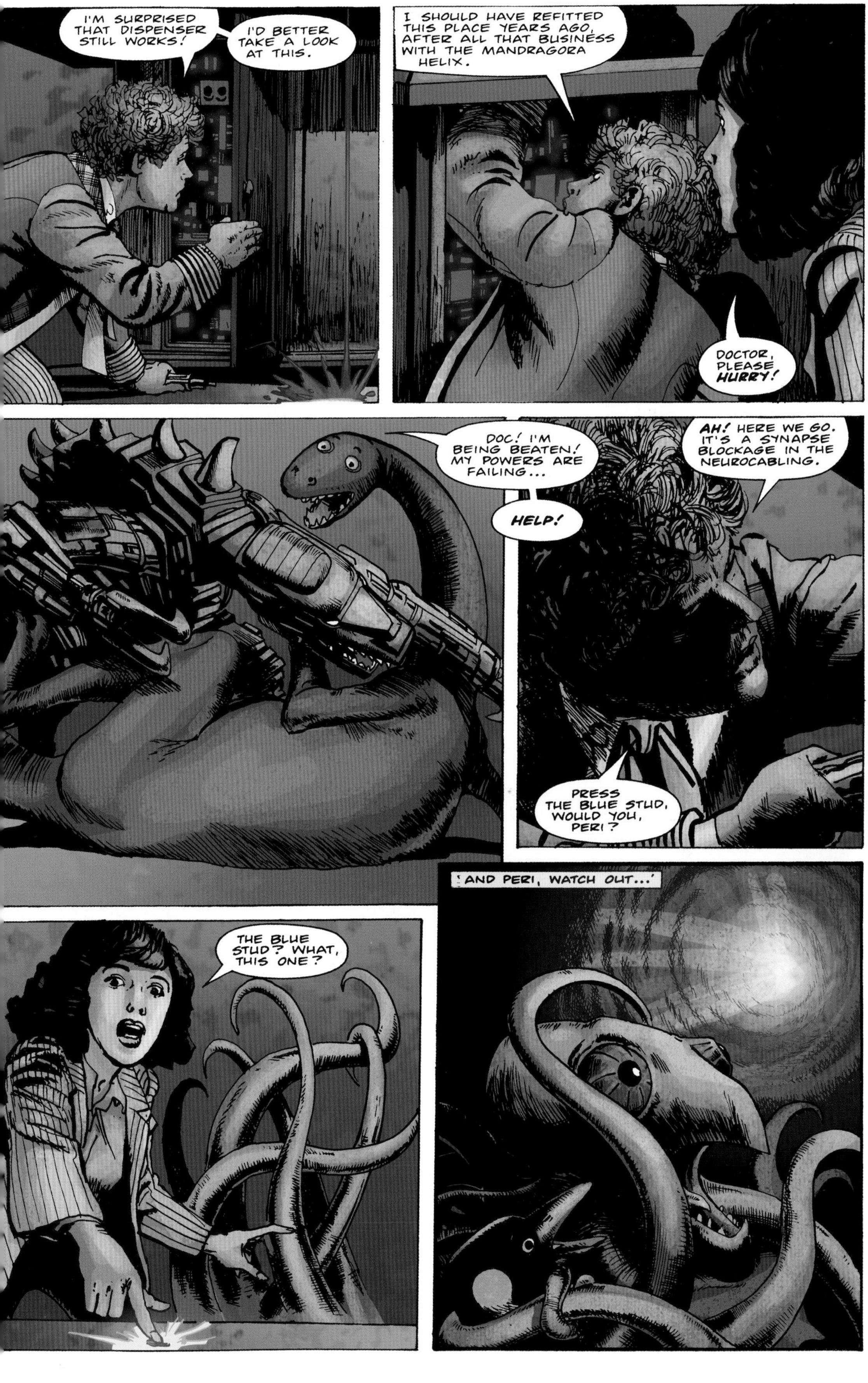

I'M SURPRISED THAT DISPENSER STILL WORKS!
I'D BETTER TAKE A LOOK AT THIS.
I SHOULD HAVE REFITTED THIS PLACE YEARS AGO, AFTER ALL THAT BUSINESS WITH THE MANDRAGORA HELIX.
DOCTOR, PLEASE **HURRY!**
DOC! I'M BEING BEATEN! MY POWERS ARE FAILING...
HELP!
AH! HERE WE GO. IT'S A SYNAPSE BLOCKAGE IN THE NEUROCABLING.
PRESS THE BLUE STUD, WOULD YOU, PERI?
THE BLUE STUD? WHAT, THIS ONE?
'AND PERI, WATCH OUT...'

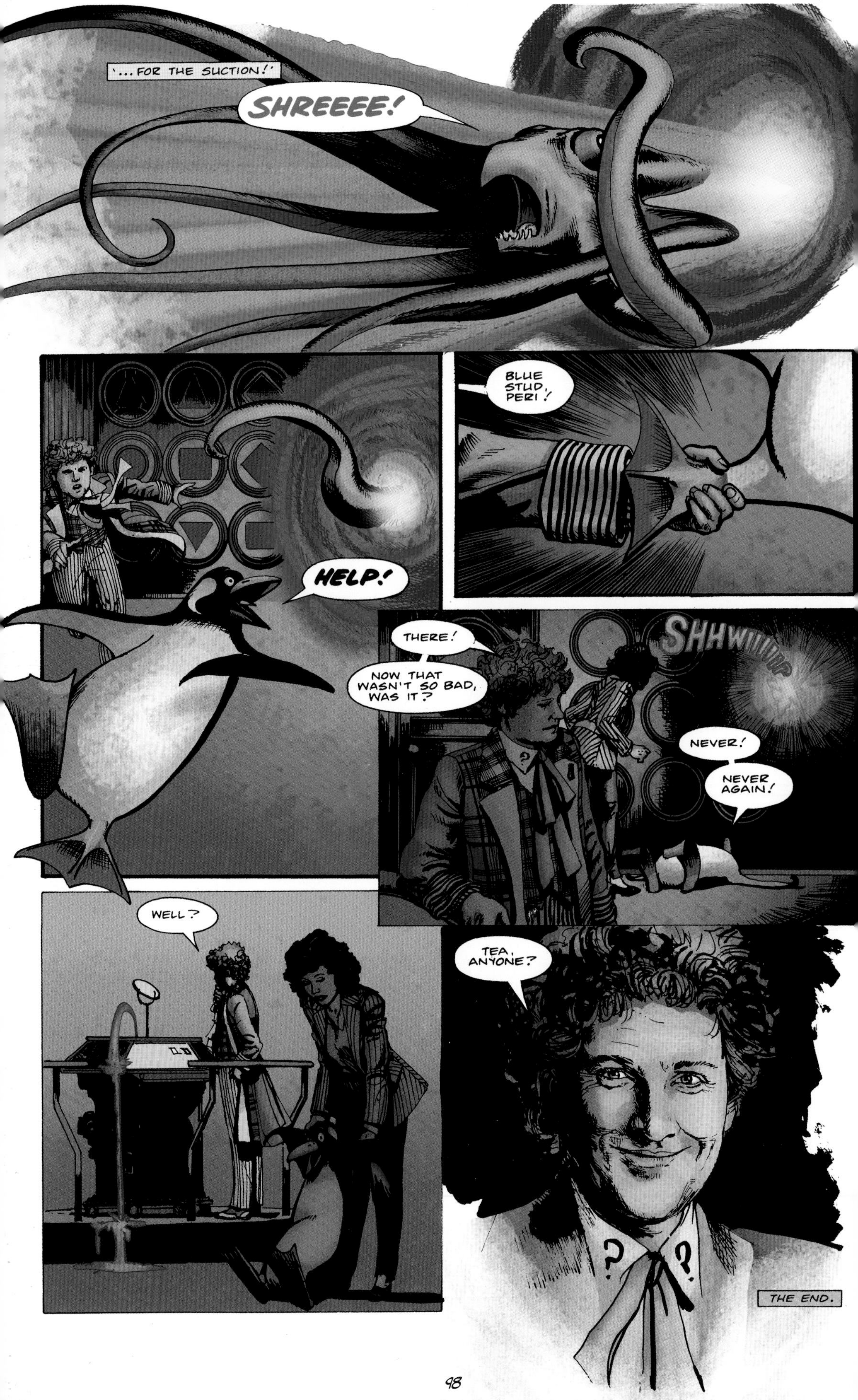

'...FOR THE SUCTION!'
SHREEEE!
BLUE STUD, PERI!
HELP!
THERE!
NOW THAT WASN'T SO BAD, WAS IT?
SHHWIIIIIP
NEVER!
NEVER AGAIN!
WELL?
TEA, ANYONE?
THE END.

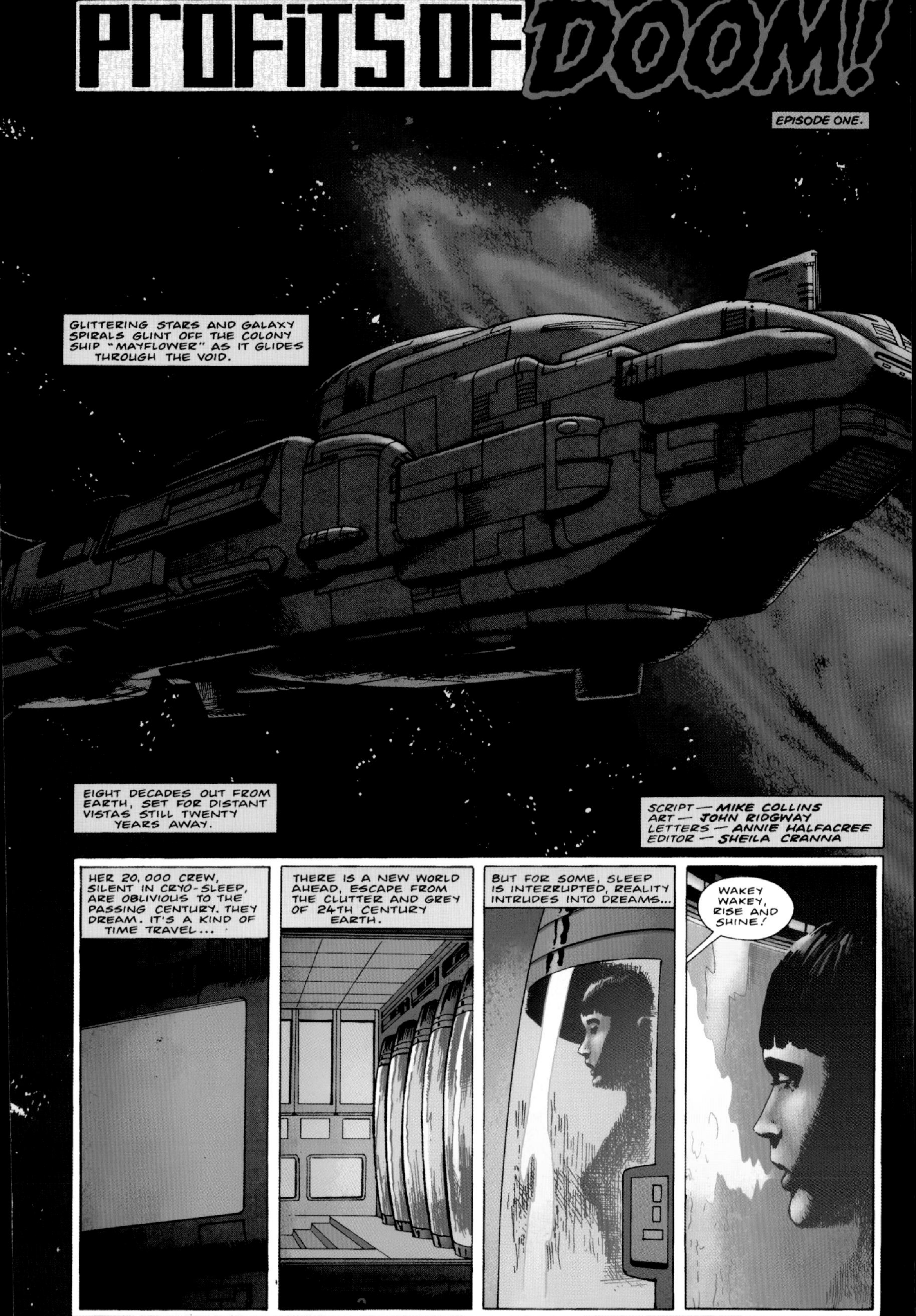
PROFITS OF DOOM!
EPISODE ONE.
GLITTERING STARS AND GALAXY SPIRALS GLINT OFF THE COLONY SHIP "MAYFLOWER" AS IT GLIDES THROUGH THE VOID.
EIGHT DECADES OUT FROM EARTH, SET FOR DISTANT VISTAS STILL TWENTY YEARS AWAY.
SCRIPT — MIKE COLLINS
ART — JOHN RIDGWAY
LETTERS — ANNIE HALFACREE
EDITOR — SHEILA CRANNA
HER 20,000 CREW, SILENT IN CRYO-SLEEP, ARE OBLIVIOUS TO THE PASSING CENTURY. THEY DREAM. IT'S A KIND OF TIME TRAVEL...
THERE IS A NEW WORLD AHEAD, ESCAPE FROM THE CLUTTER AND GREY OF 24TH CENTURY EARTH.
BUT FOR SOME, SLEEP IS INTERRUPTED, REALITY INTRUDES INTO DREAMS...
WAKEY WAKEY, RISE AND SHINE!

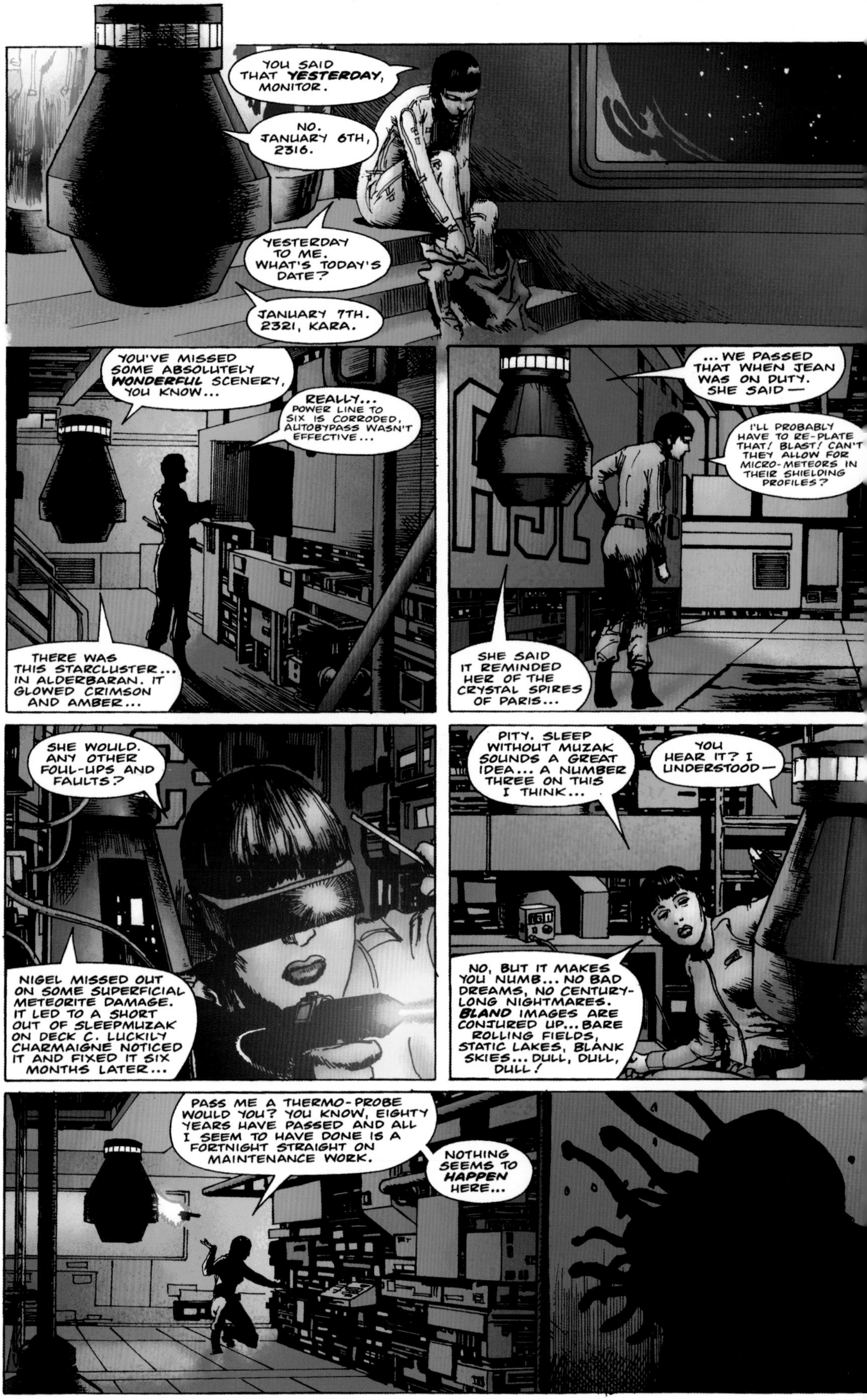
YOU SAID THAT YESTERDAY, MONITOR.
NO. JANUARY 6TH, 2316.
YESTERDAY TO ME. WHAT'S TODAY'S DATE?
JANUARY 7TH. 2321, KARA.
YOU'VE MISSED SOME ABSOLUTELY WONDERFUL SCENERY, YOU KNOW...
REALLY... POWER LINE TO SIX IS CORRODED, AUTOBYPASS WASN'T EFFECTIVE...
THERE WAS THIS STARCLUSTER... IN ALDERBARAN. IT GLOWED CRIMSON AND AMBER...
...WE PASSED THAT WHEN JEAN WAS ON DUTY. SHE SAID—
I'LL PROBABLY HAVE TO RE-PLATE THAT! BLAST! CAN'T THEY ALLOW FOR MICRO-METEORS IN THEIR SHIELDING PROFILES?
SHE SAID IT REMINDED HER OF THE CRYSTAL SPIRES OF PARIS...
SHE WOULD. ANY OTHER FOUL-UPS AND FAULTS?
NIGEL MISSED OUT ON SOME SUPERFICIAL METEORITE DAMAGE. IT LED TO A SHORT OUT OF SLEEPMUZAK ON DECK C. LUCKILY CHARMAIGNE NOTICED IT AND FIXED IT SIX MONTHS LATER...
PITY. SLEEP WITHOUT MUZAK SOUNDS A GREAT IDEA... A NUMBER THREE ON THIS I THINK...
YOU HEAR IT? I UNDERSTOOD—
NO, BUT IT MAKES YOU NUMB... NO BAD DREAMS, NO CENTURY-LONG NIGHTMARES. BLAND IMAGES ARE CONJURED UP... BARE ROLLING FIELDS, STATIC LAKES, BLANK SKIES... DULL, DULL, DULL!
PASS ME A THERMO-PROBE WOULD YOU? YOU KNOW, EIGHTY YEARS HAVE PASSED AND ALL I SEEM TO HAVE DONE IS A FORTNIGHT STRAIGHT ON MAINTENANCE WORK.
NOTHING SEEMS TO HAPPEN HERE...

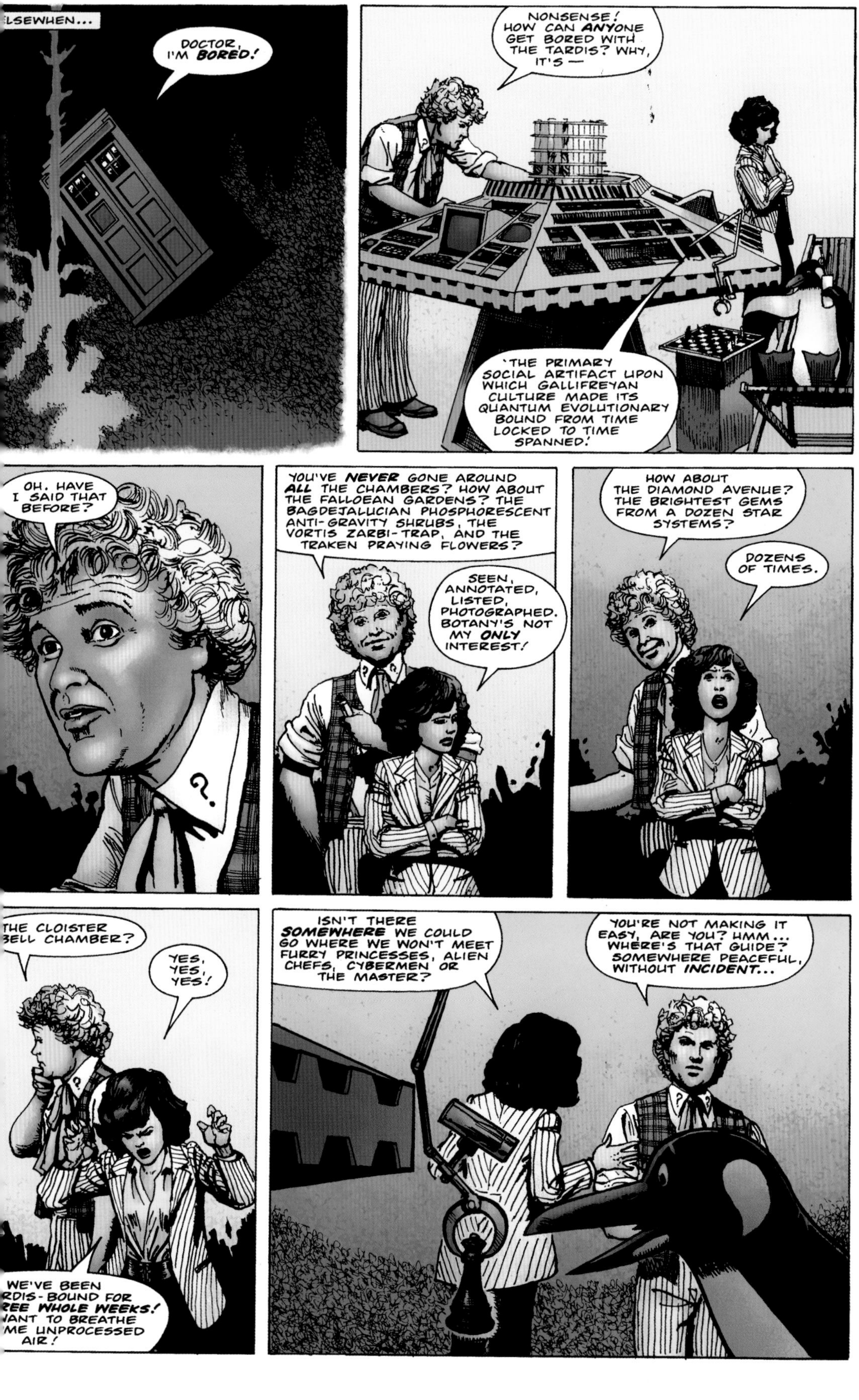

ELSEWHEN...
DOCTOR, I'M BORED!
NONSENSE! HOW CAN ANYONE GET BORED WITH THE TARDIS? WHY, IT'S —
'THE PRIMARY SOCIAL ARTIFACT UPON WHICH GALLIFREYAN CULTURE MADE ITS QUANTUM EVOLUTIONARY BOUND FROM TIME LOCKED TO TIME SPANNED.'
OH. HAVE I SAID THAT BEFORE?
YOU'VE NEVER GONE AROUND ALL THE CHAMBERS? HOW ABOUT THE FALLOEAN GARDENS? THE BAGDEJALUCIAN PHOSPHORESCENT ANTI-GRAVITY SHRUBS, THE VORTIS ZARBI-TRAP, AND THE TRAKEN PRAYING FLOWERS?
SEEN, ANNOTATED, LISTED, PHOTOGRAPHED. BOTANY'S NOT MY ONLY INTEREST!
HOW ABOUT THE DIAMOND AVENUE? THE BRIGHTEST GEMS FROM A DOZEN STAR SYSTEMS?
DOZENS OF TIMES.
THE CLOISTER BELL CHAMBER?
YES, YES, YES!
WE'VE BEEN RDIS-BOUND FOR REE WHOLE WEEKS! VANT TO BREATHE ME UNPROCESSED AIR!
ISN'T THERE SOMEWHERE WE COULD GO WHERE WE WON'T MEET FURRY PRINCESSES, ALIEN CHEFS, CYBERMEN OR THE MASTER?
YOU'RE NOT MAKING IT EASY, ARE YOU? HMM... WHERE'S THAT GUIDE? SOMEWHERE PEACEFUL, WITHOUT INCIDENT...

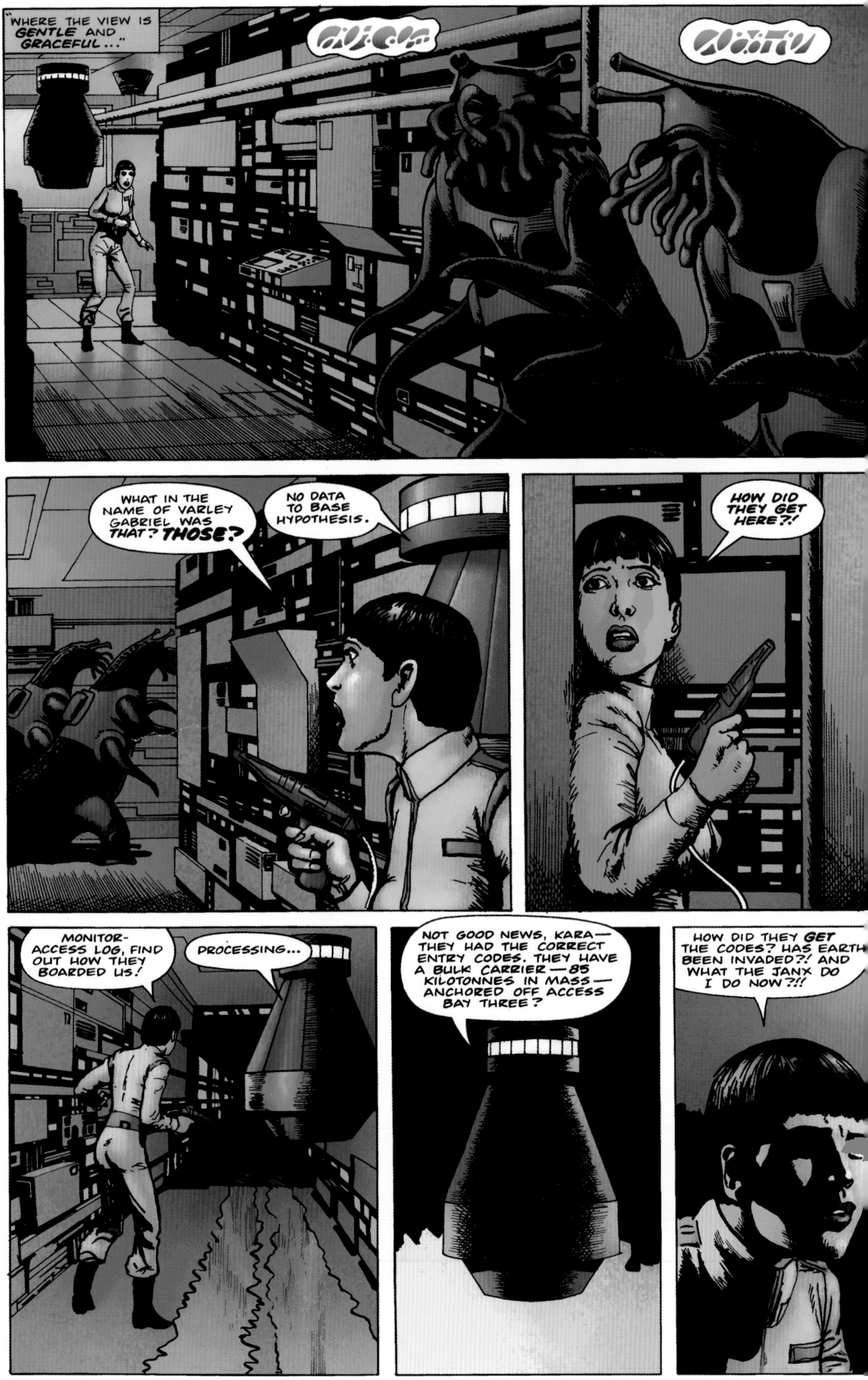
"WHERE THE VIEW IS GENTLE AND GRACEFUL..."
WHAT IN THE NAME OF VARLEY GABRIEL WAS THAT? THOSE?
NO DATA TO BASE HYPOTHESIS.
HOW DID THEY GET HERE?!
MONITOR-ACCESS LOG, FIND OUT HOW THEY BOARDED US!
PROCESSING...
NOT GOOD NEWS, KARA— THEY HAD THE CORRECT ENTRY CODES. THEY HAVE A BULK CARRIER—85 KILOTONNES IN MASS— ANCHORED OFF ACCESS BAY THREE?
HOW DID THEY GET THE CODES? HAS EARTH BEEN INVADED?! AND WHAT THE JANX DO I DO NOW?!!

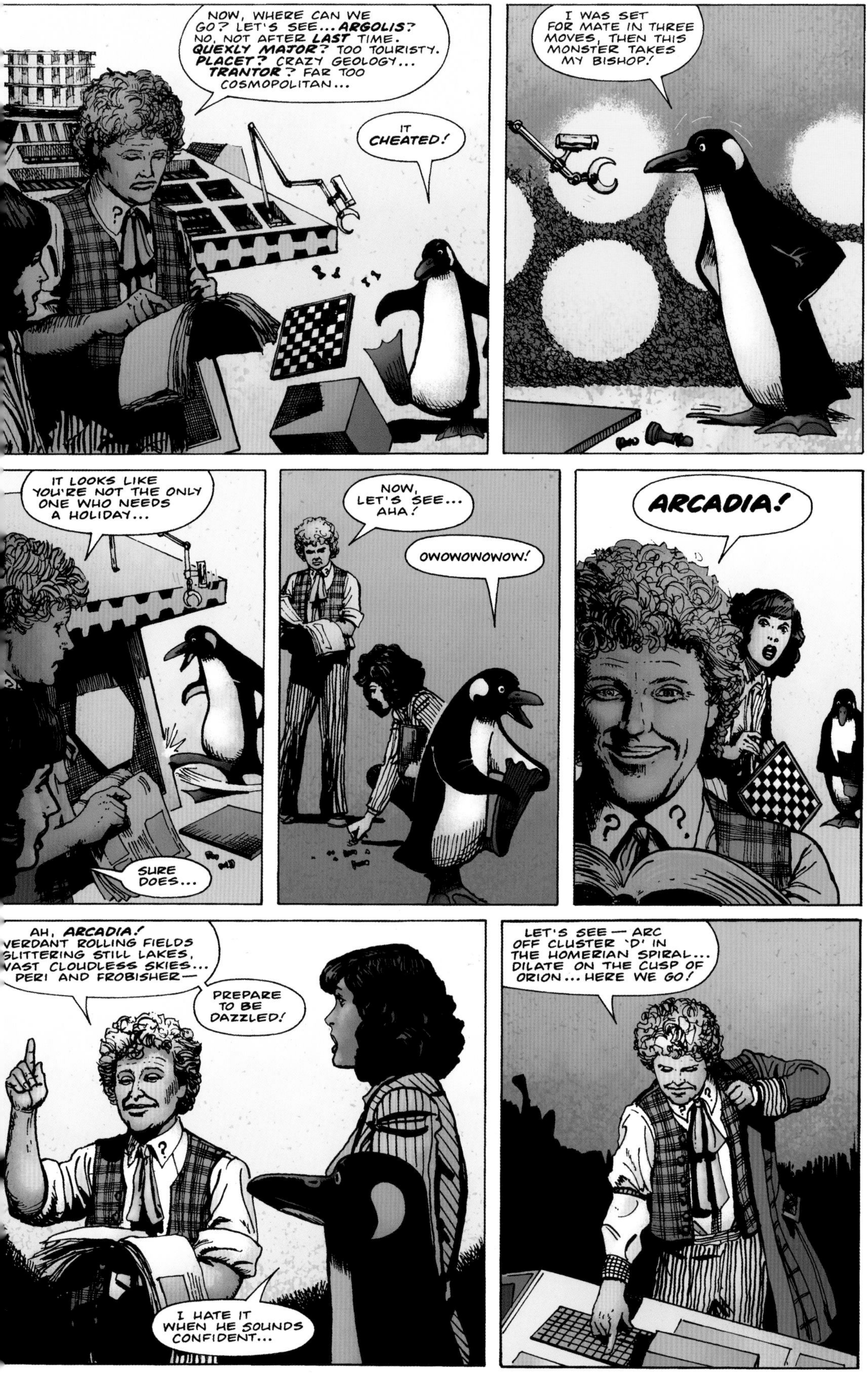

NOW, WHERE CAN WE GO? LET'S SEE... **ARGOLIS?** NO, NOT AFTER **LAST** TIME. **QUEXLY MAJOR?** TOO TOURISTY. **PLACET?** CRAZY GEOLOGY... **TRANTOR?** FAR TOO COSMOPOLITAN...
IT **CHEATED!**
I WAS SET FOR MATE IN THREE MOVES, THEN THIS MONSTER TAKES MY BISHOP!
IT LOOKS LIKE YOU'RE NOT THE ONLY ONE WHO NEEDS A HOLIDAY...
SURE DOES...
NOW, LET'S SEE... AHA!
OWOWOWOWOW!
ARCADIA!
AH, **ARCADIA!** VERDANT ROLLING FIELDS GLITTERING STILL LAKES, VAST CLOUDLESS SKIES... PERI AND FROBISHER—
PREPARE TO BE DAZZLED!
I HATE IT WHEN HE SOUNDS CONFIDENT...
LET'S SEE — ARC OFF CLUSTER 'D' IN THE HOMERIAN SPIRAL... DILATE ON THE CUSP OF ORION... HERE WE GO!

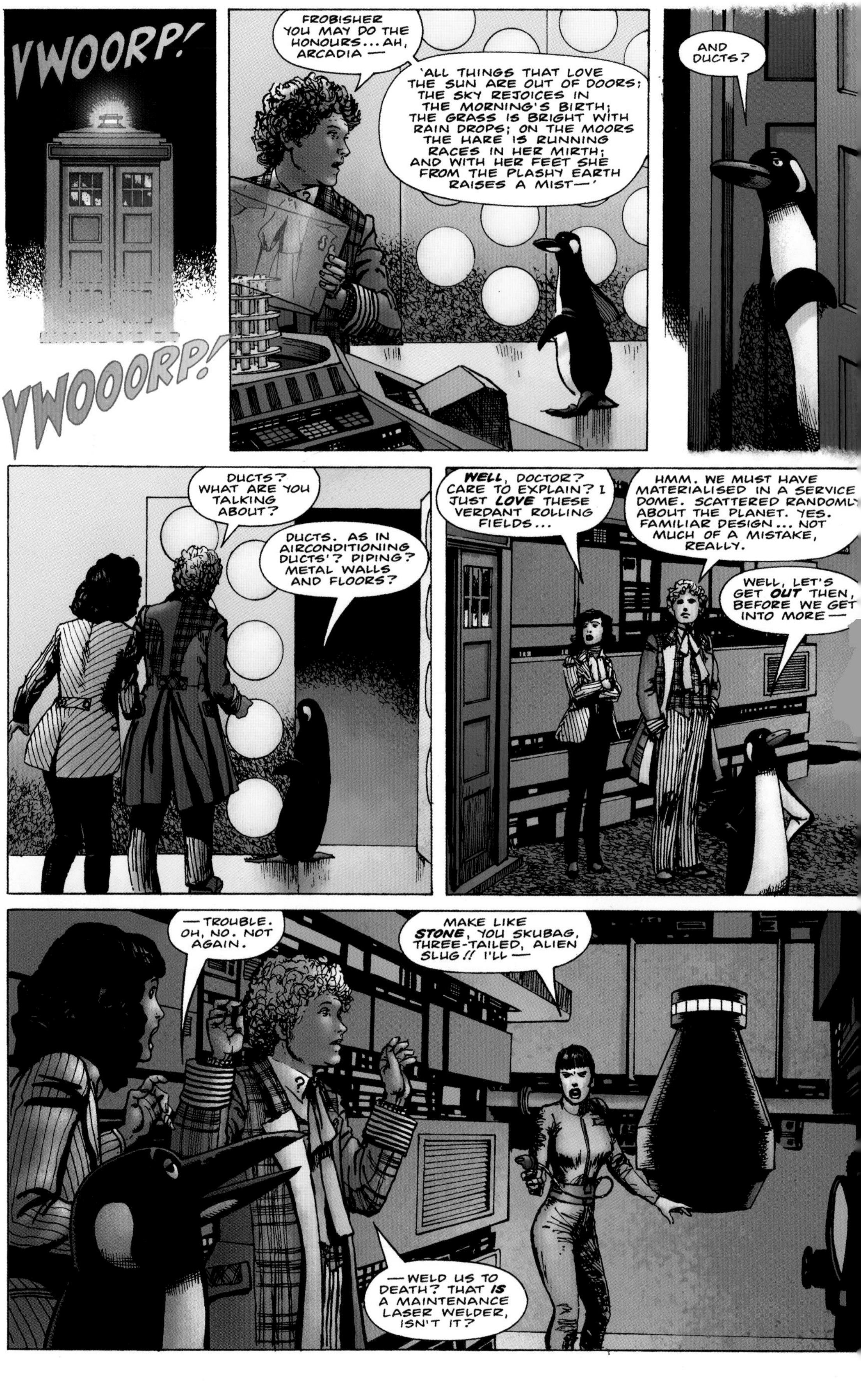
VWOORP!
VWOOORP!
FROBISHER YOU MAY DO THE HONOURS... AH, ARCADIA —
'ALL THINGS THAT LOVE THE SUN ARE OUT OF DOORS; THE SKY REJOICES IN THE MORNING'S BIRTH; THE GRASS IS BRIGHT WITH RAIN DROPS; ON THE MOORS THE HARE IS RUNNING RACES IN HER MIRTH; AND WITH HER FEET SHE FROM THE PLASHY EARTH RAISES A MIST—'
AND DUCTS?
DUCTS? WHAT ARE YOU TALKING ABOUT?
DUCTS. AS IN AIRCONDITIONING DUCTS'? PIPING? METAL WALLS AND FLOORS?
WELL, DOCTOR? CARE TO EXPLAIN? I JUST LOVE THESE VERDANT ROLLING FIELDS...
HMM. WE MUST HAVE MATERIALISED IN A SERVICE DOME. SCATTERED RANDOMLY ABOUT THE PLANET. YES. FAMILIAR DESIGN... NOT MUCH OF A MISTAKE, REALLY.
WELL, LET'S GET OUT THEN, BEFORE WE GET INTO MORE —
— TROUBLE. OH, NO. NOT AGAIN.
MAKE LIKE STONE, YOU SKUBAG, THREE-TAILED, ALIEN SLUG!! I'LL —
— WELD US TO DEATH? THAT IS A MAINTENANCE LASER WELDER, ISN'T IT?

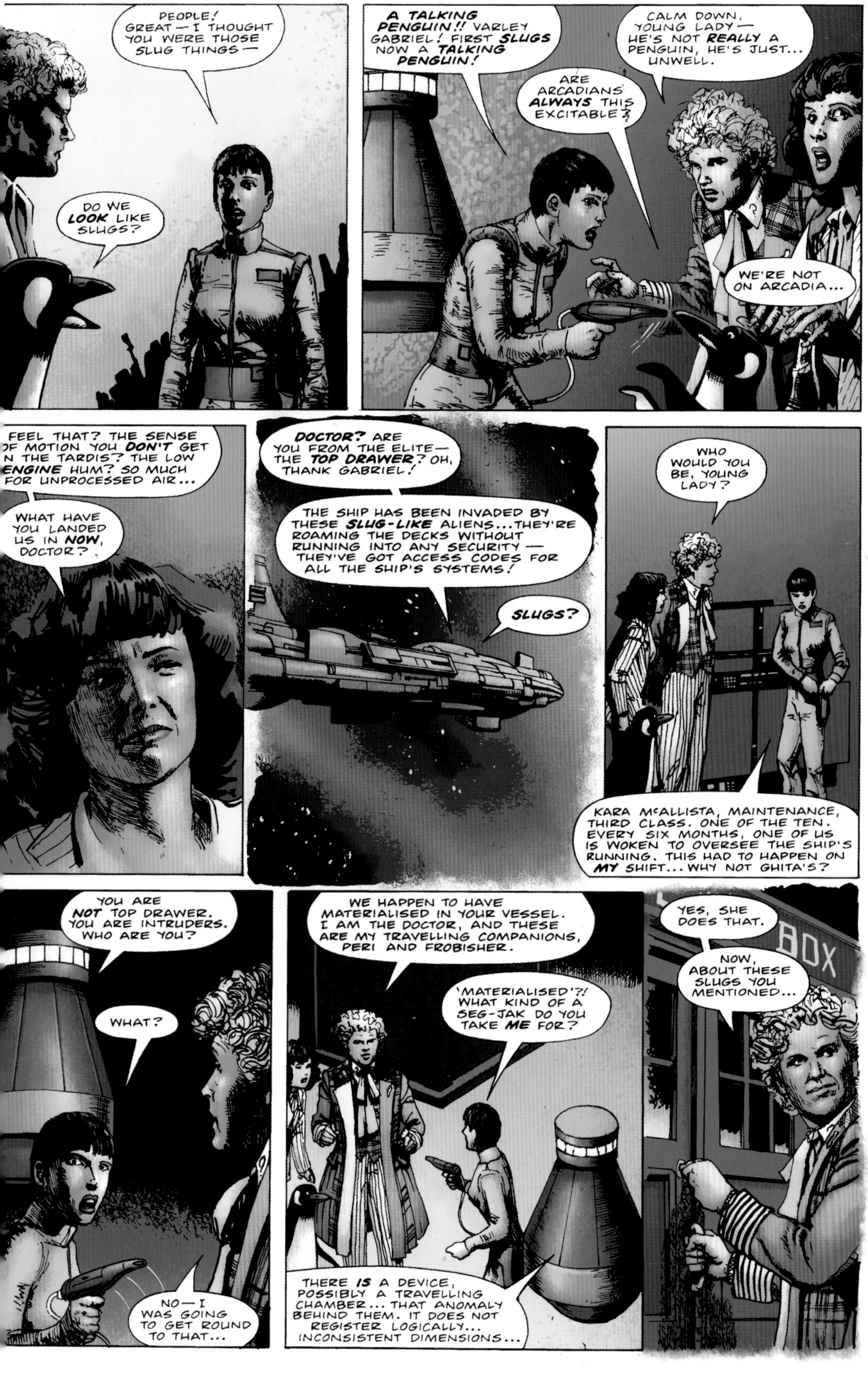

PEOPLE! GREAT — I THOUGHT YOU WERE THOSE SLUG THINGS —
DO WE LOOK LIKE SLUGS?
A TALKING PENGUIN!! VARLEY GABRIEL! FIRST SLUGS NOW A TALKING PENGUIN!
ARE ARCADIANS ALWAYS THIS EXCITABLE?
CALM DOWN, YOUNG LADY — HE'S NOT REALLY A PENGUIN, HE'S JUST... UNWELL.
WE'RE NOT ON ARCADIA...
FEEL THAT? THE SENSE OF MOTION YOU DON'T GET IN THE TARDIS? THE LOW ENGINE HUM? SO MUCH FOR UNPROCESSED AIR...
WHAT HAVE YOU LANDED US IN NOW, DOCTOR?
DOCTOR? ARE YOU FROM THE ELITE — THE TOP DRAWER? OH, THANK GABRIEL!
THE SHIP HAS BEEN INVADED BY THESE SLUG-LIKE ALIENS... THEY'RE ROAMING THE DECKS WITHOUT RUNNING INTO ANY SECURITY — THEY'VE GOT ACCESS CODES FOR ALL THE SHIP'S SYSTEMS!
SLUGS?
WHO WOULD YOU BE, YOUNG LADY?
KARA McALLISTA, MAINTENANCE, THIRD CLASS. ONE OF THE TEN. EVERY SIX MONTHS, ONE OF US IS WOKEN TO OVERSEE THE SHIP'S RUNNING. THIS HAD TO HAPPEN ON MY SHIFT... WHY NOT GHITA'S?
YOU ARE NOT TOP DRAWER. YOU ARE INTRUDERS. WHO ARE YOU?
WHAT?
NO — I WAS GOING TO GET ROUND TO THAT...
WE HAPPEN TO HAVE MATERIALISED IN YOUR VESSEL. I AM THE DOCTOR, AND THESE ARE MY TRAVELLING COMPANIONS, PERI AND FROBISHER.
'MATERIALISED'?! WHAT KIND OF A SEG-JAK DO YOU TAKE ME FOR?
THERE IS A DEVICE, POSSIBLY A TRAVELLING CHAMBER... THAT ANOMALY BEHIND THEM. IT DOES NOT REGISTER LOGICALLY... INCONSISTENT DIMENSIONS...
YES, SHE DOES THAT.
NOW, ABOUT THESE SLUGS YOU MENTIONED...
BOX

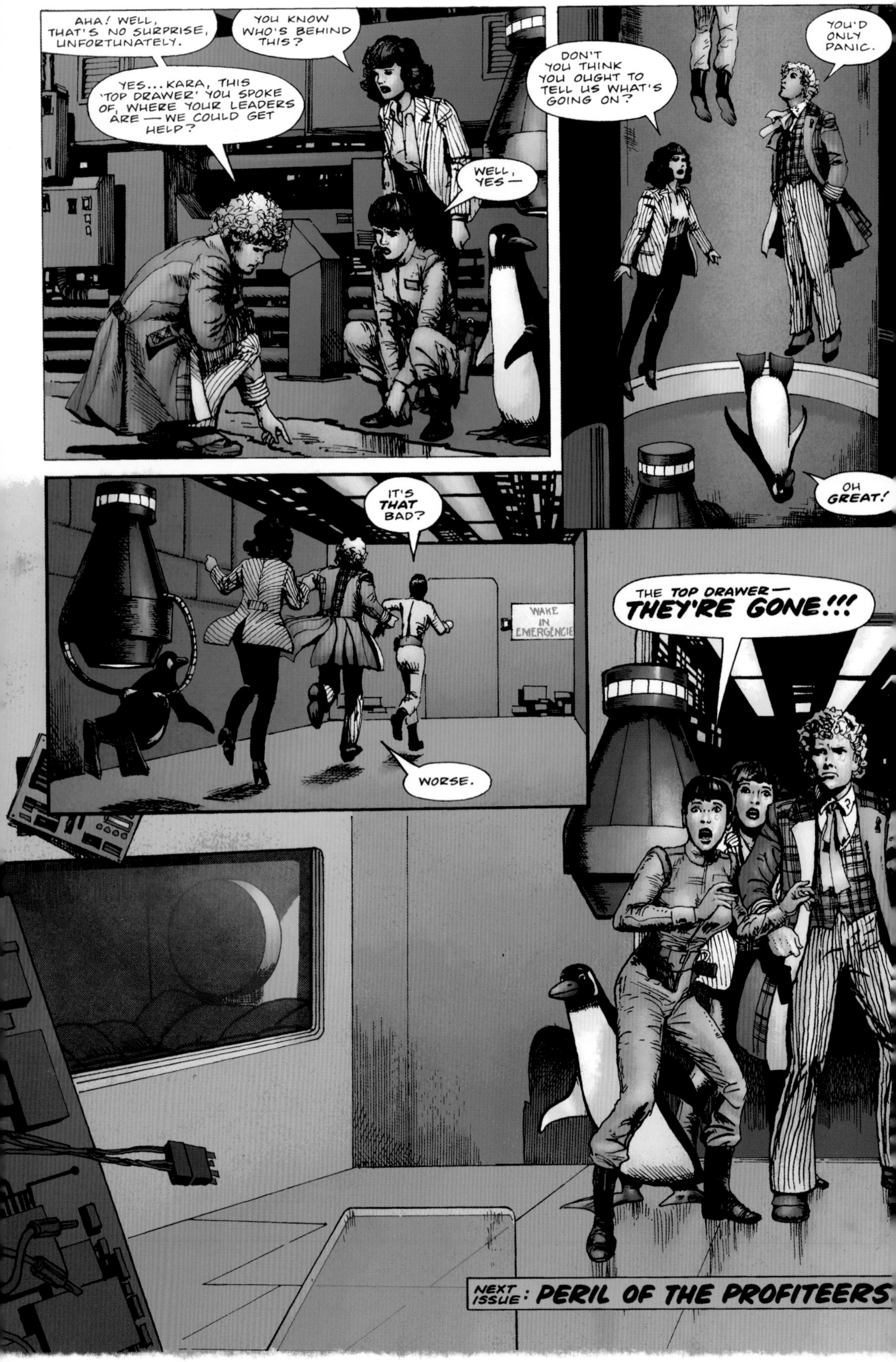

AHA! WELL, THAT'S NO SURPRISE, UNFORTUNATELY.
YOU KNOW WHO'S BEHIND THIS?
YES... KARA, THIS 'TOP DRAWER' YOU SPOKE OF, WHERE YOUR LEADERS ARE — WE COULD GET HELP?
WELL, YES —
DON'T YOU THINK YOU OUGHT TO TELL US WHAT'S GOING ON?
YOU'D ONLY PANIC.
OH GREAT!
IT'S THAT BAD?
WAKE IN EMERGENCIE
WORSE.
THE TOP DRAWER — THEY'RE GONE!!!
NEXT ISSUE: PERIL OF THE PROFITEERS

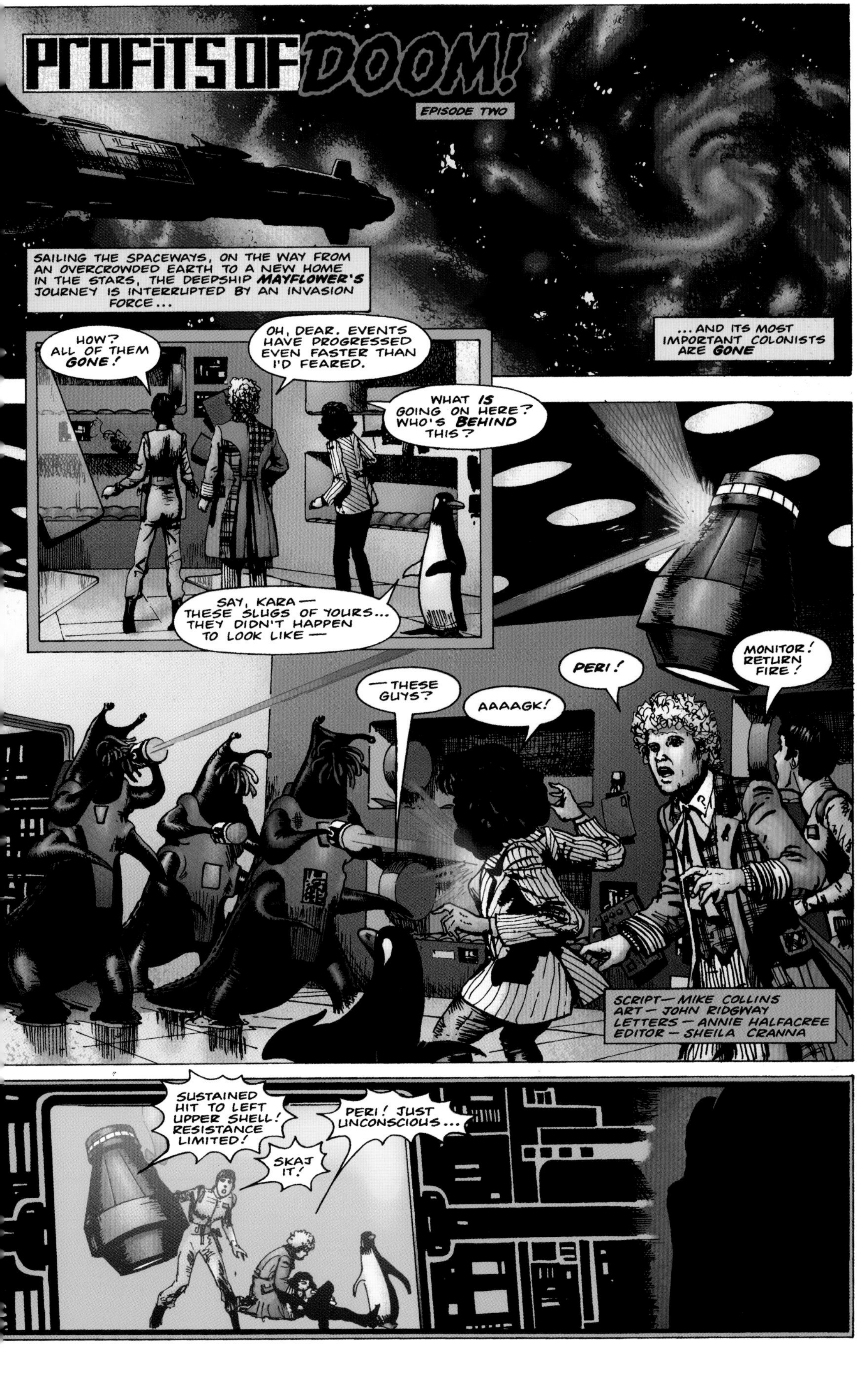
PROFITS OF DOOM!
EPISODE TWO
SAILING THE SPACEWAYS, ON THE WAY FROM AN OVERCROWDED EARTH TO A NEW HOME IN THE STARS, THE DEEPSHIP MAYFLOWER'S JOURNEY IS INTERRUPTED BY AN INVASION FORCE...
...AND ITS MOST IMPORTANT COLONISTS ARE GONE
HOW? ALL OF THEM GONE!
OH, DEAR. EVENTS HAVE PROGRESSED EVEN FASTER THAN I'D FEARED.
WHAT IS GOING ON HERE? WHO'S BEHIND THIS?
SAY, KARA— THESE SLUGS OF YOURS... THEY DIDN'T HAPPEN TO LOOK LIKE—
—THESE GUYS?
AAAAGK!
PERI!
MONITOR! RETURN FIRE!
SCRIPT— MIKE COLLINS
ART— JOHN RIDGWAY
LETTERS— ANNIE HALFACREE
EDITOR— SHEILA CRANNA
SUSTAINED HIT TO LEFT UPPER SHELL! RESISTANCE LIMITED!
SKAJ IT!
PERI! JUST UNCONSCIOUS...

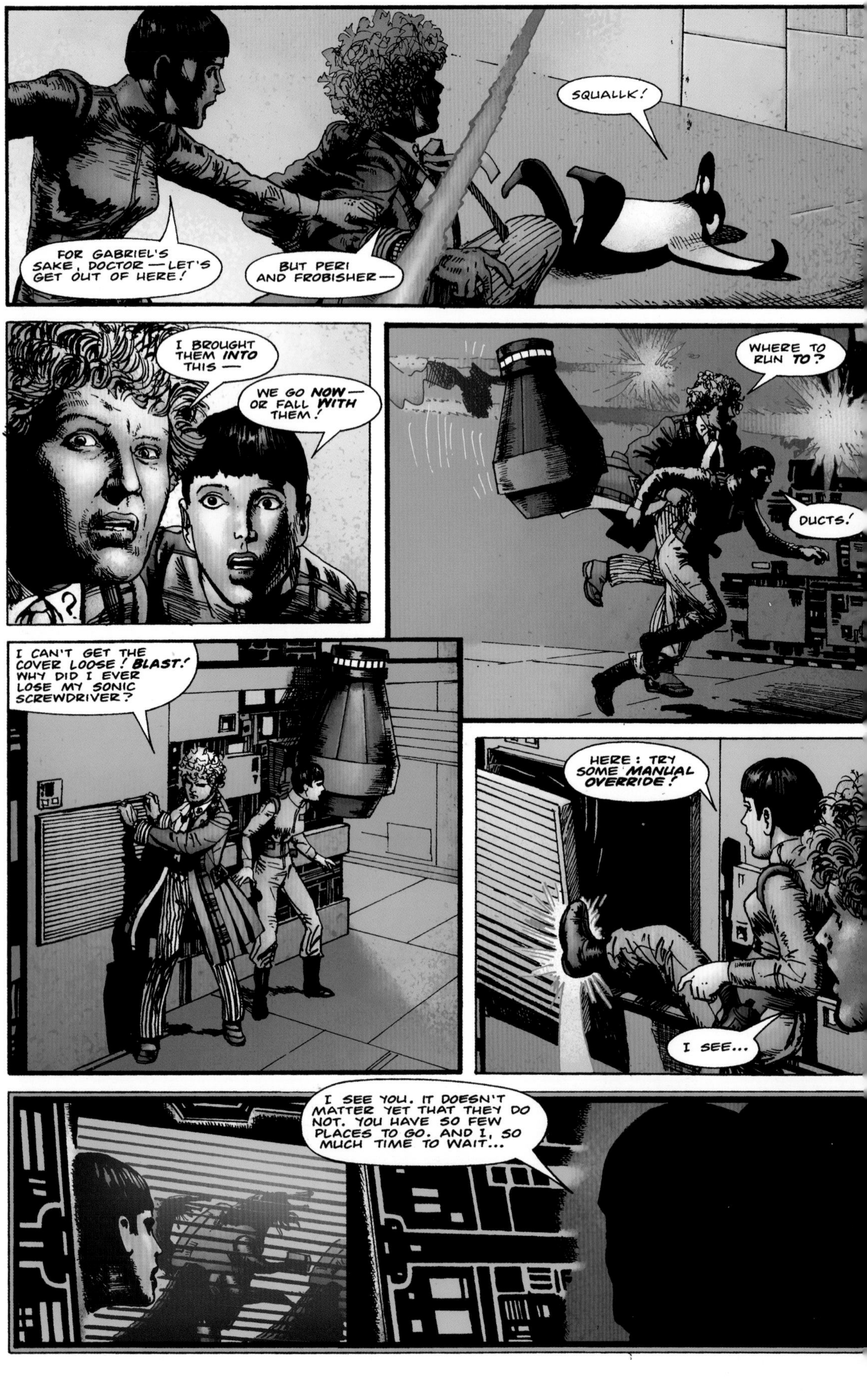
SQUALLK!
FOR GABRIEL'S SAKE, DOCTOR — LET'S GET OUT OF HERE!
BUT PERI AND FROBISHER —
I BROUGHT THEM INTO THIS —
WE GO NOW — OR FALL WITH THEM!
WHERE TO RUN TO?
DUCTS!
I CAN'T GET THE COVER LOOSE! BLAST! WHY DID I EVER LOSE MY SONIC SCREWDRIVER?
HERE: TRY SOME MANUAL OVERRIDE!
I SEE...
I SEE YOU. IT DOESN'T MATTER YET THAT THEY DO NOT. YOU HAVE SO FEW PLACES TO GO. AND I, SO MUCH TIME TO WAIT...

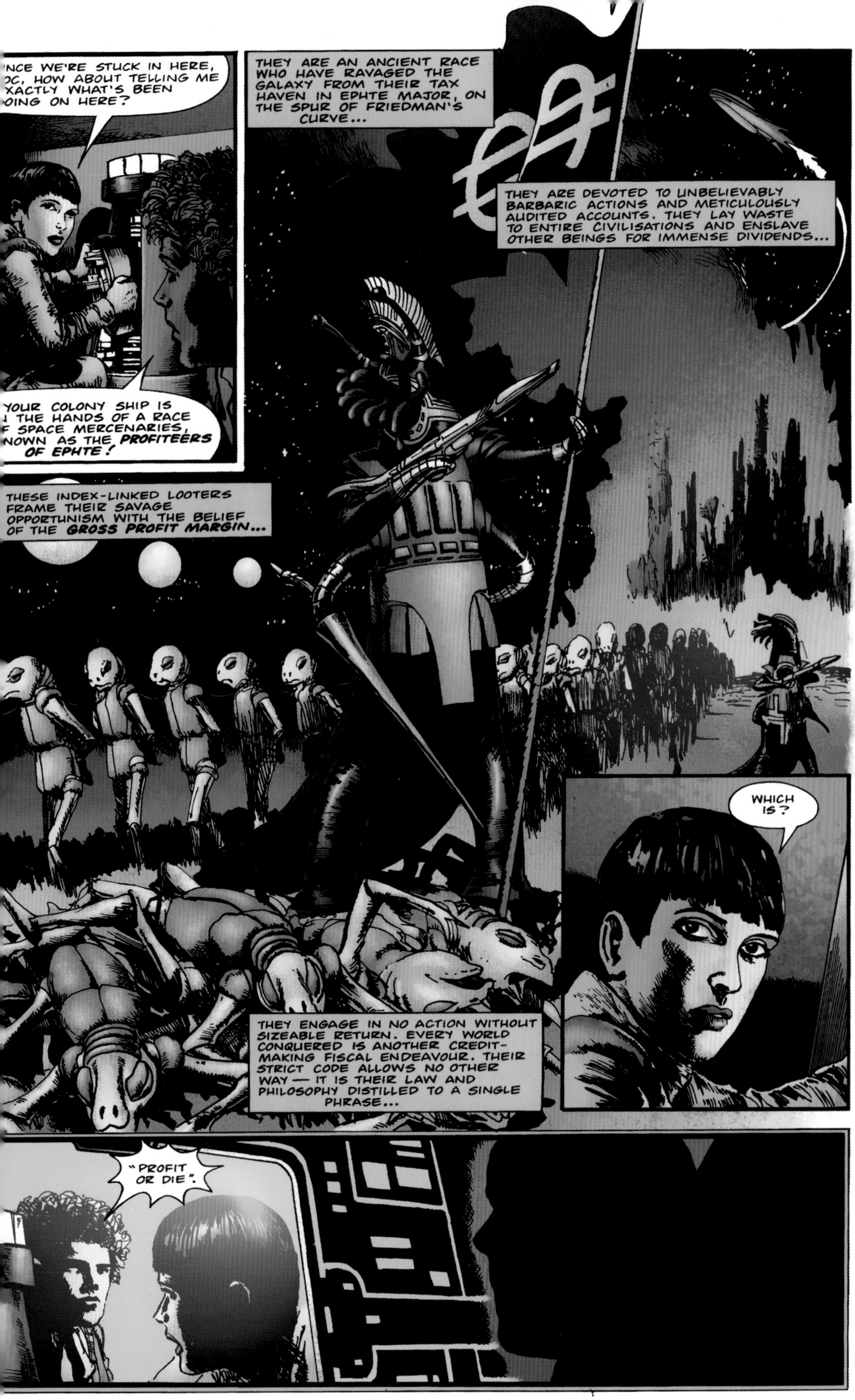
NCE WE'RE STUCK IN HERE, OC, HOW ABOUT TELLING ME XACTLY WHAT'S BEEN OING ON HERE?
YOUR COLONY SHIP IS THE HANDS OF A RACE F SPACE MERCENARIES, NOWN AS THE PROFITEERS OF EPHTE!
THEY ARE AN ANCIENT RACE WHO HAVE RAVAGED THE GALAXY FROM THEIR TAX HAVEN IN EPHTE MAJOR, ON THE SPUR OF FRIEDMAN'S CURVE...
THEY ARE DEVOTED TO UNBELIEVABLY BARBARIC ACTIONS AND METICULOUSLY AUDITED ACCOUNTS. THEY LAY WASTE TO ENTIRE CIVILISATIONS AND ENSLAVE OTHER BEINGS FOR IMMENSE DIVIDENDS...
THESE INDEX-LINKED LOOTERS FRAME THEIR SAVAGE OPPORTUNISM WITH THE BELIEF OF THE GROSS PROFIT MARGIN...
THEY ENGAGE IN NO ACTION WITHOUT SIZEABLE RETURN. EVERY WORLD CONQUERED IS ANOTHER CREDIT-MAKING FISCAL ENDEAVOUR. THEIR STRICT CODE ALLOWS NO OTHER WAY — IT IS THEIR LAW AND PHILOSOPHY DISTILLED TO A SINGLE PHRASE...
WHICH IS?
"PROFIT OR DIE".

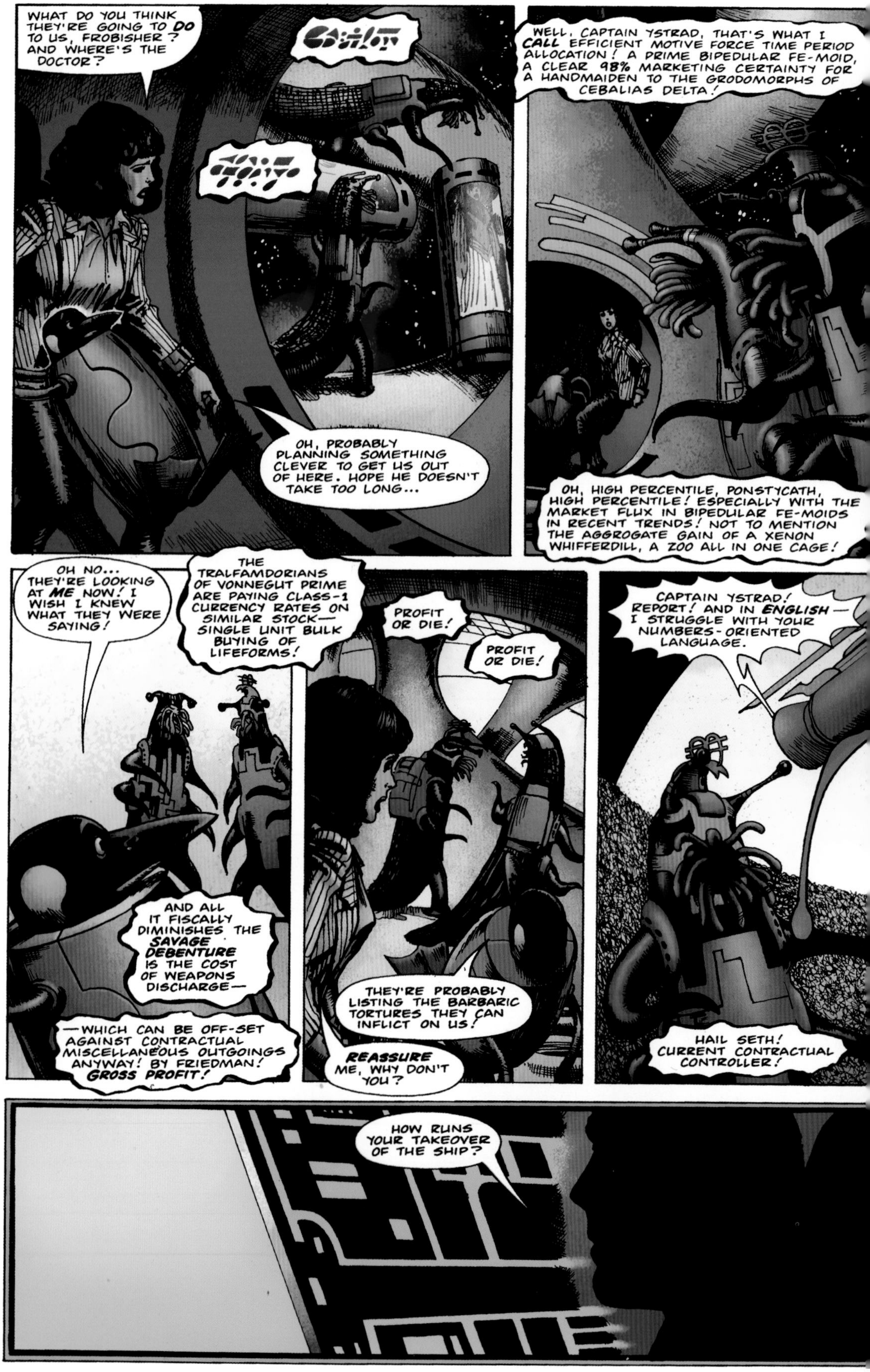

WHAT DO YOU THINK THEY'RE GOING TO DO TO US, FROBISHER? AND WHERE'S THE DOCTOR?
OH, PROBABLY PLANNING SOMETHING CLEVER TO GET US OUT OF HERE. HOPE HE DOESN'T TAKE TOO LONG...
WELL, CAPTAIN YSTRAD, THAT'S WHAT I CALL EFFICIENT MOTIVE FORCE TIME PERIOD ALLOCATION! A PRIME BIPEDULAR FE-MOID, A CLEAR 98% MARKETING CERTAINTY FOR A HANDMAIDEN TO THE GRODOMORPHS OF CEBALIAS DELTA!
OH, HIGH PERCENTILE, PONSTYCATH, HIGH PERCENTILE! ESPECIALLY WITH THE MARKET FLUX IN BIPEDULAR FE-MOIDS IN RECENT TRENDS! NOT TO MENTION THE AGGROGATE GAIN OF A XENON WHIFFERDILL, A ZOO ALL IN ONE CAGE!
OH NO... THEY'RE LOOKING AT ME NOW! I WISH I KNEW WHAT THEY WERE SAYING!
THE TRALFAMDORIANS OF VONNEGUT PRIME ARE PAYING CLASS-1 CURRENCY RATES ON SIMILAR STOCK— SINGLE UNIT BULK BUYING OF LIFEFORMS!
AND ALL IT FISCALLY DIMINISHES THE SAVAGE DEBENTURE IS THE COST OF WEAPONS DISCHARGE—
—WHICH CAN BE OFF-SET AGAINST CONTRACTUAL MISCELLANEOUS OUTGOINGS ANYWAY! BY FRIEDMAN! GROSS PROFIT!
PROFIT OR DIE!
PROFIT OR DIE!
THEY'RE PROBABLY LISTING THE BARBARIC TORTURES THEY CAN INFLICT ON US!
REASSURE ME, WHY DON'T YOU?
CAPTAIN YSTRAD! REPORT! AND IN ENGLISH— I STRUGGLE WITH YOUR NUMBERS-ORIENTED LANGUAGE.
HAIL SETH! CURRENT CONTRACTUAL CONTROLLER!
HOW RUNS YOUR TAKEOVER OF THE SHIP?

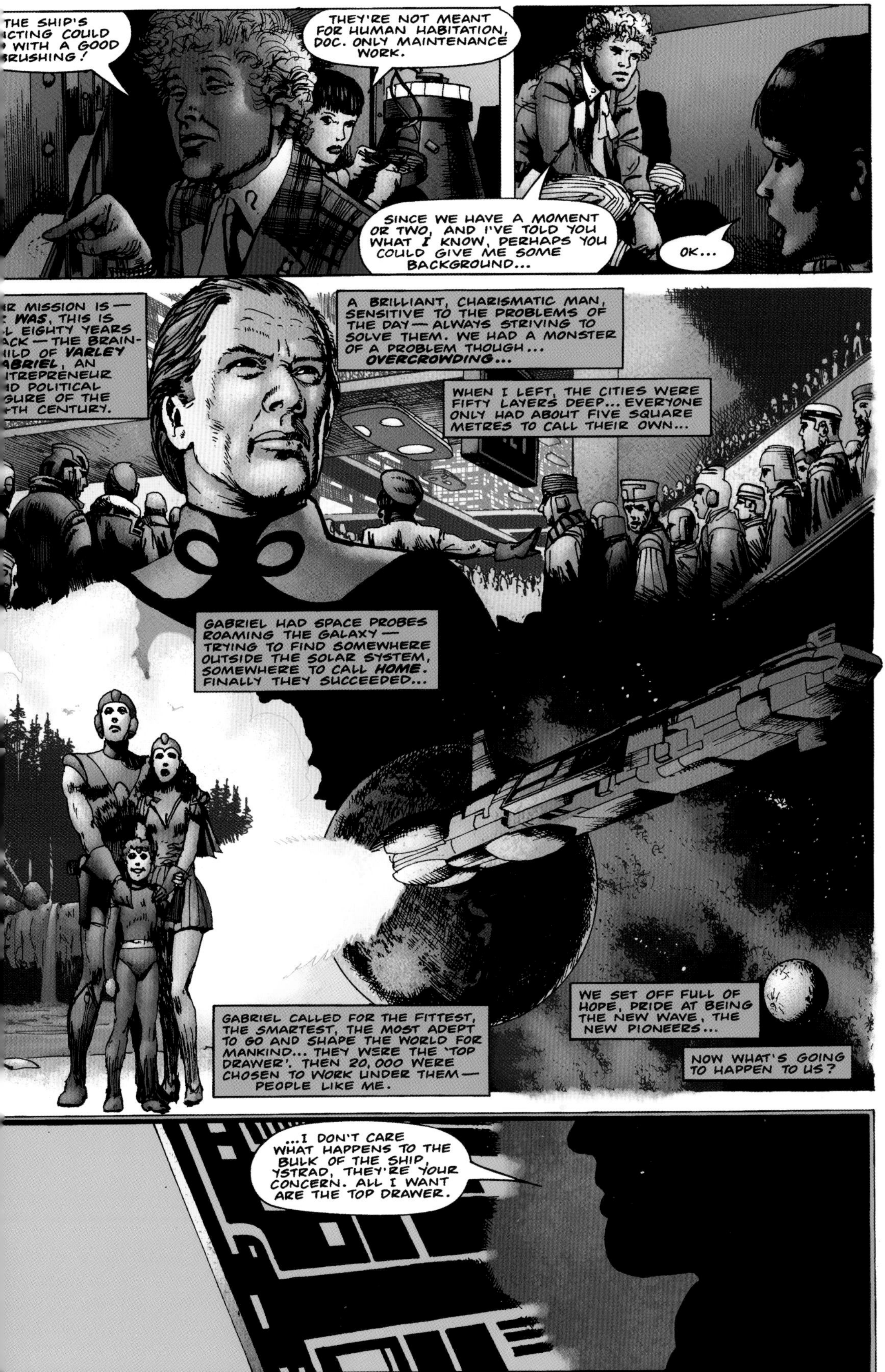

THE SHIP'S ICTING COULD O WITH A GOOD BRUSHING!
THEY'RE NOT MEANT FOR HUMAN HABITATION, DOC. ONLY MAINTENANCE WORK.
SINCE WE HAVE A MOMENT OR TWO, AND I'VE TOLD YOU WHAT I KNOW, PERHAPS YOU COULD GIVE ME SOME BACKGROUND...
OK...
R MISSION IS— WAS, THIS IS EIGHTY YEARS ACK—THE BRAIN- HILD OF VARLEY ABRIEL, AN ITREPRENEUR D POLITICAL URE OF THE TH CENTURY.
A BRILLIANT, CHARISMATIC MAN, SENSITIVE TO THE PROBLEMS OF THE DAY—ALWAYS STRIVING TO SOLVE THEM. WE HAD A MONSTER OF A PROBLEM THOUGH... OVERCROWDING...
WHEN I LEFT, THE CITIES WERE FIFTY LAYERS DEEP... EVERYONE ONLY HAD ABOUT FIVE SQUARE METRES TO CALL THEIR OWN...
GABRIEL HAD SPACE PROBES ROAMING THE GALAXY— TRYING TO FIND SOMEWHERE OUTSIDE THE SOLAR SYSTEM, SOMEWHERE TO CALL HOME. FINALLY THEY SUCCEEDED...
GABRIEL CALLED FOR THE FITTEST, THE SMARTEST, THE MOST ADEPT TO GO AND SHAPE THE WORLD FOR MANKIND... THEY WERE THE 'TOP DRAWER'. THEN 20,000 WERE CHOSEN TO WORK UNDER THEM— PEOPLE LIKE ME.
WE SET OFF FULL OF HOPE, PRIDE AT BEING THE NEW WAVE, THE NEW PIONEERS...
NOW WHAT'S GOING TO HAPPEN TO US?
...I DON'T CARE WHAT HAPPENS TO THE BULK OF THE SHIP, YSTRAD, THEY'RE YOUR CONCERN. ALL I WANT ARE THE TOP DRAWER.

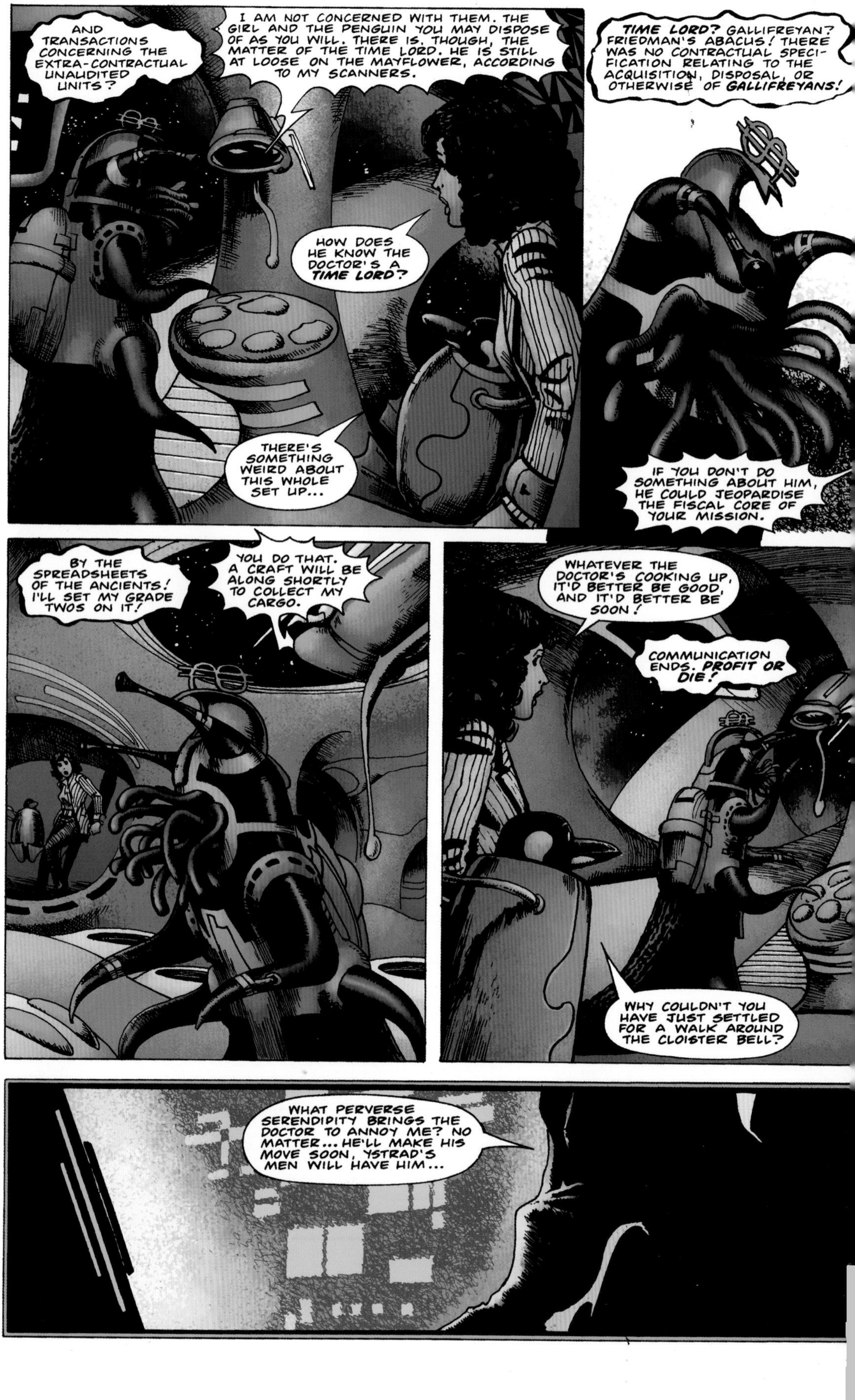
AND TRANSACTIONS CONCERNING THE EXTRA-CONTRACTUAL UNAUDITED UNITS?
I AM NOT CONCERNED WITH THEM. THE GIRL AND THE PENGUIN YOU MAY DISPOSE OF AS YOU WILL. THERE IS, THOUGH, THE MATTER OF THE TIME LORD. HE IS STILL AT LOOSE ON THE MAYFLOWER, ACCORDING TO MY SCANNERS.
HOW DOES HE KNOW THE DOCTOR'S A TIME LORD?
THERE'S SOMETHING WEIRD ABOUT THIS WHOLE SET UP...
TIME LORD? GALLIFREYAN? FRIEDMAN'S ABACUS! THERE WAS NO CONTRACTUAL SPECIFICATION RELATING TO THE ACQUISITION, DISPOSAL, OR OTHERWISE OF GALLIFREYANS!
IF YOU DON'T DO SOMETHING ABOUT HIM, HE COULD JEOPARDISE THE FISCAL CORE OF YOUR MISSION.
BY THE SPREADSHEETS OF THE ANCIENTS! I'LL SET MY GRADE TWOS ON IT!
YOU DO THAT. A CRAFT WILL BE ALONG SHORTLY TO COLLECT MY CARGO.
WHATEVER THE DOCTOR'S COOKING UP, IT'D BETTER BE GOOD, AND IT'D BETTER BE SOON!
COMMUNICATION ENDS. PROFIT OR DIE!
WHY COULDN'T YOU HAVE JUST SETTLED FOR A WALK AROUND THE CLOISTER BELL?
WHAT PERVERSE SERENDIPITY BRINGS THE DOCTOR TO ANNOY ME? NO MATTER... HE'LL MAKE HIS MOVE SOON, YSTRAD'S MEN WILL HAVE HIM...

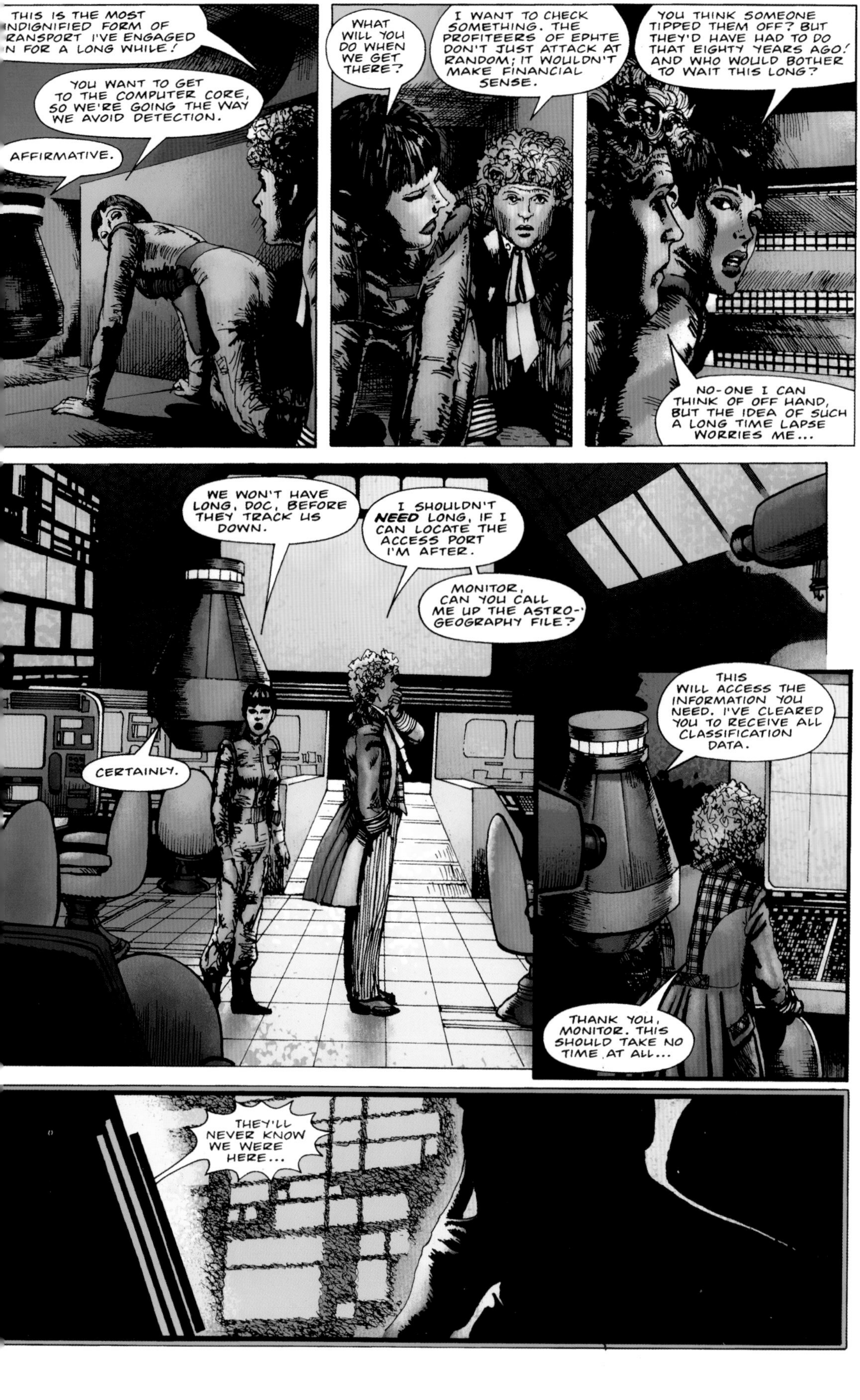
THIS IS THE MOST INDIGNIFIED FORM OF RANSPORT I'VE ENGAGED N FOR A LONG WHILE!
YOU WANT TO GET TO THE COMPUTER CORE, SO WE'RE GOING THE WAY WE AVOID DETECTION.
AFFIRMATIVE.
WHAT WILL YOU DO WHEN WE GET THERE?
I WANT TO CHECK SOMETHING. THE PROFITEERS OF EPHTE DON'T JUST ATTACK AT RANDOM; IT WOULDN'T MAKE FINANCIAL SENSE.
YOU THINK SOMEONE TIPPED THEM OFF? BUT THEY'D HAVE HAD TO DO THAT EIGHTY YEARS AGO! AND WHO WOULD BOTHER TO WAIT THIS LONG?
NO-ONE I CAN THINK OF OFF HAND, BUT THE IDEA OF SUCH A LONG TIME LAPSE WORRIES ME...
WE WON'T HAVE LONG, DOC, BEFORE THEY TRACK US DOWN.
I SHOULDN'T **NEED** LONG, IF I CAN LOCATE THE ACCESS PORT I'M AFTER.
MONITOR, CAN YOU CALL ME UP THE ASTRO-GEOGRAPHY FILE?
CERTAINLY.
THIS WILL ACCESS THE INFORMATION YOU NEED. I'VE CLEARED YOU TO RECEIVE ALL CLASSIFICATION DATA.
THANK YOU, MONITOR. THIS SHOULD TAKE NO TIME AT ALL...
THEY'LL NEVER KNOW WE WERE HERE...

LET'S SEE, ACCESS: MAYFLOWER: LOG: PRIME DATE

COME ON... COME ON...AGES SINCE I HAD TO DEAL WITH ONE OF THESE MUSEUM PIECES...

MUSEUM PIECE? THAT'S STATE OF THE ART!

THAT RATHER DEPENDS ON WHA YOU CALL *ART*... COME ON... **COME ON**...

THEY'RE HERE! THEY'LL GET IN! THEY'VE GOT THE ACCESS CODES!

THEY *DID* HAVE— I JUST CHANGED THEM! THAT SHOULD GIVE US TEN MINUTES...

BADOOM!

HOLD ON... THIS CAN'T BE RIGHT!

HURRY! THOSE BLASTS ARE GETTING MEANER AND THE SHIP ISN'T DESIGNED TO WITHSTAND AN ATTACK LIKE THIS...

MISS McALLISTA, THERE'S A VERY BIZARRE ANOMALY HERE...

NO. THAT CONFIRMS IT. BLAST! I'M AFRAID TO TELL YOU, BUT—

BADOOM! BADOOM!

WE HAVE THE UNAUDITED UNITS! PROFIT OR DIE!

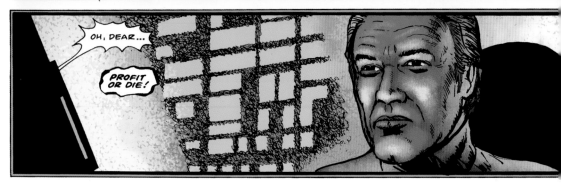

OH, DEAR...

PROFIT OR DIE!

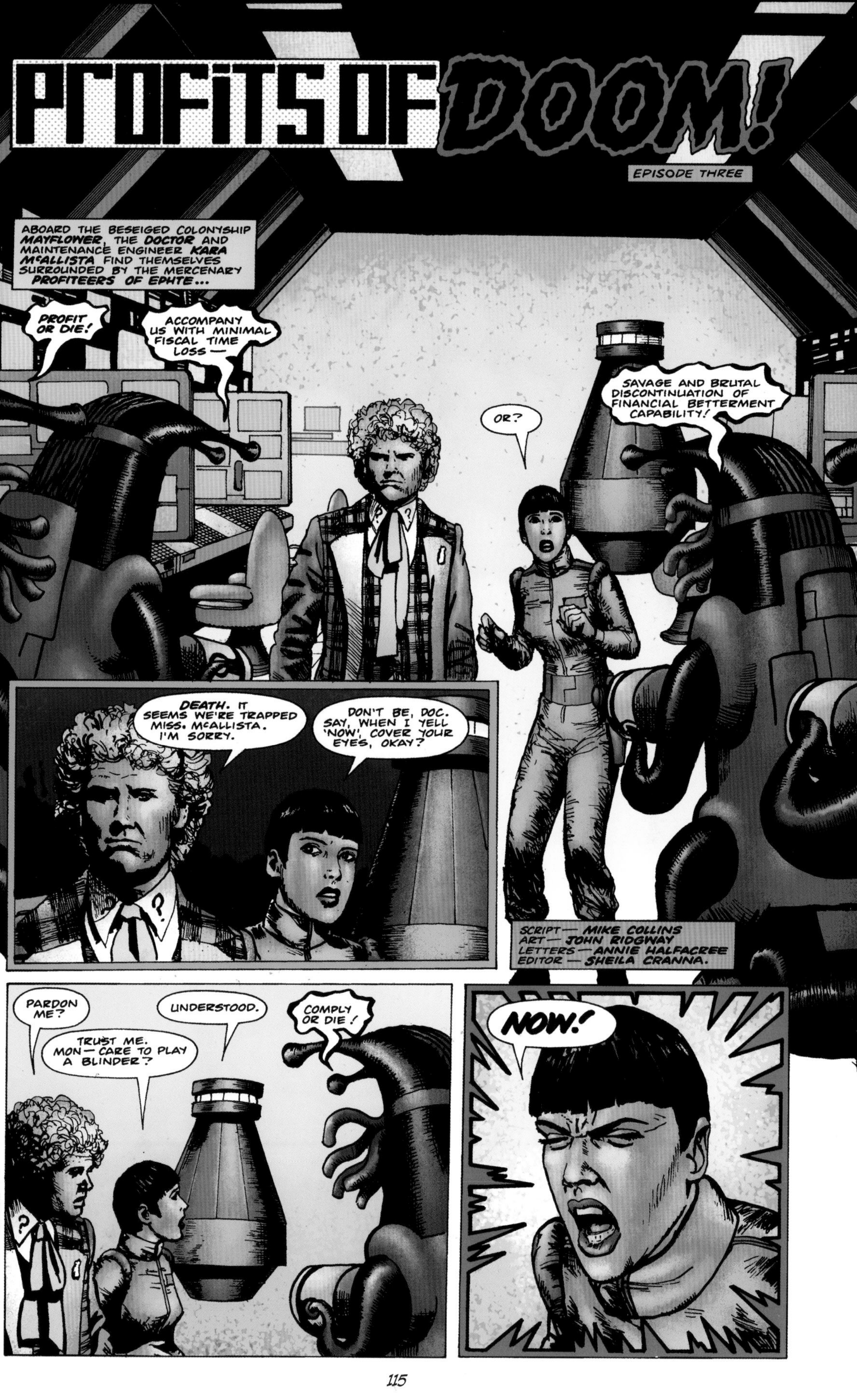
PROFITS OF DOOM!
EPISODE THREE
ABOARD THE BESEIGED COLONYSHIP MAYFLOWER, THE DOCTOR AND MAINTENANCE ENGINEER KARA McALLISTA FIND THEMSELVES SURROUNDED BY THE MERCENARY PROFITEERS OF EPHTE...
PROFIT OR DIE!
ACCOMPANY US WITH MINIMAL FISCAL TIME LOSS —
OR?
SAVAGE AND BRUTAL DISCONTINUATION OF FINANCIAL BETTERMENT CAPABILITY!
DEATH. IT SEEMS WE'RE TRAPPED MISS. McALLISTA. I'M SORRY.
DON'T BE, DOC. SAY, WHEN I YELL 'NOW', COVER YOUR EYES, OKAY?
SCRIPT — MIKE COLLINS
ART — JOHN RIDGWAY
LETTERS — ANNIE HALFACREE
EDITOR — SHEILA CRANNA.
PARDON ME?
TRUST ME. MON — CARE TO PLAY A BLINDER?
UNDERSTOOD.
COMPLY OR DIE!
NOW!

ARRRGH!

NONAUDITED UNITS HAVE ENGAGED IN SELF REMOVAL!

KEYNES' ANKLE! WHAT WILL CAPTAIN YSTRAD SAY?

UNEXPEDITED CONTRACTUAL OBLIGATION! NEGLIGENT WAGE PERIODS! NO PROFIT, NO RETURN! *FRIEDMAN'S ABACUS!!* WHAT KIND OF PROFITEERS *ARE* YOU?

THE DOCTOR'S *ELUDED* THEM AGAIN!

RUN AWAY, YOU MEAN?

BIT OF A BROAD APPLICATION OF THE WORD 'ELUDE', IF YOU ASK ME. WHEN'S HE GOING TO RESCUE US THEN, HUH? *ELUDE* US OUT OF HERE?

WILL YOU QUIT COMPLAINING? I'M SU THE DOCTOR IS PLANN FOR OUR ESCAPE AT VERY MINUTE... I HO

THANKS FOR SAVING ME AGAIN.

NO TROUBLE, DOC! LOOK, YOU WERE ABOUT TO TELL ME SOMETHING WHEN WE WERE ATTACKED. YOU'D FOUND SOMETHING IN THE FILES THAT DISTURBED YOU...

I WAS CHECKING ON THE ASTRO-GEOGRAPHY CHARTS FOR THE DESTINATION OF YOUR SHIP. IT'S SET FOR A BRAVE NEW WORLD, A LOCATION CAREFULLY CHOSEN BY YOUR SAINTLY *VARLEY GABRIEL*, YES?

LIKE I TOLD YOU. SO?

THIS LOCATION...THERE'S NOTHING THERE BUT *STARDUST*.

WHY WOULD VARLEY GABRIEL SEND A SHIP FULL OF PEOPLE OUT TO *NOWHERE*?!

INCOMPETENCE? ERROR IN ASTROGATION? NO, I THINK HE *PLANNED* FOR THE PROFITEERS TO MAKE OFF WITH THE SHIP'S *BULK* —

OH, *THANKS!*

I'M THINKING IN *HIS* TERMS, MISS McALLISTA — HE OBVIOUSLY NEEDS THE TOP DRAWER FOR SOME OFF-WORLD OPERATION... THIS ELABORATE 'COLONYSHIP' PLOY SERVED AS A COVER TO, HIS INTENTION.

IF YOU HADN'T WOKEN WHEN YOU DID, YOU WOULD HAVE COME OUT OF FREEZE AS PART-PAYMENT TO THE PROFITEERS!

THE SCALE OF THIS IS BIZARRE. WE LEFT EARTH EIGHTY *YEARS AGO* — HOW IMPORTANT MUST THE TOP DRAWER BE?

TURN THAT ON ITS HEAD — IF THE SCALE IS SO VAST, HOW *INSIGNIFICANT* IS THIS OPERATION? HOW MUCH A 'BY-THE-WAY' COMPONENT TO SOMETHING QUITE SINISTER?

OH.

AHA!

DOC, I ONLY *FIXED* MONITOR HALF-AN-HOUR PAST!

DO YOU KNOW HOW CLOSELY HE CAN LINK INTO THE COMPUTER CORE? FASCINATING. I'M PROGRAMMING HIM TO INSTRUCT THE ON-BOARD CAMERAS — WHICH WE'VE OBVIOUSLY BEEN WATCHED ON — TO INSTIGATE AUTO-MAINTENANCE ROUTINES.

AND THEN?

WHY, BACK TO THE COMPUTER CORE, TO FINISH WHAT I STARTED! THE LAST PLACE THEY'LL EXPECT TO FIND US IS THERE! NOW, MONITOR —

— COMMENCE SEQUENCE ON THE CAMERAS!

TURE SCAN IME IME: D BEAMED

LORD RUNNING: PICTURE SCAN PRIME PRIME: 2D BEAMED

SIGNALS LOST TO INSIDE THE SHIP! THAT TIMELORD'S BLASTED *MEDDLING!*

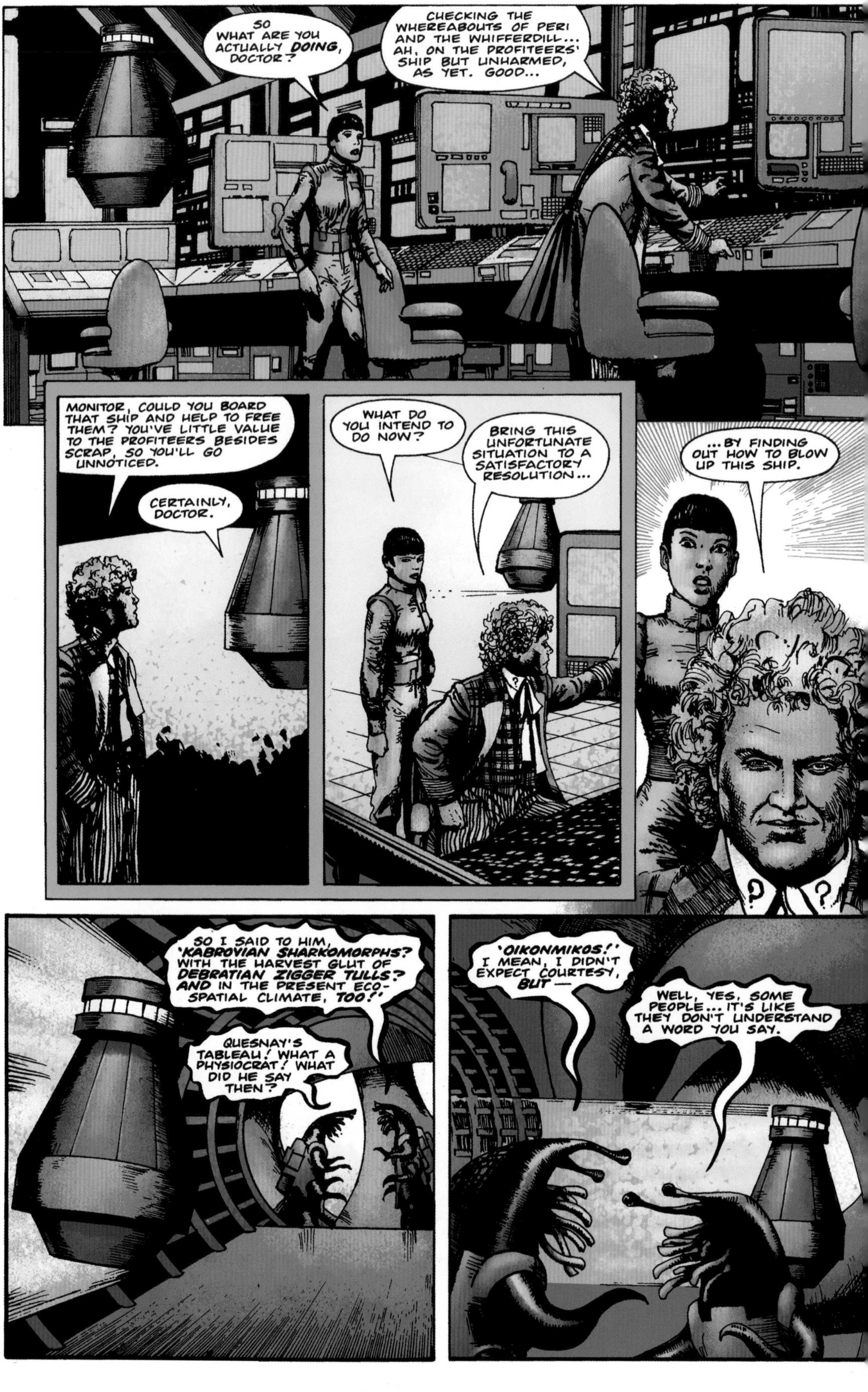
SO WHAT ARE YOU ACTUALLY DOING, DOCTOR?
CHECKING THE WHEREABOUTS OF PERI AND THE WHIFFERDILL... AH, ON THE PROFITEERS' SHIP BUT UNHARMED, AS YET. GOOD...
MONITOR, COULD YOU BOARD THAT SHIP AND HELP TO FREE THEM? YOU'VE LITTLE VALUE TO THE PROFITEERS BESIDES SCRAP, SO YOU'LL GO UNNOTICED.
CERTAINLY, DOCTOR.
WHAT DO YOU INTEND TO DO NOW?
BRING THIS UNFORTUNATE SITUATION TO A SATISFACTORY RESOLUTION...
...BY FINDING OUT HOW TO BLOW UP THIS SHIP.
SO I SAID TO HIM, 'KABROVIAN SHARKOMORPHS? WITH THE HARVEST GLUT OF DEBRATIAN ZIGGER TULLS? AND IN THE PRESENT ECO-SPATIAL CLIMATE, TOO!'
QUESNAY'S TABLEAU! WHAT A PHYSIOCRAT! WHAT DID HE SAY THEN?
'OIKONMIKOS!' I MEAN, I DIDN'T EXPECT COURTESY, BUT—
WELL, YES, SOME PEOPLE... IT'S LIKE THEY DON'T UNDERSTAND A WORD YOU SAY.

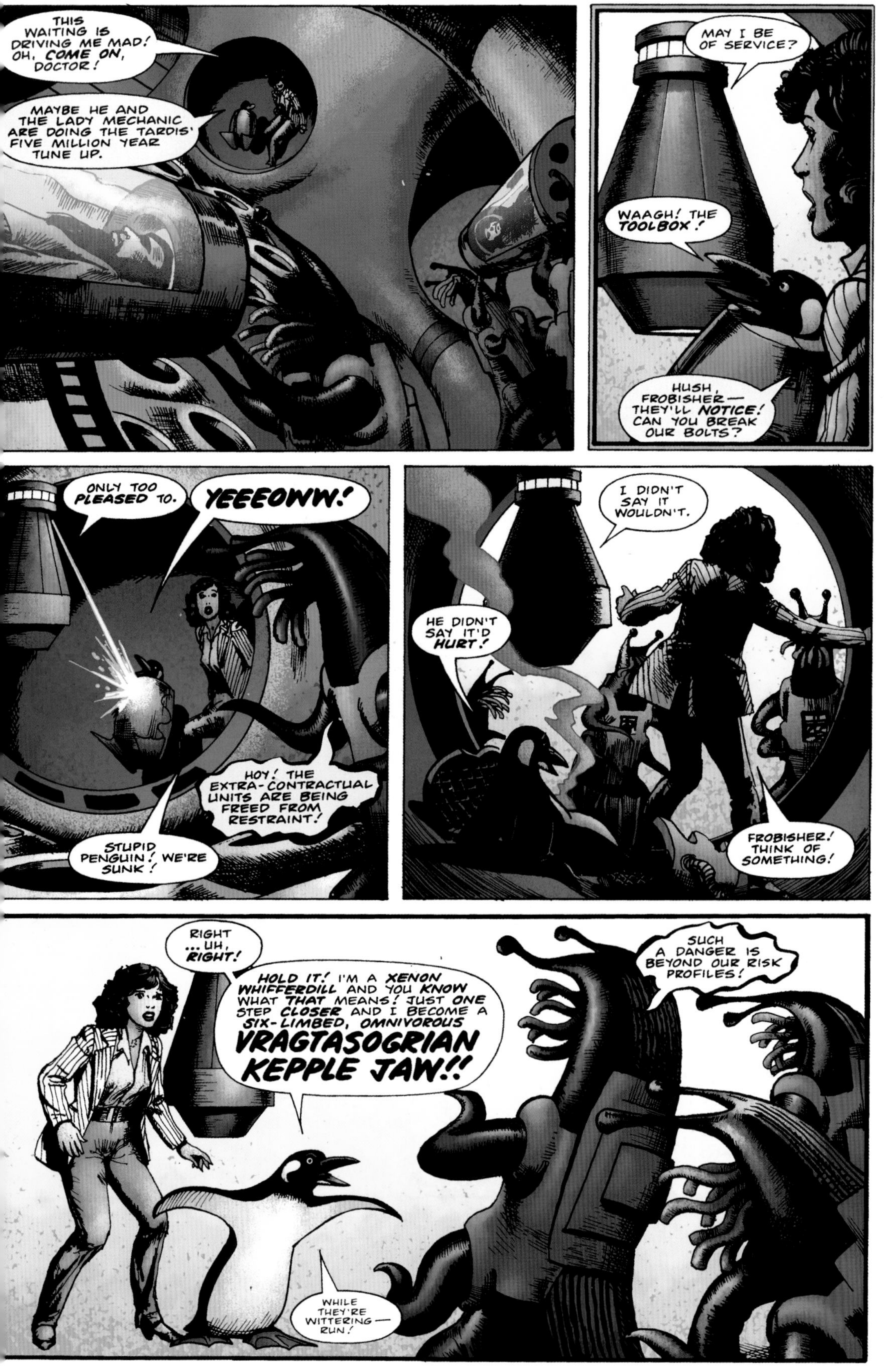
THIS WAITING IS DRIVING ME MAD! OH, COME ON, DOCTOR!
MAYBE HE AND THE LADY MECHANIC ARE DOING THE TARDIS' FIVE MILLION YEAR TUNE UP.
MAY I BE OF SERVICE?
WAAGH! THE TOOLBOX!
HUSH, FROBISHER— THEY'LL NOTICE! CAN YOU BREAK OUR BOLTS?
ONLY TOO PLEASED TO.
YEEEOWW!
HOY! THE EXTRA-CONTRACTUAL UNITS ARE BEING FREED FROM RESTRAINT!
STUPID PENGUIN! WE'RE SUNK!
I DIDN'T SAY IT WOULDN'T.
HE DIDN'T SAY IT'D HURT!
FROBISHER! THINK OF SOMETHING!
RIGHT ...UH, RIGHT!
HOLD IT! I'M A XENON WHIFFERDILL AND YOU KNOW WHAT THAT MEANS! JUST ONE STEP CLOSER AND I BECOME A SIX-LIMBED, OMNIVOROUS VRAGTASOGRIAN KEPPLE JAW!!
SUCH A DANGER IS BEYOND OUR RISK PROFILES!
WHILE THEY'RE WITTERING— RUN!

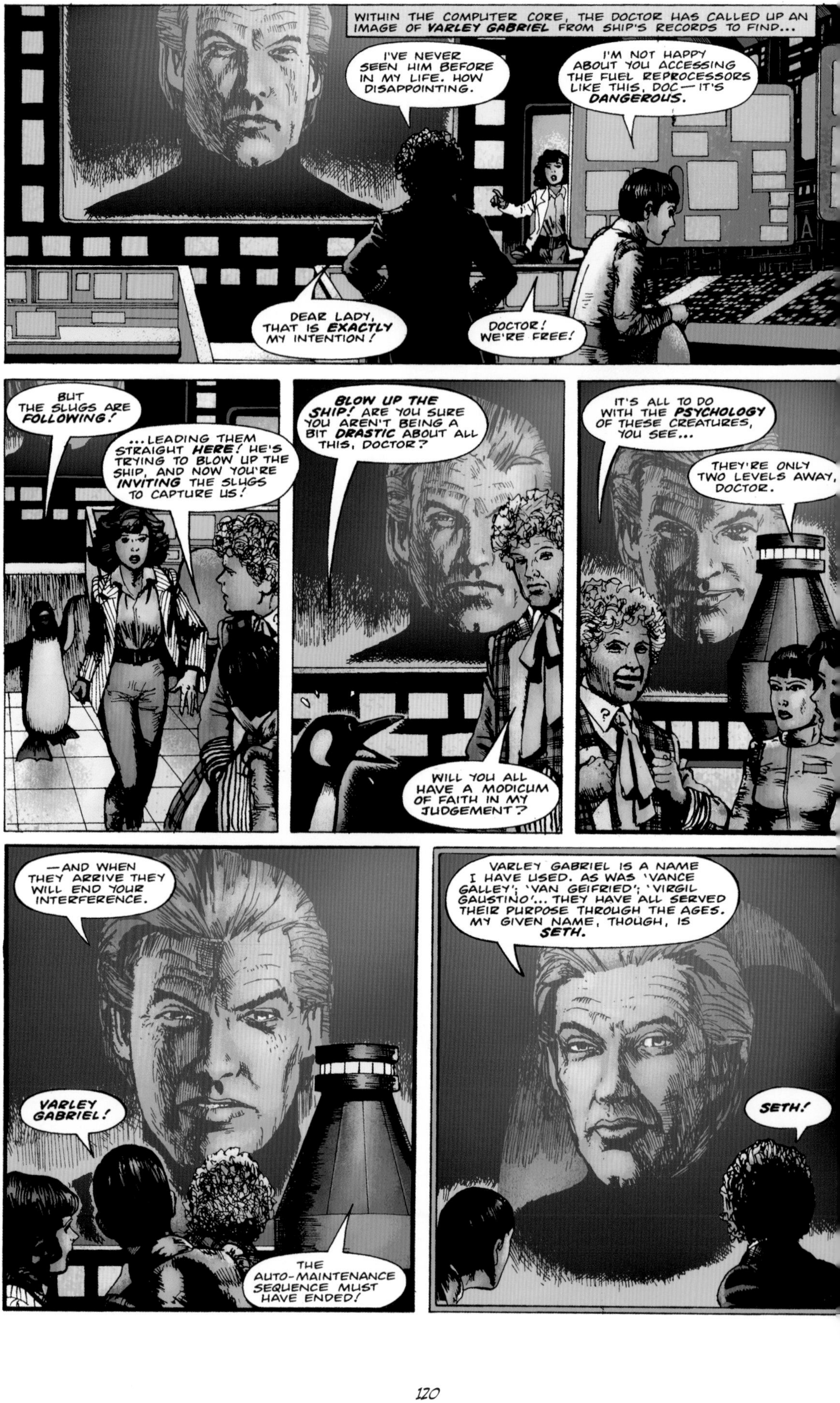
WITHIN THE COMPUTER CORE, THE DOCTOR HAS CALLED UP AN IMAGE OF VARLEY GABRIEL FROM SHIP'S RECORDS TO FIND...
I'VE NEVER SEEN HIM BEFORE IN MY LIFE. HOW DISAPPOINTING.
I'M NOT HAPPY ABOUT YOU ACCESSING THE FUEL REPROCESSORS LIKE THIS, DOC — IT'S DANGEROUS.
DEAR LADY, THAT IS EXACTLY MY INTENTION!
DOCTOR! WE'RE FREE!
BUT THE SLUGS ARE FOLLOWING!
...LEADING THEM STRAIGHT HERE! HE'S TRYING TO BLOW UP THE SHIP, AND NOW YOU'RE INVITING THE SLUGS TO CAPTURE US!
BLOW UP THE SHIP! ARE YOU SURE YOU AREN'T BEING A BIT DRASTIC ABOUT ALL THIS, DOCTOR?
WILL YOU ALL HAVE A MODICUM OF FAITH IN MY JUDGEMENT?
IT'S ALL TO DO WITH THE PSYCHOLOGY OF THESE CREATURES, YOU SEE...
THEY'RE ONLY TWO LEVELS AWAY, DOCTOR.
—AND WHEN THEY ARRIVE THEY WILL END YOUR INTERFERENCE.
VARLEY GABRIEL!
THE AUTO-MAINTENANCE SEQUENCE MUST HAVE ENDED!
VARLEY GABRIEL IS A NAME I HAVE USED. AS WAS 'VANCE GALLEY', 'VAN GEIFRIED', 'VIRGIL GAUSTINO'... THEY HAVE ALL SERVED THEIR PURPOSE THROUGH THE AGES. MY GIVEN NAME, THOUGH, IS SETH.
SETH!

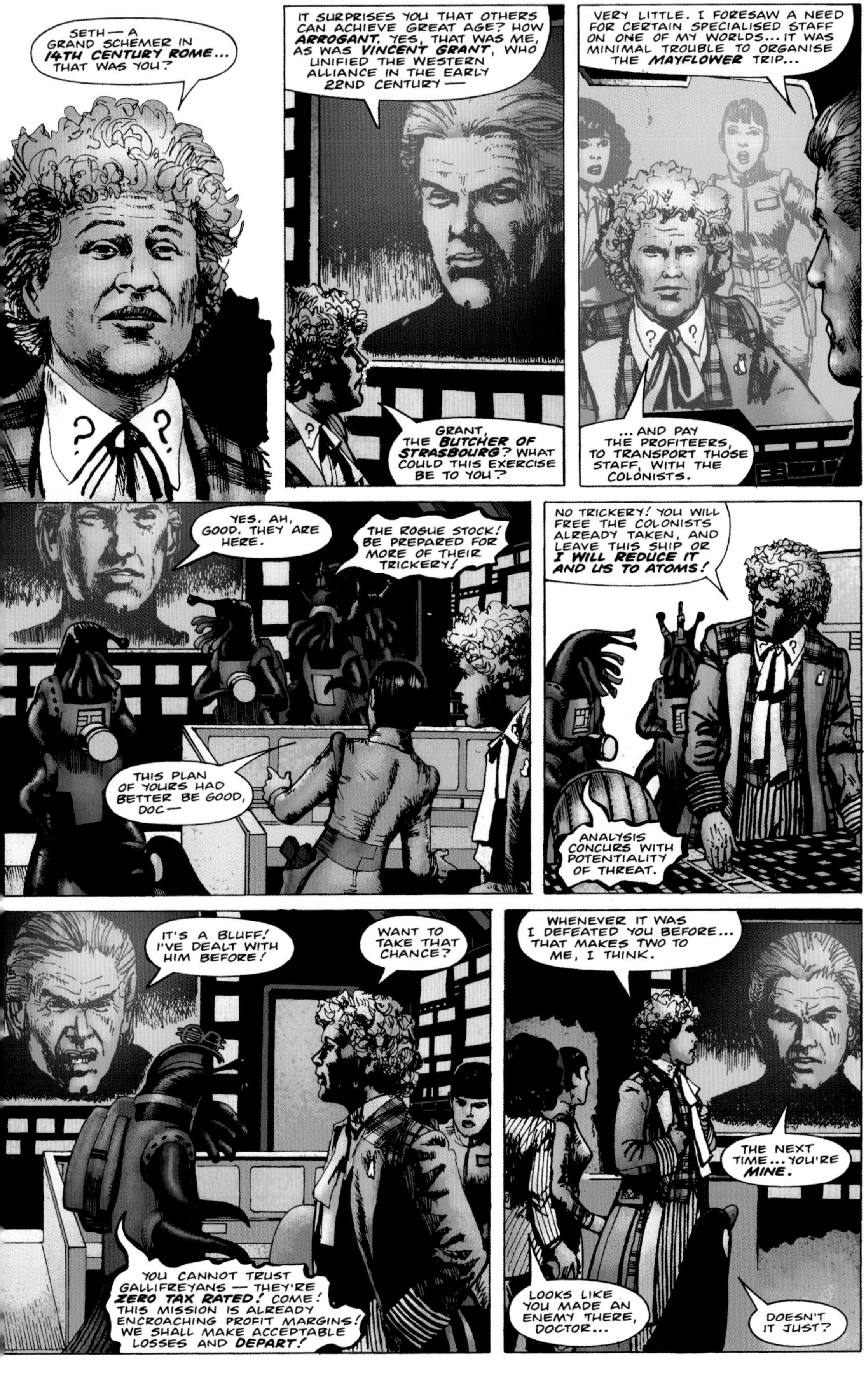
SETH — A GRAND SCHEMER IN **14TH CENTURY ROME**... THAT WAS YOU?
IT SURPRISES YOU THAT OTHERS CAN ACHIEVE GREAT AGE? HOW **ARROGANT**. YES, THAT WAS ME, AS WAS **VINCENT GRANT**, WHO UNIFIED THE WESTERN ALLIANCE IN THE EARLY 22ND CENTURY —
GRANT, THE **BUTCHER OF STRASBOURG**? WHAT COULD THIS EXERCISE BE TO YOU?
VERY LITTLE. I FORESAW A NEED FOR CERTAIN SPECIALISED STAFF ON ONE OF MY WORLDS... IT WAS MINIMAL TROUBLE TO ORGANISE THE **MAYFLOWER** TRIP...
...AND PAY THE PROFITEERS, TO TRANSPORT THOSE STAFF, WITH THE COLONISTS.
YES. AH, GOOD. THEY ARE HERE.
THE ROGUE STOCK! BE PREPARED FOR MORE OF THEIR TRICKERY!
THIS PLAN OF YOURS HAD BETTER BE GOOD, DOC—
NO TRICKERY! YOU WILL FREE THE COLONISTS ALREADY TAKEN, AND LEAVE THIS SHIP OR **I WILL REDUCE IT AND US TO ATOMS!**
ANALYSIS CONCURS WITH POTENTIALITY OF THREAT.
IT'S A BLUFF! I'VE DEALT WITH HIM BEFORE!
WANT TO TAKE THAT CHANCE?
YOU CANNOT TRUST GALLIFREYANS — THEY'RE **ZERO TAX RATED!** COME! THIS MISSION IS ALREADY ENCROACHING PROFIT MARGINS! WE SHALL MAKE ACCEPTABLE LOSSES AND **DEPART!**
WHENEVER IT WAS I DEFEATED YOU BEFORE... THAT MAKES TWO TO ME, I THINK.
THE NEXT TIME... YOU'RE **MINE**.
LOOKS LIKE YOU MADE AN ENEMY THERE, DOCTOR...
DOESN'T IT JUST?

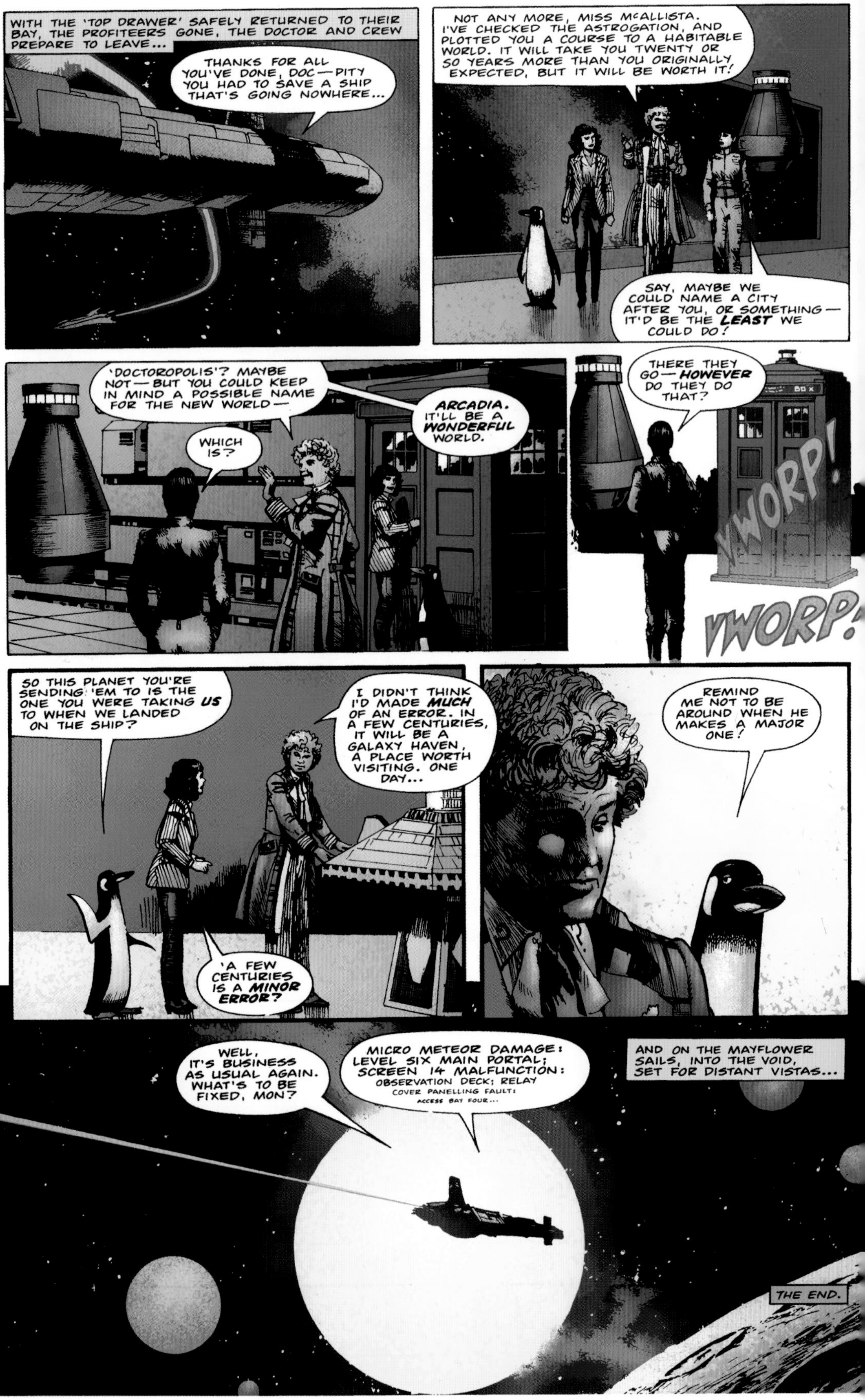

WITH THE 'TOP DRAWER' SAFELY RETURNED TO THEIR BAY, THE PROFITEERS GONE, THE DOCTOR AND CREW PREPARE TO LEAVE...
THANKS FOR ALL YOU'VE DONE, DOC—PITY YOU HAD TO SAVE A SHIP THAT'S GOING NOWHERE...
NOT ANY MORE, MISS McALLISTA. I'VE CHECKED THE ASTROGATION, AND PLOTTED YOU A COURSE TO A HABITABLE WORLD. IT WILL TAKE YOU TWENTY OR SO YEARS MORE THAN YOU ORIGINALLY EXPECTED, BUT IT WILL BE WORTH IT!
SAY, MAYBE WE COULD NAME A CITY AFTER YOU, OR SOMETHING—IT'D BE THE LEAST WE COULD DO!
'DOCTOROPOLIS'? MAYBE NOT—BUT YOU COULD KEEP IN MIND A POSSIBLE NAME FOR THE NEW WORLD—
WHICH IS?
ARCADIA. IT'LL BE A WONDERFUL WORLD.
THERE THEY GO—HOWEVER DO THEY DO THAT?
VWORP!
VWORP!
SO THIS PLANET YOU'RE SENDING 'EM TO IS THE ONE YOU WERE TAKING US TO WHEN WE LANDED ON THE SHIP?
I DIDN'T THINK I'D MADE MUCH OF AN ERROR. IN A FEW CENTURIES, IT WILL BE A GALAXY HAVEN, A PLACE WORTH VISITING. ONE DAY...
'A FEW CENTURIES IS A MINOR ERROR?
REMIND ME NOT TO BE AROUND WHEN HE MAKES A MAJOR ONE!
WELL, IT'S BUSINESS AS USUAL AGAIN. WHAT'S TO BE FIXED, MON?
MICRO METEOR DAMAGE: LEVEL SIX MAIN PORTAL; SCREEN 14 MALFUNCTION: OBSERVATION DECK; RELAY COVER PANELLING FAULT: ACCESS BAY FOUR...
AND ON THE MAYFLOWER SAILS, INTO THE VOID, SET FOR DISTANT VISTAS...
THE END.

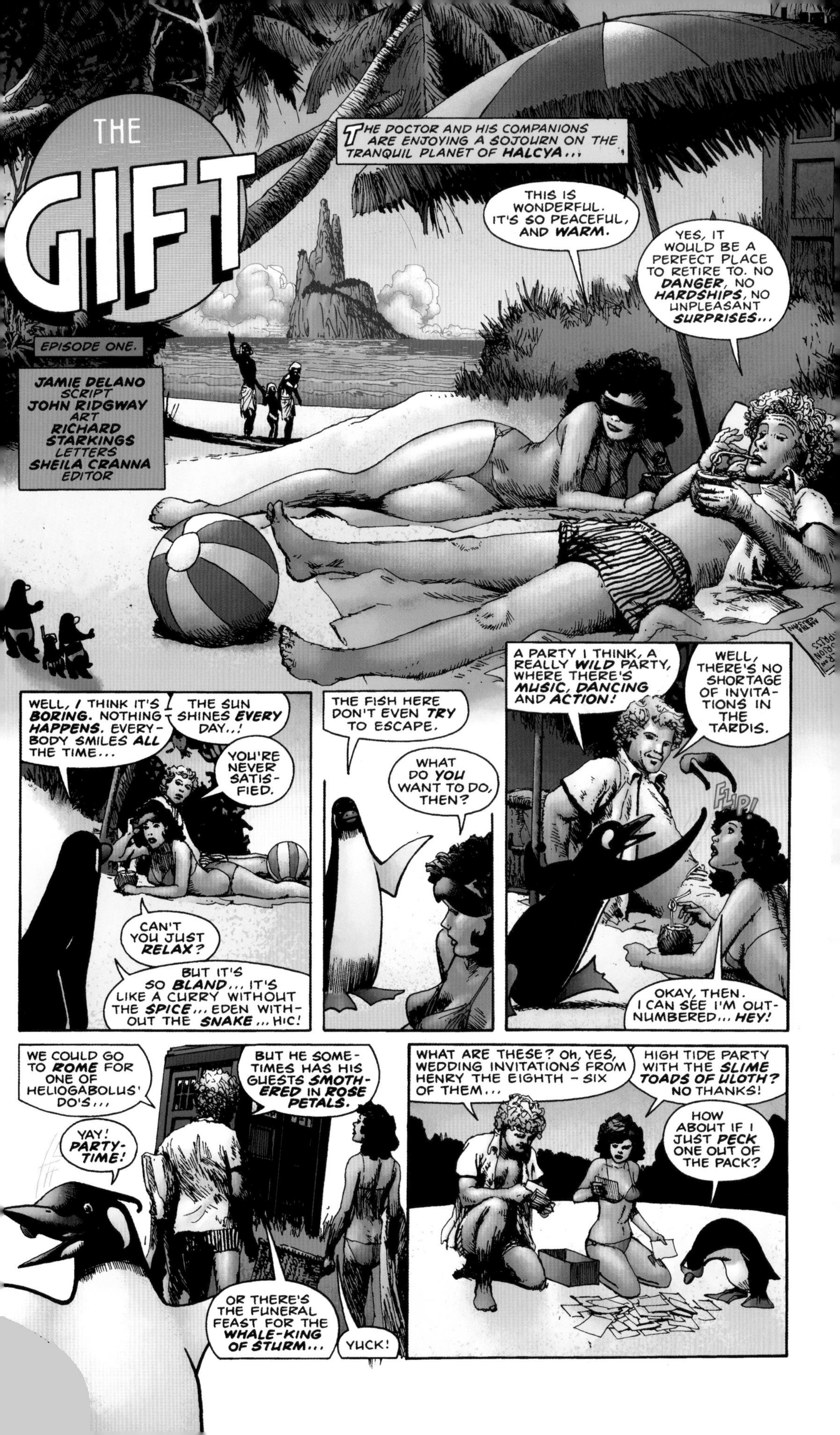
THE GIFT
THE DOCTOR AND HIS COMPANIONS ARE ENJOYING A SOJOURN ON THE TRANQUIL PLANET OF HALCYA...
THIS IS WONDERFUL. IT'S SO PEACEFUL, AND WARM.
YES, IT WOULD BE A PERFECT PLACE TO RETIRE TO. NO DANGER, NO HARDSHIPS, NO UNPLEASANT SURPRISES...
EPISODE ONE.
JAMIE DELANO SCRIPT
JOHN RIDGWAY ART
RICHARD STARKINGS LETTERS
SHEILA CRANNA EDITOR
WELL, I THINK IT'S BORING. NOTHING HAPPENS. EVERYBODY SMILES ALL THE TIME...
THE SUN SHINES EVERY DAY...!
YOU'RE NEVER SATISFIED.
CAN'T YOU JUST RELAX?
BUT IT'S SO BLAND... IT'S LIKE A CURRY WITHOUT THE SPICE... EDEN WITHOUT THE SNAKE... HIC!
THE FISH HERE DON'T EVEN TRY TO ESCAPE.
WHAT DO YOU WANT TO DO, THEN?
A PARTY I THINK, A REALLY WILD PARTY, WHERE THERE'S MUSIC, DANCING AND ACTION!
WELL, THERE'S NO SHORTAGE OF INVITATIONS IN THE TARDIS.
FLIP!
OKAY, THEN. I CAN SEE I'M OUTNUMBERED... HEY!
WE COULD GO TO ROME FOR ONE OF HELIOGABOLUS' DO'S...
BUT HE SOMETIMES HAS HIS GUESTS SMOTHERED IN ROSE PETALS.
YAY! PARTY-TIME!
OR THERE'S THE FUNERAL FEAST FOR THE WHALE-KING OF STURM...
YUCK!
WHAT ARE THESE? OH, YES, WEDDING INVITATIONS FROM HENRY THE EIGHTH - SIX OF THEM...
HIGH TIDE PARTY WITH THE SLIME TOADS OF ULOTH? NO THANKS!
HOW ABOUT IF I JUST PECK ONE OUT OF THE PACK?

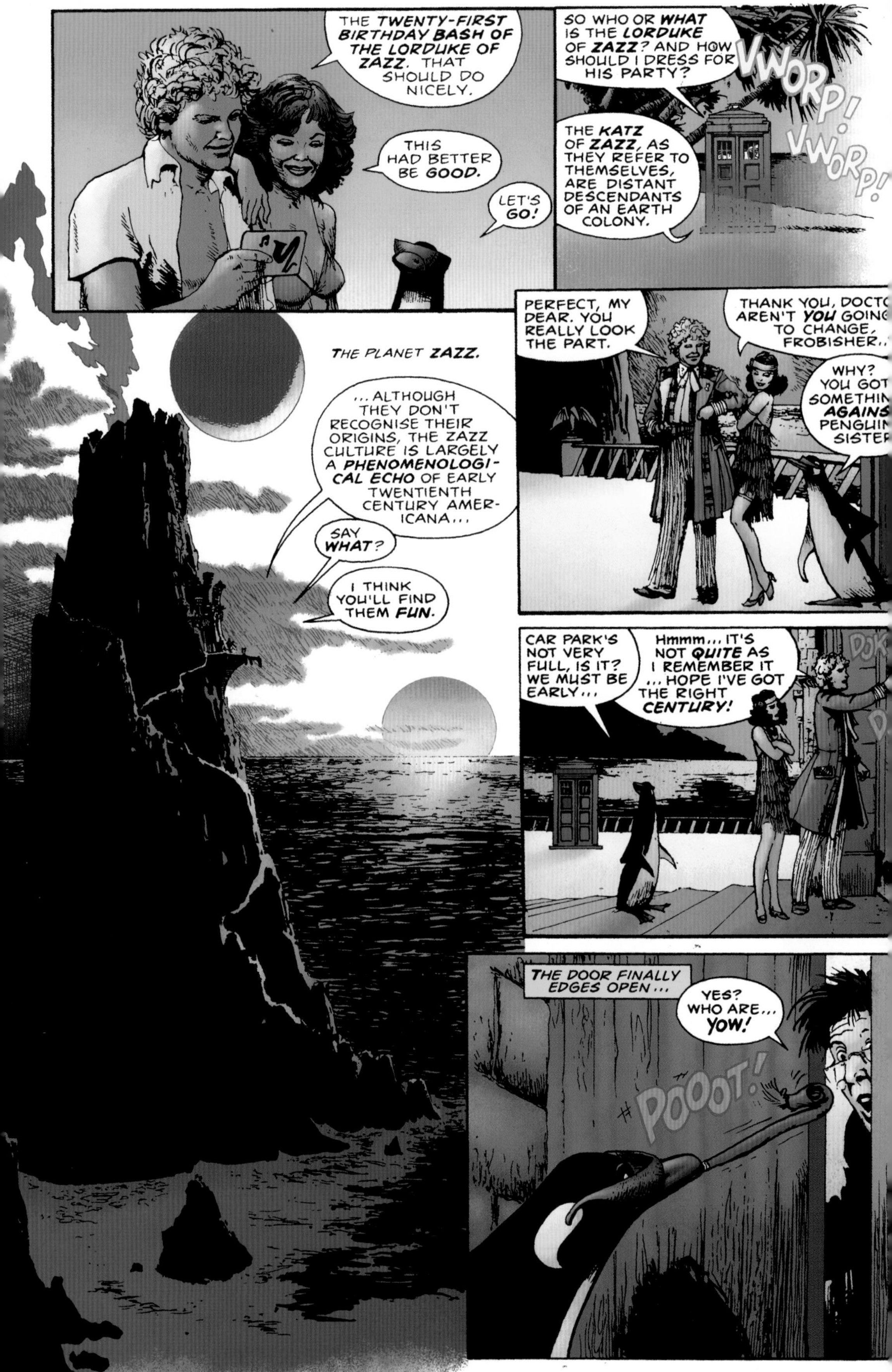

THE TWENTY-FIRST BIRTHDAY BASH OF THE LORDUKE OF ZAZZ. THAT SHOULD DO NICELY.
THIS HAD BETTER BE GOOD.
LET'S GO!
SO WHO OR WHAT IS THE LORDUKE OF ZAZZ? AND HOW SHOULD I DRESS FOR HIS PARTY?
VWORP! VWORP!
THE KATZ OF ZAZZ, AS THEY REFER TO THEMSELVES, ARE DISTANT DESCENDANTS OF AN EARTH COLONY.
THE PLANET ZAZZ.
...ALTHOUGH THEY DON'T RECOGNISE THEIR ORIGINS, THE ZAZZ CULTURE IS LARGELY A PHENOMENOLOGICAL ECHO OF EARLY TWENTIENTH CENTURY AMERICANA...
SAY WHAT?
I THINK YOU'LL FIND THEM FUN.
PERFECT, MY DEAR. YOU REALLY LOOK THE PART.
THANK YOU, DOCTO AREN'T YOU GOING TO CHANGE, FROBISHER..
WHY? YOU GOT SOMETHIN AGAINS PENGUIN SISTER
CAR PARK'S NOT VERY FULL, IS IT? WE MUST BE EARLY...
Hmmm... IT'S NOT QUITE AS I REMEMBER IT ...HOPE I'VE GOT THE RIGHT CENTURY!
THE DOOR FINALLY EDGES OPEN...
YES? WHO ARE... YOW!
POOOT!

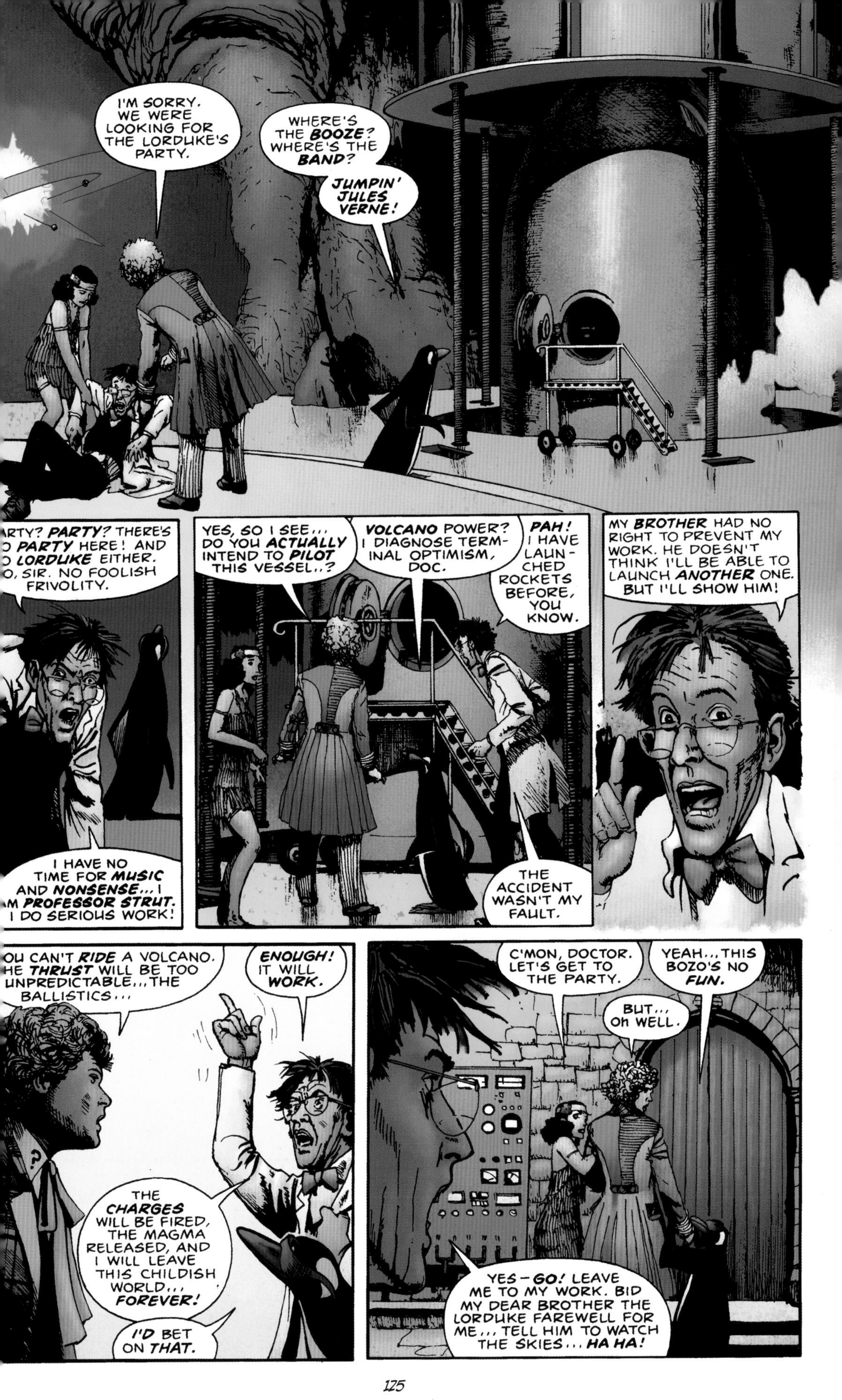
I'M SORRY. WE WERE LOOKING FOR THE LORDUKE'S PARTY.
WHERE'S THE BOOZE? WHERE'S THE BAND?
JUMPIN' JULES VERNE!
ARTY? PARTY? THERE'S O PARTY HERE! AND O LORDUKE EITHER. O, SIR. NO FOOLISH FRIVOLITY.
I HAVE NO TIME FOR MUSIC AND NONSENSE... I M PROFESSOR STRUT. I DO SERIOUS WORK!
YES, SO I SEE... DO YOU ACTUALLY INTEND TO PILOT THIS VESSEL..?
VOLCANO POWER? I DIAGNOSE TERMINAL OPTIMISM, DOC.
PAH! I HAVE LAUNCHED ROCKETS BEFORE, YOU KNOW.
THE ACCIDENT WASN'T MY FAULT.
MY BROTHER HAD NO RIGHT TO PREVENT MY WORK. HE DOESN'T THINK I'LL BE ABLE TO LAUNCH ANOTHER ONE. BUT I'LL SHOW HIM!
OU CAN'T RIDE A VOLCANO. HE THRUST WILL BE TOO UNPREDICTABLE... THE BALLISTICS...
ENOUGH! IT WILL WORK.
THE CHARGES WILL BE FIRED, THE MAGMA RELEASED, AND I WILL LEAVE THIS CHILDISH WORLD... FOREVER!
I'D BET ON THAT.
C'MON, DOCTOR. LET'S GET TO THE PARTY.
YEAH... THIS BOZO'S NO FUN.
BUT... Oh WELL.
YES—GO! LEAVE ME TO MY WORK. BID MY DEAR BROTHER THE LORDUKE FAREWELL FOR ME... TELL HIM TO WATCH THE SKIES... HA HA!

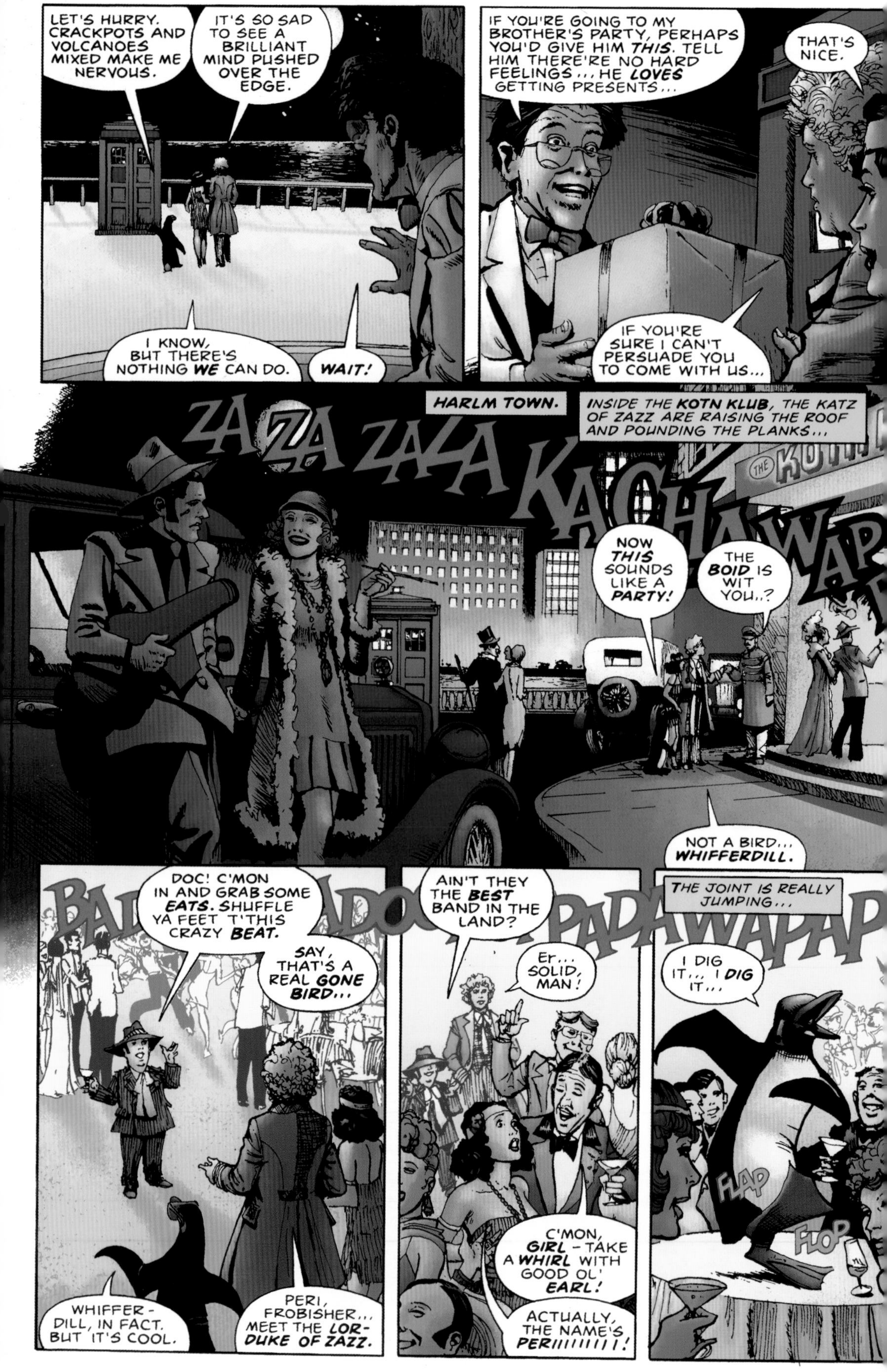
LET'S HURRY. CRACKPOTS AND VOLCANOES MIXED MAKE ME NERVOUS.
IT'S SO SAD TO SEE A BRILLIANT MIND PUSHED OVER THE EDGE.
I KNOW, BUT THERE'S NOTHING WE CAN DO.
WAIT!
IF YOU'RE GOING TO MY BROTHER'S PARTY, PERHAPS YOU'D GIVE HIM THIS. TELL HIM THERE'RE NO HARD FEELINGS... HE LOVES GETTING PRESENTS...
THAT'S NICE.
IF YOU'RE SURE I CAN'T PERSUADE YOU TO COME WITH US...
HARLM TOWN.
INSIDE THE KOTN KLUB, THE KATZ OF ZAZZ ARE RAISING THE ROOF AND POUNDING THE PLANKS...
ZAZAZAZALA KACHAWAP
NOW THIS SOUNDS LIKE A PARTY!
THE BOID IS WIT YOU..?
NOT A BIRD... WHIFFERDILL.
DOC! C'MON IN AND GRAB SOME EATS. SHUFFLE YA FEET T'THIS CRAZY BEAT.
SAY, THAT'S A REAL GONE BIRD...
WHIFFER-DILL, IN FACT. BUT IT'S COOL.
PERI, FROBISHER... MEET THE LOR-DUKE OF ZAZZ.
AIN'T THEY THE BEST BAND IN THE LAND?
Er... SOLID, MAN!
C'MON, GIRL - TAKE A WHIRL WITH GOOD OL' EARL!
ACTUALLY, THE NAME'S PERIIIIIIIII!
THE JOINT IS REALLY JUMPING...
PADAWAPAP
I DIG IT... I DIG IT...
FLAP
FLOP

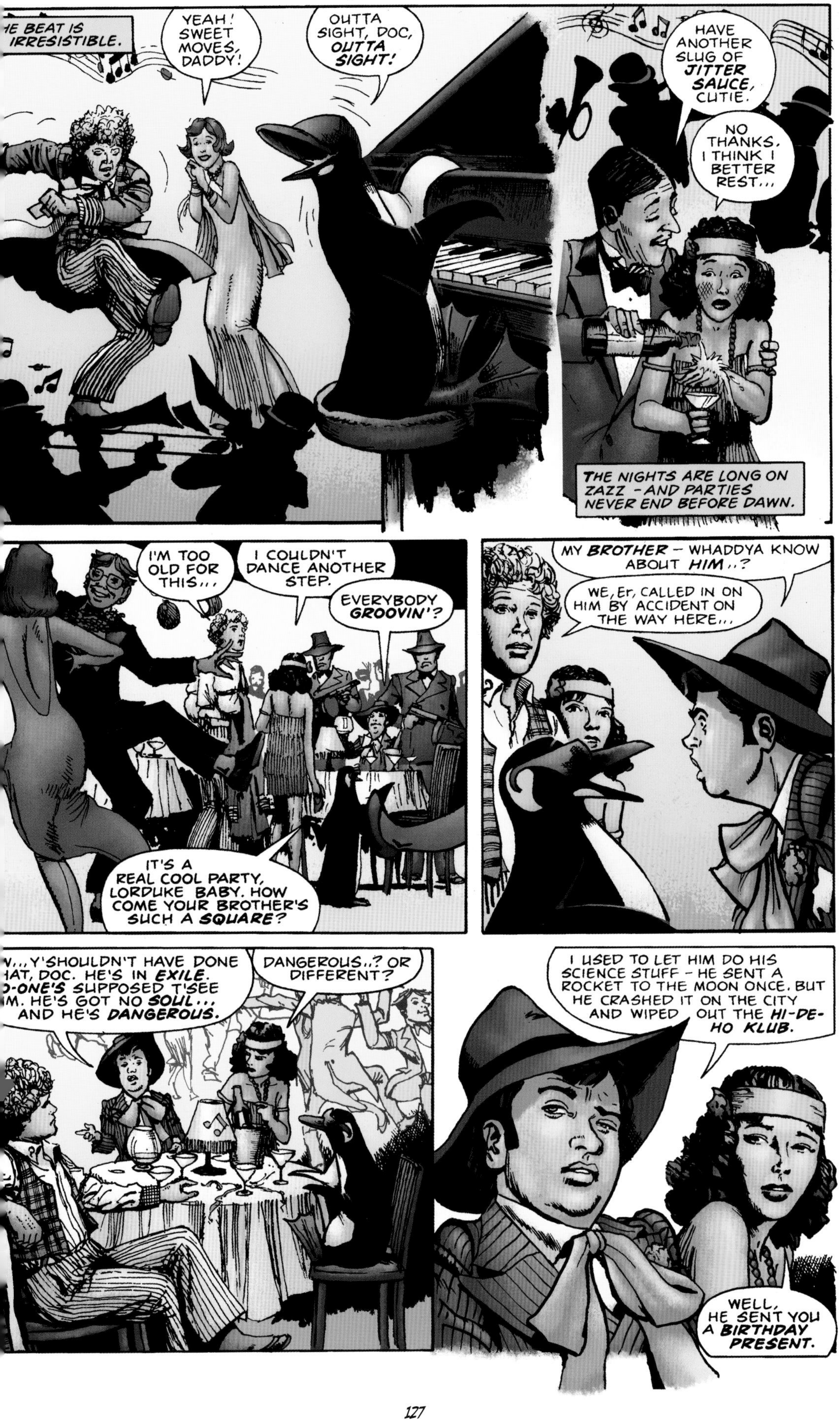

HE BEAT IS IRRESISTIBLE.
YEAH! SWEET MOVES, DADDY!
OUTTA SIGHT, DOC, OUTTA SIGHT!
HAVE ANOTHER SLUG OF JITTER SAUCE, CUTIE.
NO THANKS. I THINK I BETTER REST...
THE NIGHTS ARE LONG ON ZAZZ - AND PARTIES NEVER END BEFORE DAWN.
I'M TOO OLD FOR THIS...
I COULDN'T DANCE ANOTHER STEP.
EVERYBODY GROOVIN'?
IT'S A REAL COOL PARTY, LORDUKE BABY. HOW COME YOUR BROTHER'S SUCH A SQUARE?
MY BROTHER - WHADDYA KNOW ABOUT HIM..?
WE, Er, CALLED IN ON HIM BY ACCIDENT ON THE WAY HERE...
W...Y'SHOULDN'T HAVE DONE HAT, DOC. HE'S IN EXILE. O-ONE'S SUPPOSED T'SEE IM. HE'S GOT NO SOUL... AND HE'S DANGEROUS.
DANGEROUS..? OR DIFFERENT?
I USED TO LET HIM DO HIS SCIENCE STUFF - HE SENT A ROCKET TO THE MOON ONCE. BUT HE CRASHED IT ON THE CITY AND WIPED OUT THE HI-DE-HO KLUB.
WELL, HE SENT YOU A BIRTHDAY PRESENT.

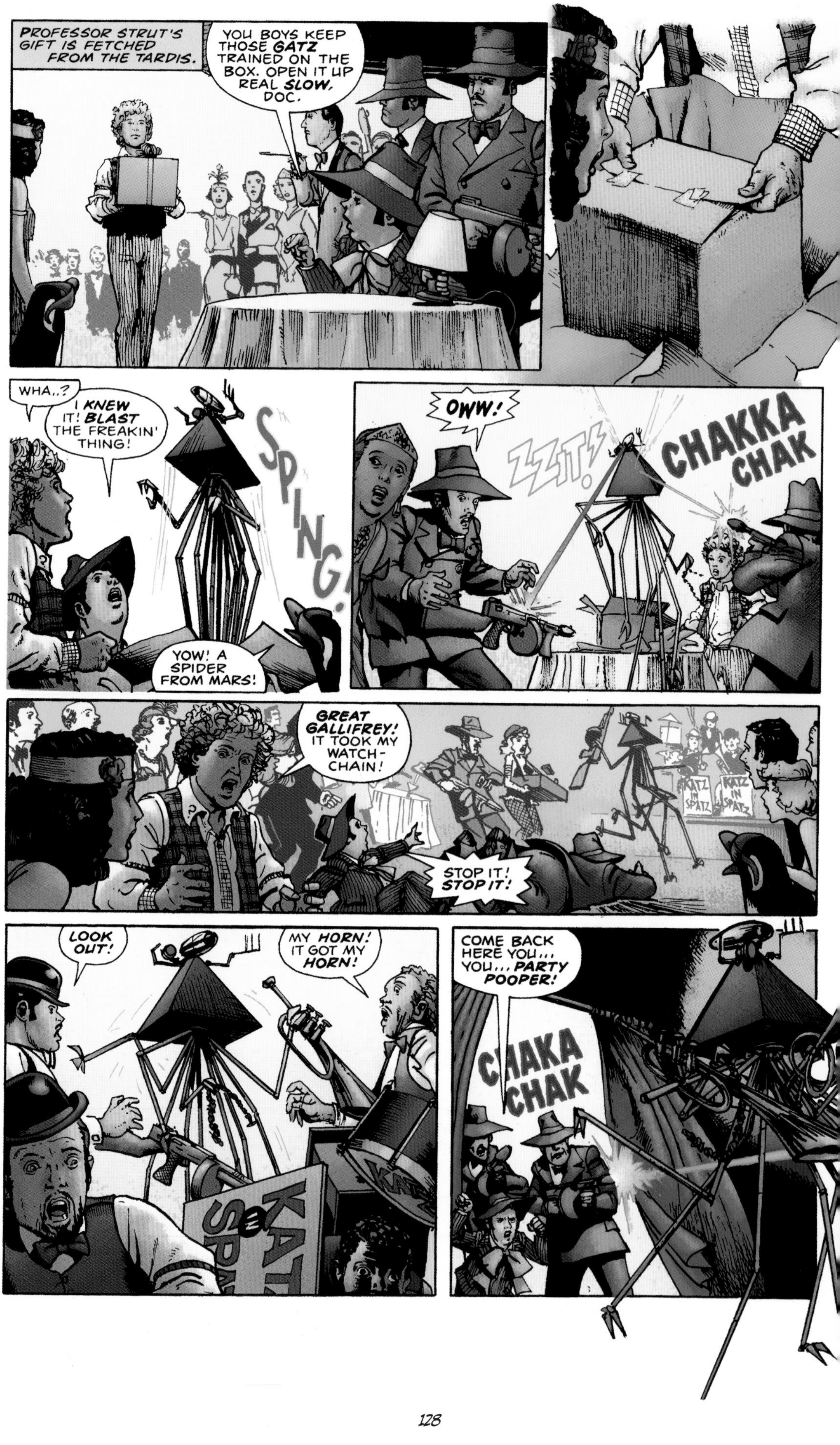
PROFESSOR STRUT'S GIFT IS FETCHED FROM THE TARDIS.
YOU BOYS KEEP THOSE GATZ TRAINED ON THE BOX. OPEN IT UP REAL SLOW, DOC.
WHA..?
I KNEW IT! BLAST THE FREAKIN' THING!
SPING!
YOW! A SPIDER FROM MARS!
OWW!
ZZIT!
CHAKKA CHAK
GREAT GALLIFREY! IT TOOK MY WATCH-CHAIN!
KATZ IN SPATZ
KATZ IN SPATZ
STOP IT! STOP IT!
LOOK OUT!
MY HORN! IT GOT MY HORN!
COME BACK HERE YOU... YOU... PARTY POOPER!
CHAKA CHAK

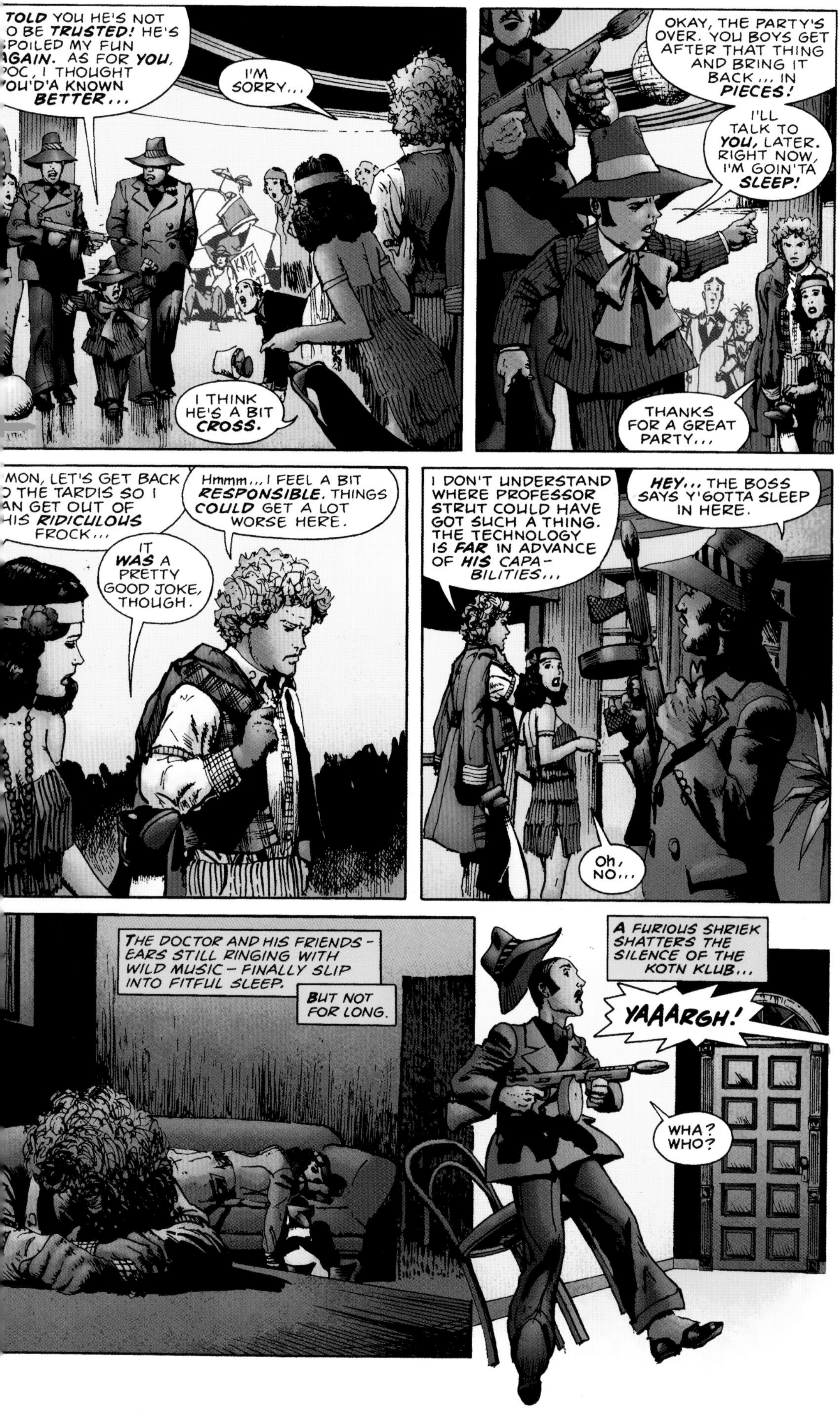
TOLD YOU HE'S NOT
O BE TRUSTED! HE'S
POILED MY FUN
AGAIN. AS FOR YOU,
OC, I THOUGHT
OU'D'A KNOWN
BETTER...
I'M SORRY...
I THINK HE'S A BIT CROSS.
OKAY, THE PARTY'S OVER. YOU BOYS GET AFTER THAT THING AND BRING IT BACK... IN PIECES!
I'LL TALK TO YOU, LATER. RIGHT NOW, I'M GOIN'TA SLEEP!
THANKS FOR A GREAT PARTY...
MON, LET'S GET BACK
O THE TARDIS SO I
AN GET OUT OF
HIS RIDICULOUS
FROCK...
IT WAS A PRETTY GOOD JOKE, THOUGH.
Hmmm... I FEEL A BIT RESPONSIBLE. THINGS COULD GET A LOT WORSE HERE.
I DON'T UNDERSTAND WHERE PROFESSOR STRUT COULD HAVE GOT SUCH A THING. THE TECHNOLOGY IS FAR IN ADVANCE OF HIS CAPA-BILITIES...
HEY... THE BOSS SAYS Y'GOTTA SLEEP IN HERE.
Oh, NO...
THE DOCTOR AND HIS FRIENDS - EARS STILL RINGING WITH WILD MUSIC - FINALLY SLIP INTO FITFUL SLEEP.
BUT NOT FOR LONG.
A FURIOUS SHRIEK SHATTERS THE SILENCE OF THE KOTN KLUB...
YAAARGH!
WHA? WHO?

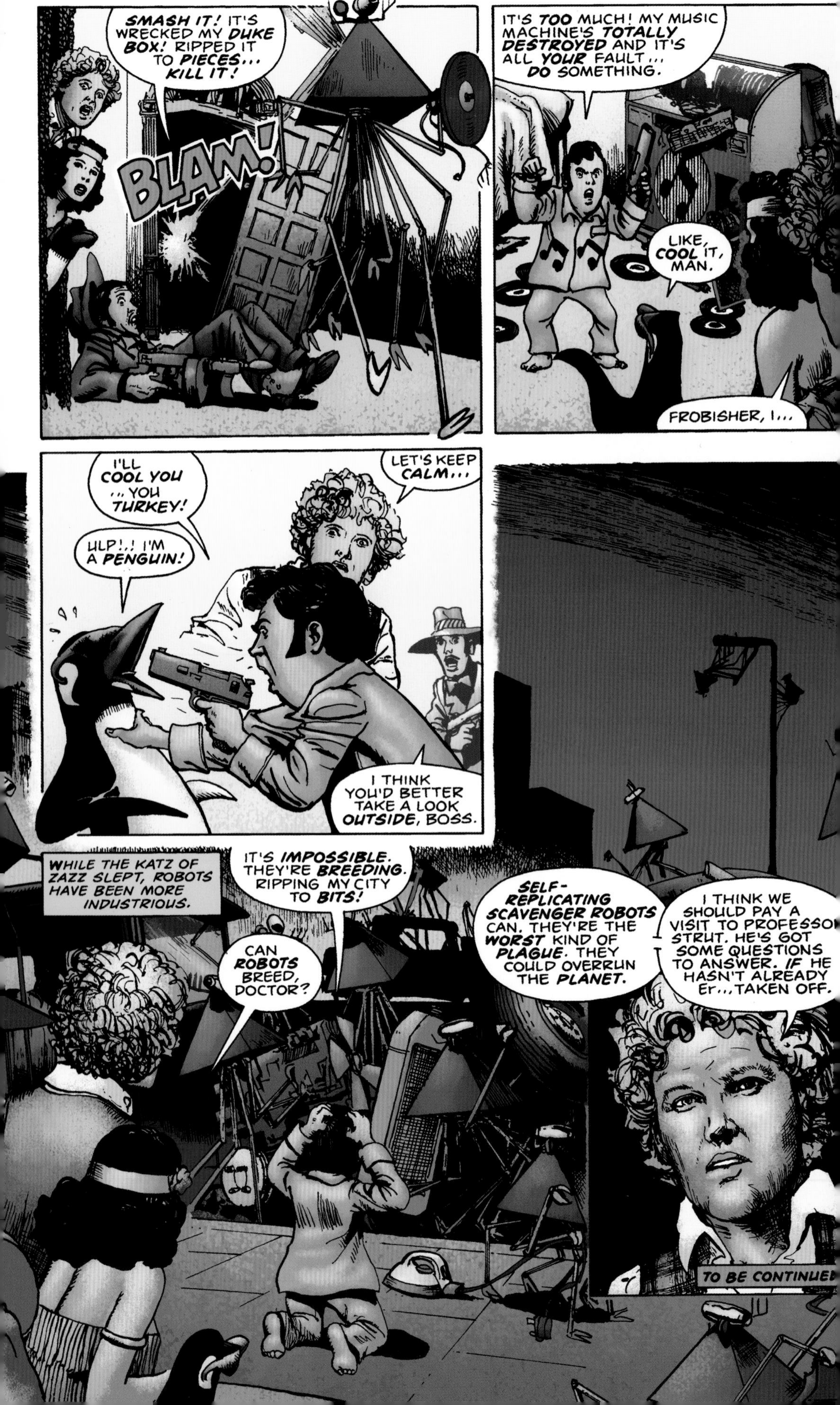
SMASH IT! IT'S WRECKED MY DUKE BOX! RIPPED IT TO PIECES... KILL IT!
BLAM!
IT'S TOO MUCH! MY MUSIC MACHINE'S TOTALLY DESTROYED AND IT'S ALL YOUR FAULT... DO SOMETHING.
LIKE, COOL IT, MAN.
FROBISHER, I...
I'LL COOL YOU ... YOU TURKEY!
LET'S KEEP CALM...
ULP!..! I'M A PENGUIN!
I THINK YOU'D BETTER TAKE A LOOK OUTSIDE, BOSS.
WHILE THE KATZ OF ZAZZ SLEPT, ROBOTS HAVE BEEN MORE INDUSTRIOUS.
IT'S IMPOSSIBLE. THEY'RE BREEDING. RIPPING MY CITY TO BITS!
CAN ROBOTS BREED, DOCTOR?
SELF-REPLICATING SCAVENGER ROBOTS CAN. THEY'RE THE WORST KIND OF PLAGUE. THEY COULD OVERRUN THE PLANET.
I THINK WE SHOULD PAY A VISIT TO PROFESSO STRUT. HE'S GOT SOME QUESTIONS TO ANSWER. IF HE HASN'T ALREADY Er...TAKEN OFF.
TO BE CONTINUE

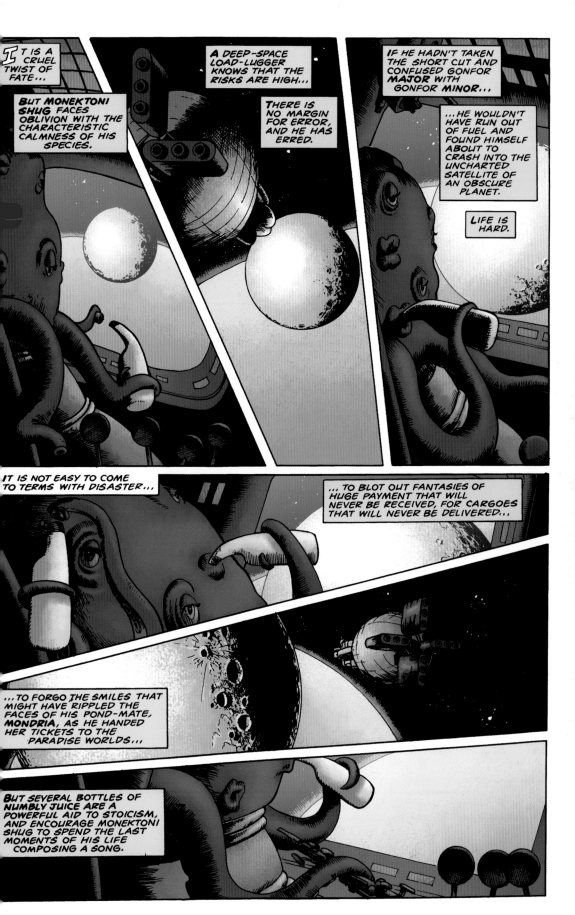

IT IS A CRUEL TWIST OF FATE...

BUT MONEKTONI SHUG FACES OBLIVION WITH THE CHARACTERISTIC CALMNESS OF HIS SPECIES.

A DEEP-SPACE LOAD-LUGGER KNOWS THAT THE RISKS ARE HIGH...

THERE IS NO MARGIN FOR ERROR, AND HE HAS ERRED.

IF HE HADN'T TAKEN THE SHORT CUT AND CONFUSED GONFOR MAJOR WITH GONFOR MINOR...

...HE WOULDN'T HAVE RUN OUT OF FUEL AND FOUND HIMSELF ABOUT TO CRASH INTO THE UNCHARTED SATELLITE OF AN OBSCURE PLANET.

LIFE IS HARD.

IT IS NOT EASY TO COME TO TERMS WITH DISASTER...

..., TO BLOT OUT FANTASIES OF HUGE PAYMENT THAT WILL NEVER BE RECEIVED, FOR CARGOES THAT WILL NEVER BE DELIVERED...

...TO FORGO THE SMILES THAT MIGHT HAVE RIPPLED THE FACES OF HIS POND-MATE, MONDRIA, AS HE HANDED HER TICKETS TO THE PARADISE WORLDS...

BUT SEVERAL BOTTLES OF NUMBLY JUICE ARE A POWERFUL AID TO STOICISM, AND ENCOURAGE MONEKTONI SHUG TO SPEND THE LAST MOMENTS OF HIS LIFE COMPOSING A SONG.

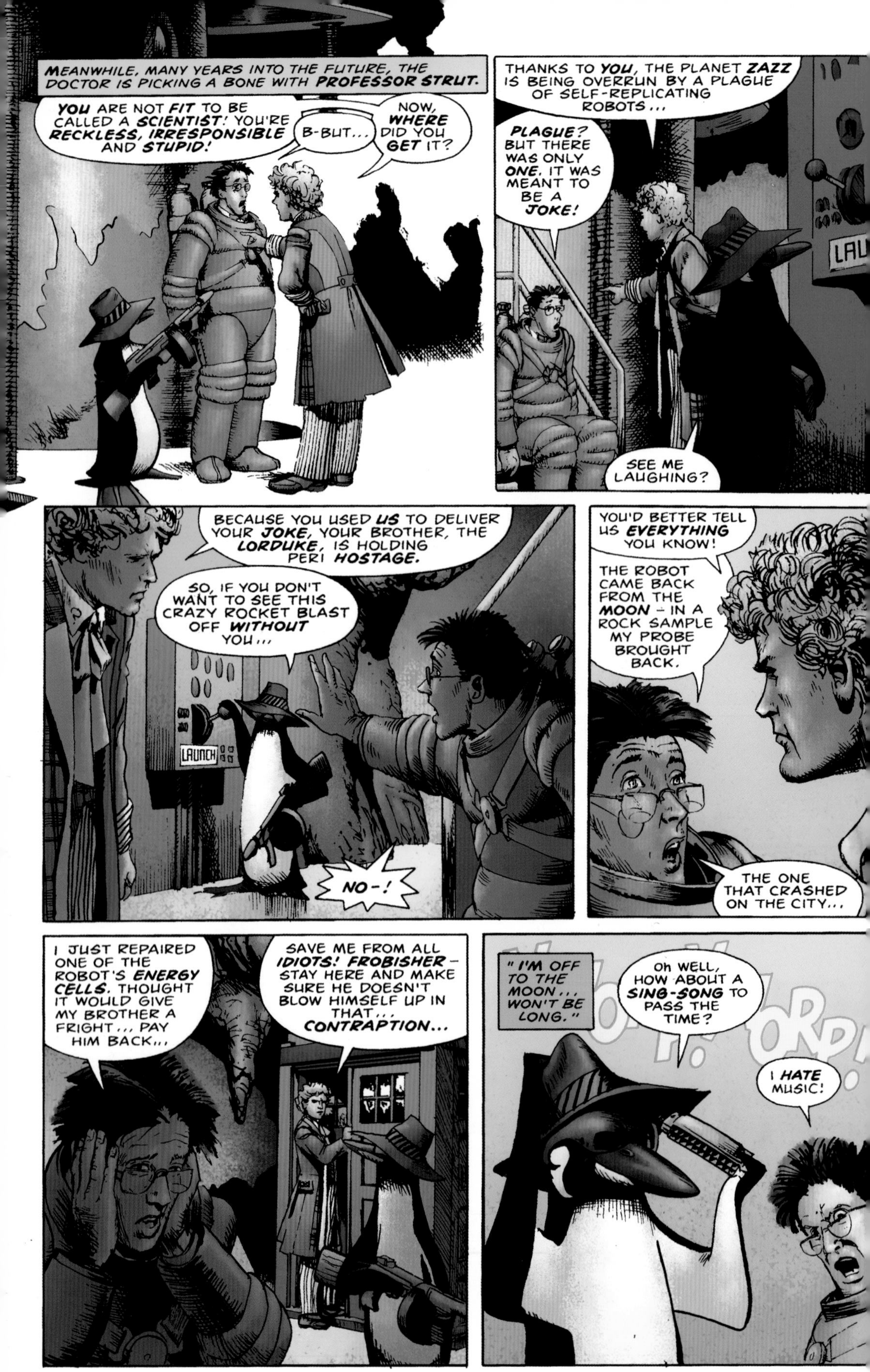
MEANWHILE, MANY YEARS INTO THE FUTURE, THE DOCTOR IS PICKING A BONE WITH PROFESSOR STRUT.
YOU ARE NOT FIT TO BE CALLED A SCIENTIST! YOU'RE RECKLESS, IRRESPONSIBLE AND STUPID!
B-BUT...
NOW, WHERE DID YOU GET IT?
THANKS TO YOU, THE PLANET ZAZZ IS BEING OVERRUN BY A PLAGUE OF SELF-REPLICATING ROBOTS...
PLAGUE? BUT THERE WAS ONLY ONE. IT WAS MEANT TO BE A JOKE!
SEE ME LAUGHING?
BECAUSE YOU USED US TO DELIVER YOUR JOKE, YOUR BROTHER, THE LORDUKE, IS HOLDING PERI HOSTAGE.
SO, IF YOU DON'T WANT TO SEE THIS CRAZY ROCKET BLAST OFF WITHOUT YOU...
LAUNCH
NO-!
YOU'D BETTER TELL US EVERYTHING YOU KNOW!
THE ROBOT CAME BACK FROM THE MOON - IN A ROCK SAMPLE MY PROBE BROUGHT BACK.
THE ONE THAT CRASHED ON THE CITY...
I JUST REPAIRED ONE OF THE ROBOT'S ENERGY CELLS. THOUGHT IT WOULD GIVE MY BROTHER A FRIGHT... PAY HIM BACK...
SAVE ME FROM ALL IDIOTS! FROBISHER - STAY HERE AND MAKE SURE HE DOESN'T BLOW HIMSELF UP IN THAT... CONTRAPTION...
"I'M OFF TO THE MOON... WON'T BE LONG."
Oh WELL, HOW ABOUT A SING-SONG TO PASS THE TIME?
I HATE MUSIC!

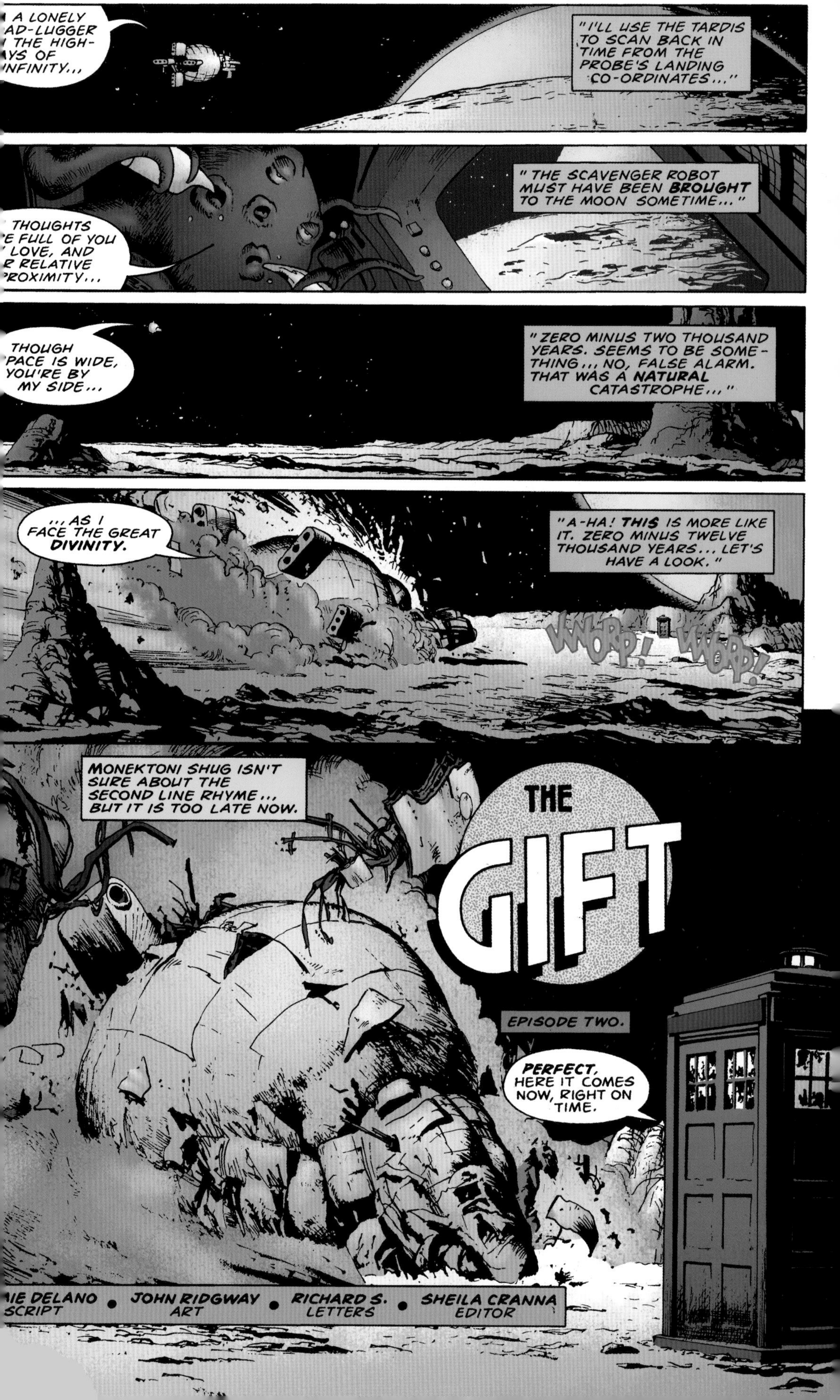
A LONELY
AD-LUGGER
THE HIGH-
YS OF
NFINITY...
"I'LL USE THE TARDIS TO SCAN BACK IN TIME FROM THE PROBE'S LANDING CO-ORDINATES..."
THOUGHTS
E FULL OF YOU
LOVE, AND
R RELATIVE
PROXIMITY...
"THE SCAVENGER ROBOT MUST HAVE BEEN BROUGHT TO THE MOON SOMETIME..."
THOUGH
PACE IS WIDE,
YOU'RE BY
MY SIDE...
"ZERO MINUS TWO THOUSAND YEARS. SEEMS TO BE SOME-THING... NO, FALSE ALARM. THAT WAS A NATURAL CATASTROPHE..."
...AS I FACE THE GREAT DIVINITY.
"A-HA! THIS IS MORE LIKE IT. ZERO MINUS TWELVE THOUSAND YEARS... LET'S HAVE A LOOK."
VWORP! VWORP!
MONEKTONI SHUG ISN'T SURE ABOUT THE SECOND LINE RHYME... BUT IT IS TOO LATE NOW.
THE GIFT
EPISODE TWO.
PERFECT, HERE IT COMES NOW, RIGHT ON TIME.
IE DELANO SCRIPT • JOHN RIDGWAY ART • RICHARD S. LETTERS • SHEILA CRANNA EDITOR

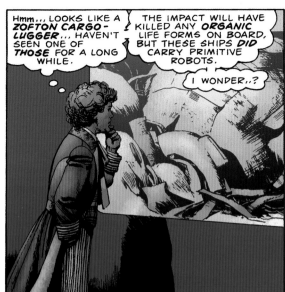

Hmm..., LOOKS LIKE A **ZOFTON CARGO-LUGGER**... HAVEN'T SEEN ONE OF **THOSE** FOR A LONG WHILE.

THE IMPACT WILL HAVE KILLED ANY **ORGANIC** LIFE FORMS ON BOARD, BUT THESE SHIPS **DID** CARRY PRIMITIVE ROBOTS.

I WONDER..?

" I THINK I'LL JUST SKIP FORWARD A BIT. "

TIME PASSES. BUT IN THE MAINTENANCE BAY OF THE SHATTERED LUGGER AN INTELLIGENCE SURVIVES...

RISING FROM ITS NEST OF DEBRIS, THE CRIPPLED SERVOTRON STRUGGLES HEROICALLY TO FULFIL ITS PRIME DIRECTIVE...

SURVEY DAMAGE AND REPAIR.

LOGIC TELLS IT THAT FIRST IT MUST RESTORE EFFICIENCY TO ITS OWN MECHANISMS...

SCAVENGING PARTS FROM THE SURROUNDING DEVASTATION, THE PHYSICIAN HEALS ITSELF.

THE DAMAGE INVENTORY TAKES TWO YEARS TO COMPILE. BUT A BASIC MODEL SERVOTRON DOES NOT THINK IN TERMS OF **TIME**.

IT BEGINS WITH BEGINNINGS AND PROCEEDS TO FULL OPERATING EFFICIENCY.

WITH PARTS SALVAGED FROM THE LUGGER'S ELECTRONIC CARGO, IT REPAIRS THE RADARSCOPES AND DISTRESS BEACON...

...AND WITHIN A YEAR, IS READY TO APPLY ITSELF TO THE SHIP'S STRUCTURAL DAMAGE...

THE SERVOTRON HAS BARELY EMBARKED UPON ITS GIGANTIC LABOURS, WHEN IT DETECTS A SUDDEN PRESENCE...

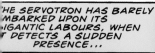
ZERO MINUS 11950 GS YEARS

Ah, *MOVEMENT!* BUT IT'S ONLY A PRIMITIVE MAINTENANCE ROBOT, THE SCAVENGERS ARE *FAR* MORE ADVANCED. THIS IS GETTING INTERESTING.

"ONWARD, EVER ONWARD."

VWORP!

VWORP!

THE PRESENCE IS AS QUICKLY GONE AGAIN. THE SERVOTRON FILES IT UNDER *ANOMALY* AND CONTINUES ITS PATIENT TOIL.

FOR CENTURIES, THE ULTIMATE *FUTILITY* OF ITS *TASK* IS LOST ON THE SERVOTRON, UNTIL A SUDDEN DYSFUNCTION CAUSES IT TO WELD A DEXTRO-LEG TO A SUPPORT BEAM...

TWO PARALLEL CALCULATIONS HAVE CONVERGED IN A LOGIC CRASH.

ACCORDING TO ITS COMPUTATIONS, IT HAS ACCOMPLISHED ONLY TWO PER CENT RESTORATION, BUT SUSTAINED SEVENTY PER CENT WEAR AND DEGENERATION OF CAPACITY.

THE TASK IS BEYOND THE DURATION OF ITS EFFICIENCY.

SHOCKED INTO STASIS LASTING SEVERAL YEARS, THE SERVOTRON STRUGGLES TO RECONCILE THE EQUATION.

SLOWLY, IT BEGINS TO COMPREHEND AN INDEFINITE QUALITY OF EXISTENCE.

TIME. THERE IS NOT ENOUGH *TIME.*

ELECTRONS FLOW IN NEW PATTERNS. A SPARK LEAPS A GAP. THE SERVOTRON DEVELOPS ABSTRACT THOUGHT.

IF ITS CAPABILITY IS NOT SUFFICIENT TO FULFIL ITS FUNCTION, IT MUST *DUPLICATE* ITS CAPABILITY.

IT MUST MULTIPLY, REGENERATE — *REPRODUCE.*

AS WITH MOST PRIMITIVE INTELLIGENCES, THE FIRST THING THE SERVOTRON TEACHES ITS OFFSPRING IS *SURVIVAL.*

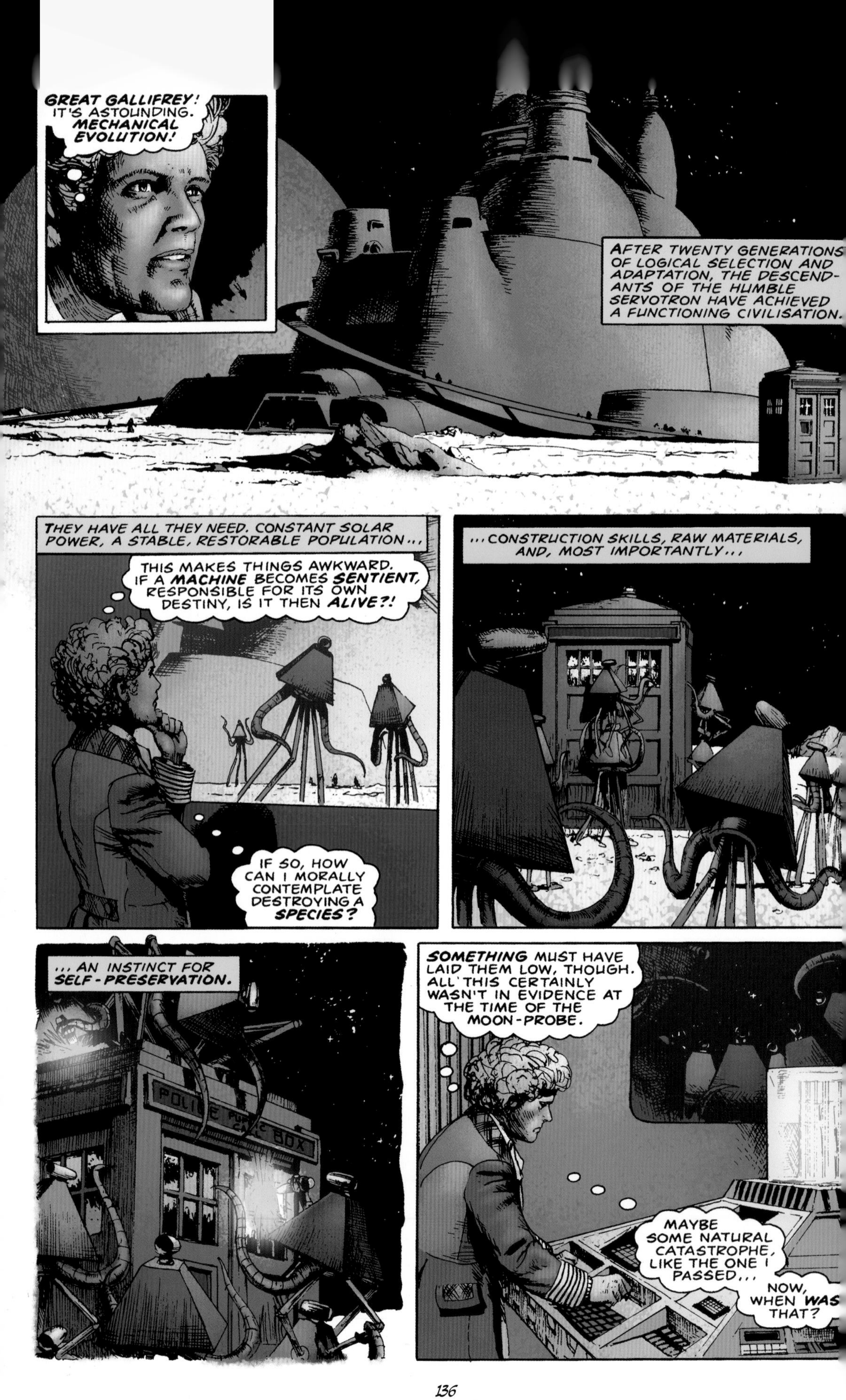
GREAT GALLIFREY! IT'S ASTOUNDING. MECHANICAL EVOLUTION!
AFTER TWENTY GENERATIONS OF LOGICAL SELECTION AND ADAPTATION, THE DESCENDANTS OF THE HUMBLE SERVOTRON HAVE ACHIEVED A FUNCTIONING CIVILISATION.
THEY HAVE ALL THEY NEED. CONSTANT SOLAR POWER, A STABLE, RESTORABLE POPULATION...
THIS MAKES THINGS AWKWARD. IF A MACHINE BECOMES SENTIENT, RESPONSIBLE FOR ITS OWN DESTINY, IS IT THEN ALIVE?!
IF SO, HOW CAN I MORALLY CONTEMPLATE DESTROYING A SPECIES?
...CONSTRUCTION SKILLS, RAW MATERIALS, AND, MOST IMPORTANTLY...
...AN INSTINCT FOR SELF-PRESERVATION.
POLICE PUBLIC CALL BOX
SOMETHING MUST HAVE LAID THEM LOW, THOUGH. ALL THIS CERTAINLY WASN'T IN EVIDENCE AT THE TIME OF THE MOON-PROBE.
MAYBE SOME NATURAL CATASTROPHE, LIKE THE ONE I PASSED...
NOW, WHEN WAS THAT?

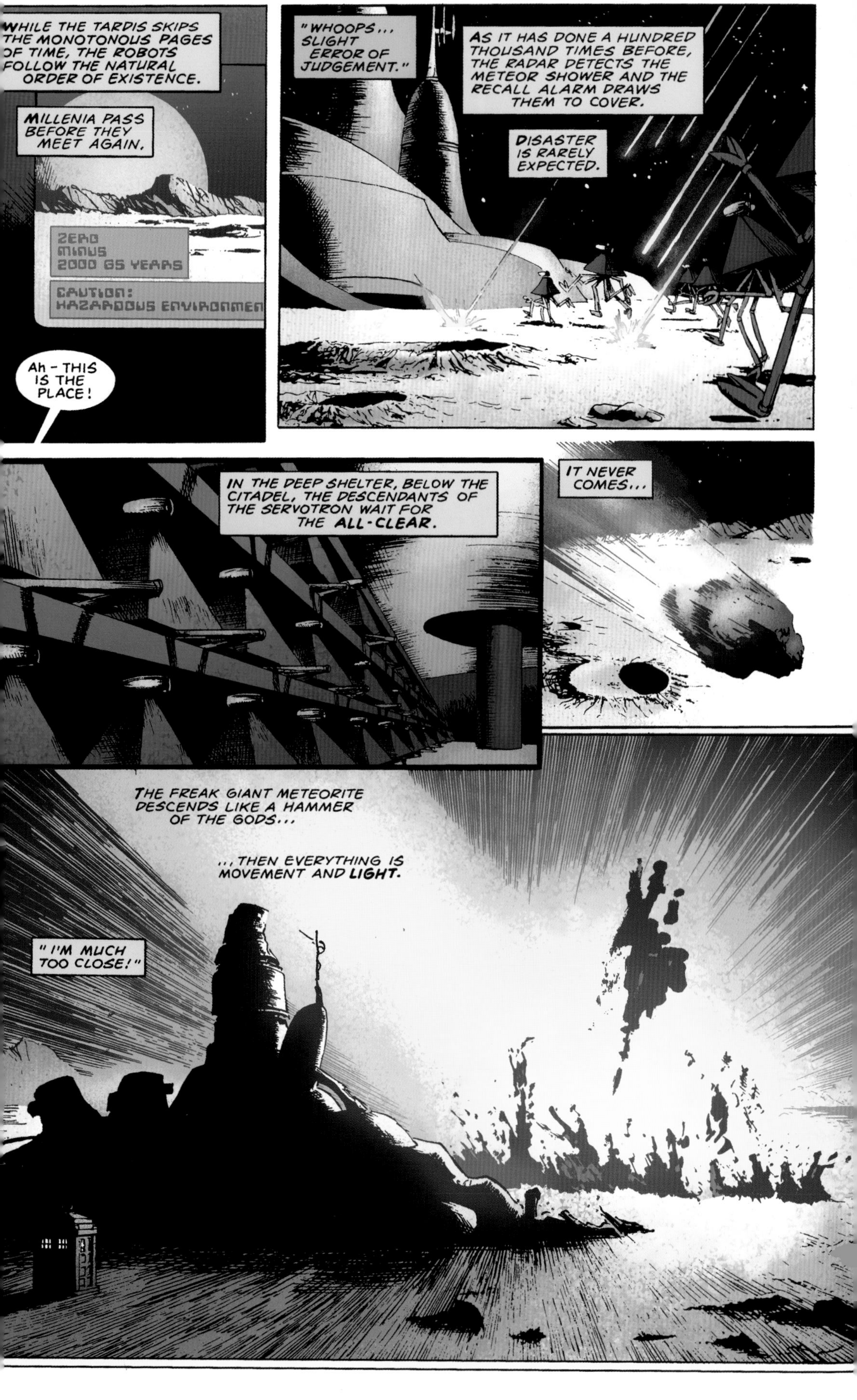
WHILE THE TARDIS SKIPS THE MONOTONOUS PAGES OF TIME, THE ROBOTS FOLLOW THE NATURAL ORDER OF EXISTENCE.
MILLENIA PASS BEFORE THEY MEET AGAIN.
ZERO MINUS 2000 GS YEARS
CAUTION: HAZARDOUS ENVIRONMEN
Ah - THIS IS THE PLACE!
"WHOOPS... SLIGHT ERROR OF JUDGEMENT."
AS IT HAS DONE A HUNDRED THOUSAND TIMES BEFORE, THE RADAR DETECTS THE METEOR SHOWER AND THE RECALL ALARM DRAWS THEM TO COVER.
DISASTER IS RARELY EXPECTED.
IN THE DEEP SHELTER, BELOW THE CITADEL, THE DESCENDANTS OF THE SERVOTRON WAIT FOR THE ALL-CLEAR.
IT NEVER COMES...
THE FREAK GIANT METEORITE DESCENDS LIKE A HAMMER OF THE GODS...
...THEN EVERYTHING IS MOVEMENT AND LIGHT.
"I'M MUCH TOO CLOSE!"

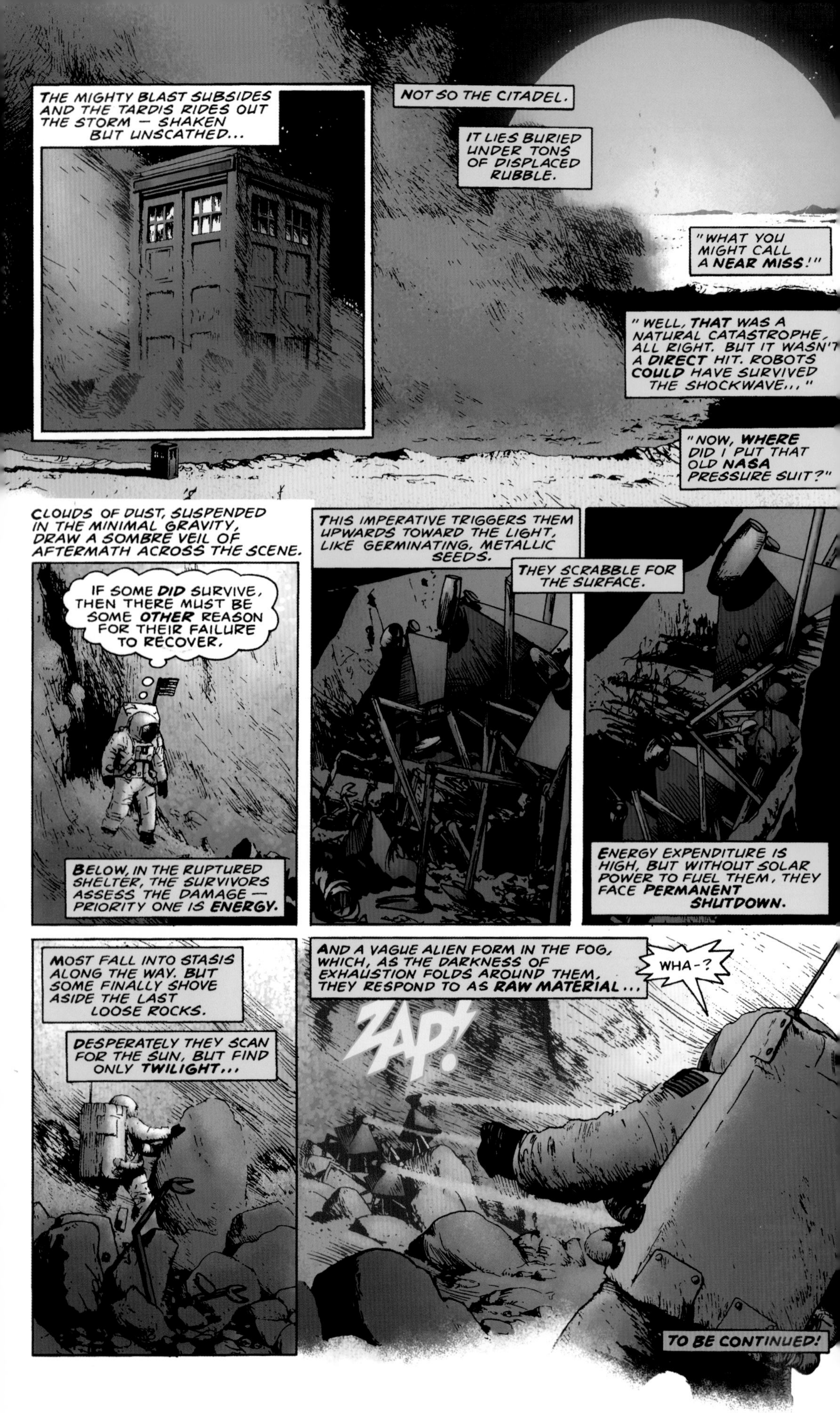

THE MIGHTY BLAST SUBSIDES AND THE TARDIS RIDES OUT THE STORM — SHAKEN BUT UNSCATHED...
NOT SO THE CITADEL.
IT LIES BURIED UNDER TONS OF DISPLACED RUBBLE.
"WHAT YOU MIGHT CALL A NEAR MISS!"
"WELL, THAT WAS A NATURAL CATASTROPHE, ALL RIGHT. BUT IT WASN'T A DIRECT HIT. ROBOTS COULD HAVE SURVIVED THE SHOCKWAVE..."
"NOW, WHERE DID I PUT THAT OLD NASA PRESSURE SUIT?"
CLOUDS OF DUST, SUSPENDED IN THE MINIMAL GRAVITY, DRAW A SOMBRE VEIL OF AFTERMATH ACROSS THE SCENE.
IF SOME DID SURVIVE, THEN THERE MUST BE SOME OTHER REASON FOR THEIR FAILURE TO RECOVER.
BELOW, IN THE RUPTURED SHELTER, THE SURVIVORS ASSESS THE DAMAGE — PRIORITY ONE IS ENERGY.
THIS IMPERATIVE TRIGGERS THEM UPWARDS TOWARD THE LIGHT, LIKE GERMINATING, METALLIC SEEDS.
THEY SCRABBLE FOR THE SURFACE.
ENERGY EXPENDITURE IS HIGH, BUT WITHOUT SOLAR POWER TO FUEL THEM, THEY FACE PERMANENT SHUTDOWN.
MOST FALL INTO STASIS ALONG THE WAY. BUT SOME FINALLY SHOVE ASIDE THE LAST LOOSE ROCKS.
DESPERATELY THEY SCAN FOR THE SUN, BUT FIND ONLY TWILIGHT...
AND A VAGUE ALIEN FORM IN THE FOG, WHICH, AS THE DARKNESS OF EXHAUSTION FOLDS AROUND THEM, THEY RESPOND TO AS RAW MATERIAL...
WHA-?
ZAP!
TO BE CONTINUED!

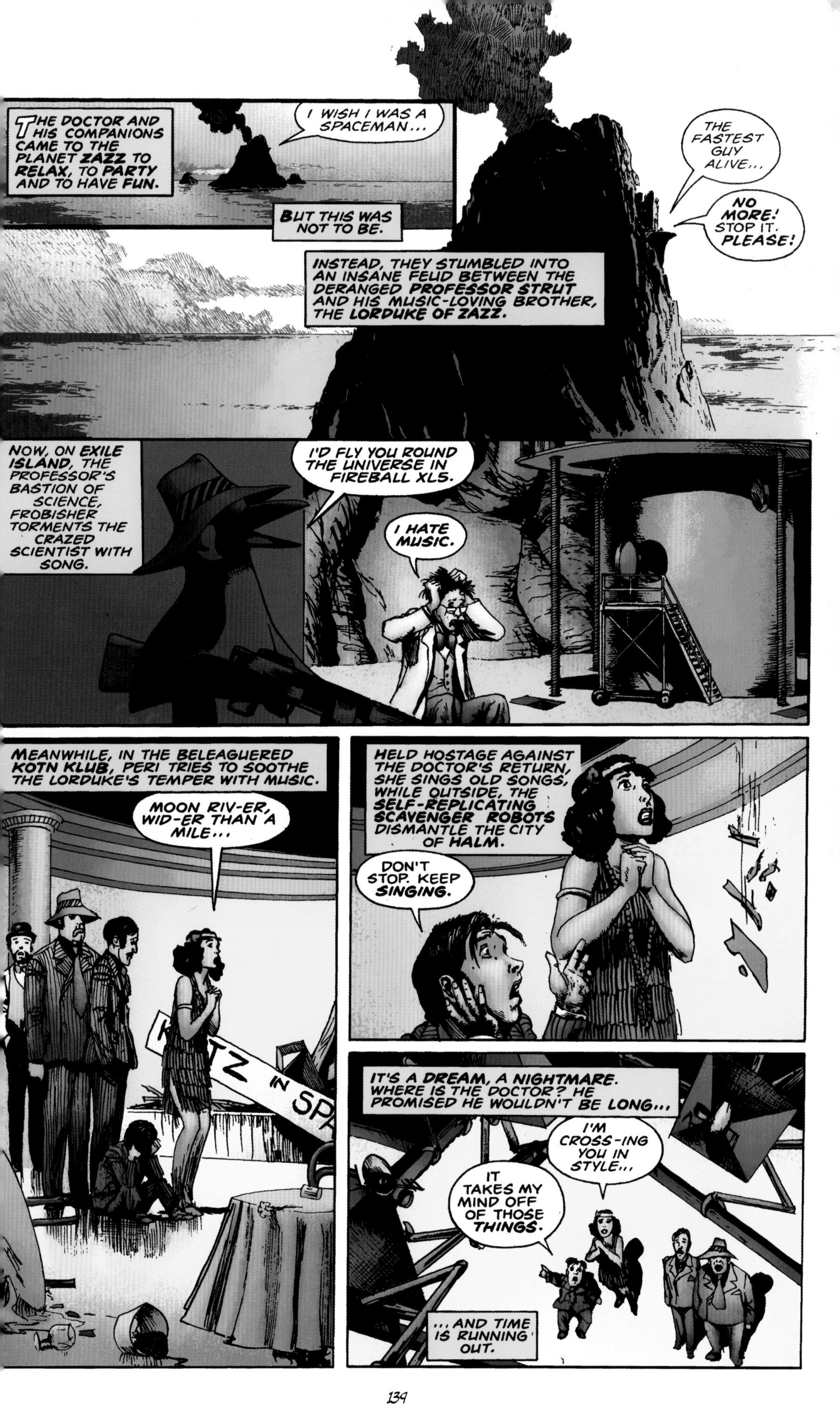

THE DOCTOR AND HIS COMPANIONS CAME TO THE PLANET ZAZZ TO RELAX, TO PARTY AND TO HAVE FUN.
I WISH I WAS A SPACEMAN...
BUT THIS WAS NOT TO BE.
THE FASTEST GUY ALIVE...
NO MORE! STOP IT. PLEASE!
INSTEAD, THEY STUMBLED INTO AN INSANE FEUD BETWEEN THE DERANGED PROFESSOR STRUT AND HIS MUSIC-LOVING BROTHER, THE LORDUKE OF ZAZZ.
NOW, ON EXILE ISLAND, THE PROFESSOR'S BASTION OF SCIENCE, FROBISHER TORMENTS THE CRAZED SCIENTIST WITH SONG.
I'D FLY YOU ROUND THE UNIVERSE IN FIREBALL XL5.
I HATE MUSIC.
MEANWHILE, IN THE BELEAGUERED KOTN KLUB, PERI TRIES TO SOOTHE THE LORDUKE'S TEMPER WITH MUSIC.
MOON RIV-ER, WID-ER THAN A MILE...
HELD HOSTAGE AGAINST THE DOCTOR'S RETURN, SHE SINGS OLD SONGS, WHILE OUTSIDE, THE SELF-REPLICATING SCAVENGER ROBOTS DISMANTLE THE CITY OF HALM.
DON'T STOP. KEEP SINGING.
IT'S A DREAM, A NIGHTMARE. WHERE IS THE DOCTOR? HE PROMISED HE WOULDN'T BE LONG...
I'M CROSS-ING YOU IN STYLE...
IT TAKES MY MIND OFF OF THOSE THINGS.
...AND TIME IS RUNNING OUT.

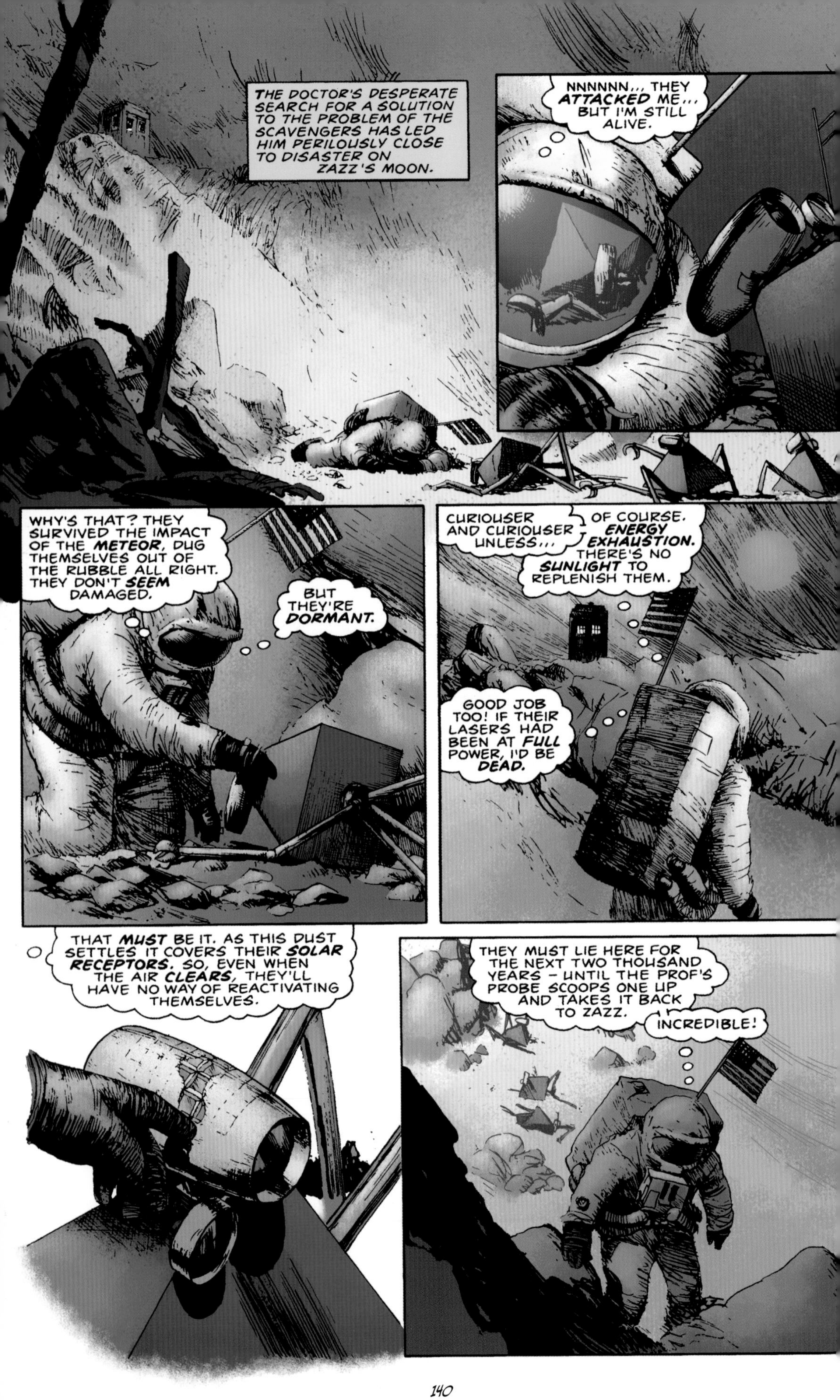
THE DOCTOR'S DESPERATE SEARCH FOR A SOLUTION TO THE PROBLEM OF THE SCAVENGERS HAS LED HIM PERILOUSLY CLOSE TO DISASTER ON ZAZZ'S MOON.
NNNNNN... THEY ATTACKED ME... BUT I'M STILL ALIVE.
WHY'S THAT? THEY SURVIVED THE IMPACT OF THE METEOR, DUG THEMSELVES OUT OF THE RUBBLE ALL RIGHT. THEY DON'T SEEM DAMAGED.
BUT THEY'RE DORMANT.
CURIOUSER AND CURIOUSER UNLESS...
OF COURSE. ENERGY EXHAUSTION. THERE'S NO SUNLIGHT TO REPLENISH THEM.
GOOD JOB TOO! IF THEIR LASERS HAD BEEN AT FULL POWER, I'D BE DEAD.
THAT MUST BE IT. AS THIS DUST SETTLES IT COVERS THEIR SOLAR RECEPTORS. SO, EVEN WHEN THE AIR CLEARS, THEY'LL HAVE NO WAY OF REACTIVATING THEMSELVES.
THEY MUST LIE HERE FOR THE NEXT TWO THOUSAND YEARS - UNTIL THE PROF'S PROBE SCOOPS ONE UP AND TAKES IT BACK TO ZAZZ.
INCREDIBLE!

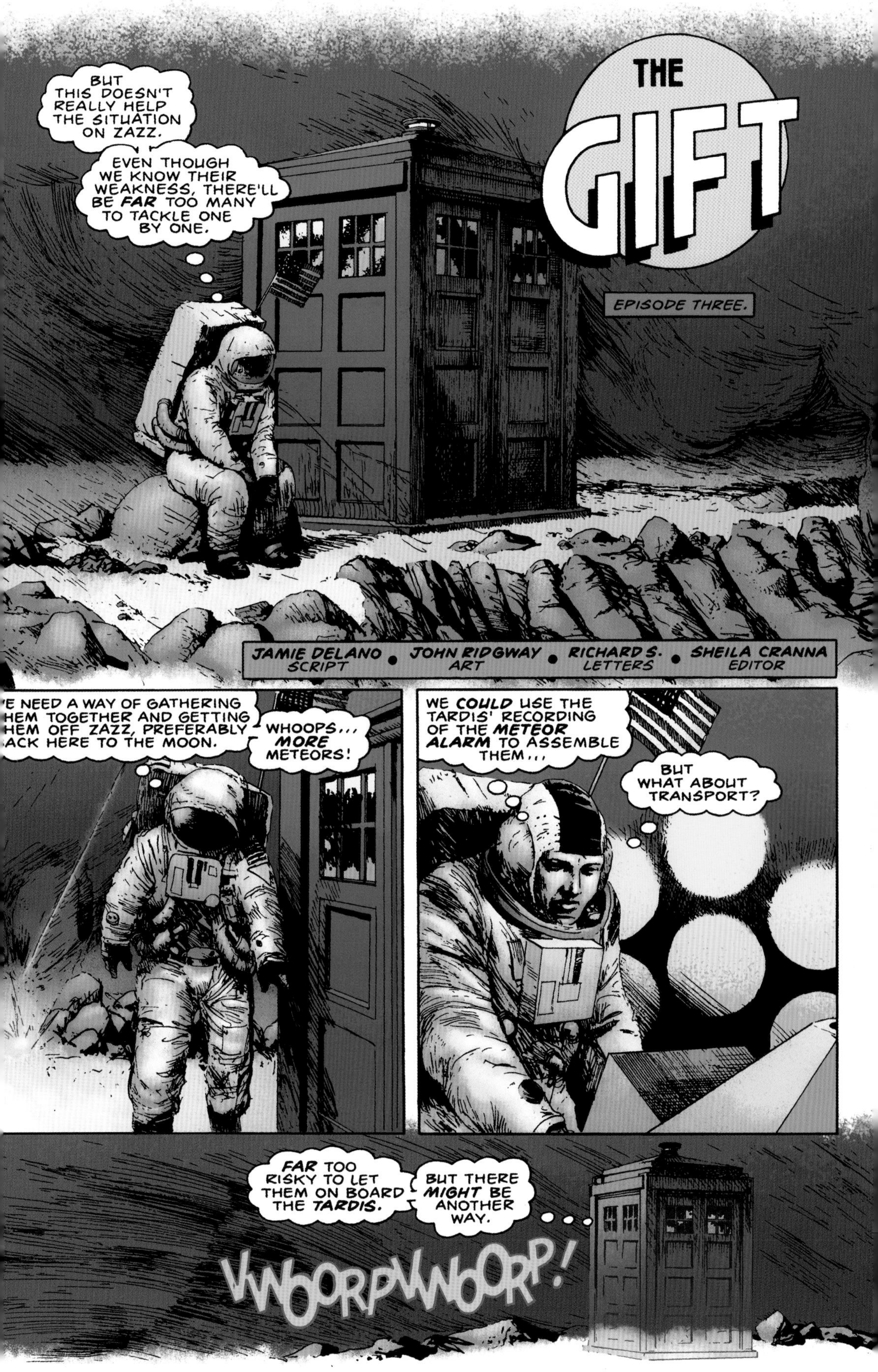
THE GIFT
EPISODE THREE.
BUT THIS DOESN'T REALLY HELP THE SITUATION ON ZAZZ.
EVEN THOUGH WE KNOW THEIR WEAKNESS, THERE'LL BE FAR TOO MANY TO TACKLE ONE BY ONE.
JAMIE DELANO SCRIPT • JOHN RIDGWAY ART • RICHARD S. LETTERS • SHEILA CRANNA EDITOR
'E NEED A WAY OF GATHERING HEM TOGETHER AND GETTING HEM OFF ZAZZ, PREFERABLY ACK HERE TO THE MOON.
WHOOPS... MORE METEORS!
WE COULD USE THE TARDIS' RECORDING OF THE METEOR ALARM TO ASSEMBLE THEM...
BUT WHAT ABOUT TRANSPORT?
FAR TOO RISKY TO LET THEM ON BOARD THE TARDIS.
BUT THERE MIGHT BE ANOTHER WAY.
VWORP VWORP!

GROUND CONTROL TO MAJOR TOM. Ah, ABOUT TIME!

VWORP

DID YOU SORT IT OUT THEN, DOC?

... NOT *EXACTLY*. NOW LET'S HAVE A LOOK A THIS CONTRAPTION

I'LL HAVE TO CHECK YOUR MATHEMATICS — AND THERE ARE SOME *OBVIOUS* ALTERATIONS TO BE MADE.

IT'S A LONG SHOT, BUT IT *COULD* JUST WORK.

WHAT COULD, DOC?

PROFESSOR, I DID YOU AN INJUSTICE. YOUR ROCKET'S NOT *TOTALLY* USELESS. IT COULD JUST FLY.

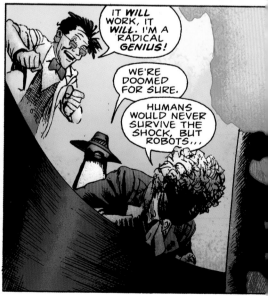

IT *WILL* WORK, IT *WILL*. I'M A RADICAL *GENIUS!*

WE'RE DOOMED FOR SURE.

HUMANS WOULD NEVER SURVIVE THE SHOCK, BUT ROBOTS...

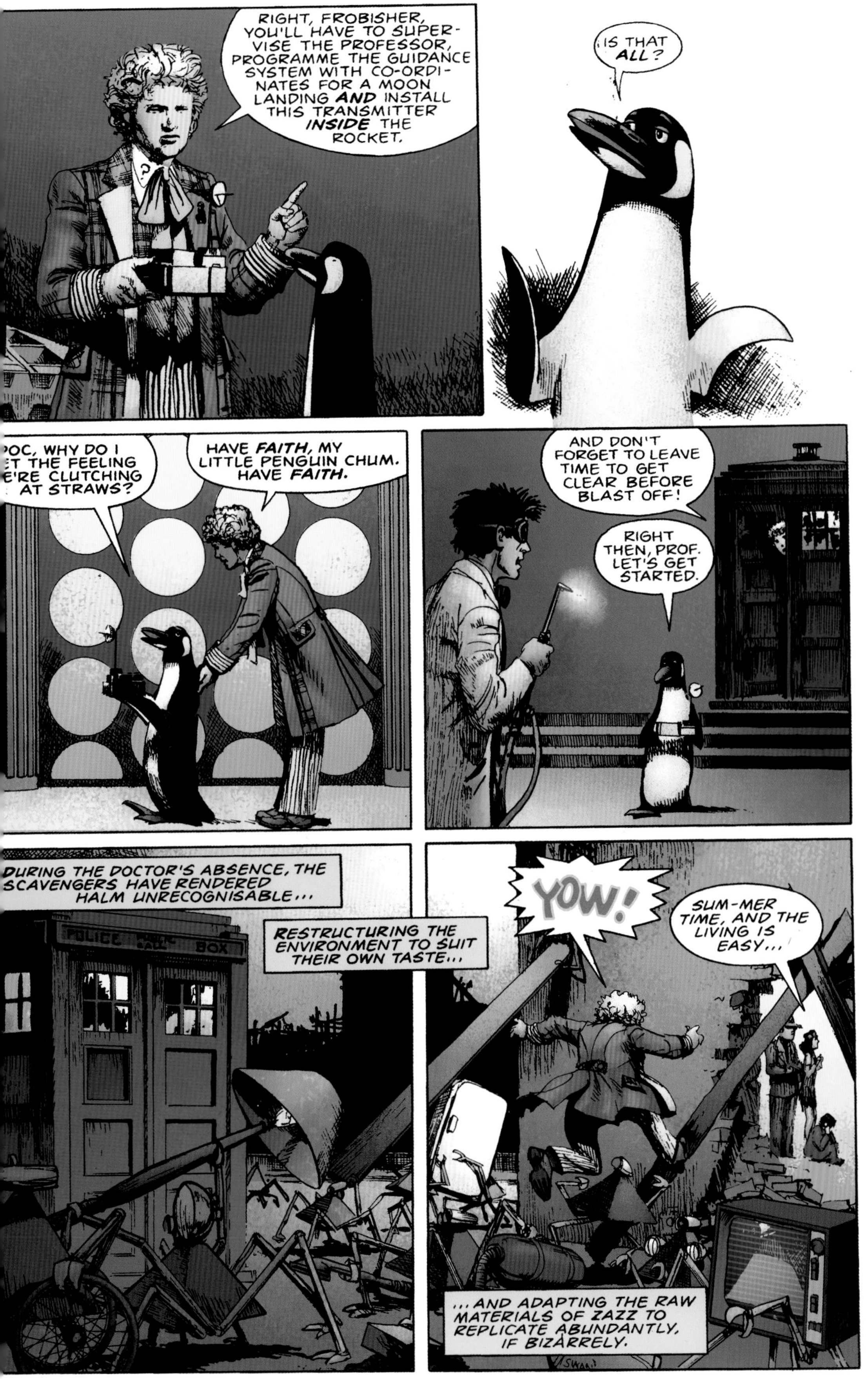
RIGHT, FROBISHER, YOU'LL HAVE TO SUPER-VISE THE PROFESSOR, PROGRAMME THE GUIDANCE SYSTEM WITH CO-ORDINATES FOR A MOON LANDING AND INSTALL THIS TRANSMITTER INSIDE THE ROCKET.
IS THAT ALL?
OC, WHY DO I ET THE FEELING E'RE CLUTCHING AT STRAWS?
HAVE FAITH, MY LITTLE PENGUIN CHUM. HAVE FAITH.
AND DON'T FORGET TO LEAVE TIME TO GET CLEAR BEFORE BLAST OFF!
RIGHT THEN, PROF. LET'S GET STARTED.
DURING THE DOCTOR'S ABSENCE, THE SCAVENGERS HAVE RENDERED HALM UNRECOGNISABLE...
POLICE BOX
RESTRUCTURING THE ENVIRONMENT TO SUIT THEIR OWN TASTE...
YOW!
SUM-MER TIME, AND THE LIVING IS EASY...
...AND ADAPTING THE RAW MATERIALS OF ZAZZ TO REPLICATE ABUNDANTLY, IF BIZARRELY.

THE KATZ OF ZAZZ ARE VERY BLUE.

FISH ARE JUMPIN' AND THE COTTON IS HIGH...

CLAP CLAP

BRAVO! BRAVO!

DOCTOR, WHERE HAVE YOU *BEEN*? I'VE SUNG THROUGH *PORGY AND BESS* SO MANY TIMES I SOUND LIKE *PAUL ROBESON*!

DIDJA SEE WHAT THEY DID T'MY CITY? *DIDJA*?

WELL, DID YOU FIND AN *ANSWER*?

I *THINK* SO. IT'S A BIT *CLUMSY* BUT IT *SHOULD* WORK.

IT'D *BETTER* WORK! OR YOU AN' ME ARE GONNA STOP BEING *FRIENDS*!

BEST KEEP OUR FINGERS CROSSED THEN.

ANY MOMENT NOW FROBISHER SHOULD START TRANSMITTIN' A SIGNAL THAT WILL CALL THE SCAVENGERS TO EXILE ISLAND.

HA, I LIKE IT! GIVE THAT LOOPY BROTHER OF MINE A DOSE OF HIS OWN MEDICINE.

SOMETHING'S GONE WRONG. THE SIGNAL'S PROBABLY TOO *WEAK*.

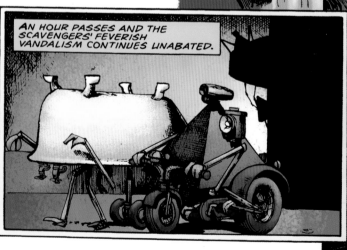

AN HOUR PASSES AND THE SCAVENGERS' FEVERISH VANDALISM CONTINUES UNABATED.

THIS IS *BAD*. NOW WE CAN'T EVEN GET INTO THE TARDIS. IF THE SCAVENGERS SNEAK INSIDE THEY COULD END UP *ANYWHERE*

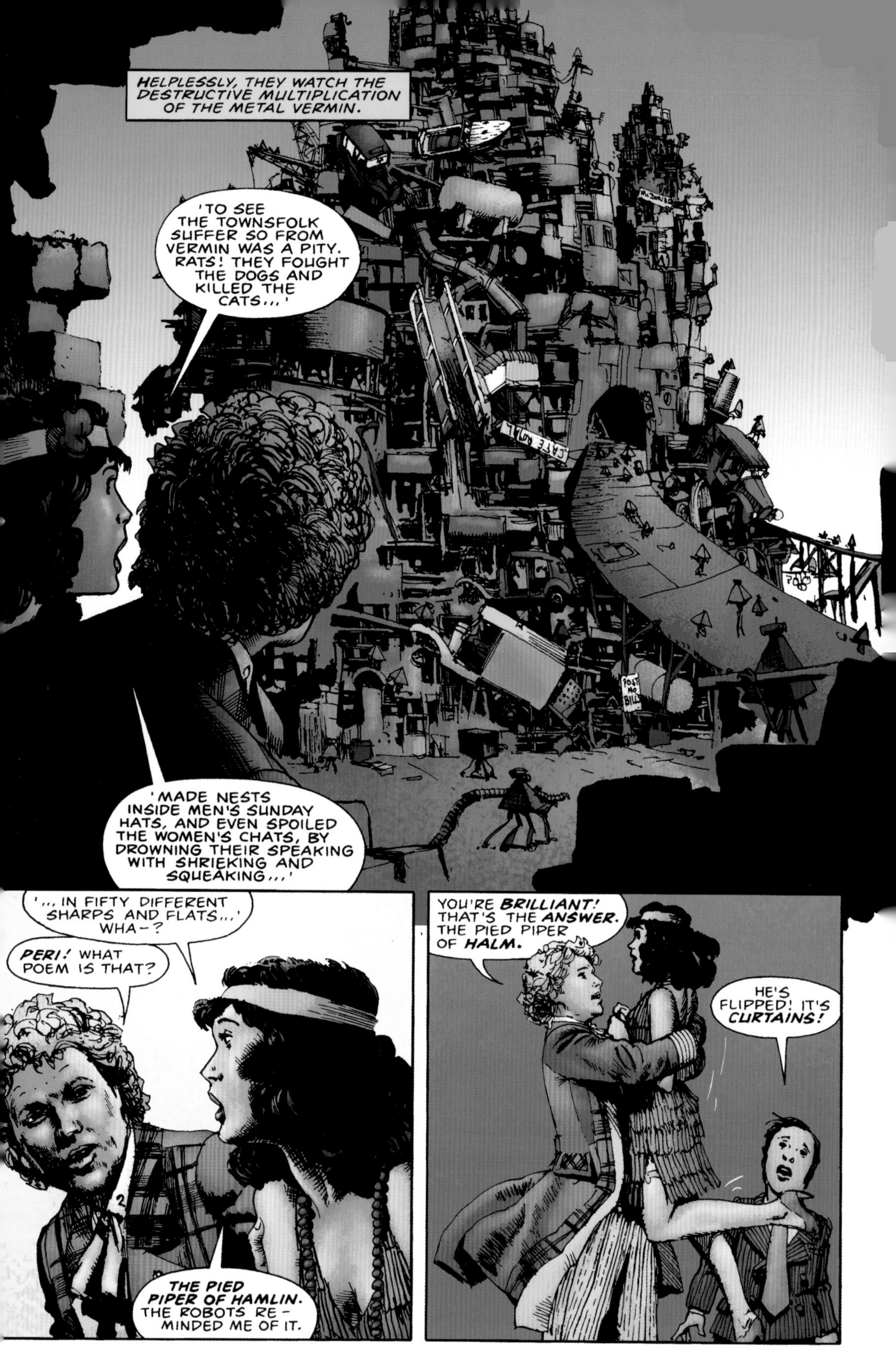
HELPLESSLY, THEY WATCH THE DESTRUCTIVE MULTIPLICATION OF THE METAL VERMIN.
'TO SEE THE TOWNSFOLK SUFFER SO FROM VERMIN WAS A PITY. RATS! THEY FOUGHT THE DOGS AND KILLED THE CATS...'
'MADE NESTS INSIDE MEN'S SUNDAY HATS, AND EVEN SPOILED THE WOMEN'S CHATS, BY DROWNING THEIR SPEAKING WITH SHRIEKING AND SQUEAKING...'
'...IN FIFTY DIFFERENT SHARPS AND FLATS...' WHA-?
PERI! WHAT POEM IS THAT?
THE PIED PIPER OF HAMLIN. THE ROBOTS RE-MINDED ME OF IT.
YOU'RE BRILLIANT! THAT'S THE ANSWER. THE PIED PIPER OF HALM.
HE'S FLIPPED! IT'S CURTAINS!

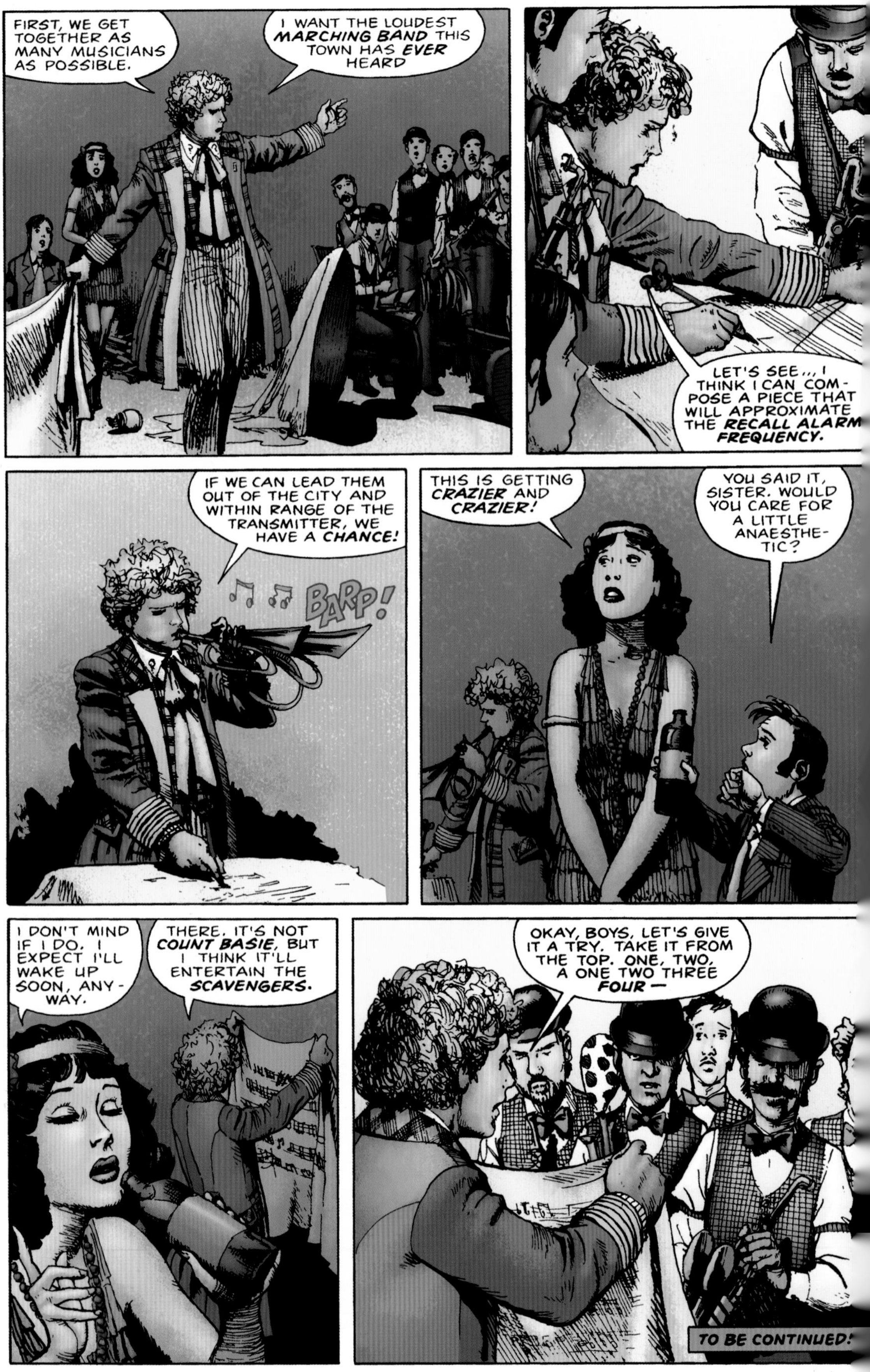
FIRST, WE GET TOGETHER AS MANY MUSICIANS AS POSSIBLE.
I WANT THE LOUDEST **MARCHING BAND** THIS TOWN HAS **EVER** HEARD
LET'S SEE..., I THINK I CAN COMPOSE A PIECE THAT WILL APPROXIMATE THE **RECALL ALARM FREQUENCY.**
IF WE CAN LEAD THEM OUT OF THE CITY AND WITHIN RANGE OF THE TRANSMITTER, WE HAVE A **CHANCE!**
BARP!
THIS IS GETTING **CRAZIER** AND **CRAZIER!**
YOU SAID IT, SISTER. WOULD YOU CARE FOR A LITTLE ANAESTHETIC?
I DON'T MIND IF I DO. I EXPECT I'LL WAKE UP SOON, ANYWAY.
THERE. IT'S NOT **COUNT BASIE**, BUT I THINK IT'LL ENTERTAIN THE **SCAVENGERS.**
OKAY, BOYS, LET'S GIVE IT A TRY. TAKE IT FROM THE TOP. ONE, TWO, A ONE TWO THREE **FOUR** —
TO BE CONTINUED!

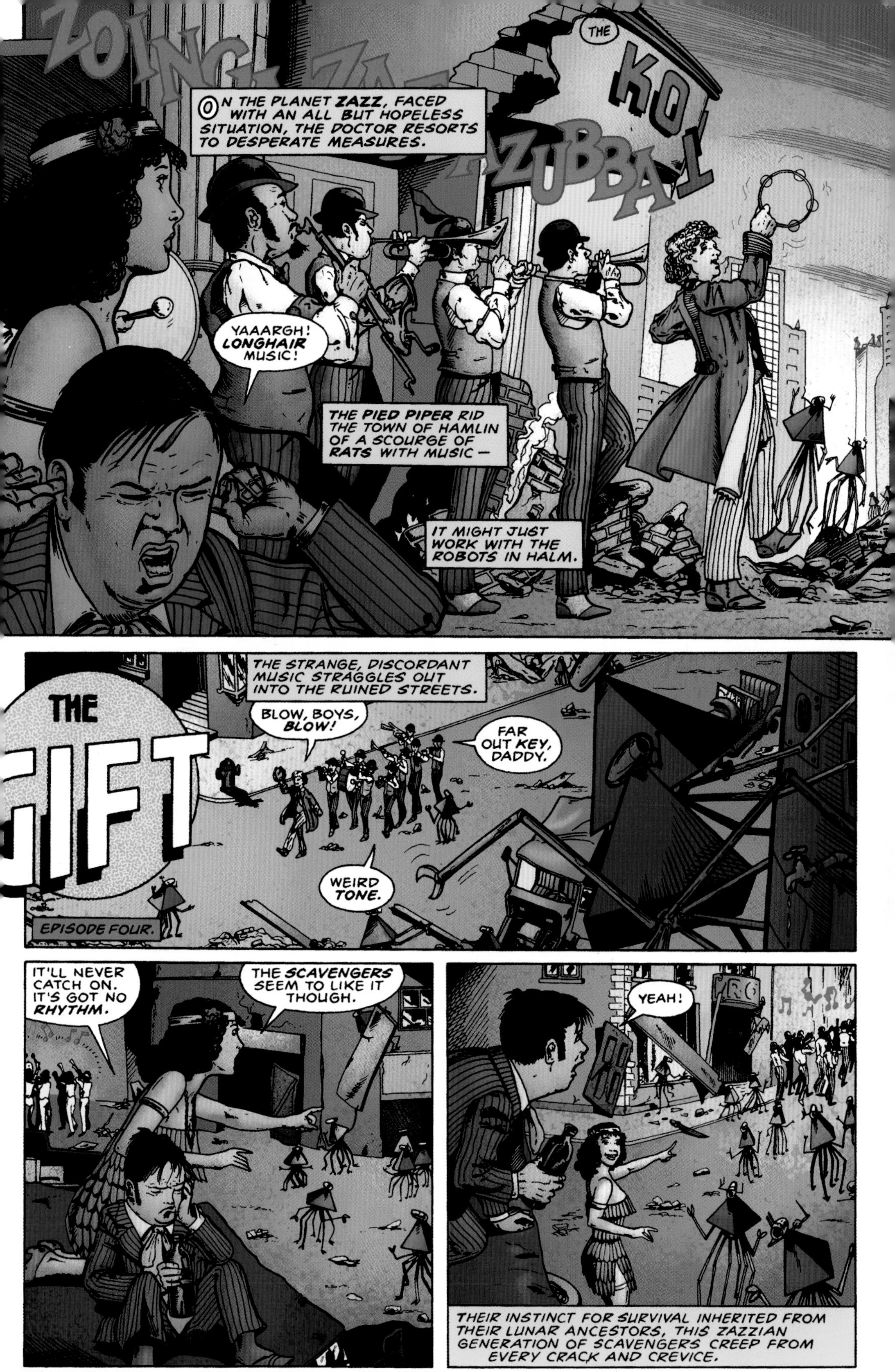
ZOING
ZAT
THE
KO
ZUBBA
ON THE PLANET ZAZZ, FACED WITH AN ALL BUT HOPELESS SITUATION, THE DOCTOR RESORTS TO DESPERATE MEASURES.
YAAARGH! LONGHAIR MUSIC!
THE PIED PIPER RID THE TOWN OF HAMLIN OF A SCOURGE OF RATS WITH MUSIC —
IT MIGHT JUST WORK WITH THE ROBOTS IN HALM.
THE STRANGE, DISCORDANT MUSIC STRAGGLES OUT INTO THE RUINED STREETS.
THE GIFT
EPISODE FOUR.
BLOW, BOYS, BLOW!
FAR OUT KEY, DADDY.
WEIRD TONE.
IT'LL NEVER CATCH ON. IT'S GOT NO RHYTHM.
THE SCAVENGERS SEEM TO LIKE IT THOUGH.
YEAH!
THEIR INSTINCT FOR SURVIVAL INHERITED FROM THEIR LUNAR ANCESTORS, THIS ZAZZIAN GENERATION OF SCAVENGERS CREEP FROM EVERY CRACK AND CREVICE.

JAMIE DELANO SCRIPT • JOHN RIDGWAY PENCILS • TIM PERKINS INKS • RICHARD STARKINGS LETTERS • SHEILA CRANNA EDITOR

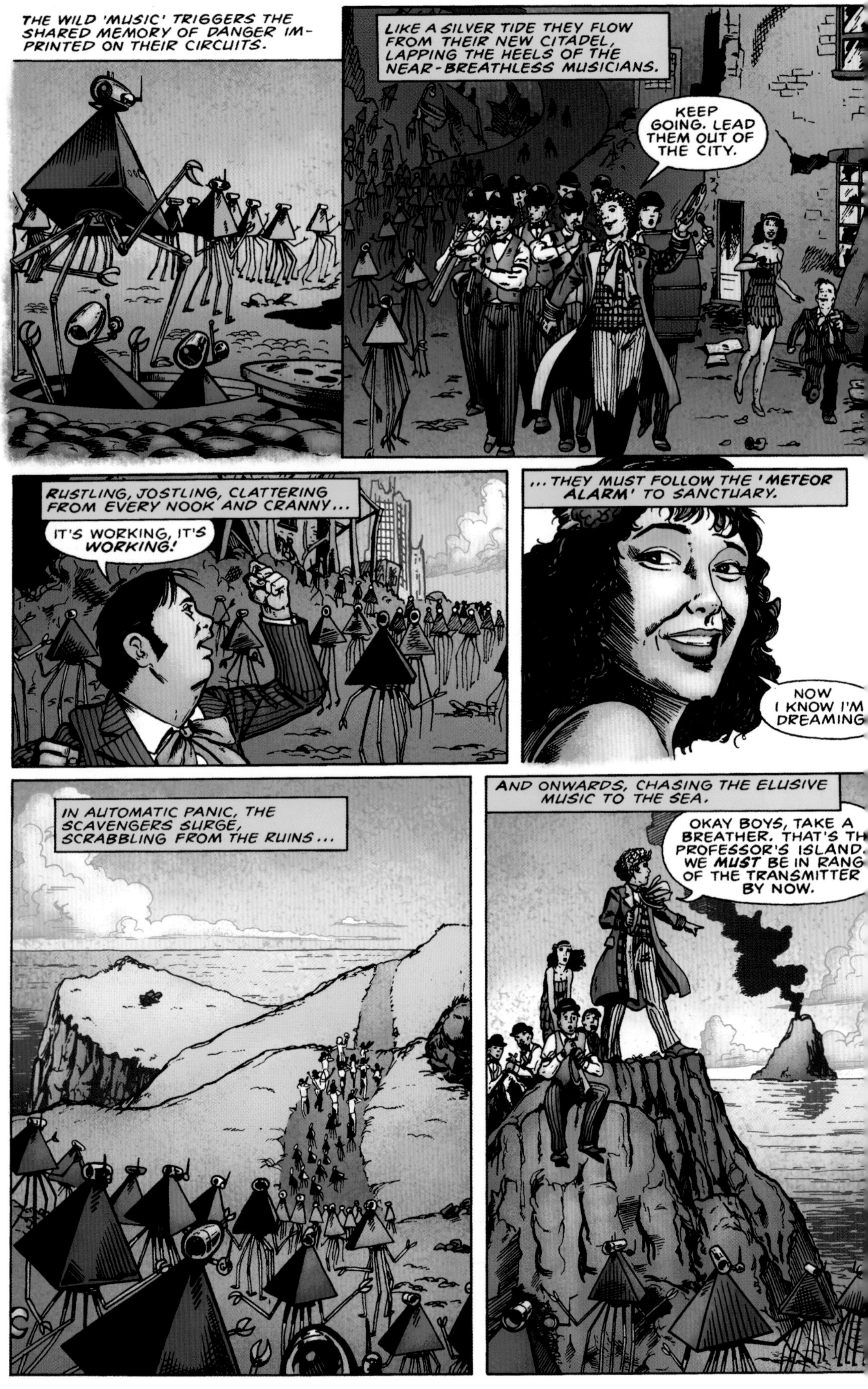
THE WILD 'MUSIC' TRIGGERS THE SHARED MEMORY OF DANGER IMPRINTED ON THEIR CIRCUITS.
LIKE A SILVER TIDE THEY FLOW FROM THEIR NEW CITADEL, LAPPING THE HEELS OF THE NEAR-BREATHLESS MUSICIANS.
KEEP GOING. LEAD THEM OUT OF THE CITY.
RUSTLING, JOSTLING, CLATTERING FROM EVERY NOOK AND CRANNY...
IT'S WORKING, IT'S WORKING!
...THEY MUST FOLLOW THE 'METEOR ALARM' TO SANCTUARY.
NOW I KNOW I'M DREAMING
IN AUTOMATIC PANIC, THE SCAVENGERS SURGE, SCRABBLING FROM THE RUINS...
AND ONWARDS, CHASING THE ELUSIVE MUSIC TO THE SEA.
OKAY BOYS, TAKE A BREATHER. THAT'S TH PROFESSOR'S ISLAND. WE MUST BE IN RANG OF THE TRANSMITTER BY NOW.

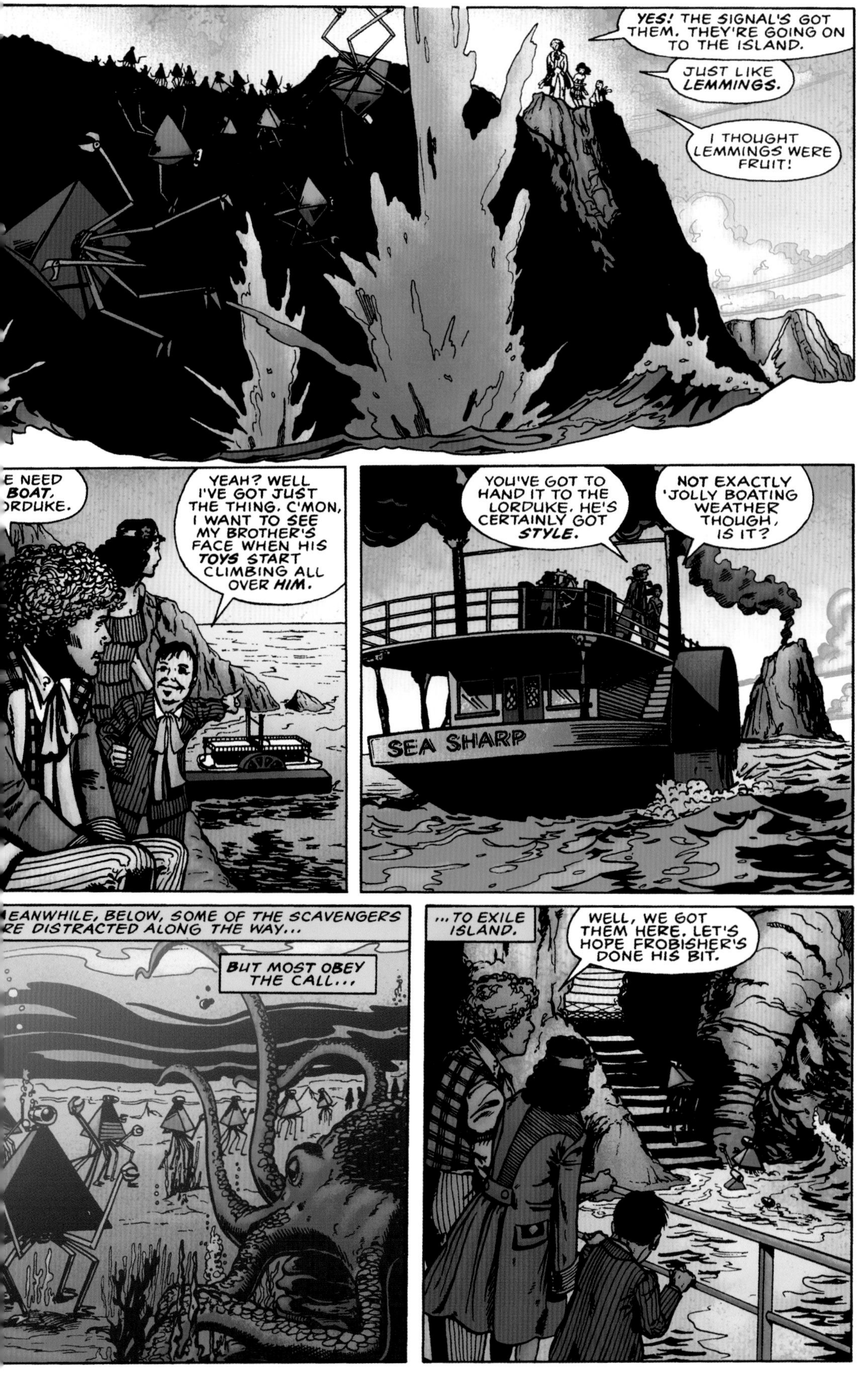
YES! THE SIGNAL'S GOT THEM. THEY'RE GOING ON TO THE ISLAND.
JUST LIKE LEMMINGS.
I THOUGHT LEMMINGS WERE FRUIT!
E NEED BOAT, ORDUKE.
YEAH? WELL I'VE GOT JUST THE THING. C'MON, I WANT TO SEE MY BROTHER'S FACE WHEN HIS TOYS START CLIMBING ALL OVER HIM.
YOU'VE GOT TO HAND IT TO THE LORDUKE. HE'S CERTAINLY GOT STYLE.
NOT EXACTLY 'JOLLY BOATING WEATHER THOUGH, IS IT?
SEA SHARP
EANWHILE, BELOW, SOME OF THE SCAVENGERS RE DISTRACTED ALONG THE WAY...
BUT MOST OBEY THE CALL...
...TO EXILE ISLAND.
WELL, WE GOT THEM HERE. LET'S HOPE FROBISHER'S DONE HIS BIT.

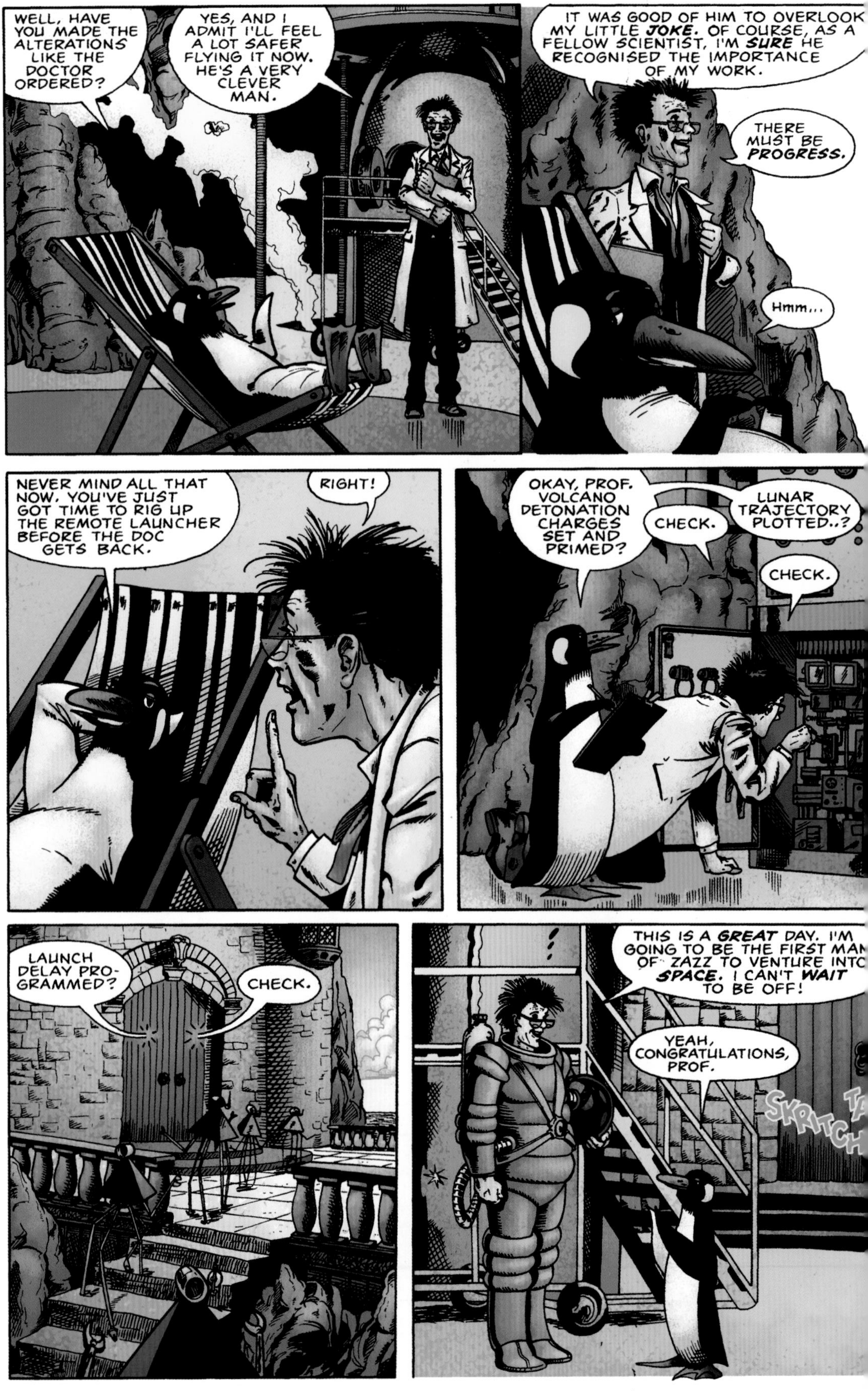
WELL, HAVE YOU MADE THE ALTERATIONS LIKE THE DOCTOR ORDERED?
YES, AND I ADMIT I'LL FEEL A LOT SAFER FLYING IT NOW. HE'S A VERY CLEVER MAN.
IT WAS GOOD OF HIM TO OVERLOOK MY LITTLE JOKE. OF COURSE, AS A FELLOW SCIENTIST, I'M SURE HE RECOGNISED THE IMPORTANCE OF MY WORK.
THERE MUST BE PROGRESS.
Hmm...
NEVER MIND ALL THAT NOW. YOU'VE JUST GOT TIME TO RIG UP THE REMOTE LAUNCHER BEFORE THE DOC GETS BACK.
RIGHT!
OKAY, PROF. VOLCANO DETONATION CHARGES SET AND PRIMED?
CHECK.
LUNAR TRAJECTORY PLOTTED..?
CHECK.
LAUNCH DELAY PRO-GRAMMED?
CHECK.
THIS IS A GREAT DAY. I'M GOING TO BE THE FIRST MAN OF ZAZZ TO VENTURE INTO SPACE. I CAN'T WAIT TO BE OFF!
YEAH, CONGRATULATIONS, PROF.
SKRITCH

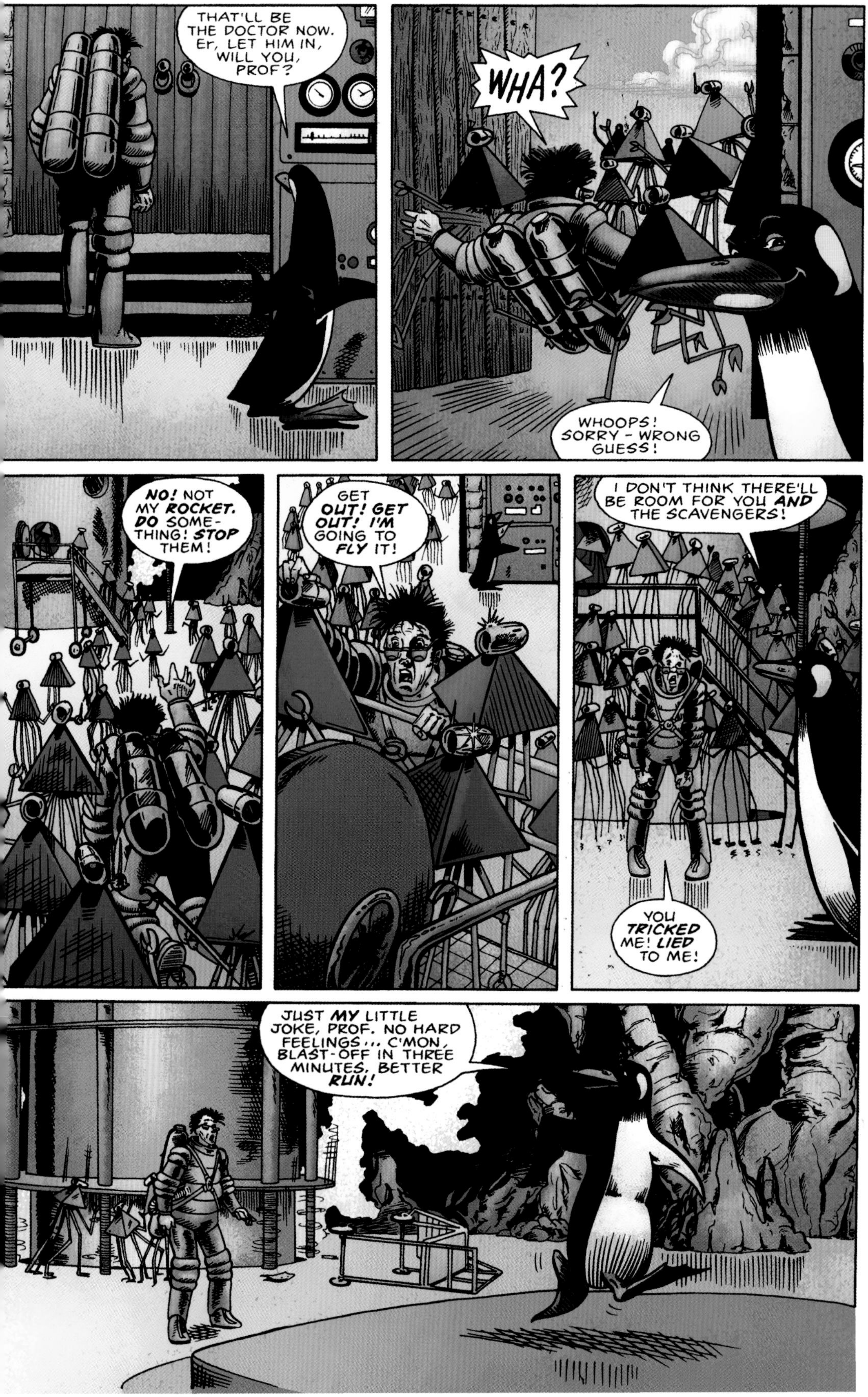
THAT'LL BE THE DOCTOR NOW. Er, LET HIM IN, WILL YOU, PROF?
WHA?
WHOOPS! SORRY - WRONG GUESS!
NO! NOT MY ROCKET. DO SOMETHING! STOP THEM!
GET OUT! GET OUT! I'M GOING TO FLY IT!
I DON'T THINK THERE'LL BE ROOM FOR YOU AND THE SCAVENGERS!
YOU TRICKED ME! LIED TO ME!
JUST MY LITTLE JOKE, PROF. NO HARD FEELINGS... C'MON, BLAST-OFF IN THREE MINUTES, BETTER RUN!

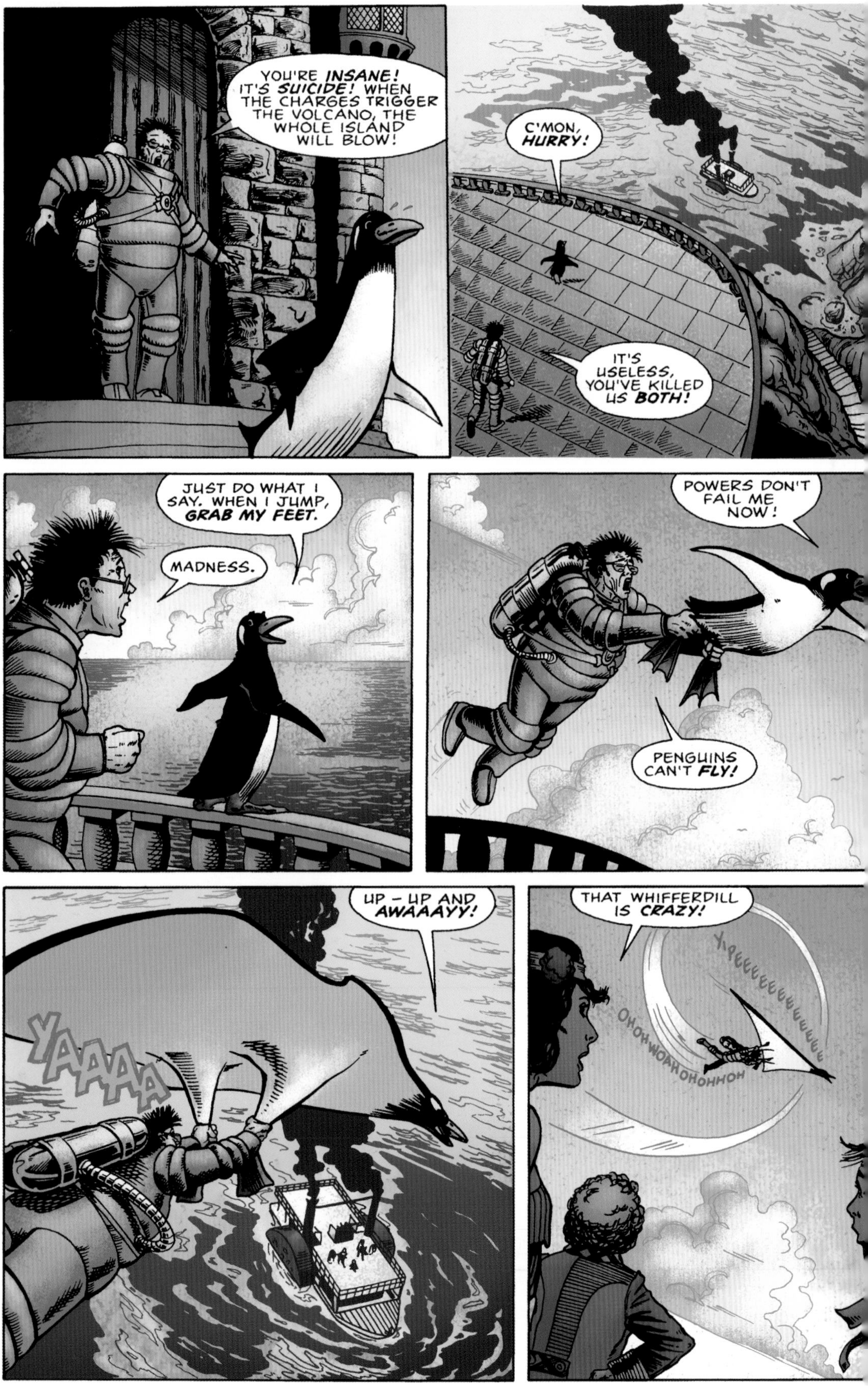
YOU'RE INSANE! IT'S SUICIDE! WHEN THE CHARGES TRIGGER THE VOLCANO, THE WHOLE ISLAND WILL BLOW!
C'MON, HURRY!
IT'S USELESS, YOU'VE KILLED US BOTH!
JUST DO WHAT I SAY. WHEN I JUMP, GRAB MY FEET.
MADNESS.
POWERS DON'T FAIL ME NOW!
PENGUINS CAN'T FLY!
UP - UP AND AWAAAYY!
YAAAA
THAT WHIFFERDILL IS CRAZY!
YIPEEEEEEEEEEEE
OHOHWOAHOHOHHOH

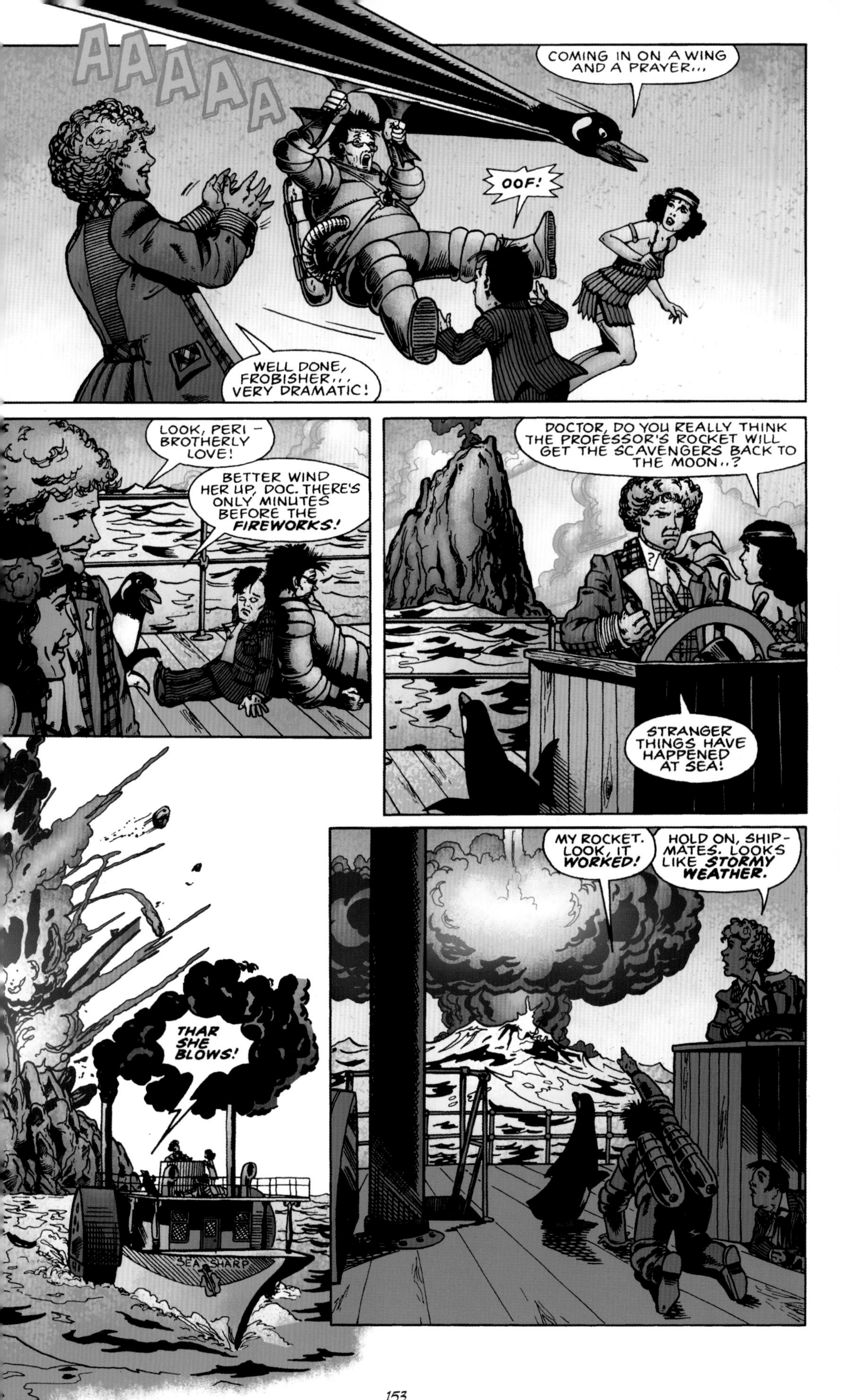
AAAAA
COMING IN ON A WING AND A PRAYER...
OOF!
WELL DONE, FROBISHER... VERY DRAMATIC!
LOOK, PERI – BROTHERLY LOVE!
BETTER WIND HER UP, DOC. THERE'S ONLY MINUTES BEFORE THE FIREWORKS!
DOCTOR, DO YOU REALLY THINK THE PROFESSOR'S ROCKET WILL GET THE SCAVENGERS BACK TO THE MOON..?
STRANGER THINGS HAVE HAPPENED AT SEA!
THAR SHE BLOWS!
SEA SHARP
MY ROCKET. LOOK, IT WORKED!
HOLD ON, SHIPMATES. LOOKS LIKE STORMY WEATHER.

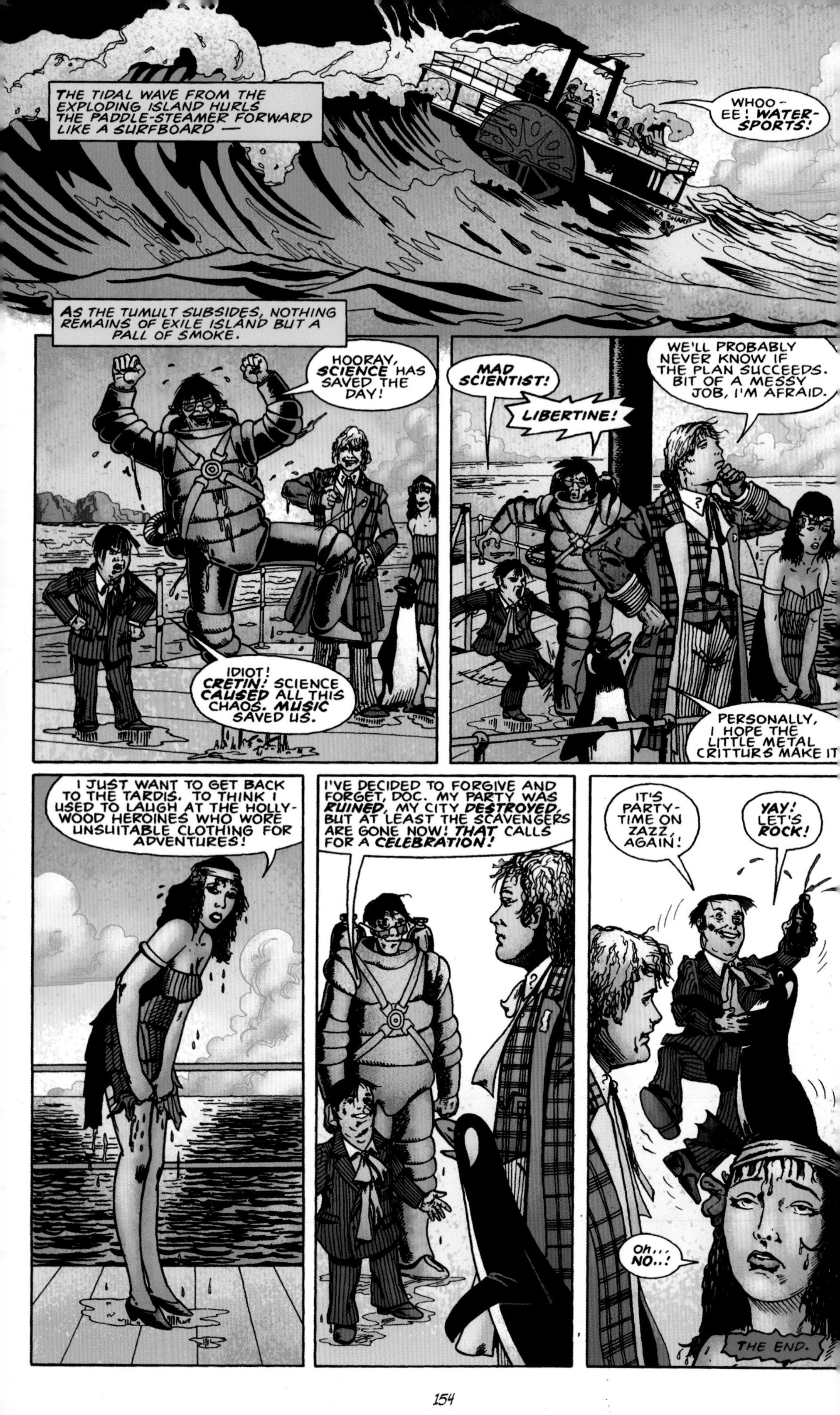

THE TIDAL WAVE FROM THE EXPLODING ISLAND HURLS THE PADDLE-STEAMER FORWARD LIKE A SURFBOARD —
WHOO-EE! WATER-SPORTS!
SEA SHARP
AS THE TUMULT SUBSIDES, NOTHING REMAINS OF EXILE ISLAND BUT A PALL OF SMOKE.
HOORAY, SCIENCE HAS SAVED THE DAY!
IDIOT! CRETIN! SCIENCE CAUSED ALL THIS CHAOS. MUSIC SAVED US.
MAD SCIENTIST!
LIBERTINE!
WE'LL PROBABLY NEVER KNOW IF THE PLAN SUCCEEDS. BIT OF A MESSY JOB, I'M AFRAID.
PERSONALLY, I HOPE THE LITTLE METAL CRITTURS MAKE IT
I JUST WANT TO GET BACK TO THE TARDIS. TO THINK I USED TO LAUGH AT THE HOLLY-WOOD HEROINES WHO WORE UNSUITABLE CLOTHING FOR ADVENTURES!
I'VE DECIDED TO FORGIVE AND FORGET, DOC. MY PARTY WAS RUINED, MY CITY DESTROYED, BUT AT LEAST THE SCAVENGERS ARE GONE NOW! THAT CALLS FOR A CELEBRATION!
IT'S PARTY-TIME ON ZAZZ, AGAIN!
YAY! LET'S ROCK!
Oh... NO...!
THE END.

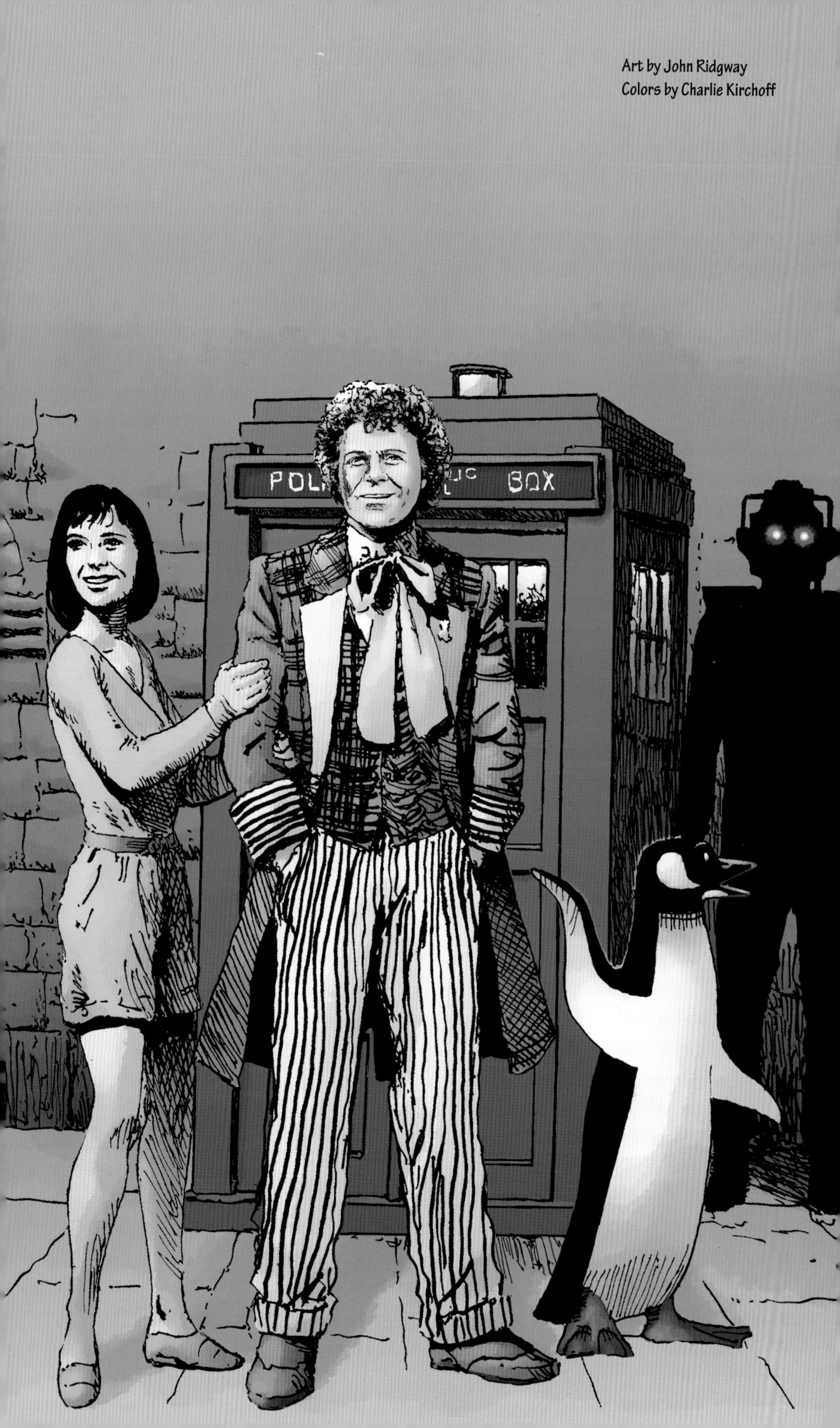
BOX

Art by John Ridgway
Colors by Charlie Kirchoff

Art by John Ridgway
Colors by Charlie Kirchoff

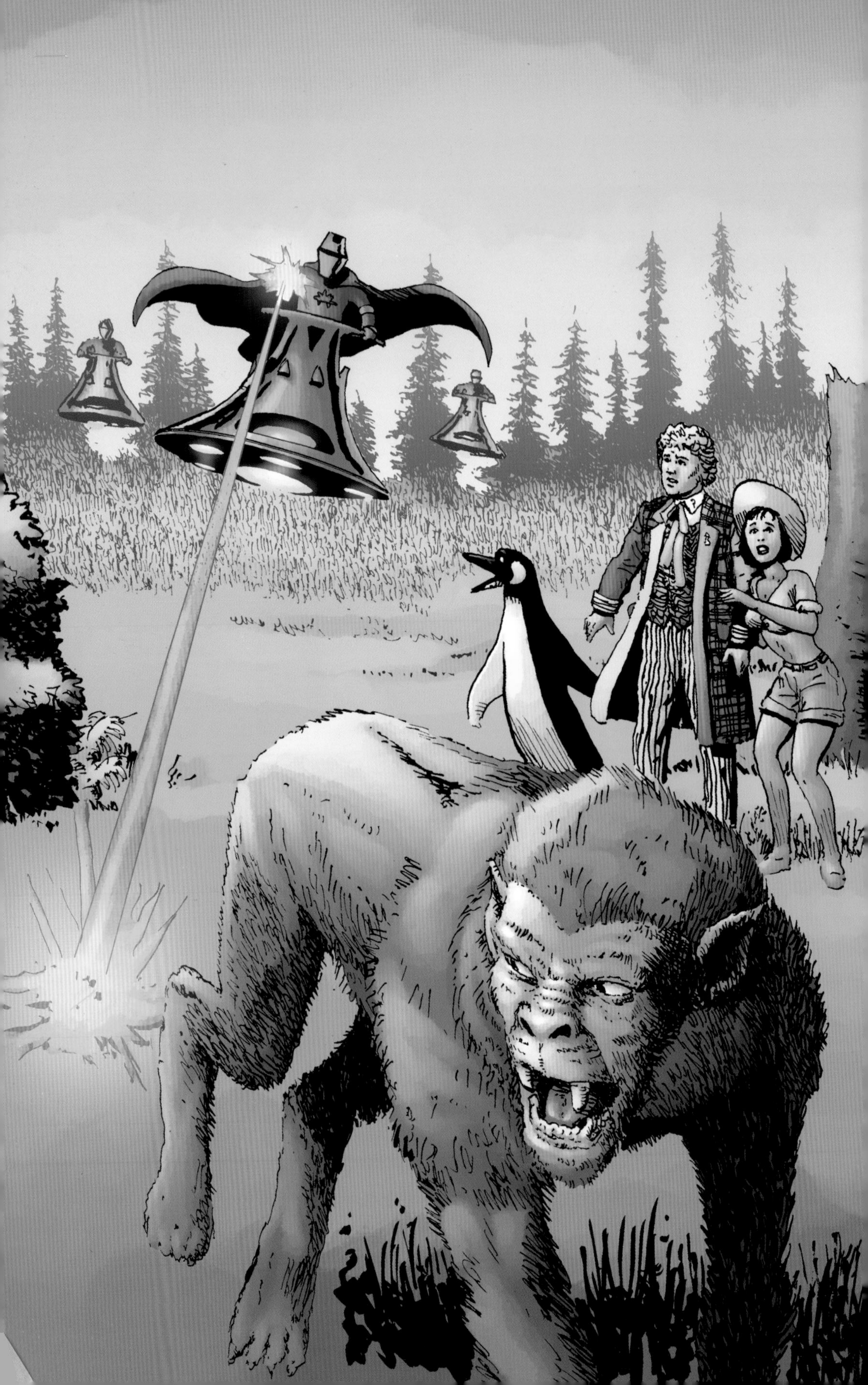

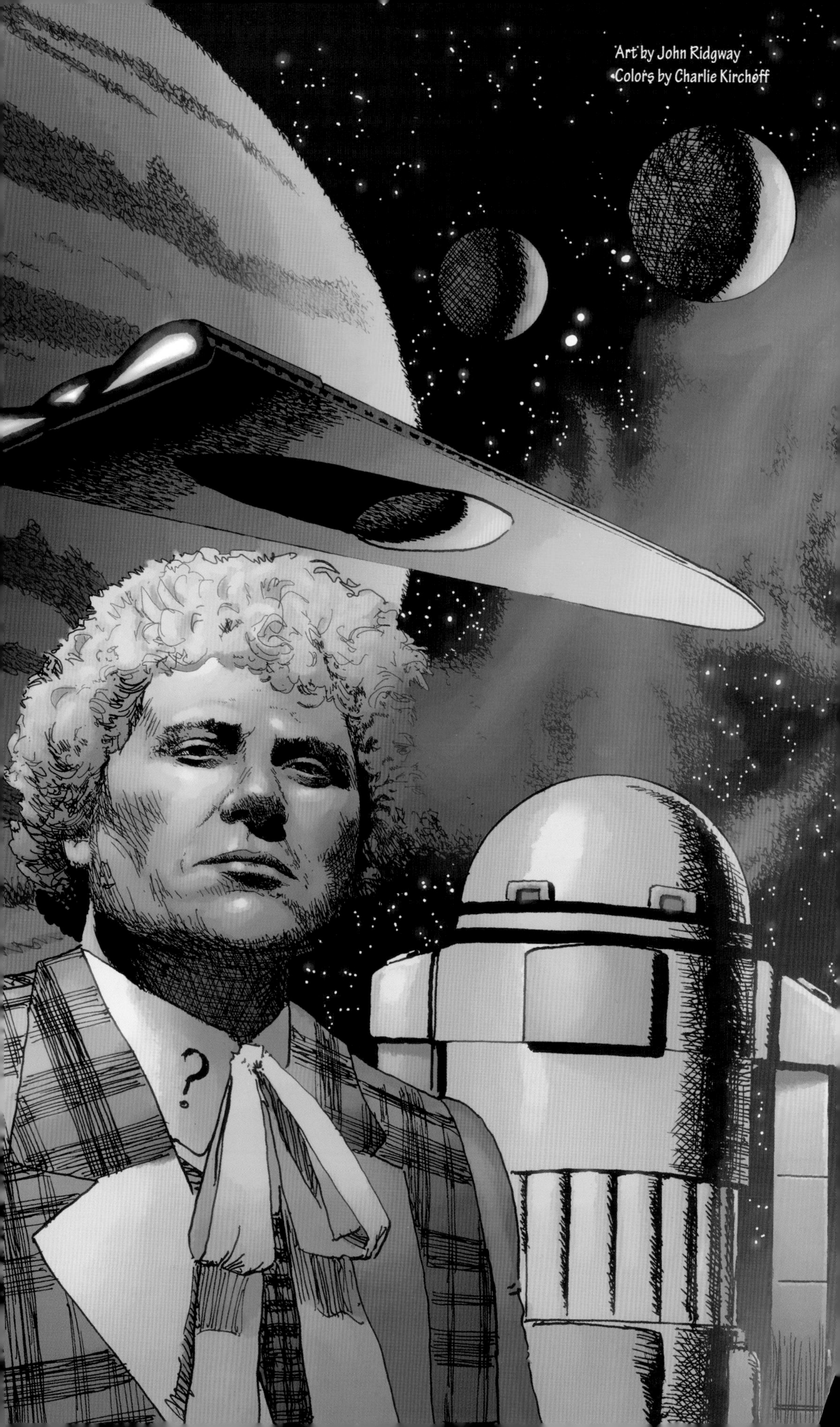
Art by John Ridgway
Colors by Charlie Kirchoff

Art by John Ridgway
Colors by Charlie Kirchoff

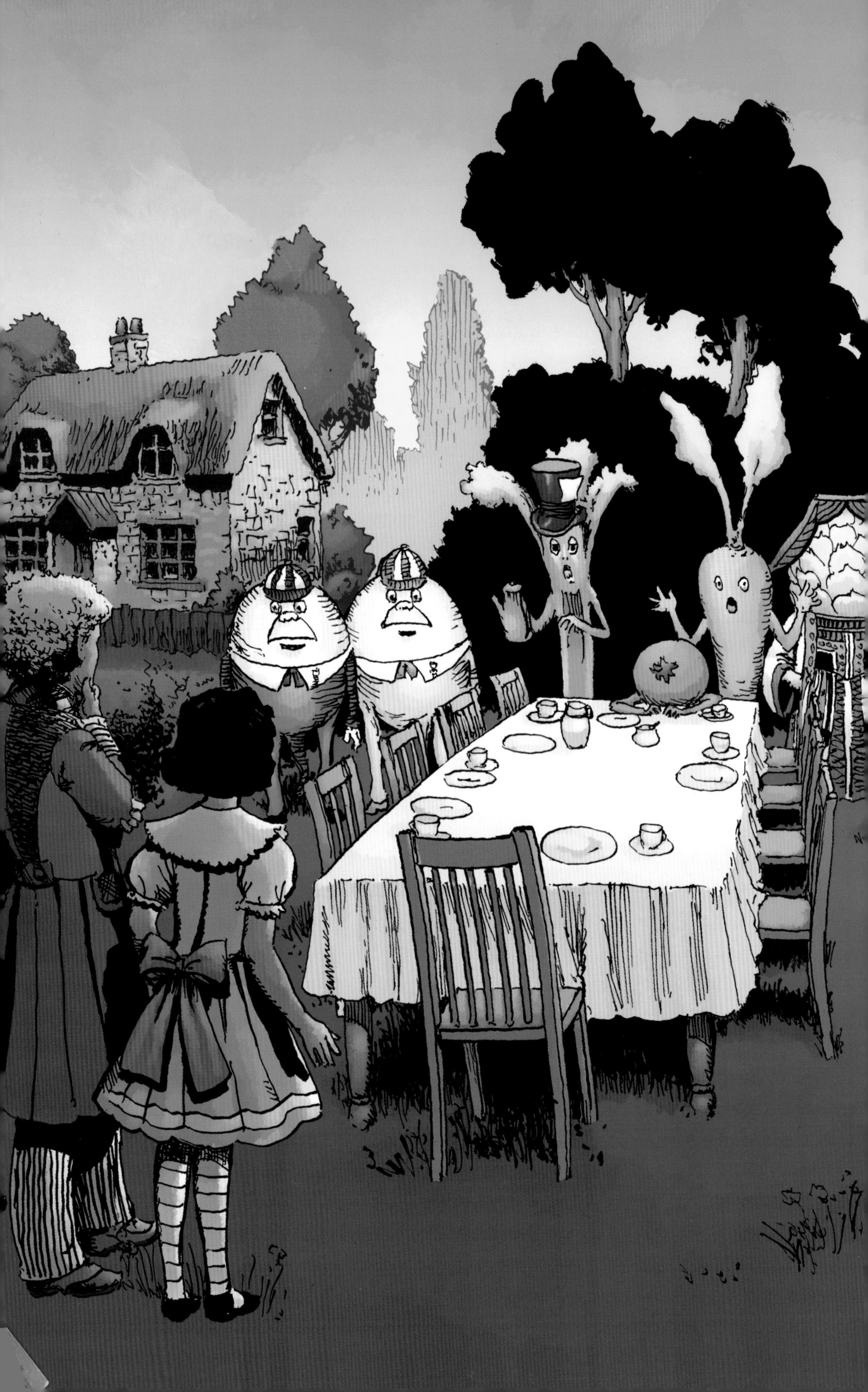

Art by John Ridgway
Colors by Charlie Kirchoff

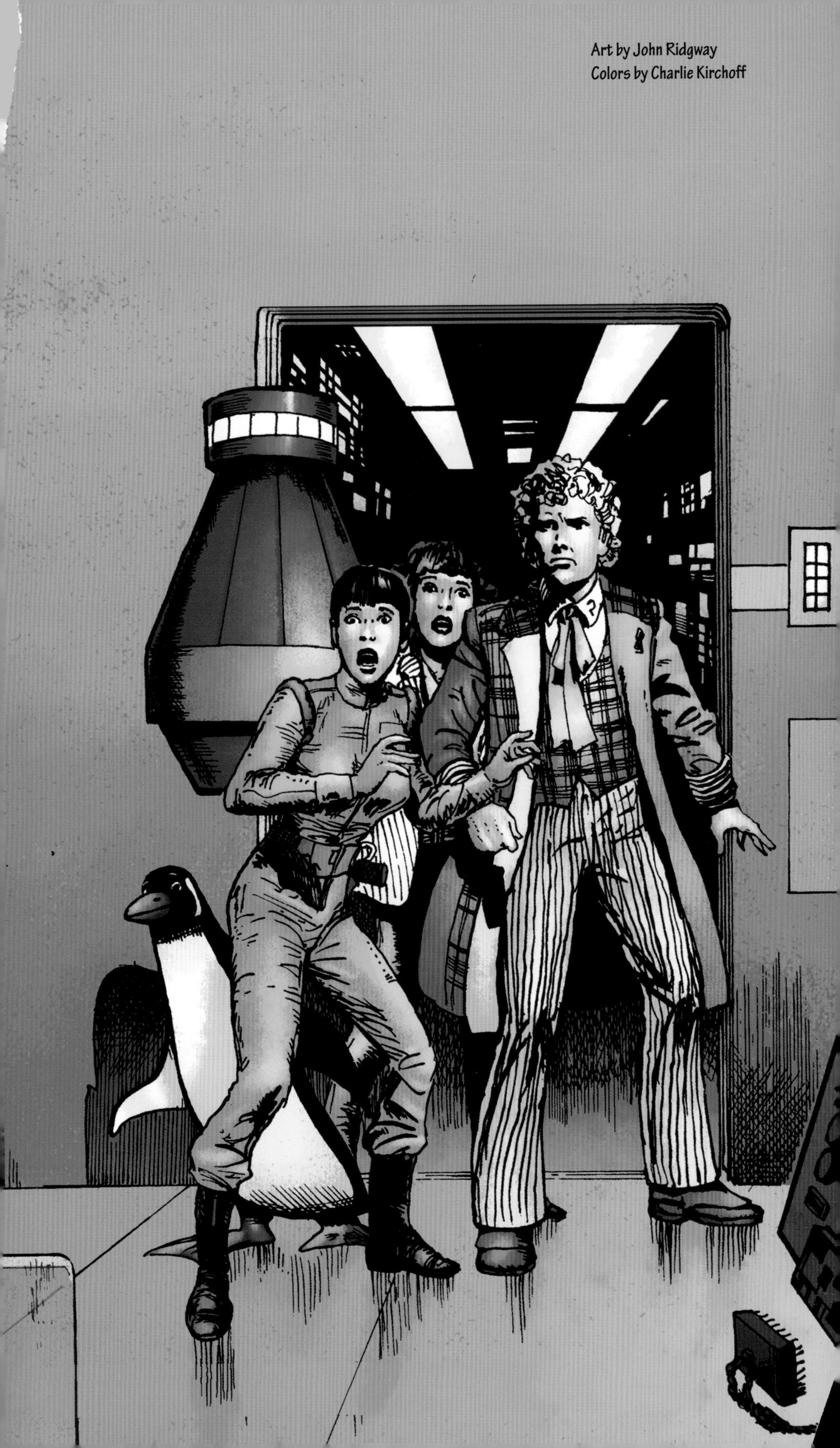

DOCTOR DW WHO

Doctor Who:
Agent Provocateur
ISBN: 978-1-60010-196-0

Doctor Who:
A Fairytale Life
ISBN: 978-1-61377-022-1

Doctor Who:
The Forgotten
ISBN: 978-1-60010-396-4

Doctor Who:
Through Time And Sp
ISBN: 978-1-60010-575-

Doctor Who Series 1,
Vol. 1: The Fugitive
ISBN: 978-1-60010-607-1

Doctor Who Series 1,
Vol. 2: Tessaract
ISBN: 978-1-60010-756-6

Doctor Who Series 1,
Vol. 3: Final Sacrifice
ISBN: 978-1-60010-846-4

Doctor Who Series
Vol. 1: The Ripper
ISBN: 978-1-60010-974-